CHRISTIAN RITE AND
CHRISTIAN DRAMA
IN THE MIDDLE AGES

CHRISTIAN RITE AND CHRISTIAN DRAMA IN THE MIDDLE AGES

*Essays in the Origin
and Early History
of Modern Drama*

By

O. B. HARDISON, Jr.

The Johns Hopkins Press, Baltimore, Md.

To
MARIFRANCES

Preface

THE FOLLOWING ESSAYS are an attempt to reassess the knowledge available concerning the early history of medieval drama. They are not an attempt to write a history of this drama. If the conclusions here presented have any merit, they show that before a new history can be attempted, a great many texts must be re-examined and questions must be explored that were beyond the scope of earlier scholarship. In addition, it would be useful to relate what can be known about drama of the early Middle Ages to the considerable revaluation of the drama of the later Middle Ages found in the work of scholars such as Father Harold Gardiner, Eleanor Prosser, Arnold Williams, F. M. Salter, and Glynne Wickham.

As will be evident from the Contents, my studies have led me along several previously untrodden paths. The position taken by E. K. Chambers in *The Mediaeval Stage* and expanded by Karl Young in *The Drama of the Medieval Church* is so well established as to have attained the status of dogma. The only challenge of any importance has been offered by proponents of the pagan derivation of medieval drama, most notably Robert Stumpfl, Benjamin Hunningher, and John Speirs; and this challenge, because it begins by ignoring the obvious, has come to nothing in spite of some useful peripheral contributions. I have therefore found it necessary to begin with an examination of the critical principles on which the Chambers-Young hypothesis is based. Like all other scholars, including the present author, Chambers and Young wrote in accordance with their conceptions of the nature of drama and the normative mode of literary development. Any scholar who enters the field of medieval Latin drama will confess a heavy debt to their labors. Their data are invaluable, but their interpretations of the data rest on assumptions now generally discredited. In the first essay I have tried to show what these assumptions were, why they were attractive, and what their general effect has been on the direction of later studies.

If there is a single defining difference between the attitude of the nineteenth-century literary scholar and the scholar writing after World War II, it is the greater willingness of the contemporary to recognize the close bond between the huge area of experience conventionally labeled "religion" and that labeled "literature." Although Chambers and Young both recognized that medieval drama developed out of a religious context, neither was willing to accept the implications of this fact. In the second, third, and fourth essays I have attempted to show that in the ninth century the boundary that Chambers and Young posited between religious ritual (the services of the Church) and drama did not exist. Religious ritual *was* the drama of the early Middle Ages and had been ever since the decline of the classical theater. The most valuable source for our knowledge of ninth-century attitudes is the *Liber officialis* of Amalarius of Metz, who died around 850 but whose influence can be discerned in liturgical commentaries throughout the later Middle Ages. The *Liber officialis* shows, first, that the Mass was consciously interpreted as drama during the ninth century, and second, that representational ceremonies were common in the Roman liturgy long before the earliest manuscripts of the *Quem quaeritis* play.

The essays on the Mass and the Church year attempt not only to document attitudes, but also to reconstruct the services on which they were based. This has entailed what I feel is a long overdue examination of the dramatic elements in the ninth-century liturgy. The subject is large, highly specialized, and complicated by the vicissitudes of manuscript survival and variations in the practices of the churches of different regions and even of different towns. In spite of these hazards, it is an important part of the history of drama and, I believe, essential to a valid understanding of the characteristic dramatic forms of postclassical Western culture. Since the ninth-century liturgy was different in content and tone from the liturgy of the later Middle Ages, even a rudimentary account of it is better than none. The reconstruction here offered is based as far as possible on ninth-century texts and commentaries, supplemented by reference to liturgical historians. Father Joseph Jungmann's *Mass of the Roman Rite*, at present the definitive treatment of the subject, has been particularly helpful. The reconstruction is, I hope, both accurate and adequate to the needs of the historian of drama, but I am aware of my own limitations in the field of liturgical history and trust that many of its details will be improved by subsequent scholars.

The essay on the *Quem quaeritis* explores the relation between that famous play and the liturgical context previously described. It shows, among other things, that the accepted theory of the evolution of the play is inconsistent with the chronology and content of the earliest manuscripts. Some alternative is necessary, and the one tentatively offered is based on both chronology and certain persistently recurring ceremonial elements found in the later manuscripts. The theme of the development of Latin drama carries forward into the next essay, which moves from examination of chronology to analysis of the content of three texts that can be dated with some certainty in the eleventh and twelfth centuries. The emphasis of this essay falls on the evident shift from ritual to representational modes, and an effort is made in the conclusion to summarize the principles that appear to have determined the way in which the shift occurred.

The last essay turns from Latin drama to the earliest vernacular dramas, the *Mystère d'Adam* and the *Seinte Resureccion*, both dated in the twelfth century. Examination of these two plays shows that there existed a vernacular tradition in the twelfth century, and that this tradition was already independent of the Latin drama from which it is usually said to be derived. Although the history of this tradition is unknown and probably unknowable, its characteristics can be determined from the plays themselves. The evidence indicates that they are consciously composed works, written for a theater that already possessed definite traditions of staging and acting, and conceived from the beginning as representation. The existence of this early and independent vernacular tradition has never been recognized, much less taken into account, in efforts to write the history of later vernacular drama. If my conclusions about it are valid, the neat theory of a drama that moves from the church to the church portal, from the church portal to the plaza in front of the church, and from there to movable pageant cars, changing its language from Latin to vernacular in the process, badly needs revision. The work of revision is, however, beyond the scope of the present volume.

Perhaps the most persistent theme in the following essays is the question of what constitutes the nature and modes of dramatic form. The study of early medieval drama is not a dry, tedious pursuit of facts remote from the great questions of literary criticism. Facts are important, and, like any other subject worth study, medieval drama demands patience and effort. What makes it unique is that it is the only area of literary history in which a literary form can be traced from origin to complex manifestations on the basis of something more than conjecture. At present, the most persuasive accounts of the transition from ritual to drama are based on the early Greek theater. But knowledge of the religion and drama of preclassical Greece is fragmentary. Few facts are certain, and those that are must be linked by long chains of conjecture. On the other hand, we possess a rich fund of information about the religion, the liturgy, and the ceremony of the ninth and tenth century. The gaps between the facts are smaller (though gaps still exist), and the conjectures are correspondingly fewer.

In many cases, instead of discussing how a given development *might* have occurred, we can describe how, in fact, it *did* occur. Another limitation to the study of early Greek drama is that the Greek theatrical tradition is somewhat different from the tradition behind the modern theater. Certain elements—some of them should probably be called archetypes—are common to both traditions. Many others are not. For better or worse, modern Western drama is the product of a Christian, not a pagan, culture. Its forms, its conventions, and its characteristic tonalities are shaped by this fact. To study early medieval drama is to study the way in which these forms, conventions, and tonalities came into being. A better understanding of them should be of value in attempts to understand any later drama—one thinks especially of Spanish and English Renaissance drama —in which the Christian heritage remains a shaping influence.

The methodology of the following essays is pragmatic. Different techniques are required for different questions, and I have tried to avoid a Procrustean accommodation of the subjects treated to the demands of a single system. Two critical methods have proved especially useful. Much of my terminology is derived from Aristotle's *Poetics*, and the terminology, in turn, reflects a generally Aristotelian orientation on matters such as the importance of imitation, the differentiation of drama from lyric and narrative, the nature and function of plot, the proper division of the parts of the drama, and the like. I have not turned to Aristotle because the *Poetics* is an "authoritative" document, but because time and again the *Poetics* provides the only critical method adequate to the problems that occur. This is so because Aristotle's approach is intrinsic. It begins with the inner nature of drama—its entelechy—and builds outward, in contrast to the extrinsic approach used, for example, by J. M. Manly and Karl Young.

The second critical method I have found especially useful complements the *Poetics*. In Chapter IV of the *Poetics* Aristotle suggests that poetry begins in a natural human delight in imitation. The passage has always intrigued commentators. Not until the work of Sir James Frazer, however, was it possible to surmise why human beings should be delighted by imitation, what constitutes primitive imitation, or why both primitive and civilized societies appear to delight in imitations that involve conflict, brutality, suffering, and death. To Frazer belongs the credit of demonstrating that primitive imitation is essentially religious; and this in spite of Frazer's scorn for what he considered the barbaric superstition revealed by the customs he so laboriously collected. Frazer's work was first used in relation to the history of drama by Gilbert Murray and F. M. Cornford. Enlarged and modified by the assimilation of the concept of archetypes, it has become an invaluable tool for the analysis of both ritual and literary forms, a point equally apparent in Father Hugo Rahner's studies of the Roman Mass and Northrop Frye's *Anatomy of Criticism*. The method cannot be ignored in an attempt to deal with the early history of medieval drama and is used here without apology.

To write about medieval literature is to face the problem of quotations in Latin. There is no ideal solution to this problem. My own solution has been a compromise. I have translated quotations from commentaries and used authoritative translations of liturgical texts when available. In Essay II, I have included the Latin passages from Amalarius in the notes because of their great interest to students of the history of drama. In later essays, two different practices have proved desirable. Passages of liturgical commentary have been translated, and their source (but not the original Latin) has been given in the notes. On the other hand, literary passages whose wording is important to the argument have, of necessity, been given in the original language. Most of these are short and relatively simple. In the few longer passages, the reader is referred to Appendix I for the translation.

The following essays are the result of an interest in liturgical drama first stimulated by the late Professor George R. Coffman and sustained through many years of reading, teaching, and meditation. The debt of gratitude that I owe Professor Coffman is great. Although my conclusions differ from his, they are offered as a tribute to his ability to communicate to those around him his own enthusiasm for an important but neglected subject.

The writing of the present volume was made possible by a grant from the John Simon Guggenheim Foundation. The grant provided a year's release from teaching, without which the task of collecting and organizing the relevant materials would have been unthinkable. The Foundation's policy of freeing grantees from progress reports, visitations, and other minor harassments has been particularly appreciated.

Among the many friends and colleagues who have encouraged or assisted me in my work, I wish particularly to thank Professor Ernest Talbert, Professor Dougald MacMillan, Mr. Kevin Kerrane, and Father Robert Brophy, S.J., all of the University of North Carolina; Father Thomas Porter, S.J., of Columbière Seminary in Michigan; and Professor John L. Lievsay of Duke University. As ever, my debt to my wife is too great to be expressed in words.

CHAPEL HILL, N.C.
May, 1965

Table of Contents

PREFACE   *vii*

Essay I: DARWIN, MUTATIONS, AND
THE ORIGIN OF MEDIEVAL DRAMA   *1*

Essay II: THE MASS AS SACRED DRAMA   *35*

Essay III: THE LENTEN AGON:
FROM SEPTUAGESIMA TO GOOD FRIDAY   *80*

Essay IV: *CHRISTUS VICTOR:*
FROM HOLY SATURDAY TO LOW SUNDAY   *139*

Essay V: THE EARLY HISTORY OF
THE *QUEM QUAERITIS*   *178*

Essay VI: FROM *QUEM QUAERITIS* TO
RESURRECTION PLAY   *220*

Essay VII: THE VERNACULAR TRADITION:
FORM, EPISODE, DIALOGUE   *253*

Epilogue: A NOTE ON THE CONTINUITY OF
RITUAL FORM IN EUROPEAN DRAMA   *284*

Appendix I: TRANSLATIONS   *293*

Appendix II: CHRONOLOGICAL INDEX OF
EARLY LITURGICAL PLAYS   *307*

INDEX   *317*

CHRISTIAN RITE AND
CHRISTIAN DRAMA
IN THE MIDDLE AGES

ESSAY I

Darwin, Mutations, and
the Origin of Medieval Drama

I

IN THE LAST fifty years literary criticism has experienced a series of major revolutions. During this period, however, the history of early medieval drama has retained the basic form established in 1903 by E. K. Chambers' *The Mediaeval Stage*. Karl Young's *The Drama of the Medieval Church*, published in 1933, sharpens the definition of the subject, modifies several important details, and adds a wealth of fresh documentation. In these respects it is a revision and supplement, not a new departure. Since 1933 scholarship has continued to accumulate new records and to suggest modifications in regard to influences and modes of transmission without seriously questioning the frame within which the new material is to be placed. Both *The Mediaeval Stage* and *The Drama of the Medieval Church* were reprinted in the 1950's—a striking testimony to their continuing authority in view of the swift obsolescence of many other studies once considered definitive. The most recent full-scale study, Hardin Craig's *English Religious Drama of the Middle Ages*, assimilates much fresh data but remains fundamentally aligned with what Craig refers to as the "two great books in the field of religious drama"—i.e., Chambers and Young.[1]

The continuing authority of Chambers and Young is in one respect both inevitable and proper. *The Mediaeval Stage* and *The Drama of the Medieval Church* are compendiums of texts and information essential to the subject and difficult or impossible to obtain elsewhere. In another respect, however, the situation is less satisfactory. Is it possible that the methods and approaches which in the last thirty years have had such a profound effect on the study of postmedieval literature have nothing to contribute to the study of the drama of the Middle Ages?

This question has been raised sporadically in the past—particularly in the last decade—by scholars as diverse as Eleanor Prosser, J. S. Purvis,

[1] Hardin Craig, *English Religious Drama of the Middle Ages* (London, 1960), p. v. Hereafter cited as *ERD*.

1

John Speirs, and A. P. Rossiter, to name only four;[2] but thus far no comprehensive re-examination of the materials treated by Chambers and Young has appeared.

To speak of a re-examination of Chambers and Young is to recognize that *The Mediaeval Stage* and *The Drama of the Medieval Church* are more than anthologies of facts. In both works the materials are selected and arranged in accordance with assumptions which were widespread at the time of their composition. As Henry Adams discovered in the course of his arduous self-education, "Historians undertake to arrange facts,— called stories, or histories—assuming in silence a relation of cause and effect. Their assumptions, hidden in the depths of dusty libraries, have been astounding but commonly unconscious . . . ; so much so that if any captious critic were to drag them to light, historians would probably reply, with one voice, that they had never supposed themselves required to know what they were talking about."[3] The phrasing is facetious and probably unfair to the historians Adams had in mind, but the concern with assumptions is proper. Chambers and Young wrote in an atmosphere which encouraged the belief that one approach to literature is correct and that others are either wrong or trivial. The assumptions inherent in this approach were regarded, at least by scholars, as self-evident. But it is increasingly clear that they are not self-evident. They are the product of a particular moment in the history of scholarship, and one with major limitations as well as outstanding virtues.

In 1894 John Addington Symonds observed that "if we attempt to seize the main fact in the intellectual development of the last half of the nineteenth century, we shall find that this may be described as the triumph of the scientific method in relation to all man's thoughts about the universe."[4] In the field of literary scholarship, as distinct from belles-lettres, the scientific method was indeed triumphant. Many factors contributed to its success. The underlying cause was probably a wholly natural desire on the part of humanists to associate themselves with the noble enterprise of leading mankind "ever onward, ever upward, down the ringing grooves of change." The discoveries of the brothers Grimm, of Verner, Scherer and the "jung Grammatiker" had demonstrated that one

[2] See Prosser, *Drama and Religion in the English Mystery Plays* (Stanford, Calif., 1961), and Purvis (ed.), *The York Cycle of Mystery Plays: A Complete Version* (London, 1957), who agree that the literary and dramatic quality of the plays has been overlooked by historical scholars. Speirs, *Medieval English Poetry: The Non-Chaucerian Tradition* (London, 1957), pp. 307–18, and Rossiter, *English Drama from Early Times to the Elizabethans* (London, 1950), approach medieval drama from a "myth-ritual" point of view.

[3] *The Education of Henry Adams* (New York, 1931), p. 382.

[4] "The Philosophy of Evolution," *Essays, Speculative and Suggestive* (London, 1907), p. 1.

branch of literary study—philology—could be elevated to the status of *Strengwissenschaft*. A more ambitious program aimed at the creation of a science of culture began in France with Madame de Staël's *De la littérature considérée dans ses rapports avec les institutions sociales* (1801) and culminated in Taine's Introduction to his *History of English Literature* (1864). This Introduction, which may be considered almost a manifesto of historical scholarship, buttressed Madame de Staël's rather elementary sociological notions with ideas drawn from Comte, Sainte-Beuve, Stendhal, and Hegel.[5] History, Taine asserted, is "but a mechanical problem; the total effect is a result, depending entirely on the magnitude and direction of the producing causes."[6]

Most historical scholars in the generation following Taine subscribed to his scientific ideal while substituting a methodology based upon the accumulation of "fact" for the Hegelian metaphysics. Empiricism, the no-nonsense philosophy of Mr. Gradgrind, which, as T. H. Huxley explained, "is nothing but the expression of the necessary mode of working of the human mind,"[7] easily overcame all rival approaches to the study of culture. Among the influential expressions of the empirical approach are August Boeckh's *Encyclopädie und Methodologie der philologischen Wissenschaft* (1877), Georges Renard's *La méthode scientifique de l'histoire littéraire* (1900), and Langlois and Seignobos' *Introduction aux études historiques* (1897), a work of sufficient stature to be reprinted in English translation as late as 1925.[8]

During the last quarter of the nineteenth century, the course of empirical criticism was modified, to a degree not always recognized by its

[5] For comment on Taine see René Wellek, "Hippolyte Taine's Theory and Criticism," *Criticism*, I (1959), 1–18. More general commentaries on the scientific mode of criticism include E. Cassirer, *The Logic of the Humanities*, trans. Clarence S. Howe (New Haven, Conn., 1961); H. A. Needham, *Le développement de l'esthétique sociologique en France et en Angleterre au XIXᵉ siècle* (Paris, 1926); and H. H. Clark, "The Influence of Science on American Literary Criticism, 1860–1910," *Transactions of the Wisconsin Academy*, XLIV (1956), 109–64.

[6] "Introduction," *History of English Literature*, trans. H. Van Laun (Philadelphia, 1908), I, 23. As Henry James noted in his 1872 review of the first edition of this translation, Taine's theory is often refuted by his own text. See "Taine's English Literature," *Literary Reviews and Essays of Henry James*, ed. Albert Mordell (New York, 1957), pp. 61–67. The truth of James's view is so evident today that it requires an act of imagination to appreciate the great seriousness with which Taine was taken by his contemporaries. For evidence that Taine—or at least Taine's ideal—remains influential, see Harry Levin, "Literature as an Institution," *Literary Opinion in America*, ed. M. D. Zabel (New York, 1951), pp. 655–66.

[7] "The Method by Which the Causes . . . of Organic Nature Are to Be Discovered," *Victorian Prose*, ed. Frederick W. Roe (New York, 1947), p. 475.

[8] Charles V. Langlois and Charles Seignobos, *An Introduction to the Study of History*, trans. G. G. Berry (New York, 1925). This edition includes the introduction written by F. Y. Powell for the 1898 edition.

proponents, by the concept of evolution. At the end of *The Origin of Species* (1859), Darwin called for an evolutionary treatment of subjects relating to man. Within the next twenty years Darwinian concepts became pervasive in studies of culture, including literary scholarship.[9] In France, Taine and Zola were both influenced by Darwin, but it was Ferdinand Brunetière who made the most important large-scale application of Darwin to literary history in his *L'Évolution des genres dans l'histoire de la littérature* (1890). Brunetière's Introduction to the English edition of the *Manual of the History of French Literature* (1897) fairly represents the temper of the age. The *Manual*, says Brunetière, is simply "an application of the doctrine of Evolution to the history of a great literature. In this way the work is placed under the auspices of the great name of Charles Darwin."[10]

One of the examples of Darwinian evolution cited by Brunetière is "English drama in the sixteenth century." In retrospect, it can be seen that English drama provides an ideal subject for evolutionary investigation. It appeared to have developed in relative isolation from outside influences, and its development appeared to be continuous—the sort of gradual, incremental growth demanded by biologists in the days when *Natura non facit saltus* was considered an essential evolutionary postulate. Moreover, the evolutionary hypothesis gave scientific respectability to a theory already widely held. Ever since Thomas Warton's *History of English Poetry*, the history of drama had been regarded as organic. Drama had "arisen" from simple medieval beginnings, had "flowered" in the work of Marlowe, Shakespeare, and Ben Jonson, and had then passed into a phase of "decadence" until its expiration in 1642.

In England, E. B. Tylor, Herbert Spencer, and T. H. Huxley were particularly influential in popularizing the application of Darwin's ideas to cultural study. In 1884 J. A. Symonds offered an evolutionary interpretation of English drama in *Shakespeare's Predecessors*; in 1894 he generalized his findings in an influential essay "On the Application of Evolutionary Principles to Art and Literature."[11] At about the same time Karl

---

[9] The impact of Darwin is studied by Richard Hofstadter, *Social Darwinism in American Thought* (New York, 1955); William Irvine, *Apes, Angels, and Victorians* (New York, 1955); and Lionel Stevenson, *Darwin among the Poets* (Chicago, 1932). Darwinian influences on criticism are examined by René Wellek, "The Concept of Evolution in Literary History," *Concepts of Criticism* (New Haven, Conn., 1963), pp. 37–53.

[10] Reprinted in *Modern Continental Literary Criticism*, ed. O. B. Hardison, Jr. (New York, 1962), p. 97.

[11] *Essays, Speculative and Suggestive*, pp. 26–52. Spencer and Huxley were evidently (p. 27) Symonds' chief sources. The view taken is "organic," and English drama is cited as an especially clear example of organic evolution. The citation restates the position taken earlier by Symonds in *Shakespeare's Predecessors* (London, 1904), pp. 2–9. For Symonds' influence on several important American scholars, see H. H. Clark, "The Influence of Science on American Literary Criticism," pp. 109–38.

Pearson, the eminent mathematician and biologist, included an important essay on the German Passion play in a collection entitled *The Chances of Death and Other Studies in Evolution.* Here Pearson combined Taine's idea that cultural phenomena are relative to their socioeconomic milieu with the theory that "a study of the medieval passion-plays will . . . bring before us an intermediate link in the chain of evolution" from savagery to "liberal faith."[12]

It is against the background of nineteenth-century historical scholarship and, in particular, the theory of evolution, that the work of Chambers and Young must be appraised.

II

E. K. Chambers was a far-ranging, deeply learned scholar, exemplary of all that is best in the English tradition. Resisting the Germanic impulse toward narrow specialization, he wrote poetry, belletristic essays, and studies of figures as remote from the Middle Ages and Renaissance as Coleridge and George Meredith. In his later life he apparently came to feel that the historical method had dangers as well as virtues. His presidential address to the English Association, delivered in 1940, is a discussion of "The Timelessness of Poetry." In this paper he suggests that literary history is a discipline of secondary importance and that the real issue is the confrontation of reader and text: "Many of my hearers are no doubt teachers of English literature, accustomed to classify it by periods.... That is no doubt a useful exercise. Anything, indeed, will do as scaffolding, so long as it is not forgotten that the dominant purpose is to bring the young mind, in one way or another, directly into contact with poetry, itself. But there are dangers to the historical method. The categories may become too rigid."[13]

On the other hand, in the period from 1895 to 1903, when *The Mediaeval Stage* was being written, the historical method was in the ascendancy and Chambers embraced it with enthusiasm. "The Study of English Litera-

<hr/>

[12] "The German Passion-Play: A Study in the Evolution of Western Christianity," *The Chances of Death and Other Studies in Evolution* (London, 1897), II, 250. That the word "evolution" is used in the technical Darwinian sense and not simply as a synonym for "history" is evident from the essay, as well as from the general orientation of Pearson's two volumes. By 1903 the idea that English drama had "evolved" in the technical sense had penetrated the popular handbooks, e.g., Richard Garnett and Edmund Gosse, *English Literature, an Illustrated Record* (London, 1903), I, 221.

[13] *The English Association Presidential Address, 1940*, p. 6. Reprinted in *A Sheaf of Papers* (Oxford, 1942), pp. 109–25. For details of Chambers' career, see F. P. Wilson and J. D. Wilson, "Obituary Notice," in *Proceedings of the British Academy*, XLII (1956), 267–85.

ture," written in 1896, takes a position generally parallel to that of Taine, though without Hegelian elements. Chambers takes a strong stand against reducing literature to "lessons in philology and grammar," on the narrow Germanic pattern. In place of philology he advocates study of the socio-economic milieu within which literature is produced; for ". . . no writer, however great, stands absolutely alone; each is the child of his own age . . . nor is a complete understanding of any man's work possible, without some knowledge of the conditions under which it had its being, of the influences which helped to shape its form and inspire its purpose. This is an universal law."[14] The Preface to *The Mediaeval Stage* reflects Chambers' practical commitment to this "universal law." A. W. Ward, author of the most extensive English study of medieval drama prior to Chambers', is criticized, along with other, unnamed scholars, because "while dealing excellently with medieval drama as literature, [they] have shown themselves but little curious about the social and economic facts upon which the medieval drama rested. Yet from a study of such facts, I am sure, any literary history, which does not confine itself entirely to the analysis of genius, must take a start."[15]

[14] "The Study of Poetry," *A Sheaf of Papers*, p. 101. Like Taine, Chambers at this time believed that the critic is a reader "not of books only, but of souls" (p. 108).

[15] *The Mediaeval Stage* (Oxford, 1903), I, v. Hereafter cited as *MS*. The distinction between "literary history" and "analysis of genius" echoes an important nineteenth-century debate. Because of the nature of aesthetic creativity, Kant argued in the *Critique of Judgment* (trans. J. H. Bernard [New York, 1951], pp. 150–63) that genius is the capacity to create without the guidance of general principles. Romantic writers inflated this idea into the cult of genius unflatteringly described by Irving Babbitt in *Rousseau and Romanticism* (New York, 1959), pp. 39–66. The rise of sociological criticism and Darwinism created acute problems: (1) Sociological criticism could account for the typical, the traditional, for sources and influences, but if genius was the ability to be absolutely original, could it account for the very element supposedly responsible for artistic greatness? (2) Darwinian critics of the early school insisted that literary change was organic and continuous; hence they were led to discount the importance of individual artists, a viewpoint which seemed to work in connection with folk litera-ture and anonymous material such as liturgical drama. Solutions varied. Taine (*History*, pp. 34–35) reinterpreted literary genius. To him genius was a superior capacity for reflecting the essence of one's age. Thus the sociological critic finds "classics" his best documents—a viewpoint apparently echoed by Erich Auerbach in *Mimesis*. Taine, of course, wanted to use literature to discover society; most later historical critics had the opposite goal in mind. Thus Brunetière ("Introduction," in Hardison [ed.], *Modern Continental Literary Criticism*, pp. 97–99) defended the historical method because it allowed the critic to peel away the conventional elements in a work of genius, leaving the truly original elements all the more visible. This view has its parallel in the contemporary notion that the more we study the theatrical conventions of Shakespeare's day, the more we appreciate his innovations. The position is, of course, two-edged. It pays lip service to genius while justifying concentration on everything but genius. Chambers' condescending statement that Ward was "but little curious about the social and economic facts" on which "any literary history, which

The scholars cited approvingly by Chambers in his "List of Authorities" further illustrate his commitment to historical methodology. The list is a roster of the outstanding historical scholars of the last quarter of the nineteenth century. Not a single purely theoretical or critical work is included. Ward and J. A. Symonds, who deal with the "literary" as well as the historical aspects of the subject, are dismissed with a condescending "of value." Foremost among Chambers' authorities is Wilhelm Creizenach's *Geschichte des neueren Dramas*, complete to volume three by 1903. Next there is J. M. Manly, whose *Specimens of Pre-Shakespearean Drama* had appeared in 1897 in two volumes with the promise of a third (of commentary) to follow.[16] Finally, among major authorities, there is L. Petit de Julleville, whose *Histoire du théâtre en France au Moyen Age* had been published in four volumes between 1880 and 1890. The minor authorities cited with approval in Chambers' footnotes (e.g., Sepet, du Méril, Cloetta, Duchesne [for liturgy]) are also for the most part historical scholars, with an occasional reference to psychologists and anthropologists in connection with Book II. As far as methodology is concerned, Chambers complains, perhaps half in fun, that "Oxford, my most kindly nurse, maintained in my day no *École des Chartes*, and I had to discover the rules of method as I went along."[17] He adds that he had as a guide the "remorseless ideal" of Langlois and Seignobos.

The references to an *École des chartes* and Langlois and Seignobos are significant. No less a figure than Frederick York Powell, Regius Professor of Modern History and a member of the editorial board of the Clarendon Press at the time when the *Mediaeval Stage* was submitted for consideration, had called publicly in 1897 for the establishment of an English *École des chartes*.[18] In 1898, the same year that Chambers' still incomplete work was

does not confine itself solely to the analysis of genius, must make a start" (*MS*, I, v) places him in this group. It was for this very reason that the American Darwinian critics sought for an alternative to organic evolution. To Manly, and even more emphatically, to John P. Hoskins, the mutation theory allowed for a reconciliation of evolution and genius. See John P. Hoskins, "Biological Analogy in Literary Criticism: I. Variation and Personality" (*MP*, VI [1908–9], 416–18), for a Darwinian discussion of genius. Significantly, Hoskins finds an ally in Sainte-Beuve and strongly attacks Zola's naturalistic theory, expounded in *Le roman expérimental*. After 1910 the discussion of genius became increasingly Freudian, with special emphasis on the relation of genius to neurosis.

[16] *MS*, I, xiii.
[17] *MS*, I, vii.
[18] Oliver Elton, *Frederick York Powell* (Oxford, 1906), I, 250–53. The nineteenth-century effort to collect and publish documents was encouraged by Ranke, Froude, Motley, and the Abbé Migne, to name only the most prominent figures. Among the monuments to this effort are the 112 volumes of the *Colección de documentos inéditos*, the over 200 of the *Collection des documents inédits*, the English Rolls series, and, in English literature, the publications of the Early English Text Society.

accepted by Clarendon, Powell had contributed an enthusiastic Preface to the English translation of Langlois and Seignobos' *Introduction to the Study of History*. In view of Powell's immense prestige in the area of medieval history and literature, Chambers could hardly afford to ignore the work and, in fact, was strongly influenced by it.

The *Introduction to the Study of History* is an epitome of historical method as understood at the end of the nineteenth century. It is resolutely empirical, and its authors, with Powell's hearty approval, dismiss "curious Hegelianisms" as vestigial survivals of a religious—hence unscientific—world view.[19] Powell boasted that the authors "have the temerity to view history as a scientific pursuit. . . . They are bold enough to look forward to a day . . . when a sensible or honest man will no more dare to write history unscientifically than he would to-day be willing to waste his time and that of others observing the heavens unscientifically."[20] Like other empiricists of their generation, Langlois and Seignobos consider the accumulation of "fact" the first and most important task of the scholar. The first half of the *Introduction* deals with the reading interpretation, and evaluation of documents, which are the "facts" of the historian. These "facts" have an intrinsic value, quite apart from any interpretation which may be placed upon them. The possibility of an organic relation between "fact" and interpretation—the idea that the "facts" elicited in any investigation may be a function of the questions posed—is not even considered.

This overriding, almost Gradgrindian concern for documentary fact dominates *The Mediaeval Stage* to such a degree that Chambers himself felt the need to apologize. "The burden of my notes and appendices," he wrote, "sometimes appears to me intolerable." His excuse for such an accumulation was that facts have an intrinsic worth quite apart from the uses to which they are put: "I wanted to collect, once for all, as many facts . . . as possible. These may, perhaps, have a value independent of any conclusions which I have founded upon them."[21] Since Karl Young, the consensus has been that Chambers' pursuit of fact did, indeed, lead him astray: "It is out of scale, and he knew it," wrote F. P. Wilson.[22] The

---

[19] Pp. vii, 286–87.

[20] P. vi. It is amusing to compare Powell's statement with Whitman's poem "When I Heard the Learned Astronomer."

[21] *MS*, I, vii. In a generally laudatory review contributed to *The Pelican* in 1903, Chambers' close friend Oliver Elton expressed the hope that he "would not bind himself against appreciating the plays as literature" when he reached Elizabethan drama (see Wilson and Wilson, "Obituary Notice," pp. 277–78).

[22] "Obituary Notice," p. 277.

result is a structural weakness: disproportionate emphasis on minstrels and folk plays tends to obscure the main line of development being traced. A still more serious weakness is the fact that the "main line" traced by Chambers does not emerge in classical empirical fashion "from the data themselves," but is assumed before the data are discovered and thus serves as an unconscious criterion for the selection. A circularity commonly associated with naïve empiricism is evident. Having been selected on the basis of evolutionary theory, the data can hardly fail to illustrate this theory when assembled.

The second half of Langlois and Seignobos deals with "synthetic operations," the process of ordering the "facts." In this section there is no questioning the sufficiency of the empirical method. Christian and Hegelian metaphysical ideas are ruled out. When the "facts" are collected, a pattern will inevitably emerge, and this pattern will be the form of history. Although the pattern will be vague in places because of lacunae in surviving documents, its outline will be beyond dispute. Consequently, Langlois and Seignobos reach the striking conclusion that the future of history-writing, except in the area of recent history, is limited: "History has at its disposal a limited stock of documents; this very circumstance limits the possible progress of historical science. When all the documents are known, and have gone through all the operations which fit them for use, the work of critical scholarship will be finished. In the case of some ancient periods, for which documents are rare, we can now see that in a generation or two it will be time to stop."[23] What remains is the essentially mechanical task of co-ordination: certain "workers of experience should be found to renounce personal research and devote their whole time to . . . comprehensive works of historical construction."[24]

Obviously, no research, even of the most trivial sort, can be carried forward in such a vacuum of general concepts as that suggested by the more doctrinaire passages of Langlois and Seignobos. As might be expected, several hypotheses are offered for guidance in the "synthetic" phase of research. One of the key hypotheses is that fundamental human desires and impulses remain the same in all ages; this assumption may be invoked to explain historical causality when detailed information is lacking. Another hypothesis—and perhaps the most important one—is that of evolution.[25] Langlois and Seignobos accept the idea that cultures grow organically by continuous fine gradations, and that a general pattern of birth, growth, and decline can be observed in most cultural phenomena.

[23] P. 316.
[24] P. 318.
[25] Pp. 244–49.

The *Introduction* ends with the assertion that "if the result of these labors were to bring out clear and certain conclusions as to the nature and causes of social evolution, a truly scientific 'philosophy of history' would have been created, which historians might acknowledge as legitimately crowning historical science."[26]

In its simplest form, Chambers' concept of the evolution of drama is an updated version of an idea prominent in English thought as early as Roger Ascham. The humanists of the Renaissance accepted a rudimentary theory of history according to which the brilliance of classical literature was obscured by a long night of Gothic barbarism, which, in turn, was gradually dispelled by the Revival of Learning. In the seventeenth and eighteenth centuries it was often assumed that the progress initiated by the humanists was—and would be—continuous.[27] In spite of the Gothic Revival, Thomas Warton complacently admitted in his *History of English Poetry* that "our reflections on this subject are accompanied with a conscious pride, arising in great measure from a tacit comparison of the infinite disproportion between the feeble efforts of remote ages, and our present improvements in knowledge."[28] The concept of evolution adopted by nineteenth-century literary scholarship modified this view without fundamentally changing it. The earlier position assumed a pattern of gradually increasing complexity, together with a teleological bias involving progress toward a goal considered ideal. Nineteenth-century scholars incorporated both of these ideas in a synthesis based on the analogy between culture and biological organisms. Literatures, periods, and literary types were compared to living creatures. In *Shakespeare's Predecessors*, J. A. Symonds discovers three phases in the history of English drama. These are growth (from the "germ" of liturgical drama to

---

[26] P. 318.

[27] J. B. Bury, *The Idea of Progress: An Inquiry into Its Origin and Growth* ([London, 1921] pp. 260–349), discusses nineteenth-century progressivism. His last chapter (pp. 334–49) is devoted to "progress in the light of evolution." The idea of progress must be balanced against theories of history as a decline from an ideal norm or Golden Age. Among historical critics of literature the progressive idea was generally adopted. "Organicism" in the later nineteenth century encouraged the sort of growth-blossoming-decadence cycle found in Symonds. Since medieval drama was considered the prelude to Elizabethan drama, the emphasis, naturally, was on progress, with sixteenth-century religious dramas conveniently explained as vestiges or degenerate survivals of earlier forms. The idea that primitive ages produce the finest poetry—popular among students of epic and espoused by Vico, Herder, Macaulay, and Renan, to name only a few authors—was not applied to medieval drama, probably for the reason that medieval drama contradicted it.

[28] *History of English Poetry* (London, 1824), I, 3. Warton's idea is parallel to the scientific views of Lamarck and Erasmus Darwin. See Stevenson, *Darwin among the Poets*, pp. 25–27.

Marlowe), maturity (Marlowe, Shakespeare, Ben Jonson), and "decadence and dissipation" (the Jacobeans to 1642). As in the case of an organism, "the completion of the process was inherent in its earliest embryonic stages."[29] Symonds' terminology makes the teleological bias of his work readily apparent. The mature state of the organism is its "ideal" form. Thus early forms of drama are interesting only as they lead to Shakespeare; later ones, only as they are consequences of the Shakespearean moment. Symonds concludes that "the more we study Shakespeare, the more do we perceive that his predecessors, no less than his successors, exist for him."[30]

The conceptual frame of *The Mediaeval Stage* may be understood as the fusion of the concept of progress with the organic analogy evident in Symonds' work. While at Oxford, Chambers had been a student of classics. His sense of the contrast between classical civilization and medieval ignorance could only have been intensified by his undergraduate studies. After graduation, and probably with the encouragement of his close friend Oliver Elton, he decided to devote himself to English literature. The project which he set himself was "a little book . . . about Shakespeare," and *The Mediaeval Stage* began as an attempt to write "a short account of the origins of play-acting in England and its development during the Middle Ages."[31] In other words, *The Mediaeval Stage* was, in its initial conception, teleological. That it remained teleological is indicated by Chambers' Preface, in which the final goal of the work is defined as "to state and explain the pre-existing conditions which, by the latter half of the sixteenth century, made the great Shakespearean stage possible."[32] Chambers did not carry his project beyond Shakespeare. His essay on "The Disenchantment of the Elizabethans"[33] indicates, however, that if he had, the composite image would have been one of organic evolution, maturity, and "decadence and dissipation," an image varying little from that offered by J. A. Symonds.

Instead of beginning with liturgical drama, Chambers began his history with the decay of the ancient world. Neither Roger Ascham nor Thomas Warton—nor, for that matter, Edward Gibbon—would have quarreled with his picture of "the onslaught of Christianity and the indifference of barbarism" which broke down the tradition of classical drama. Chambers' second book, insofar as it is not wholly digressive, endeavors to show that

[29] Pp. 2–3.
[30] P. 14.
[31] I, v.
[32] I, v–vi.
[33] *Sir Thomas Wyatt and Some Collected Studies* (London, 1933), pp. 181–204.

in spite of the hostility of the Church a "mimetic instinct" continued to manifest itself in the form of *spectacula*, ludi, folk dramas, and irreligious offshoots of church ceremony such as the Feast of Fools. Strongly influenced by Sir James Frazer's recently published *Golden Bough*, Chambers associated the "mimetic instinct" and its various products with paganism. The folk drama, in fact, is the detritus of ancient pagan ceremonies never completely eradicated by the Church.

In the third book, which is the central one insofar as Chambers' influence is concerned, the evolutionary analogy becomes explicit. Words like "growth," "development," and "process" are frequent, and the book opens with a formal bow to Darwin. Its subject, Chambers remarks, "is of the highest importance as an object lesson in literary evolution. The historian is not often privileged to isolate a definite literary form throughout the whole course of its development, and to trace its rudimentary beginnings, as may be done, beyond the very borders of articulate speech."[34]

The existence of a spectrum of forms from the *Quem quaeritis* to the enormous Corpus Christi cycles doubtless made the evolutionary hypothesis inevitable. Yet even in *The Mediaeval Stage* defects are visible. The distribution and chronology of the existing documents was (and is) highly erratic. Simple forms occur at late dates, and not infrequently the earliest surviving example of a type is more complex than later examples. No country exhibits the full range of forms, and gaps in the English record must be filled with examples from other countries, principally France and Germany. To preserve the idea of a gradual, uniform development from simple to complex, documents must be chronologically displaced. To preserve the idea of the development of varieties of a species from a single archetype, complex lines of influence must be postulated between Germany and France, and France and England. The exact manner in which the influences operated is left vague, but traveling monks and *clerici vagantes* are suggested as possibilities. Although Chambers admits that it is impossible "to isolate the centres and lines of diffusion of that gradual process of accretion and development through which the *Quem quaeritis* gave ever fuller and fuller expression to . . . dramatic instincts," he also believes that if all texts were available, apparent anomalies "would not improbably be removed."[35] Since only fifteen examples of the fully

---

[34] II, 3. Cf. Symonds, *Shakespeare's Predecessors*, p. 2.

[35] II, 27–28; also 64, 73, 109, etc. The theory of transmission by monks and *clerici vagantes* was given substance by George R. Coffman's suggestion, in *A New Theory concerning the Origin of the Miracle Play* (Menasha, Wis., 1914), that the Cluniac reform accounted for at least some of the necessary consolidation and travel between monasteries.

expanded *Quem quaeritis* and only two full medieval Latin texts of the *Pastores* were known to Chambers, the evolutionary hypothesis was not, in fact, an empirically justifiable theory.[36]

Although Chambers used the evolutionary hypothesis *passim*, he appears to have been dissatisfied with it. After commenting on the problem of establishing a chronological line of development for the *Quem quaeritis*, he suggests that "disregarding . . . in the main the dates of the manuscripts, it is easy so to classify the available versions as to mark the course of a development."[37] The classification system moves from simple to complex. Obviously, it does not abandon the concept of evolution, but it does shift attention from stemma and lines of influence to content. Later, when discussing the plays of the Epiphany cycle, Chambers claims only that he has reproduced "at least the logical order of their development."[38] Thus, along with the dominant evolutionary element in *The Mediaeval Stage*, there is a subdominant current of scepticism. Considering Chambers' evidence, this sceptical strain seems more in keeping with his scientific ideals, a fact clearly recognized by J. M. Manly and Karl Young.[39]

In his fourth book Chambers almost entirely abandons evolution to assume another stance typical of nineteenth-century historians. The fourth book crosses the line between Middle Ages and Renaissance. It describes with muted but unmistakable enthusiasm the "transformation" of the medieval stage by humanism and the emergence of "a new class of professional actors, in whose hands the theatre was destined to recover a stable organization upon lines which had been departed from since the days of Tertullian."[40] As the quotation indicates, Chambers' emphasis is on discontinuity rather than continuity. The idea of the Renaissance as a radical departure from medievalism—a concept encouraged by Hegel as well as by Hallam, Taine, Burckhardt, and Symonds—is evident. Paradoxically, Chambers considered the break in the evolutionary process particularly sharp in the case of drama: ". . . hardly any branch of human activities was destined to be more completely transformed by the new

---

[36] *MS*, II, 31, 43. Cf. A. W. Ward, *A History of English Dramatic Literature* (London, 1899), I, 37: "it is easier to detach the successive stages [of liturgical drama] from one another in accordance with an *a priori* theory than to arrange the sequence in proved chronological order." The source for Chambers' arrangement is Carl Lange, *Die Lateinischen Osterfeiern* (Munich, 1887). Lange makes no evolutionary claim for his arrangement, which he evidently regarded simply as a convenience.

[37] II, 28, 32.

[38] II, 50.

[39] See below, pp. 20, 26–27.

[40] I, vi.

forces than the drama."[41] The consequence of this transformation is that Chambers' history becomes compartmentalized. If it is true that *Natura non facit saltus*, the evolutionary hypothesis breaks down. The discussion of medieval drama may be agreeable to an antiquarian, but, by Chambers' own admission, it casts little light on "the pre-existing conditions which . . . made the great Shakespearean stage possible."

Two other features of *The Mediaeval Stage* can be traced to characteristic nineteenth-century attitudes. The first is Chambers' attitude toward Christianity. In dealing with medieval subjects, he was continuously involved with religious subject matter. Yet he lived in an age when Christianity was suspect. Matthew Arnold's definition of religion as "morality touched by emotion" is both an expression of scepticism and a profession of faith in ethics as opposed to theological dogma. Ironically, although Arnold strongly criticized historical scholars in his Introduction to Ward's *The English Poets* (1880), his religious views aligned him with them.[42] The scientific student of culture, according to Taine, should examine questions of right and wrong in the same dispassionate spirit as that of the chemist examining sugar or sulphuric acid. Chambers' mentors Langlois and Seignobos insist throughout the *Introduction to the Study of History* that the historian must take no sides, espouse no causes, and shun the outmoded providential view of history inherited from the Christian Middle Ages. In practice, such "objectivity" was often a disguise for contempt, or even active hostility, toward religion. Sir James Frazer, from whom Chambers derived his ideas about folk drama, took unfailing delight in pointing out the primitive origins of Christian ritual, most notably in the excursus on "The Crucifixion of Christ" appended to volume nine (*The Scapegoat*) of *The Golden Bough*. The implied conclusion of Frazer's excursus—like the work of such nineteenth-century anthropologists and critics as David Strauss, Rudolf Seydel, and J. M. Robertson—is that Christianity is nothing more than a tissue of barbaric superstitions redeemed here and there by some useful moral truths.[43]

---

[41] II, 206; still more emphatic, II, 180: "It is the object of the present book [Book IV of *MS*] briefly to record the rise, also in the fifteenth century, of *new dramatic conditions*, which, after existing side by side with those of mediaevalism, were destined ultimately *to become a substitute for them and to lead up directly to the magic stage of Shakespeare*" (italics mine).

[42] The essay is the famous "Study of Poetry" essay, in which Arnold proposes the theory of touchstones. It was reprinted in 1888 as the first essay of *Essays in Criticism, Second Series*.

[43] Frazer believed the reader of his treatment would "reduce Jesus of Nazareth to the level of a multitude of other victims of a barbarous superstition, and will see in him no more than a moral teacher whom the fortunate accident of his execution invested with the crown not merely of a martyr, but of a God" (quoted in John B. Vickery, "*The Golden Bough*: Impact and Archetype," *VQR*, XXXIX [1963], 52–53).

Thus it is that a dramatic element enters the conceptual framework of *The Mediaeval Stage*. The clergy is consistently cast in the role of the villain who opposes the "mimetic instinct," which is associated with such terms as "healthy," "human," and "pagan." Classical drama was, by definition, "pagan." Christians, allied with "barbarian invaders," attacked the theater. By the seventh century, "the bishops and the barbarians had triumphed."[44] Yet the mimetic instinct lived on. Minstrels "braved the ban of the church, and finally won their way."[45] Folk plays, "the last sportive stage[s] of ancient heathen ritual," were enacted, although they "remained to the last alien and distasteful to the Church."[46] Unfortunately, liturgical drama is almost impossible to explain within the framework of a struggle between Christianity and the "mimetic instinct." Chambers was therefore forced to describe it as "an audacious . . . attempt to wrest the pomps of the devil to a spiritual service, or as an inevitable and ironic recoil of a barred human instinct within the hearts of the gaolers themselves."[47] Such a view, it may be noted, is unlikely to encourage scholars to seek explanations of the form or effect of medieval drama within the framework of medieval Christianity.

At any rate, liturgical drama was at first "a mere spectacle, devised by ecclesiastics," but in time it "broke the bonds of ecclesiastical control" and appealed to a "deep-rooted native instinct"—clearly a pagan instinct, since Chambers stresses the popularity and elaboration of scenes featuring devils.[48] Pagan instinct again triumphs over Christianity in the secularization of the drama, which Chambers describes as a "reaction of the temper of the folk upon the handling of the plays, the broadening of their human as distinct from their religious aspect." As a result, "*officia* for devotion and edification" give way to "*spectacula* for mirth, wonder, and delight."[49]

For a concise review of anticlerical anthropology in the nineteenth and early twentieth centuries, see Thomas J. Thornburn, *The Mythical Interpretation of the Gospels* (New York, 1916), pp. xiii–xviii.

[44] I, 22.

[45] II, 179.

[46] II, 2.

[47] II, 3. Cf. Pearson, "The German Passion-Play," p. 284: "Thus the scenic ritual, and ultimately the religious plays, indirectly owe their origin to the very heathen ceremonies which their introduction was designed to suppress."

[48] II, 147–48.

[49] II, 69. Chambers' rhetoric exhibits a strong polarity. The passages cited in the text can be tabulated in two columns, labeled Christian (pejorative) and pagan (favorable). In the first column, along with "Church," would go "bishops," "barbarians," "gaolers," "ban," "triumphed," and "barred." In the second, along with "pagan," would go "braved," "won," "sportive," and "deep-rooted instinct." Note that "religious" is distinguished from "human," and "devotion and edification" from "mirth, wonder, and delight."

Clearly, Chambers' anticlericalism is complemented by a pronounced sympathy for things pagan. The same sympathy is evident in Karl Pearson's studies of witchcraft and of the German Passion play, where it is associated with a bias toward "Aryanism" reminiscent of Nietzsche. The association is worth mentioning because it has reappeared in the twentieth century in the attempts by Stumpfl, Pascal, Hunningher, and others to show that almost all dramatic elements in medieval drama are derived from survivals of Aryan ritual and folk custom.[50] In Chambers the sympathy toward paganism is never so extreme. It does, however, divert attention from Christian backgrounds. And since the "Renaissance" popularized by Taine, Burckhardt, and Symonds was primarily a "pagan" Renaissance, it also contributed something to the sense of discontinuity between medieval and sixteenth-century drama. With the advent of humanism, Chambers observes, drama at last "put off its exclusively religious character, and enter[ed] upon a new heritage."[51] Yet even in the new era, ecclesiastical authorities remained bitterly hostile. Just as Catholics were beginning to accommodate themselves to drama, the Lollard author of *A Tretise of Miraclis Pleyinge* (*ca.* 1400) raised the old objections anew, and bequeathed his attitudes to sixteenth-century Puritans. The first volume of *The Mediaeval Stage* closes with the melancholy observation that "it is a far cry from Tertullian to Bishop Grosseteste to Archbishop Grindal, but each alike voices for his own day the relentless hostility of the austerer clergy during all ages to the ineradicable *ludi* of pagan inheritance."[52]

Although F. P. Wilson's suggestion that Chambers "writes about religious drama and leaves out religion"[53] is not wholly serious, it contains an important truth. The view encouraged by *The Mediaeval Stage* is that drama originated in spite of Christianity, not because of it. In addition to

---

[50] The celebration of "Aryan" and "folk" elements of culture began with German romanticism (Herder) and gained momentum from the work of Fichte and Schleiermacher, the operas of Wagner, and Nietzsche's attack on Christianity. Chambers may have absorbed some of this admiration for things Aryan from Otto Schraeder, *Pre-Christian Antiquities of the Aryan People* (trans. F. B. Jevons [London, 1890]), which is cited in his bibliography. Karl Pearson believed strongly in both the importance and the fundamental health of pagan survivals in Christian religious drama (see above, n. 47). English and American criticism quietly dropped the Aryan theory of the origins of drama, but it was revived briefly during the 1930's by Robert Stumpfl (*Kultspiele des Germanen als Ursprung des mittelalterlichen Dramas* [Berlin, 1936]). Also, R. Pascal, "On the Origins of Liturgical Drama in the Middle Ages," *MLR*, XXXVI (1941), 369–87; and B. Hunningher, *The Origin of the Theatre* (New York, 1961).

[51] II, 181.

[52] I, 419. Cf. II, 102–3.

[53] "Obituary Notice," p. 277.

distorting the understanding of medieval drama itself, this view encourages emphasis on discontinuity between medieval and Renaissance drama and prepares the way for (or complements) a reading of Shakespeare which ignores or actively denies the religious elements in his plays.

If Chambers exhibits the anticlericalism of his age, he also manifests the historical scholar's impatience with literary theory. The first edition of A. W. Ward's *History of English Dramatic Literature*, published in 1875, begins with an extended theoretical discussion of the nature of drama. In the second edition of 1898, the theoretical introduction is dropped "to make room for more ample treatment of various passages in the body of the work."[54] In effect, Ward joined the apostles of fact. Chambers, on the other hand, never threatened apostasy. At no point in *The Mediaeval Stage* is there a discussion of what constitutes drama, and Chambers' definition must be reconstructed from various more or less casual observations.

Evidently Chambers believed in the existence of a mimetic instinct. While the phraseology suggests Aristotle, there is a strong tendency to regard the mimetic instinct as non- or even anti-Christian.[55] After defining drama as a mimetic art, Chambers offers a few suggestions for differentiating it from other mimetic forms such as lyric poetry, minstrelsy, and dance. Minstrelsy, he observes, employs dialogue, which is "the first condition of drama," but it does not use two other essential elements, "impersonation and a distribution of roles between at least two performers."[56] In other words, there are three criteria for differentiating the dramatic from the nondramatic. These are dialogue, impersonation, and "action" in the sense of role-playing. Each of them is important, and presumably Chambers did not feel that they could be ranked. Although they owe something to the discussion of "modes of imitation" in the *Poetics* 1147ᵃ–48ᵇ, they grossly oversimplify Aristotle's concept and disregard his equally important discussion of the six "parts" of tragedy. In particular, they ignore his comments on such subjects as unity, plot, and character. They are external criteria that are useful in selecting documents but that contribute little to the interpretation of the documents selected.

In retrospect, *The Mediaeval Stage* is a composite of the often contradictory ideas shaping nineteenth-century historical scholarship. It is a

---

[54] A. W. Ward, *A History of English Dramatic Literature*, I, v.

[55] I, 90ff., associates the mimetic instinct with "the folk" and appears to be based on Frazer. *MS*, I, 147, however, appears to be indebted to the somewhat different ideas of Karl Groos, *The Play of Man*, trans. E. L. Baldwin (London, 1901), pp. 280–319. See below, pp. 31–32.

[56] I, 77, 81. Cf. II, 6.

triumph of the effort to collect documentary facts, but many of the facts are, by common agreement, tangential. It is strongly influenced by the analogy between biological and literary evolution, but the evolutionary hypothesis is contradicted by Chambers' sense of the Renaissance as an antithesis to medieval culture, and weakened in respect to medieval drama by the impossibility of establishing a chronology of the movement from *Quem quaeritis* to Corpus Christi cycle. It attempts to understand the social and economic milieu of medieval drama, but it is affected by anti-clericalism to such a degree that the dramatic elements in religious drama are treated as a rebellion against religion rather than as attempts to express it. Finally, its definition of drama is inadequate. Unfortunately, the limitations of *The Mediaeval Stage* have had as much influence as its virtues on Chambers' successors.

III

Karl Young's *Drama of the Medieval Church* was published in 1933. A considerable amount of scholarship had accumulated during the thirty years since Chambers' *Mediaeval Stage*, but nothing had appeared to threaten Chambers' pre-eminence. Young wrote in his Preface, "I take pleasure in pointing to my use of his *Mediaeval Stage* in most of the chapters that follow."[57]

Young's most obvious contribution is his sizable addition to the documentary facts made available by Chambers. His work began as "a slight volume . . . in the way of an exposition," but grew into a thirteen-hundred-page corpus of medieval Latin drama. Like Chambers, Young felt that documents were more important than interpretations. He invites the reader "to centre his attention upon the plays themselves, and to assign to the accompanying exposition only such secondary importance as may seem to him appropriate."[58] Thus, says Young, if he fails in what he has written himself, he may "still hope to 'merit the thanks of the antiquarian,' through putting into his hands a considerable body of originals either freshly verified, or now brought forward for the first time."[59]

There can be no question of Young's success in this endeavor. On the other hand, Young's theoretical contributions are considerably more important than his modest Preface indicates. In terms of content, *The Drama of the Medieval Church* is an advance beyond Chambers in the

[57] *The Drama of the Medieval Church* (Oxford, 1933), I, xv. Hereafter cited as *DMC*.
[58] I, vii.
[59] I, viii. It is perhaps significant that Young is quoting Thomas Warton.

direction of definition. The decline of classical drama and the varieties of semidramatic spectacle are dealt with in a twelve-page Introduction. Conversely, almost two hundred pages are devoted to the Roman liturgy and the dramatic ceremonies associated with it in the Middle Ages. Chief emphasis falls on the development of three major types of liturgical drama: the Passion plays, the Nativity plays, and various extrabiblical and legendary plays. Young makes no effort to follow the plays from Latin into the vernacular.

Young's method is empirical in a sense which Langlois and Seignobos would have heartily approved. He promises a "descriptive" treatment of the material, and explicitly rejects aesthetic analysis, which is defined by a reference to the "aesthetic and spiritual aspects of the liturgy—its majesty, its charm, and its significance."[60] Evidently, aesthetic analysis has to do with the appeal of artistic forms to an audience. Since this sort of appeal is "subjective," it has no place in "descriptive" (i.e., objective) criticism. On the credit side, Young's approach avoids anticlericalism. Chambers had considered the devils of medieval drama as evidence of the recrudescence of pagan instinct; Young observes only that they were "undoubtedly . . . an object of derision as well as of fear, but in a particular dramatic situation we may not be able to say confidently which effect was intended or achieved."[61] Chambers—and a good many of his followers—had stressed the comic aspects of the liturgical plays; Young considers the plays for the most part "serious," even down to Balaam's ass, and attributes their early expansion to "those who were especially ambitious for the development of religious drama" rather than to the anti-Christian demands of "the folk."[62]

On the debit side, Young's "objectivity" creates two serious problems. To consider it apart from the stereotyped debate over subjectivity versus objectivity, his refusal to discuss aesthetic matters—matters involving "majesty, charm, and significance"—is a refusal to discuss the reasons why the liturgy and liturgical drama appealed to the medieval audience. Hence the second problem: unless these reasons are considered, it is impossible to interpret medieval drama in terms of the forces which actually shaped it, and there is a tendency to fall back on the presuppositions evident in Chambers. In spite of Young's cautionary statements, his approach encourages a reading of the history of medieval drama as a process of "secularization," with a complementary stress on tangential

[60] I, viii. Young's principles, summarized on pp. ix–xii, show the same concern for documents evident in Langlois and Seignobos.

[61] II, 406–7.

[62] II, 422.

action, minor characters, and comic farce. That he himself accepted this general view is indicated by his reference to an "impulse toward increasing the worldly appeal of the plays through the comic element," which manifested itself in medieval vernacular drama, although not evident in the Latin plays. [63]

The problem of the development of medieval drama leads directly to the problem of evolution. In his Preface Young appears to reject the evolutionary concept in favor of the method of logical classification which had been subdominant in *The Mediaeval Stage*. He will group the plays, he says, in "the *logical* order of development, from the simplest to the most complex and elaborate. Presumably this is, in general, also the *historical* order, but from the dates of the manuscripts a demonstration is usually impossible." [64] Even in this statement, however, the logical order is related to the historical order. The evolutionary hypothesis was too well established and too attractive to be surrendered lightly. After duly expressing his reservations, Young contradicts them with the assertion that "presumably" the evolutionary model is historically true. The same belief is evident in his vocabulary. Although his organization is apparently logical, he frequently employs terms and ideas suggesting biological analogies, among them "process," "development," "developments from a single form," "transition," and "growth." Toward the end of his Introduction, Young expresses his general view of early drama. It is the same one that Chambers had expressed thirty years earlier. Medieval drama, he asserts, "presents to the historian a unique opportunity for isolating a literary form and observing its development from almost inarticulate origins, through centuries of earnest experiment, into firmly conceived results." [65]

The influence of evolutionary theory on Young is both deeper and more pervasive than this echo of Chambers might indicate. Young's Darwinism is not a restatement of tired organic analogies; rather, it is a fundamentally revised theory in which the concept of mutations—sudden, radical changes—has replaced the concept of development by minute variations.

Like England, America had produced a large number of social Darwinists and evolutionary historians during the last quarter of the nineteenth century. William Dean Howells espoused Darwin's cause in *Harper's Magazine* and later in *Criticism and Fiction* (1892). William Graham Sumner taught Darwinian sociology at Yale, and Thomas S. Perry risked (and

[63] II, 422.
[64] I, viii–ix.
[65] I, 12. Cf. *MS*, II, 3.

lost) his Harvard professorship for the sake of Darwinian ideas in criticism. Thereafter the literary application of evolutionary ideas in America spread rapidly. John Fiske, E. C. Stedman, W. M. Payne, and Kuno Franke, chairman of the Harvard German Department, supported the use of evolution as a theory of criticism. In 1898 Felix Schelling recognized the application of Darwinism to the history of drama in an article in the University of Pennsylvania *Bulletin* entitled "Studies in the Evolution of Dramatic Species from the Beginnings of English Drama to the Year 1660."

Most of this early criticism is organic. A significant new departure was made by Professor John M. Manly in an article published in 1907 in the fourth volume of *Modern Philology*, titled "Literary Forms and the New Theory of the Origin of Species." At that time and for some years to come, Professor Manly was the outstanding American authority on medieval drama. He was also the teacher of Karl Young and of several other scholars destined to become major figures in American medieval studies. For both reasons his article had—and continues to have—considerable influence. It led immediately to three lengthy essays in Darwinian criticism by John P. Hoskins of Princeton; it was quoted approvingly by such scholars as P. S. Allen, George C. Taylor, H. S. V. Jones, and George R. Coffman; it was referred to in 1955 by Hardin Craig, at the beginning of *English Religious Drama*, as "brilliant and original"; and it is cited at the beginning of the entry on drama in the revised Thrall, Hibbard, and Holman *Handbook to Literature*, published in 1960. In other words, it is still a living influence today.[66]

[66] For the spread of Darwinism in American criticism, see especially H. H. Clark, "The Influence of Science on American Literary Criticism," pp. 109–38. Clark makes it clear that the chief sources of literary evolutionism prior to Manly were Taine, Brunetière, and J. A. Symonds. See also Elton Miles, "The Influence of Darwin on American Literary Criticism," in *The Impact of Darwinian Thought on American Life and Culture* (Austin, Texas, 1959), pp. 27–36. Manly's article is "Literary Forms and the New Theory of the Origin of Species" (*MP*, IV [1906–7], 577–95). Its influence can be traced in: John P. Hoskins, "Biological Analogy in Literary Criticism: I. Variation and Personality" (pp. 408–34); Hoskins, "II. The Struggle for Existence and the Survival of the Fittest" (*MP*, VII [1909–10], 61–82); Hoskins, "The Place and Function of a Standard in a Genetic Theory of Literary Development" (*PMLA*, XV [1910], 379–402); P. S. Allen, "The Medieval Mimus, Part II" (*MP*, VIII [1910–11], 126); George C. Taylor, "The Middle English Religious Lyric" (*MP*, V [1907–8], 16); H. S. V. Jones, "The Plan of the *Canterbury Tales*" (*MP*, XIII [1915], 45–48); George R. Coffman, *A New Theory concerning the Origin of the Miracle Play* (pp. 9–12); Hardin Craig, *ERD* (p. 19). The fact that all of these studies are of medieval literature is obviously significant. For other uses of Manly's definition, see, e.g., Thomas M. Parrott and Robert H. Ball, *A Short View of Elizabethan Drama* (New York, 1958), pp. 4–5; William F. Thrall *et al.*, *A Handbook to Literature* (rev. ed.; New York, 1960), p. 150.

Manly's success stems from the fact that he significantly altered the co-ordinates of Darwinian critical method. He explains (perhaps with Chambers explicitly in mind) that "the historians of literature . . . like the thinkers in all fields of thought, have come under the pervasive, dominating influence of a great zoological theory, and under this influence have been blind to some of our facts, have distorted others, and have allowed ourselves to substitute catchy phrases for a real understanding of the processes." His experience with medieval drama convinced him that the accepted concept of organic growth was inadequate: "the conditions of change had been very different from what the theory presupposed."[67] Manly did not, however, abandon evolutionary analogies. Instead he turned to the new theory of evolution by mutation. This theory, an outgrowth of the nineteenth-century study of genetics, had been explained by Charles A. White in an article on "The Mutation Theory of Professor de Vries," published in the *Smithsonian Report* for 1901.[68] In de Vries's theory, evolution proceeds in two ways, by "fluctuating" variation, which accounts for gradual improvements within species, and by "sudden and unaccountable differences" or mutations, which account for the development of new species. Accordingly, new literary species develop "not by gradual accumulation of insensible differences, but by a sudden definite change . . . because certain literary forms, like certain species of plants, owe their distinctive character to the presence of one essential element."[69]

[67] Pp. 580–81, 591–92. Manly aptly expresses the appeal of Darwinian thought in the early twentieth century: ". . . even if we try to keep steadily before us the fallacy of reading in such terms as 'organism' or 'evolution,' it is practically impossible to speak or think of any unified body of facts showing progressive change as men habitually spoke and thought before 1860" (p. 580). Like other neoevolutionists, Manly objected to (1) the organic analogy and (2) the *Natura non facit salus* idea (see Cassirer, *Logic of the Humanities*, p. 179). It is important to realize that although neoevolutionists occasionally seem to attack evolution, they themselves believed that they were improving on earlier efforts. Hoskins wrote: "We have no quarrel with the theory of evolution, we are rather convinced that it is almost the only theory which gives any promise of bringing order out of the chaos of aesthetic, biographical, and historical monographs, which form the bulk of critical production today" ("The Struggle for Existence," p. 80). Craig is merely paraphrasing Young and Manly when he writes: "literary forms do not arise out of a welter of circumstances and influences, approximations and imitations, but each literary form is a special discovery or invention" (*ERD*, p. 19).

[68] Manly, "Literary Forms," p. 577. De Vries addressed a convocation at the University of Chicago in 1904, and his talk was subsequently reprinted in the *Annual Report of the Smithsonian Institute*, 1904, pp. 389–96. Manly does not mention hearing the 1904 talk, but he does tell us that he read White's article in 1903.

[69] "Literary Forms," pp. 590–91. Cf. Hugo de Vries, *Mutation Theory* (trans. J. B. Farmer and A. D. Darbishire [Chicago, 1909], I, 3): "I define mutation theory as the thesis that the characteristics of organisms are built from wholes sharply distinct from each other . . . species do not flow [into one another] but have originated from one another in a step-wise fashion. Each new whole coming from the old constitutes the new form as a species independent from the species from which it came."

The Darwinian axiom *Natura non facit saltus* is replaced by the de Vriesian axiom *Natura semper facit saltus*.

To apply the mutation theory, it was necessary to improve on earlier definitions of drama. As long as drama was considered an "organism" in continuous development from the protozoan *Quem quaeritis* to *Hamlet*, labeling was sufficient. As Manly recognized, however, the mutation theory required literary forms to be regarded as bundles of "characteristics." In this view, a new species is formed when an established characteristic changes or a new one is added to the original complex.[70] Medieval drama, Manly believed, is a perfect illustration of the mutation theory. Drawing on Chambers, he equated the elements of dialogue, action, and impersonation with the characteristics of species in mutation theory. Dialogue is the least important of these characteristics, but action and impersonation are essential. A literary form which does not employ action and impersonation may be dramatic or theatrical, but it is not drama. In the same way the miracle play, the morality play, pastoral drama, and the heroic couplet are seen as evolutionary "jumps" rather than as products of a "gradual accumulation of insensible differences."[71]

Karl Young used Manly's theory as the basis for the theoretical framework of *The Drama of the Medieval Church*. Unlike Chambers, he believed that "no satisfying study . . . can be made without . . . a candid and practical definition of the term *drama*." With a footnote bow to Manly, he continued, "A play . . . is, above all else, a story presented in action, in which the speakers or actors impersonate the characters concerned."[72] Impersonation is still more important for Young than for Manly. Dialogue, while important, is not necessary, for monologue and pantomime are "true though limited" forms of drama. It is the criterion of impersonation that leads Young to make an emphatic separation between the liturgy and the drama proper, which he believes to have emerged first in the ceremony of the *Visitatio Sepulchri*. Young quotes medieval authorities who call the Mass a drama only in order to reject their testimony. The Mass does not involve impersonation but is a "true sacrifice." It is not pretense but a literal repetition of the original sacrifice, according to Catholic

[70] "Literary Forms," pp. 580–86. See the comment on this by Hoskins, "Biological Analogy: I," pp. 409–10. Hoskins' only objection to Manly is that the "Literary Forms" article is too "impersonal." In fact, Manly's reform of evolutionary theory had the effect of emphasizing the individual's part in the process of developing new species, as Hardin Craig rightly insists (*ERD*, p. 19). Temporarily, at least, it was possible to discuss genius (see Hoskins, "Biological Analogy: I," pp. 414–20; "II," pp. 65–68).

[71] "Literary Forms," pp. 583–90.

[72] *DMC*, I, 79–80. Young first used Manly's definitions in studying liturgical drama in "Observations on the Origin of the Mediaeval Passion-Play" (*PMLA*, XXV [1910], 309–54).

doctrine: "What takes place at the altar is not an aesthetic picture of a happening in the past, but a genuine renewal of it"; "it is not a representation of an action, but an actual re-creation of it."[73]

A clearer understanding of Young's classification scheme is now possible. It is only in part a logical device based on the wish to be descriptive. It is also (perhaps primarily) a schematic elaboration of the mutation theory. Recurring theatrical elements, with emphasis on dialogue and action, are discovered in a variety of ceremonies, including the Easter Introit, the *Depositio* and *Elevatio Crucis*, the procession on Palm Sunday, and the ceremony for the consecration of a church. These are merely "dramatic" because they lack impersonation. They are what Manly called "futile variations."[74] Then in the *Visitatio Sepulchri* impersonation appears, and the new species called drama is formed. Once formed, it can develop. The development, however, is not perfectly smooth. It occurs by a series of increments (Manly's "fluctuating variations"), which, since they do not involve the essential characteristic, improve the species without changing it. The *Visitatio* manuscripts are divided into the three large "stages" originally proposed by Chambers. Stage one includes only the three Marys and the angels. Stage two adds the apostles Peter and John; stage three adds the risen Christ. Between stages the increments are dramatic episodes. There is also evolution within stages. Each stage contains "groups" arranged from simple to complex. The placing of a drama within a group depends on the absence or presence of "additions," such as the antiphon *Venite et videte*, the sequence *Victimae Paschali*, and the *Planctus Mariae*. The additions are the smallest evolutionary increment considered.

Chronology must be disregarded in Young's arrangement, but we recall his belief that "presumably" if all manuscripts were recovered anomalies

---

[73] *DMC*, I, 84–85, 110. The radical effect of the mutation theory on literary history is apparent from this arbitrary rejection of medieval testimony concerning the Mass. The same line of thought is apparent in Young's 1910 article: "To many an intelligent and sensitive observer . . . it must have occurred . . . that the addition of the merest suggestion of impersonation . . . would transform the dramatic dialogue into true drama." Other followers of Manly also seem arbitrary. Allen, for example, refuses to consider Hroswitha's plays dramas because they are not written for "impersonation." They are therefore "nothing but *legends in dialogue form*" ("Mimus," p. 25). Other scholars were encouraged to postulate evolutionary "jumps" to account for previously unexplained literary changes. Coffman, for example, explained the medieval saint's play as an evolutionary jump; Jones invoked the theory to account for the "new species" created by Chaucer in his *Canterbury Tales;* Taylor discovered evolutionary jumps in the introduction of nondramatic lyric material into Middle English drama; Hoskins found mutation at work in the formation of the Renaissance drama of personality and nineteenth-century naturalistic drama, as well as an example of the extinction of "unfit" literary forms in the decline in reputation of *Paradise Lost*.

[74] "Literary Forms," p. 581.

would disappear. The result is strikingly similar to a biological classification chart showing the origin of a species, its variants, and its pattern of evolution toward its most recent (and, in drama, its most complex) members. In *The Drama of the Medieval Church* the most recent "member" considered is the Passion play. In *English Religious Drama* Hardin Craig extends the survey to the cycle plays and moralities. The result, says Craig, is "not unlike the meticulously perfect range of colours seen in the breeding of the fruit-fly: every possible colour is realized, but not by a sequential transition from one shade to another."[75]

Because of Young's *terminus ad quem*, the question of continuity between medieval and Renaissance drama does not occur in *The Drama of the Medieval Church*. It does arise in Craig's *English Religious Drama*, which in this respect may be considered a logical continuation of Young's work. The lacuna apparent in Chambers' theory persists. His dislike for the critical emphasis on "comic realism" leads Craig to insist that "medieval religious drama existed for its own self, and not as an early stage of secular drama,"[76] a position clearly at odds with evolutionary teleology. Although the idea of viewing medieval drama "for its own self" has suggestions of aesthetic formalism, as used by Craig it serves chiefly to emphasize the discontinuity between medieval and Renaissance drama. The mysteries, says Craig, "were medieval in their essence, and the Middle Ages were passing."[77] If any influence persists, it is not via comic realism but in the backwaters of sixteenth-century Latin Biblical drama, Jesuit school drama, and vestigial survivals like Bale's Protestant mystery cycle and the Stonyhurst pageants.[78] Morality plays have a more obvious influence, but for Shakespeare, even their influence is indirect—it is limited to "a quality of moral earnestness" common among sixteenth-century Englishmen. Chambers had hoped for a history of medieval drama which would "explain the pre-existing conditions which, by the latter half of the sixteenth century, made the great Shakespearean stage possible." The failure of this ideal was inherent in his assumptions. Its epitaph is Craig's observation that "there is only the faintest possibility that there was any tangible influence of the moral interlude on Shakespeare when he wrote *Macbeth*. . . . It is not therefore a matter of the formal and often thin thing called literary influence that makes Macbeth remind one of Everyman, but a community of race and purpose that found expression in the drama of two different though still closely connected ages."[79]

[75] P. 6. For Craig's use of the action-dialogue-impersonation trilogy, see *ibid.*, pp. 3–4.
[76] P. 7.
[77] P. 363.
[78] *ERD*, pp. 367–71.
[79] P. 389.

IV

At this point we may legitimately proceed to summary and evaluation. Chambers, Young, and Craig agree that the chronology of medieval drama is difficult to trace, but the outline and logic of the development is clear. After a long period of quiescence, a dramatic instinct asserted itself in the *Quem quaeritis* trope of the Easter liturgy. The trope grew, was detached from the liturgy, and eventually became genuine drama. Similar dramas developed in connection with Christmas and other Church festivals. At first the dramas were given in the church and in Latin. Later they were presented in the churchyard, and vernacular began to be used. In the course of this development they were expanded, and much comic and farcical material was added.

Although there is disagreement about the steps in the process, all authorities agree that the individual plays tended to be collected and presented in groups. By the early fourteenth century large-scale cycles had been created which form the basis of the Passion plays and Corpus Christi cycles of the fifteenth century. In northern England the cycles were most popular; in the south and on the Continent the Passion play became dominant.

We may pause here, for the time being, to ask what the history sketched in the preceding paragraphs amounts to. No one who reads Chambers and Young can fail to be impressed by their energy. If their theory is a skeleton, they have created an enormous body around it. No available document has remained unread, no known allusion has been overlooked, no surviving fragment of dialogue has been ignored. If later scholars have gleaned a good many new facts after the harvest, their findings have added fresh confirmation or modified details without affecting the whole.

The structure created by Chambers and Young gives the sense of being unshakably solid—of being objective and empirical in the best sense of those terms. Yet on examination it proves to be arbitrary. Buried among the facts and protestations of objectivity are assumptions peculiar to a specific age and group of thinkers. In the first place, the empiricism radically limits the type of question which can be asked. The focus is on the "what" rather than the "why." The resulting form is closer to a chronicle than a history in the true sense of the word. From Thucydides and Polybius to Collingwood, historians have recognized that the number of facts available to them is limited only by the patience of their readers and the affluence of their publishers. The historian must select and discriminate, and his highest achievement is to create a coherent structure which explains the "why" of history as well as the "what." J. M. Manly asked the question, "Can we not lay aside all theories and merely collect the facts of literary development, and then enquire what they mean?" His reply is a challenge to the most fundamental assumption of nineteenth-century empirical scholarship: "We cannot. The whole history of science tells us in unmistakable tones that no man who merely collected facts and then inquired into their meaning has ever succeeded in dealing with any problem but the tiniest."[80]

Even as Manly made this point, historical scholarship was being challenged from several other directions. Humanists following in the path of Matthew Arnold and James Russell Lowell complained that "scientism" in cultural study was destroying the very values which justified the emphasis placed on it in higher education.[81] A quite different group, in the tradition of Schiller and Coleridge, argued with equal vehemence that historical criticism was based on a fundamental misconception of the nature of art. The most telling expression of this view, Croce's *Aesthetic*, first appeared in 1901 and was published in English translation in 1909, followed almost immediately by Joel Spingarn's announcement in "The New Criticism" (1911) that "we have done with the 'evolution' of literature. . . . The later nineteenth century gave a new air of verisimilitude to this old theory by borrowing the term 'evolution' from science; but this too involves a fundamental misconception of the free and original movement of art."[82]

A question of a seemingly different sort, and one directly pertinent to the history of medieval drama, was being raised by the cultural historians themselves. The study of primitive culture had begun on a confidently progressivist note with Fontanelle a century and a half before Darwin. Primitive society was of interest chiefly as it revealed the abysmal depths from which humanity had dragged itself. Although Vico and Herder qualified this view, it persisted and actually gained strength in the generation following Darwin.[83]

[80] "Literary Forms," p. 592.

[81] Typical of "neohumanist" invective against historical criticism are Irving Babbitt's *Literature and the American College* (New York, 1956), first published in 1908, and Norman Foerster's *The American Scholar* (Chapel Hill, N.C., 1929).

[82] *Visions and Revisions in American Literary Criticism*, ed. B. Oldsey and A. Lewis, Jr. (New York, 1962), p. 19. There is no satisfactory history of aesthetic criticism in the later nineteenth and early twentieth century. A useful but partial survey of the earlier period is given by Benedetto Croce, "History of Aesthetic," in *Aesthetic*, trans. D. Ainslie (New York, 1960), pp. 155ff. Bosanquet is unsatisfactory. For excerpts and brief comment, see Hardison, *Modern Continental Literary Criticism*, pp. xi–xix, 141–224.

[83] For the history of the study of primitive culture, see Richard Chase, *The Quest for Myth* (Baton Rouge, La., 1949), pp. 7–12, 38–65. For the Victorian anthropologists and Frazer, see John B. Vickery, "*The Golden Bough*: Impact and Archetype," pp. 37–40; James Kissane, "Victorian Mythology," *Victorian Studies*, VI (1962), 5–28.

E. B. Tylor, Andrew Lang, W. Robertson Smith, and James Frazer were (or began as) evolutionists, but the very nature of their material forced them to relax their doctrinaire position. Max Muller, father of the idea that myth is a "disease of language," had contributed, both by his theory that primitive society is a degeneration from a higher culture and by his editions of oriental texts, to an awareness that society is not evolutionary in the biological sense. The "primitive" mentality which produced the Upanishads may be different from the modern one, but it is certainly not simpler. E. B. Tylor's *Primitive Culture* (1871) was a direct response to *The Origin of Species* and was praised by Darwin himself in a letter following its publication. Yet to understand primitive myth Tylor was forced to attempt to see the world from the primitive point of view, and he thus anticipated in some measure the nonevolutionary stance of modern comparative anthropology.[84] The same may be said of James Frazer.[85] A firm rationalist who never tired of ironic descriptions of primitive superstitions, he was directly responsible for the Cambridge school of anthropologists, contributed significantly to the thought of Freud and Jung, and continues to influence such diverse thinkers as Clyde Kluckhohn, Stanley Hyman, T. H. Gaster, and Northrop Frye, none of whom would accept the straightforward evolutionism which Frazer himself believed in.[86]

If there is any meaning to the work of these anthropologists, psychologists, and critics, it is that rather than clarifying cultural phenomena, the evolutionary analogy obscures them. Therefore, although the documents accumulated by Chambers and Young remain valuable, the evolutionary history of the drama—whether organic or in terms of mutation—needs to be re-examined. As Spingarn was insisting in 1911, "art has no origin separate from man's life. . . . The simple art of early times may be studied with profit; but the researches of anthropology have no vital significance for Criticism, unless the anthropologist studies the simplest forms of art in the same spirit as its highest. . . ."[87]

The need for a new perspective on medieval drama rests on far more than the mere desire to substitute modern for nineteenth-century views. It arises from failures inherent in, and often recognized by, the his-

---

[84] E.g., Tylor: ". . . myth is the history of its authors, not of its subjects; it records the lives not of superhuman heroes, but of poetic nations" (*Primitive Culture* [London, 1871], I, 416).

[85] Vickery, "*The Golden Bough:* Impact and Archetype," p. 51.

[86] For a review of some phases of Frazer's influence, see Stanley E. Hyman, "The Ritual View of Myth and the Mythic," in *Myth: A Symposium*, ed. Thomas A. Sebeok (Bloomington, Ind., 1955), pp. 84–94. See also Henry Murray (ed.), *Myth and Mythmaking* (New York, 1960).

[87] "The New Criticism," pp. 19–20.

torians of medieval drama themselves. Thus it is a truism of the historical method that the scholar must seek understanding of the literary work in the context of the age which produced it and, as far as possible, from the point of view of its contemporaries. Yet Chambers and Young clearly violate this principle. Chambers' teleology leads him to write about medieval forms as though they existed as transitional points on the road to "the great Shakespearean stage." His hostility to the Church leads him to ignore the religious content of the plays and to stress "secularization." In the same way Young refuses as a matter of principle to examine the plays aesthetically—that is, in terms of the very elements which might explain their popularity. And perhaps most obvious of all, Young quotes elaborate medieval discussions of the dramatic nature of the Mass only to reject them because the Mass does not conform to his twentieth-century definition of drama.

A second problem is the evident failure of the evolutionary approach to achieve its own goals. The gap between medieval and Renaissance drama remains as wide as ever in spite of numerous demonstrations that in other areas of culture the contrast between Middle Ages and Renaissance is far less emphatic than Burckhardt imagined.[88] As Craig admitted in 1955, no real influences of the type recognized by historical scholarship have been demonstrated between religious drama and Shakespeare. The best that one can say on the basis of the standard histories is that first there was medieval drama and then there was Elizabethan drama. In practice, the introductions and handbooks to English drama do just that, devoting a chapter or two to summaries of Chambers and Young, and then proceeding to the sixteenth century with scarcely a backward glance. Or—if the author belongs to the minority still demanding influences—continuity is found in "comic realism." Craig properly complains, "Critics of the medieval religious drama have treated excrescences and aberrations as if such things, thought of as looking forward to the dramatic masterpieces of the Renaissance, were the end and purpose of dramatic activity. They have been interested in devils, raging tyrants, and clowns, in the shrewishness of Noah's wife, and the sheep-stealing episode of the Townley Second Shepherds' Play, and have sometimes been indifferent to the fact that

[88] See Wallace K. Ferguson, *The Renaissance in Historical Thought* (Boston, 1948); E. M. W. Tillyard, *The English Renaissance: Fact or Fiction* (Baltimore, 1952). Representative of the best work stressing the continuity between the Middle Ages and the Renaissance is Ernst Robert Curtius, *European Literature and the Latin Middle Ages*, trans. W. Trask (New York, 1953). See also the retrospective comments by Kristeller and Weinberg in *The Renaissance: A Reconsideration of the Theories and Interpretations of the Age*, ed. Tinsley Helton (Madison, Wis., 1961).

medieval religious drama existed for itself . . . and not as an early stage of the secular drama."[89]

The need to stress "excrescences and aberrations" is such a clear demonstration of the failure of historical scholarship to live up to its own ideals that perhaps nothing more need be said on this score. But there is another critique of the Chambers-Young approach which needs to be made. The terms action, dialogue, and impersonation appear quite simple at first glance, but the more closely they are examined, the more questionable they become. Generally speaking, they are understood as externals by Chambers and his successors. Thus action does not refer to plot or Aristotelian praxis, but to stage activity, perhaps akin to *actio* as used by Elizabethan rhetoric in reference to the lore of delivering orations. Action occurs whenever there is movement on the stage which mimics the movements or gestures of characters who, because they are imitated, are conceived to be more "real" than the flesh and blood players. Discounting the curious idea that fictitious characters are more real than actors, all performances—pageants, dances, orations, ceremonies—may be said to have action. Such action is independent of dramatic structure. It is part of what Aristotle called spectacle, and if taken seriously as a differentia for drama, would imply that a play ceases to be a play when it is read rather than performed. At any rate, as utilized, the criterion of action confuses the issue by directing attention away from dramatic form and focusing it on externals—stage directions, costumes, machinery, and the like. It has the same effect on the criticism of the drama that the classification of a whale as a fish would have on a system of zoology.

The criterion of dialogue is no less slippery. Young discounted it because it would have caused the exclusion of monologue and pantomime from the ranks of drama. Add to this point the agonies of critical indecision caused by the *débat*, and it is apparent that an emphasis on dialogue creates more problems than it solves.

Finally there is the criterion of impersonation, which, since Manly, has been the most important of the three differentiae. The most authoritative definition (Young's) asserts: "As to the nature of impersonation in itself there can scarcely be any substantial disagreement. It consists in physical imitation. In some external and recognizable manner the actor must pretend to be the person whose words he is speaking, and whose actions he is imitating. The performer must do more than merely *represent* the chosen personage; he must also *resemble* him, or at least show his intention of doing so. It follows, then, that the dialogue and physical movements of those who participate in the liturgy will be transformed from the *dramatic*

[89] *ERD*, pp. 6–7.

into *drama* whenever these persons convey a story and pretend to be the characters in this story."[90]

The definition is complex, but certain features stand out. Evidently, impersonation is closely related to the criterion of action. Like action, it is conceived as something physical—a "physical imitation." The point is important. Young is clearly not thinking of literary texts but of performances, not of what appears in manuscripts but of what would presumably occur if the manuscript were acted out.[91] Whatever else it may be, this is an extremely limiting view of drama. Discussions of drama are often weakened by ignorance of stagecraft, but acting and staging procedures are certainly not essential elements of the theory of drama. A knowledge of the habits of Elizabethan players, for example, is useful to a reader of *Hamlet*, but lack of it will not prevent him from understanding and appreciating the play. Charles Lamb's preference for *Lear* as read to *Lear* as performed is a case in point.

In addition to placing undue stress on performance, "impersonation" connotes artificiality. It suggests make-believe in contrast to reality. Both Chambers and Young approved of this suggestion. Chambers explicitly endorsed the "play" theory of art in the formulations of Herbert Spencer and Karl Groos.[92] According to the play theory, man's activities are

---

[90] *DMC*, I, 80–81.

[91] In his 1910 article in *PMLA* (p. 313) Young cites "a gesture, a change of facial expression, a bit of costume" as examples of impersonation. The triviality of this view is evident when we note the questions which could arise if it were taken seriously. Would Hroswitha's "legends in dialogue form" become dramas if they were acted today? Or is it the intention of the author which determines whether a work is drama or not? If so, how do we ascertain the intention of an author long dead, e.g., Hroswitha? The answer would probably be "by the probabilities of the age; for since Hroswitha wrote at a time when nobody composed dramas, she herself could not have composed them." But this answer, of course, assumes what is to be proved and, in addition, gets away from impersonation altogether. Again, if the Mass is not drama because it is too real (i.e., Christ is not "represented" but is actually present, as Young has it), then is the Episcopal Communion service a drama? Or the Protestant Lord's Supper? Or do we not shift from the intentions of the author to the intentions of the performer (or spectator), and if so, which performer (or spectator)? These questions are not facetious. They illustrate the inadequacy of the criterion of "impersonation" to even the simplest demands placed upon it. Since Young studied drama with George Baker of Harvard before coming under Manly's influence, he should have known better.

[92] *MS*, I, 147–48. That the idea can lead to genuine insight is illustrated by Schiller's *Letters on the Aesthetic Education of Man* and Huizinga's *Homo Ludens*. However, in the theories of Herbert Spencer and Karl Groos, which Chambers drew upon, art occupies only a minor place, and the play idea becomes another way of saying that art is trivial and/or childish (see Spencer's *Principles of Psychology* [New York, 1890], II, 629). Groos (*The Play of Man*, pp. 389–95) is somewhat more sophisticated, but remarks, "The more earnest is a man's life, the more will he enjoy the refuge afforded by play when he can engage in sham occupations, chosen at will, and unencumbered by serious aims" (p. 389).

divided into the practical and utilitarian on the one hand, and the useless on the other. Work, whether physical or intellectual, is utilitarian and is the normal lot of mature men. Occasionally, however, human beings undertake "unprofitable activities ... serving no end beyond themselves."[93] These activities are play. Children's games, dancing, all forms of make-believe, and art—particularly poetry—are varieties of play. Needless to say, drama is also a variety of play. That Young agreed is indicated by his use of words like "pretend" and "pretense" as synonyms for the actor's art and by his insistence that the Mass is not "drama" because the participants actually become what they represent—i.e., the ceremony literally becomes too real.

Right or wrong, the play theory of art echoes the nineteenth-century debate between science and poetry. In this debate the key words for science were "objective," "real," "fact," and "common sense," while the key words for art were "imagination," "emotion," "play," and "suspension of disbelief." Impersonation is therefore a nineteenth-century concept, and one which is in marked contrast to medieval and Renaissance attitudes. One needs only to recall the list of confessions attributed to the effect of drama in Thomas Heywood's *Apology for Actors* to realize that during the Renaissance the line between art and reality was much less definite than it was in the nineteenth century. Hamlet's plot to trap the conscience of a king is another example; and even in the midst of the Age of Reason, Tom Jones's friend Partridge "fell into so violent a trembling that his knees knocked together" on seeing the ghost of the elder Hamlet. Even today the experience of great drama is much more than make-believe. There would seem to be no reason to deny to medieval man watching a dramatization of the Passion of Christ experiences which modern man can have while watching *Oedipus Rex*. The folklore of such survivals as the Oberammergau Passion play is rich in examples of the curious mingling of art and reality which medieval drama seems to have encouraged.[94]

If it is conceded that no simple line can be drawn between art and life, the principle applies to the actor as well as the spectator. One of the basic concepts of the study of primitive customs, accepted since Frazer, is that of identification. The priest does not represent the god, he *is* the god. That identification is a common experience among actors is attested to

---

[93] *MS*, I, 147.

[94] The curious association between particular professions and particular plays (e.g., Goldsmiths and the Magi; the Shipmen and Noah, etc.) also serves to illustrate the point.

by numerous sources.[95] If Manly or Young had consulted professional actors, in fact, they would have discovered that far from being beyond "substantial disagreement," the idea of impersonation had been hotly debated since it was first suggested—as a novelty—by Diderot.[96] It was the subject for an early (1888) psychological study by William Archer, in which actors were asked to describe their attitudes toward their roles. By far the greatest number agreed that "contagion" (i.e., identification) was necessary for successful acting. "In this sympathetic contagion," concludes Archer, ". . . the poet—say Shakespeare—fecundates the imagination of the actor—say Salvini—so that it bodies forth the great passion-quivering phantom of Othello. In the act of representation, this phantom is, as it were, superimposed on the real man . . . the passion of the moment informs him to his fingertips, and his portrayal of a human soul in agony is true to the minutest detail. His suffering . . . cannot be called other than real."[97] Stanislavski's "method" has similar elements. Assuming that "the actor must first of all believe in everything that takes place on the stage,"[98] Stanislavski designed his famous "method" exercises to facilitate generation of this belief. It may be said, therefore, that the criterion of impersonation used by Manly and Young is at odds not only with probable medieval attitudes but with the impassioned testimony of nineteenth- and twentieth-century actors as well.

In sum, the standard historians of medieval drama have followed the procedure used by early evolutionary anthropologists in connection with the study of myth. They have attributed present concepts and attitudes to a culture of the past. They have assumed that medieval man thought like nineteenth-century man, or ought to have done so. The result has been serious distortion. History has become teleological, interpreted both intentionally and unconsciously in terms of what texts anticipate rather than what they are. The texts themselves have been read as though they were intended for production under conditions vaguely foreshadowing Covent Garden and for audiences vaguely like the rowdies in the Victorian gallery.

Chambers, Young, and Craig believed deeply that medieval drama constitutes a unique opportunity for the study of literary form. If they

---

[95] See William Archer, *Masks or Faces? A Study of the Psychology of Acting* (London, 1888), *passim*, for actual case histories and testimonials from living actors.

[96] *Ibid.*, pp. 1–11.

[97] *Ibid.*, pp. 200–1.

[98] Quoted in Toby Cole and Helen Krich Chinoy (eds.), *Actors on Acting* (New York, 1949), p. 435.

were right, the opportunity deserves to be exploited. The documents and facts which they so painstakingly assembled should be used creatively. In 1929 Norman Foerster complained of the scholarly "mystique of the brick," according to which each new literary monograph is a brick stored in a gigantic brickyard for use by an architect who never comes. The section of the yard marked "History of English Drama" is particularly rich in bricks. It is high time that scholars began building with them.

ESSAY II

The Mass as Sacred Drama

I

IN 1511 ALBRECHT DÜRER planned a series of woodcuts on the theme *salus animae*. To illustrate the importance of the Holy Eucharist in this theme, he turned naturally to the Mass of St. Gregory. A popular subject in the late Middle Ages, it became especially prominent in the art of the fifteenth and sixteenth centuries, when papal indulgences were offered to those illustrating it.

The story on which it is based is apparently rather late, but an analogue may be found in the *Legenda aurea*. During a Mass at St. Peter's, a Roman matron scoffed at the idea that the Host is transformed into the body of Christ at the moment of Consecration. Appalled by her skepticism, St. Gregory placed the consecrated Host on the altar and prayed devoutly. Suddenly the Host was transformed. According to the later story (which locates the events in Santa Croce), the risen Christ appeared, displaying the stigmata and surrounded by the instruments of the Passion. The skeptic was immediately converted and received Communion. The Mass then concluded in normal fashion.[1]

In Dürer's illustration the naïve legend becomes the basis for a vivid pictorial statement of the central meaning of the Roman Mass. The veil which normally falls between the truth of faith and the tangible realities of an imperfect life has been pierced. Christ, powerfully alive, with the cerements still clinging to him, rises from a retable which has suddenly become the *sepulchrum Domini*. The altar cross has changed from gold to the wood of the True Cross. The walls of the basilica have vanished, exposing the cloud-filled space beyond. Two angels—related perhaps to the "angels and archangels" of the prayer *Vere dignum*—appear as they did to the Marys on the morning of the Resurrection. Indifferent attendants and onlookers, including a venerable bishop, fade into an obscurity from which only Gregory's tiara and the papal cross shine forth. The two

---

[1] The tradition is summarized and fifteen examples from late medieval art are listed by Louis Réan, *Iconographie de l'art chrétien* (Paris, 1958), III, chap. ii, 614–15. The source of the late medieval amplification of the legend is not identified. Réan speculates that it may have originated in an imaginative fusion of the image of Christ over the altar in Byzantine churches with the ceremony of the Mass.

deacons assisting Gregory see nothing—their eyes are fixed on the physical symbol, the Host. We have a sense of bearing witness with St. Gregory to a timeless event, and we realize suddenly, and with a sense of shock, that as onlookers we have been placed in the position of the skeptic for whom the miracle is intended. It is our *salus animae* which concerns Christ and St. Gregory, and, incidentally, Albrecht Dürer.

The selection of a legend about St. Gregory to illustrate the meaning of the Mass is appropriate. Gregory is one of the four "Doctors" of the Latin Church and is more closely associated than the other three with the history of the liturgy. Gregory is credited with initiating the movement to establish a uniform ritual throughout Western Christendom. His Sacramentary was the basis for the liturgical reform movement of the eighth and ninth centuries and today remains the foundation of the Roman rite.[2]

In his Dialogues Gregory also helped to establish what has since become the orthodox interpretation of the Mass. "Let us meditate," he wrote, "what manner of sacrifice this is, ordained for us, which for our absolution doth always represent the passion of the only Son of God: for what right believing Christian can doubt that in the very hour of the sacrifice, at the words of the Priest, the heavens be opened, and the quires of Angels are present in that mystery of Jesus Christ; that high things are accomplished with low, and earthly joined to heavenly, and that one thing is made of visible and invisible."[3] This passage does not imply that the Mass as a whole is a joining of the visible with the invisible. Gregory's successors, however, were accustomed to regard Scripture as a fusion of a literal (i.e., "visible") meaning with three kinds of symbolic meaning: the allegorical, the tropological, and the anagogical.[4] By the ninth century this system of analysis was being used to explain the invisible realities of the Mass.[5]

---

[2] F. H. Dudden, *Gregory the Great* (London, 1905), I, 264–71.

[3] *The Dialogues of Gregory the Great . . . Translated by P. W.*, ed. Edmund Gardner (London, 1911), p. 256 (dialogue IV, chap. lviii).

[4] For a convenient set of definitions and comment on this well-known method of analysis, see *The Catholic Encyclopedia* (New York, 1909), V, 690–6, 701–4 (s.v. "Exegesis"). A useful essay on medieval allegory is included in C. S. Lewis, *The Allegory of Love: A Study in Medieval Tradition* (London, 1953), pp. 41–111.

[5] Dramatic symbolism was discovered in specific parts of the Mass long before the ninth century. As might be expected, the earliest extended allegorical readings are Eastern; for example, in a Syriac homily ascribed to Narsai (d. 502), the reader is advised during the procession in which the bread and wine are brought to the altar to

"put away all anger and hatred and . . . see Jesus who is being led to death on our account. On the paten and in the cup He goes forth with the deacon to suffer. The bread on the paten and the wine in the cup are the symbols of His death. A symbol of His death these [deacons] bear on their hands and when they have set it on the

Full-scale allegorical interpretation may be said to have begun with Amalarius, Bishop of Metz (780?–850). A prominent figure at the courts of Charlemagne and Louis the Pious, an ambassador to Constantinople, and a lifelong student of the liturgy, Amalarius wrote two, and perhaps three, interpretations of the Mass. The first is the *Eclogae de ordine Romano* (814), and the most influential is the *Liber officialis*, which Amalarius saw through three editions between 821 and 835.[6]

Explaining, as it did, Gregory's belief that in the Mass "one thing is made of visible and invisible," the work of Amalarius was immediately popular. The editions which he prepared circulated widely throughout France and neighboring regions. In only one place did it meet with strong opposition. Amalarius had been sent to Lyons in 834 by Louis the Pious

---

altar and covered it, they typify His burial: not that these bear the image of the Jews, but rather of the watchers [i.e., the angels] who were ministering to the passion of the Son. He was ministered to by the angels in His passion and the deacons attend the body which is suffering mystically. . . . The priest who celebrates bears in himself the image of our Lord in that hour. All the priests in the sanctuary bear the image of the Apostles who met together at the sepulchre. The altar is a symbol of our Lord's tomb, and the bread and wine are the Body of the Lord which was embalmed and buried."

"Homily XVII (A)," trans. Dom. R. H. Connelly, *The Liturgical Homilies of Narsai*, Vol. VIII of *Texts and Studies, Biblical and Patristic Literature* (Cambridge, 1909), 3–4. The tradition of allegorical interpretation has often been examined. For an illuminating summary discussion see Joseph A. Jungmann, S.J., *The Mass of the Roman Rite, Its Origins and Development*, trans. F. A. Brunner (New York, 1950), I, 87–92, 177–95. Of more specialized studies, two are particularly helpful: J. Mason Neale and Benjamin Webb, *The Symbolism of Churches and Church Ornaments* (London, 1906)—a translation of Book I of the *Rationale divinorum officiorum* of Durandus of Mende—and Sister Teresa Clare Goode, *Gonzalo de Berceo, El sacrificio de la Misa: A Study of Its Symbolism and of Its Sources* ("Catholic University of America Studies in Romance Language and Literature," Vol. VII; Washington, 1933). Sister Goode points out that Gonzalo's thirteenth-century interpretation is a collection of commonplaces "already the common property of the people" (p. 28). She makes the further interesting point that Calderón's *Misterios de la Misa* repeats the allegorical interpretation during the *siglo de oro* (p. 28 n.). For important instances of allegorical interpretation in Middle English literature, see Sister Loretta McGarry, *The Holy Eucharist in Middle English Homiletic and Devotional Verse* (Washington, D.C., 1936). Before Trent, opposition to allegorical interpretation was infrequent and was confined to professional theologians such as Albertus Magnus. Thomas Aquinas supported it (see Jungmann, *Mass*, I, 113–14). The most notable counterstatement to the allegorical school appeared in the eighteenth century (see Claude de Vert, *Explication simple, littérale et historique des cérémonies de l'Église* [4 vols.; Paris, 1706–13]).

[6] The facts of Amalarius' somewhat obscure life are summarized by Allen Cabaniss, *Amalarius of Metz* (Amsterdam, 1954). Cabaniss deserves credit for being one of the very few scholars to recognize the importance of Amalarius to the history of drama (see pp. 64–65). The works of Amalarius are accessible in the *Patrologia Latina* (hereafter cited as *PL*), CV, 815–1360, and in the recent scholarly edition by J. M. Hanssens, *Amalarii episcopi opera liturgica omnia* (3 vols.; Vatican City, 1948–50). For Hanssens' summary of Amalarius' life, see I, 58–82.

to settle a political dispute in which the Lyons clergy had become deeply involved.[7] Instead of attacking Amalarius' politics, the Lyons clergy, led by a certain Deacon Florus, attacked his liturgical theories. In 838 Louis the Pious summoned a council at Quiercy to examine his writings, and the council duly pronounced them heretical.

Unfortunately from their point of view, the enemies of Amalarius failed to halt, or even delay, the spread of his ideas. This failure is evident from a document written three years after his death. In spite of the adverse verdict of the Synod of Quiercy, in 849 Amalarius had been appointed, along with Scotus Erigena, to investigate the increasing influence of the Saxon monk Gottschalk of Fulda. In 853 either Remigius of Lyons or Deacon Florus himself complained of this scandal and incidentally admitted that Amalarius "has by his words, his lying books, his errors, and his fanciful and heretical discussion infected and corrupted almost all the churches in France and many in other regions. . . . All of his books should have been burned after his death so that the more simple folk [simpliciores], who are reputed to love them and read them assiduously, might not be thus foolishly occupied and so dangerously deceived."[8]

The statement corroborates the idea, which can be inferred from the almost universal diffusion of Amalarius' system among later writers, that the Liber officialis was a major success. Evidently, it answered a strongly felt need for an interpretation of the Mass which emphasized its immediate, as against its historical, significance. Of particular interest are the assertions that it appealed to the simpliciores and that its influence was especially strong in France.[9] Already in 853 there is a suggestion that allegorical interpretation can be appreciated by the illiterate and semi-literate, for whom historical details and theological subtleties are meaningless. The need of the simpliciores for a vivid, dramatic understanding of the

[7] Cabaniss, Amalarius, pp. 79–93.

[8] I have quoted the translation of Cabaniss, Amalarius, p. 93, who attributes it to Deacon Florus rather than Remigius, to whom it is attributed in Migne. The Latin may be consulted in PL, CXXI, 1054. Hanssens (Amalarii opera, I, 83–91) lists the numerous references to, and borrowings from, Amalarius, fully documenting the case for his extraordinary influence. Edmund Bishop (Historica liturgica [Oxford, 1918], p. 262) calls Amalarius a "high priest of symbolism."

[9] Seven manuscripts of Amalarius' works or portions of them are in the library of the monastery of St. Gall, which is also the source of one of the earliest manuscripts of the Quem quaeritis trope (Hanssens, Amalarii opera, I, 33, 123; Cabaniss, Amalarius, p. 65). Of equal interest is the fact that an eleventh-century version of Pseudo-Alcuin's De divinis officiis (Bibliothèque Nationale, Paris, MS lat. 2402, fol. 83ʳ–83ᵛ) incorporates a description of the Elevatio Crucis, indicating the compatibility of Amalarius with extraliturgical dramatic ceremonies. Young (DMC, I, 555) suggests that this text "may be associated" with the famous Elevatio of the tenth-century Regularis concordia of St. Ethelwold, Bishop of Winchester. For the De divinis officiis, see Hanssens, I, 52–53.

Roman rite inevitably increased as the separation between the clergy and the laity became more pronounced and as the language of the Church became ever more remote from the vernacular. Hence it is not surprising that a long succession of interpreters, including Walafrid Strabo, Hugh of St. Victor, Honorius of Autun, Sicardus of Cremona, John Beleth, Durandus of Mende, Thomas Aquinas, and Innocent III, carried on and elaborated the tradition initiated by Amalarius.[10] Dürer's "Mass of St. Gregory" demonstrates its vitality in the period just preceding the Reformation. Although the Council of Trent opposed allegorical excess in both Scripture and liturgy, traces of the influence of Amalarius can still be found in popular devotional manuals of the twentieth century.[11]

That there is a close relationship between allegorical interpretation of the liturgy and the history of drama becomes apparent the moment we turn to the Amalarian interpretations. Without exception they present the Mass as an elaborate drama with definite roles assigned to the participants and a plot whose ultimate significance is nothing less than a "renewal of the whole plan of redemption" through the re-creation of the "life, death, and resurrection" of Christ.[12] Perhaps the most remarkable expression of this idea is found in the *Gemma animae*, written about 1100 by Honorius of Autun:

> It is known that those who recited tragedies in theaters presented the actions of opponents by gestures before the people. In the same way our tragic author [i.e., the celebrant] represents by his gestures in the theater of the Church before the Christian people the struggle of Christ

[10] The principal writers of the allegorical tradition are listed by Goode (*Gonzalo de Berceo*, pp. xv–xvii and 26–28) and Hanssens (*Amalarii opera*, I, 83–91). Hanssens' catalogue demonstrates that Amalarius remained popular during the sixteenth century, declining only in the seventeenth, presumably as a result of Tridentine reforms.

[11] Compare, e.g., Godfrey Diekmann, O.S.B., *The Masses of Holy Week and the Easter Vigil* ("The Popular Liturgical Library"; Collegeville, Minn., 1956). On Palm Sunday, remarks Father Diekmann, "In spirit we are joining the enthusiastic crowds that accompanied Christ into Jerusalem. . . . We acclaim Him our King, marching with Him, we are an army rallied around its Commander" (p. 16). Concerning the lesson of Tuesday of Holy Week (Jer. 11:18–20), we are told that "Jeremias has been traditionally regarded as a 'type' of Christ; i.e., in the persecution for justice which he suffered, he personally prefigured the Messias: he too was as a meek lamb led off to slaughter" (p. 52). On Maundy Thursday, "We are gathered in spirit with the Apostles, to receive from Jesus the great Gift of His own flesh and blood, as it were for the first time" (p. 73). Among the special ceremonies still used during Easter Week and bearing an allegorical explanation may be cited the procession with palms, the restoration of the Gloria and Alleluia at the first Mass of Easter, the "Maundy rite" (restored in 1955 by Pius XII), the reservation of the Sacrament on Maundy Thursday, and the various special rites of Good Friday and the Easter vigil.

[12] Goode, *Gonzalo de Berceo*, pp. 64–65.

and teaches to them the victory of His redemption. Thus when the celebrant [*presbyter*] says the *Orate* [*fratres*] he expresses Christ placed for us in agony, when he commanded His apostles to pray. By the silence of the *Secreta* he expresses Christ as a lamb without voice being led to the sacrifice. By the extension of his hands he represents the extension of Christ on the Cross. By the chant of the Preface he expresses the cry of Christ hanging on the Cross. For He sang [*cantavit*] ten Psalms, that is, from *Deus meus respice* to *In manus tuas commendo spiritum meum*, and then died. Through the secret prayers of the Canon he suggests the silence of Holy Saturday. By the *Pax* and its communication [i.e., the "Kiss of Peace"] he represents the peace given after the Resurrection and the sharing of joy. When the sacrifice has been completed, peace and Communion are given by the celebrant to the people. This is because after our accuser has been destroyed by our champion [*agonotheta*] in the struggle, peace is announced by the judge to the people, and they are invited to a feast. Then, by the *Ite, missa est*, they are ordered to return to their homes with rejoicing. They shout *Deo gratias* and return home rejoicing.[13]

The *Gemma animae* is too late to be a reliable guide to attitudes prevalent during the ninth and tenth centuries, when, presumably, the *Quem quaeritis* originated. It does, however, indicate the importance of liturgical allegory to the history of drama. The standard literary histories of the high Middle Ages, which are doubtless correct, agree that during this period understanding of secular drama was rudimentary. The respect accorded the hopelessly confused *Paraphrase of the Poetics of Aristotle*, translated from the Arabic by Hermannus Alemannus around 1250, fully confirms the traditional view.[14] Yet Honorius not only uses the vocabulary of dramatic criticism, he uses it with considerable sophistication. The church is regarded as a theater. The drama enacted has a coherent plot based on conflict (*duellum*) between a champion and an antagonist. The plot has a rising action, culminating in the Passion and entombment. At its climax there is a dramatic reversal, the Resurrection, correlated with the emotional transition from the Canon of the Mass to the Communion. Something like dramatic catharsis is expressed in the *gaudium* of the Postcommunion.

---

[13] Translation mine. Text in Migne, *PL*, CLXXII, 570. William Prynne took exception to this passage in *Histrio-mastix* (London, 1633), pp. 112–14.

[14] The place of this curious document in medieval criticism is discussed by Hardison in *The Enduring Monument: The Idea of Praise in Renaissance Literary Theory and Practice* (Chapel Hill, N.C., 1962), pp. 34–36 and notes. For medieval theories about the nature of secular drama, especially tragedy, see Willard Farnham, *The Medieval Heritage of Elizabethan Tragedy* (Berkeley, Calif., 1936). Farnham's discussion makes it apparent that the terms tragedy and comedy, in their secular application, refer to narratives (e.g., Boccaccio's *De casibus*, Lydgate's *Fall of Princes*, Dante's *Comedy*).

Whatever else may be said about Honorius, one fact stands out: he understood the Mass as a living dramatic form. The contrast between his views and those found in discussions of secular literature could hardly be more pronounced. The conclusion seems inescapable that the "dramatic instinct" of European man did not "die out" during the earlier Middle Ages, as historians of drama have asserted. Instead, it found expression in the central ceremony of Christian worship, the Mass. This being the case, an understanding of the medieval interpretation of the Mass should illuminate many hitherto obscure aspects of the history of European drama. The works of Amalarius of Metz initiated allegorical interpretation, and they were particularly influential in France in the century just preceding the emergence of the *Quem quaeritis* trope. It is appropriate, therefore, to begin with Amalarius. A few general considerations must, however, precede discussion of the *Liber officialis*.

In the first place, the service on which his interpretation is based is quite different from the contemporary Mass. Amalarius conscientiously followed the liturgy of a Roman *ordo*, a *libellus Romanus*, but occasionally his discussion refers to practices, such as the singing of the Credo, which were Gallican rather than Roman.[15]

More important, the Roman Sacramentary used by Amalarius was intended for a Solemn stational Mass. Although private Masses were permitted during the ninth century, both the Roman and Gallican Churches disapproved of them. Church regulations stipulated that clergy and laity alike should attend Solemn Mass on the great festivals of the Church.[16]

[15] The principal sources are the Gregorian Sacramentary and the first or second *Ordo Romanus—Ordo Romanus* II, according to A. Franz, *Die Messe im deutschen Mittelalter* (Freiburg i. Br., 1892), 353, and Hanssens (ed.), *Amalarii opera*, II, 271, 273, 282, 285ff. However, M. Andrieu, *Les Ordines Romani du haut moyen age*, Vol. II: *Les textes* (Louvain, 1948), 181, emphatically states that Amalarius had before him a copy of the *Ordo Romanus* I and that Amalarius' work was itself one of the sources of *Ordo Romanus* V (Mabillon's *Ordo Romanus* II). See also Jungmann, *Mass*, I, 469–74; Goode, *Gonzalo de Berceo*, p. 78. Pope Benedict VIII (1012–24) introduced the Credo into the Roman liturgy. Amalarius lists several differences between the Gallican and Roman rites at the end of the *Praefatio altera* of the *Liber officialis* (Migne, *PL*, CV, 991–92; Hanssens, II, 17–18).

[16] As will be apparent during the following discussion, I have relied heavily for details concerning the history of the Mass on Jungmann's *Mass of the Roman Rite*, cited previously. This remarkable work supersedes the earlier studies of F. Cabrol, *Les origines liturgiques* (Paris, 1906), *La Messe en Occident* (Paris, 1932); Louis Duchesne, *Christian Worship, Its Origin and Evolution*, trans. M. L. McClure (London, 1927); A. Fortescue, *The Mass, a Study of the Roman Liturgy* (New York, 1912); and N. Gihr, *The Holy Sacrifice of the Mass* (St. Louis, Mo., 1931). A more specialized work, bearing particularly on the service described by Amalarius, is Oswald J. Reichel, *Solemn Mass at Rome in the Ninth Century* (London, 1895). For ecclesiastical disapproval of private Masses on feast days, see Reichel, pp. 5 and 20–22. For a detailed description of the sort of stational Mass forming the basis of Amalarius' work, see also Jungmann, I, 67–74.

The controlling idea of Solemn Mass as performed in the ninth century is that it is "the corporate and collegiate celebration of the Holy Mysteries in which the priesthood of the whole Christian family is directly and not vicariously exercised."[17] Representatives of each of the orders of the clerical hierarchy must participate. The *episcopus* or *archiepiscopus* is celebrant (*sacerdos*) or presides at the throne while a presbyter is allowed to celebrate. The practice of concelebration was irregularly followed, according to which all of the presbyters joined the celebrant in reciting the Canon or portions thereof.[18] Deacons, subdeacons, and the acolytes assist the celebrant, and the laity are expected to participate in both ceremony and responses. The deacon's part is especially important. His function is "to make the offering upon which the Divine Spirit is about to be invoked representative of a people united among themselves as one body united to Christ as their head."[19] The deacon receives and prepares the offerings, he participates in the Consecration, he holds the chalice during the commingling, and he distributes the Communion wine, which in the ninth century was still offered to the laity. Among many other distinctive features of Solemn Mass, the symbolism of the unity of all Christians in the mystical body of Christ is predominant. The church is a major basilica or cathedral capable of holding large crowds (symbolic of the whole Christian community) and hallowed by the presence of a martyr's grave or the relics of a saint. The participation of all orders of the clergy and the practice of concelebration are symbols of unity. The collects, in which the celebrant "sums up" the individual wishes and prayers of the people, are stressed. The Kiss of Peace is given by the deacon to the highest-ranking assistant, and eventually extended to the congregation, which completes it by a series of mutual embraces. Additional corporate symbolism is provided by the now-forgotten "sancta" ceremony. A bit of preconsecrated Host (the sancta), reserved from a previous Solemn Mass, is worshipped by the celebrant on the altar at the beginning of Mass and later, at the commingling, mixed with the consecrated wine "in order that by commixture all who partake of the cup may be brought into communion . . . with all who have been in the communion of the Church from the beginning."[20] Other details of the ninth-century Solemn Mass

---

[17] Reichel, *Solemn Mass*, p. 4; Jungmann, *Mass*, I, 195–97.

[18] Jungmann, *Mass*, I, 196, and note.

[19] Reichel, *Solemn Mass*, p. 16.

[20] *Ibid.*, p. 30. The fermentum ceremony had a parallel significance. Since there is some difference of opinion on whether or not the sancta (or fermentum) ceremony was employed, it should be noted that in the *Eclogae* (PL, CV, 1317 d and 1319 e) Amalarius twice states that the bishop "prima . . . adorat sancta" and does not leave the altar during the Introit ceremonies until "postquam adoraverit sancta." See also n. 116.

will be mentioned as they occur. Those cited should amply warn against application of Amalarius' comments to the modern forms of the Mass.

A second point of importance to an understanding of allegorical interpretation is that Amalarius and his followers were not theologians in the sense in which the word is applied to the Scholastics of the high Middle Ages. In modern terms, their work is closer to literary criticism than to theology.[21] They sought to express the felt significance of an event which is at the center of Catholic life in language which would both explain it and make it ever more widely available to the *simpliciores*. Sister Teresa Goode has aptly called this effort a "search for reality."[22] Gregory had taught that in the Mass "one thing is made of visible and invisible"; and Christ had asked His followers to "do these things in remembrance of me." In the medieval mind the idea of commemoration fused with the doctrine of the Real Presence: if the bread and wine are truly changed at the moment of Consecration into the flesh and blood of the Savior, then Christ must be literally present at every Mass. Allegorical interpretation moved outward from this insight to find dramatic significance in each of the major prayers and ceremonies. Ultimately, every detail of the service was considered symbolic. Many of the interpretations seem appropriate and beautiful. But there are also many which seem at best trivial; for example, the speculations on the significance of the number of crosses made during the Consecration prayers and the quibbles over the number of "sacrifices" actually performed by the celebrant.

But allegorical interpretation is more than a transient fashion. Both Catholic and non-Catholic scholars agree today that the Mass has important similarities to dramatic rituals which are apparently universal in primitive societies and which were widespread among the various mystery cults that flourished in the West between the first and fifth centuries. The implications of these similarities are, of course, disputed. Perhaps the most balanced position is that taken by the Jesuit scholar Hugo Rahner, who regards the Mass as a unique blend of "common

---

[21] They were, as is clear from their writings, learned men. Amalarius was a student of Alcuin. Later, he used his travels to Constantinople and Rome to observe varying practices at first hand. Although he remarks frequently that he is following his own convictions and even claims divine inspiration for some ideas, he drew heavily on a variety of sources. The most important of these are the Bible, the *libellus Romanus*, and the writings of Cyprian, Augustine, Gregory, and Bede. His most original achievement is not so much the devising of new interpretations as it is the collecting of a miscellany of ideas expressed previously and working them into a system which explained the whole service of the Mass with relative consistency. See n. 5 for an example of a sixth-century interpretation anticipating some of Amalarius' central theories; also, Jungmann, *Mass*, I, 86–87.

[22] *Gonzalo de Breceo*, p. 26.

archetypal elements" whereby man has always instinctively sought contact with the divine, minor cultural borrowings, and revelation.[23] The ninth-century interpretation may be considered an imperfectly expressed analogue of such modern theories; that is, both medieval and modern students agree that the Mass is drama, but the medieval author could only express his insight by speaking of a "plot" and assigning to the participants the roles which they played in the history from which the "plot" is derived. The medieval writer, unable to say that the Mass was a ritual drama, was forced to say simply that it was a drama. The vocabulary is awkward, but the concept is valid. To this extent, the ninth-century interpretation may be as true to its subject as the more sober historical investigations of the post-Tridentine era of Catholic scholarship.

The impossibility of explaining the felt experience of the Mass in terms other than those of drama is in itself adequate to account for the inconsistencies which may be found in allegorical interpretation. The situation is further complicated by the desire of Amalarius and his followers to find not one but several levels of allegory. Some events of the Mass are interpreted as moral lessons and some as re-enactments of Old Testament practices; some refer to the life of Christ, and some have an eschatological significance. Not infrequently, a single event bears two or more interpretations simultaneously. By the same token, the roles of the participants are fluid. At times the celebrant is the High Priest of the Temple sacrificing the holocaust on the Day of Atonement, at other times he is Christ, and at one point he is Nicodemus assisting Joseph of Arimathea at the entombment. The congregation can be the Hebrews listening to prophecies of the Messiah, the crowd witnessing the Crucifixion, the Gentiles to whom the Word was given after it had been rejected by the Hebrews, and the elect mystically incorporated into the body of Christ. Numerous conflicts among levels of interpretation, inconsistencies of chronology, and abrupt shifts of meaning are apparent. On the other hand, in the midst of these anomalies one element stands out sharply. From beginning to end, but especially during the Canon and Communion, the Mass is a rememorative drama depicting the life, ministry, crucifixion, and resurrection of Christ. Although other elements vary according to the ingenuity of the interpreter, rememorative allegory is always present. It is central to the interpretations of Amalarius, Honorius, and Durandus, and evidently it was still central when Albrecht Dürer designed his woodcut of St. Gregory's Mass.

[23] "The Christian Mystery and the Pagan Mysteries," in *Pagan and Christian Mysteries,* ed. Joseph Campbell (New York, 1955), pp. 146–210, esp. pp. 152–53.

II

The chapter headings of Amalarius' *Eclogae de officio missae* provide a convenient outline of the rememorative allegory of the Mass.[24] The service is divided into two major parts. The prayers and ceremonies which precede the Gospel represent Christ's life "from His birth to the time when He hastened to Jerusalem to suffer."[25] The Introit is the chorus of Old Testament prophets foretelling the coming of the Messiah, and the Kyrie is the voice of the more recent prophets, especially Zacharias and John. The Gloria (omitted from the beginning of Lent to the Mass of the Easter vigil) announces the Nativity. It echoes the song of the angels (Luke 2:14), and it is chanted antiphonally to suggest a dialogue between heaven and earth. The collect represents Christ in the Temple at twelve years of age. The reading—whether from the Old or the New Testament—is the preaching and prophecy of John. The responsory depicts the good will (*benevolentiam*) of the apostles, who, when summoned, came freely. The Alleluia (omitted from the beginning of Lent to the Mass of the Easter vigil) expresses the happiness which the apostles felt when they heard Christ's promises and saw miracles performed in His name. The first "act" of the drama concludes with the Gospel, which makes manifest the words and deeds of Christ during His ministry. The second "act" extends from Palm Sunday to Pentecost. The prayers from the *Secreta* to the *Nobis quoque peccatoribus* represent the prayers of Jesus in the garden of the Mount of Olives, and what follows commemorates His death and entombment. The commingling of the Host and consecrated wine marks the return of Christ's soul to His body. The next action (the Kiss of Peace) is the greeting of the disciples and their joy on learning of the Resurrection. The Fraction is not a "slaughtering of Christ," as it was sometimes considered during the baroque period,[26] but, in the *Eclogae*, the breaking of bread by Christ at Emmaus.

This outline, although not entirely reliable as a guide to the *Eclogae* or *Liber officialis* as written, illustrates the dimensions of rememorative allegory and allows some preliminary conclusions. The separation between the "Mass of the Catechumens" and the "Mass of the Faithful" has resulted in an articulation of the drama in terms of a rising action from

[24] For convenience, citations of Amalarius' works will be to both the *Patrologia* edition and that by Hanssens, abbreviated "H." The outline of the *Eclogae de officio missae* is in *PL*, CV, 1315–16, and in H, III, 229–31.

[25] "Ad primum adventum Domini usque ad illud tempus quando properabat Hierusalem passurus" (*PL*, CV, 1315; H, III, 229).

[26] Jungmann, *Mass*, I, 184–85 and note.

Introit to Gospel[27] that reflects the rising excitement of the service itself. The elaborate ceremony called for by the rubrics has provided opportunities for further allegorical interpretation and for stylized gestures of the sort which Honorius of Autun evidently had in mind when he compared the gestures of actors in the theater with those of the celebrant.[28] The second phase of the drama continues the rising action through the events of the Passion, reaches a crisis at the entombment, and undergoes a sharp reversal, punctuated by the commingling and the Kiss of Peace. The Resurrection is the climax of the drama. It is parallel to the shift in the mood of the service from the *tristia* induced by the memory of Christ's death to the *gaudium* of the Communion. The positioning of the climax of the Mass at the beginning of the Communion is typical of the ninth century but was gradually modified in later times by the emphasis on the Passion and the related practice of elevating the Host and chalice immediately after the Consecration. It gives the Mass a "comic" rather than a "tragic" structure because it becomes an action that (to quote a late classical definition) "begins in adversity and ends in peace."[29]

The structure of allegorical interpretation, then, parallels the natural emotional rhythm of the Mass. The allegory does not conflict with the rubrics or tone of the Sacramentaries. The initial emphasis on expectation —the sense that the Messiah is coming and will soon be not only among us but united with us—is admirably calculated to express (or engage) the emotions of the participants. The congregation is immediately involved in the drama in the role of the Chosen People longing for the fulfillment of prophecy. On certain feast days this role-playing is intensified by explicitly mimetic actions: on Palm Sunday, for example, there is a formal procession with palms—identifying the congregation with the crowds who welcomed Jesus into Jerusalem—and hymns of praise echoing the Gospel accounts of his entry. During the Gloria the congregation becomes the shepherds and humble folk of Bethlehem who, in the second part of the antiphon, answer the angels, either directly or vicariously through the cantors. During the reading of the Gospel the people stand to bear living witness, as soldiers of Christ, to the events of His life. They bow their heads in sorrow during the terrible events leading to the Crucifixion. They

[27] The Gospel was considered a part of the Mass of the Faithful by both the Roman and Gallican Churches, although Amalarius calls the practice of dismissing the catechumens before it is read, "consuetudo nostra" (*PL*, CV, 1156[b]; H, II, 371). For discussion, see Jungmann, *Mass*, I, 433–34.

[28] Quoted above, pp. 39–40.

[29] Euanthius, *De comoedia et tragoedia*, in *Donatus*, ed. Paul Wessner (Leipzig, 1902), I, 21.

stand bowed before the Cross with the holy women as Christ dies and blood and water pour from His side into the chalice.[30] Following the Communion, the congregation assumes still another role. Allegorically, it becomes the disciples and apostles receiving the blessing of Christ before the Ascension. At the same time, it is, in literal truth, the Gentile nations who have received Christ and who, through him, are gathered into the mystical body. In the period between the Communion and the *Deo gratias*, the congregation enters an eschatological world. It lives in a timeless present, sharing the fellowship of the apostles whose images decorate the nave and of the angels who bring the sacrifice to the throne of God.

The role-playing demanded of the congregation by Amalarius exemplifies what can only be called "sliding time." This sort of time is familiar enough in Shakespeare and, in fact, is more common in drama than the strictly chronological time demanded by the ideal of the three unities. What is surprising is the dimension of the time encompassed. We allow Shakespeare to compress into three hours five years of history in *Henry V* and sixteen years in *The Winter's Tale*, but the Mass is a truly cosmic drama, which begins with the Mosaic prophesies of Exodus and ends with a vision of the New Jerusalem. The same fluidity is evident in the "character" of Christ. Christ is represented at different points by the bishop, the celebrant (*sacerdos*), the Host, the cross, the altar, and even (at one point) the thurible. This fascinatingly Protean behavior is evident almost in spite of the efforts of Amalarius to maintain a fixed association between Christ and the celebrant. It illustrates the inadequacy of the vocabulary of allegorical interpretation and prefigures the lesser but still serious difficulties encountered by rationalistic critics of Elizabethan drama.

The *Liber officialis* is Amalarius' most ambitious work, and Book III, devoted entirely to the Mass, is justly its most famous section.[31] The long *Praefatio altera* or *Proöemium*, written after his trip to Rome in 832, makes it clear that Amalarius considered his commentary on the Mass to be his most important achievement. The parallel between the celebrant and Christ is first noted in the *Praefatio:* "Sacraments should have likeness to the things for which they are sacraments. Therefore the celebrant should be like Christ, just as the bread, wine and water are similar to the body

---

[30] This idea is vividly realized in the "Allegory of the Mass" painted by Lucas Cranach the Elder. See also below, pp. 68–71.

[31] The title of the work in the *Patrologia* is *De ecclesiasticis officiis libri IV*. I have followed Hanssens in preferring the title *Liber officialis*, which is evidently the one intended by Amalarius. Book III is found in *PL*, CV, 1101–64, and H, II, 255–399. Unless otherwise noted, the quotations follow Hanssens' readings.

of Christ."[32] For clarity, the following account will be divided into the major phases of the Mass as Amalarius understood them.

1. Introit Ceremonies: From Introit to *Lectio*

The Introit ceremonies are extremely important. As described in the *Liber officialis*, they constitute a frame drama, eschatological in emphasis, which foreshadows the entire service. Amalarius assumes a full procession with bishop, presbyters, deacons, subdeacons, acolytes, and chorus. The bishop is the vicar of Christ. His entry "recalls the advent of Christ himself to memory" and his actions suggest "the office which Christ performed on earth when incarnate." He dominates the service until his "seating" just before the *Lectio*.[33]

As he enters, the chorus antiphonally intones the Introit hymn. Because the hymn is derived from the Psalms, the chorus is at this point the prophets of the Old Testament who "with sweet and musical voice led the people to worship one God." All stand gladly during this ceremony, testifying to their readiness to hear God's call. Amalarius was particularly interested in church music, having written a treatise on the antiphonary,[34] and consistently emphasizes the appeal of chants and hymns. Here, the music expresses the joy of God's servants by its beauty, and the universality of His summons by its loudness.[35] In terms of eschatological symbolism, the singing is "the glory of the Lord filling the House of the Lord." Having heard the voice of His prophets, the bishop, personifying Christ, begins the procession. In this action he resembles Christ entering His chariot to descend to mankind. The chariot, on the basis of Augustine's commentary on Psalm 67, is "the multitude of the saints and the faithful"

[32] "Sacramenta debent habere similitudinem aliquam earum rerum quarum sacramenta sunt. Quapropter similis sit sacerdos Christo, sicut panis et liquor similia sunt corpori Christi" (*PL*, CV, 989[a]; H, II, 14).

[33] "Introitus episcopi ad missam, qui vicarius est Christi, ipsius adventum nobis ad memoriam reducit et populi adunationem ad eum. . . . Introitus episcopi celebratur usque ad sessionem suam; tangit enim ex parte officium quod Christus corporaliter gessit in terra, sive discipuli eius, usquequo ascendit ad sedem paternam" (*PL*, CV, 1108[c]; H, II, 271–72). Amalarius does not discuss the use of Psalm 42, the prayers at the foot of the altar, or the censing of the altar. He does indicate that the bishop prays after his arrival, and the fact that the thurible is used in the Introit procession suggests that it may have been used for censing. Here, as elsewhere, Jungmann's historical observations are helpful (*Mass*, I, 290–320).

[34] *De ordine antiphonarii*, composed *ca.* 836, in *PL*, CV, 1243–1316; H, III, 13–109.

[35] *PL*, CV, 1109[b]; H, II, 273. The Psalm text was one "which taken as a unit (in the sense of the allegorizing psalm-exegesis of the period), could best fit the occasion" (Jungmann, *Mass*, I, 327).

who accompany Him—i.e., the clergy and (apparently) members of the congregation accompanying the bishop.[36]

The order of the procession provides numerous opportunities for further exegesis. The deacons, subdeacons, and acolytes are "the prophets, the wise men, and the scribes," respectively.[37] The thurible, which is carried first, is "the body of Christ" in the sense of the Crucifixion, which must be preached to all nations as the first order of salvation.[38] Next come the acolytes carrying candles, and then the subdeacons. The candles symbolize learning and the subdeacons, wisdom. The candles come first because learning must enlighten wisdom. Behind them is the Gospel, carried by a deacon, and behind the Gospel, the bishop, who must meditate the life of Christ first and last, and who is pledged on the basis of Matt. 16:24 to "take up his cross, and follow me." There should be seven deacons (prophets) in the procession, and the bishop should be in their midst because he is the vicar of Christ.[39] The fact that the deacons follow the subdeacons shows that prophecy should always be controlled by wisdom.

The arrival of the bishop at the altar identifies him with Christ incarnate. His bow (genuflection was infrequent in the ninth century) recalls that Christ "took upon him the form of a servant" and was "obedient unto death" (Phil. 2:7–8). The Roman Sacramentary used by Amalarius included prayers of preparation (the modern prayers at the foot of the altar), but Amalarius does not discuss them, and they were evidently not considered mandatory by the Gallican clergy.[40] While still inclined, the bishop "gives the *Pax*"—the embrace symbolizing the Kiss of Peace—to the ministers on the right and left, for through Christ the Church, both of the Old and New Testaments, was reconciled to God.[41] This is the first

[36] *PL*, CV, 1109ᵉ; H, II, 274. For the Augustine reference, see *Enarratio in psalmo LXVII*, *PL*, XXXVI, 828–29.

[37] *PL*, CV, 1109–10; H, II, 275–77. Amalarius speculates on the proper number of deacons. Seven are ideal, but five, three, or one are acceptable. If there are seven, the bishop represents the Gospels and the deacons, the Law, Prophets, and Psalms of the Old Testament and the Acts, the non-Pauline Epistles, the Pauline Epistles, and the Book of Revelation of the New. Amalarius does not mention carrying the cross at the head of the procession.

[38] *PL*, CV, 1109–10ᵃ; H, II, 274–75.

[39] *PL*, CV, 1110ᵇ; H, II, 275.

[40] Preparatory prayers were said in the sanctuary. The bishop also prays and adores the sancta (see n. 20), but there are no set texts mentioned. In the ninth century the prayers were called *apologiae*. They assume a definite form, anticipating the modern one, in the tenth century (Jungmann, *Mass*, I, 291).

[41] "In ipsa inclinatione dat pacem ministris qui a dextris levaque sunt. Ipse est enim pax per quam reconciliatur ecclesia Deo, sive de novo testamento, sive de veteri" (*PL*, CV, 1111ᵉ; H, II, 278). The kiss and the later kissing of Gospel and altar are included in the seventh-century *Ordo Romanus* I, n. 8 (*PL*, LXXVIII, 937–48; Andrieu (ed.), *Ordines Romani*, II, 83).

instance of positional symbolism, which is an important factor in the unfolding drama. The right side of the altar, the favored position, is associated by Amalarius with paradise, the elect, the Gentiles, and with safety. Conversely, the left side is associated with hell, the temporal world, the Hebrews, strife, and danger. The ninth-century practice of placing women on the right and men on the left was explained by the rationalization that women, being the weaker sex, should be protected. The movement of the Gospel from left to right for the reading was interpreted as symbolic that Christ preached first to the Jews and then, when rejected by them, was accepted by the Gentiles. Its return to the left at the end of the service foreshadows the conversion of the Jews.[42]

As the bishop extends the *Pax Christi* to the chorus, its role changes. It has felt the effects of the Lord's blessing and, accordingly, shifts from texts derived from the Old Testament to a praise of the Trinity, the *Gloria Patri et Filio et Spiritu Sancto*. The deacons, who have been quietly praying with the bishop, now come forward two by two to kiss the altar. The kiss represents the peace brought by Christ, and the altar represents the hearts of the elect, an interpretation supported by a quotation from Gregory to the effect that "the tables of God are the hearts of the saints."[43] Now the bishop approaches the altar and kisses first it, and then the Gospel. The first kiss commemorates Christ's entry into Jerusalem and His love of the Jews. The second symbolizes His Word as received by the nations. The

---

[42] Interpretations vary, of course. The whole matter of positional symbolism is greatly complicated by three facts: (1) Early churches were not all oriented, and hence until the eleventh century commentators usually speak of the right and left side of the altar rather than the north and south, or the Gospel and Epistle sides. (2) Practice varied according to the architecture of the church, the position of the episcopal throne, and local custom. (3) When speaking of right and left, commentators usually take the clerical point of view (looking from the altar toward the congregation), and sometimes the congregation's point of view, so that accounts that are, in reality, descriptions of the same practice often seem to conflict. In the present discussion, the clerical point of view is consistently assumed because it is the one taken by Amalarius. For historical discussion, see Jungmann, *Mass*, I, 110, 411–19 (with diagrams). Whatever the difficulty for the modern reader, positional symbolism was a factor of major importance for all allegorists and for medieval church architects as well, a fact strikingly demonstrated by the first book of the *Rationale divinorum officiorum* by Durandus, Bishop of Mende. See Neale and Webb, *The Symbolism of Churches and Church Ornaments*, pp. lxxiv–cv, and the translation of Durandus, pp. 1–151, *passim*; Sister Goode, *Gonzalo de Berceo*, pp. 76–78. The idea that the moving of the Gospel represents the transition of Christ from the Jews to the Gentiles is offered by Ivo of Chartres, Sicardus of Cremona, Hugh of St. Victor, Durandus, and Gonzalo himself.

[43] *PL*, CV, 1112ᶜ; H, II, 280. The quotation ("Corda itaque sanctorum mensae Dei sunt") is from Gregory's *Homiliae in Ezechiel*, *PL*, LXXVI, 1047ᵇ. At the *sicut erat* the deacons raise their bowed heads, proceed to the altar, and stand facing the bishop. They are now the apostles who gave themselves to death to be united with Christ's body (*Eclogae*, *PL*, CV, 1318; H, III, 236).

Gospel is on the left of the altar and will remain there until read because "from the time of Christ's entry the Gospel resounded in Jerusalem."[44] The movement of the bishop to the right side of the altar is, by positional symbolism, a movement toward paradise, hence, a re-enactment of the Resurrection. Meanwhile, the deacons stand between him and the congregation, three on the left and four on the right, representing the Old and New Testaments and also the readiness of the disciples to follow Christ even to death. The candles held by the acolytes act as a reminder to teach by deeds and not by words alone.[45]

The tableau imagined by Amalarius is an emblem under which many features to be acted out more fully in the Canon and Communion are subsumed. Its effectiveness would be limited in a cathedral of the high Middle Ages. In an early basilica or Romanesque church, however, it would be striking.[46] The congregation would have a clear view of the altar No rood screen would obscure its view, since the cancelli of the ninth century was simply a low railing separating the choir from the central aisle. The altar itself would be small. In comparison to the Gothic altar with its enormous reredos, it would still resemble the "mensa" of the primitive church.[47] Behind it might be the semicircle of seats that were used by the bishop and presbyters before it became general practice to move the altar into this space (presbyterium). The cross would be simple, lacking the now-familiar figure of Christ. Above the altar, on the dome of

[44] There are thus three kisses in all. Each recalls Christ (the following text is found in *PL*, CV, 113ª; H, II, 282):

Vicarius Christi haec omnia agit in memoriam primi adventus Christi. Osculatur altare, ut ostendat adventum Christi fuisse Hierusalem; osculatur evangelium, in quo duo populi ad pacem redeunt. . . . Oscula vicarii Christi osculo Christi congruunt. Sicut Christus primo osculum his praebuit qui primo crediderunt, sic episcopus ministris primis; et sicut Christus his se offert ultro, quibus dicit: *Missus sum ad oves quae perierant domus Israhel*, sic se episcopus altari, per quod recolimus Hierusalem . . . ; et sicut Christus asscivit sibi postea gentilium populum, qui reconciliatus est Deo in novo testamento, sic episcopus evangelium, quod est novum testamentum. . . . Remanet evangelium in altari ab initio officii, usque dum a ministro assumatur ad legendum, quia ab initio adventus Christi evangelica doctrina resonuit in Hierusalem.

[45] *PL*, CV, 1113ᶜ; H, II, 282.

[46] For a sketch of the basilican arrangements, see Reichel, *Solemn Mass*, p. 49. Much more detailed comment, with numerous floor plans, may be found in Banister Fletcher, *A History of Architecture on the Comparative Method* (New York, 1938), 211–33, 261–323. For comment from the liturgical point of view, see Jungmann, *Mass*, I, 68–71, 256–58.

[47] Jungmann, *Mass*, I, 109–10, 257–58. Although the altar itself has retained approximately its original dimensions, in later churches it tends to become lost in the masses of decoration behind it. From the standpoint of the dramatic features of the liturgy, the less ornate altar obviously lends itself more fully to impressive representation. In the Gothic cathedral the enormous dimensions of the chancel and the altar decorations dwarf the human figures almost to the point of insignificance.

the apse, there would be an image of Christ the Good Shepherd, the Glorified Cross, or perhaps Christ (or the Lamb) triumphant. The echo of the image of Christ in the vestments and actions of the bishop would be evident.

The singing of the Kyrie eleison shifts the mood from expectant joy to sorrow over human unworthiness. Having rejoiced at the glad tidings of the Introit, chorus and congregation alike seek deliverance from the deceit of philosophy and fallacious doctrine.[48] While the Kyrie is being chanted, the motif of humiliation is further developed by the placing of candles on the floor (in terram) on either side of the altar, with one in the center to remind the congregation that in spite of good works we are "dust and ashes."[49] Not more than seven candles are used because both Christ and the Holy Spirit are "septiform." When the bishop ascends his throne, all candles except the one in the center are arranged in a line to symbolize the unity of the Holy Spirit which manifests itself in endless good works.

At the Gloria in Excelsis there is an abrupt reversal of mood. The celebrant—evidently still the bishop—"sings in a loud voice looking to the east [i.e., toward the presbyterium with its sedes, in an oriented church] . . . as though his proper sedes were there, although we know it to be everywhere."[50] The fusion of drama with setting—the throne of Christ with the sedes episcopi—is striking. Equally striking is the imaginative feat which enables Amalarius to transcend the rather limited interpretation that he had offered in the Eclogae. The Gloria is not only the song of the Nativity; it is at the same time the song of the angelic choir at the Ascension. The connection is based on the fact that the bishop, by his movement to the right of the altar, has become an image of Christ after the Resurrection. The text of the Gloria is thus related by its words to the birth of the Savior, and by its context, to the song of the angels receiving Christ into heaven. This double triumph is underscored by the abrupt emotional transition from the sadness of the Kyrie to the exultation of the Gloria. The fact that the chorus has for the moment assumed the role of the angels

[48] PL, CV, 1113–14; H, II, 283. A second (alio modo) interpretation suggests that the priest must have God's mercy for three reasons: (1) to obtain calm understanding, (2) to be as worthy as possible to address God, (3) so that if he fails in any particular God will still accept his prayer. The prayer referred to is the oratio prima, just before the Lectio.

[49] PL, 1114ᵉ; H, II, 285. The elaborate symbolism of candles cannot be examined in detail here. It is most evident in the "blessing of the new fire" and "paschal candle" ceremonies of the Easter vigil.

[50] "Sacerdos quando dicit 'Gloria in excelsis Deo,' orientes partes solet respicere, in quibus ita solemus Dominum requirere, quasi ibi propria eius sedes sit, cum potius eum sciamus ubique esse" (PL, CV, 115ᵇ; H, II, 286–87).

already hints that "under one Lord the earthly and the heavenly are united." Birth and death are one, and the words *in terra pax hominibus bonae voluntatis* look forward to the *osculum pacis* of the Communion.[51]

The *Dominus vobiscum* which follows is a transition to the first prayer, or collect. The bishop turns to the congregation with the form of salutation used by Boaz (Ruth 2:4) and Christ. The reply (II Tim. 4:22) is enthusiastically shouted in the manner of an acclamation by the entire congregation. It signifies the spiritual unity of the people with the bishop, which is an important point because the term "collect" refers to prayers by the priest representing or "collecting" the individual prayers of the people.[52] The bishop then turns back to the east to pray. His words recall the benediction given to the disciples by the risen Christ at the Ascension (Luke 24:50). The auditors must be careful to join the bishop in saying the *Amen*, for their response is a form of confirmation and participation.

The Introit ceremonies end with the "seating" of the bishop. In the ninth century this sometimes occurred to the accompaniment of shouts of triumph, known as *laudes gallicanae*, which were derived from the pagan custom for celebrating the enthroning of a ruler.[53] Whether punctuated by shouts of triumph or not, the "seating of the bishop" is a dramatic moment. In a basilican church the bishop moves to an elevated throne at

---

[51] "Dominus qui ubique est, secundum formam servi in Bethleem erat; quae Bethleem nostram ecclesiam signat, quae est domus panis. Angeli ad orientem cecinerunt.... Diximus superius transitum episcopi de altari in dexteram partem significare Christi transitum de passione ad aeternam vitam, ac ideo hoc in loco dicimus 'Gloria in excelsis Deo' cantandum, quoniam gloria ineffabilis in excelsis facta est, quando Christus transitu suo animas sanctorum copulavit consortio angelorum. . . . quando gloria resurrectionis eius caelebrata est, tunc in terra pax hominibus fuit. . . . Pax magna est, quando sub uno domino copulantur caelestia et terrena" (*PL*, CV, 1115°; H, II, 287). Compare Jungmann, *Mass*, I, 349–52, and for the ceremonial, p. 357. For the *osculum pacis*, see below, p. 74. Note the repetition of the association between the *osculum pacis* and (1) the Resurrection, and (2) corporate symbolism—here expressed in the phrase "copulantur caelestia et terrena."

[52] The participation of the congregation is not mentioned by Amalarius, but contemporary evidence indicates that it occurred. The tradition that it was shouted is also contemporary with Amalarius and was, in fact, characteristic of Gallican ritual (Jungmann, *Mass*, I, 365 and notes; for the collect, pp. 372–88).

[53] "After the oration, two (or six) knights stood forth, or, in their place an equal number of clerics; they began: *Christus vincit, Christus regnat, Christus imperat*. The choir repeated. Then the song became a declaration of fealty and homage . . . and then it became a plea to Christ, *Exaudi Christe*, and to a series of saints. . . . If the bishop who was named was present, the whole assembly arose, and the special singers who were chanting the acclamations mounted the steps of his throne, kissed his hand and received his blessing. The *Laudes* closed with a repetition of *Christus vincit . . .*" (Jungmann, *Mass*, I, 389; also E. Kantorowicz, *Laudes Regiae* [Berkeley, Calif., 1946]). The sense of drama is intensified by the fact that the *Laudes* are an ecclesiastical adaptation of the ancient ceremony for acclaiming a ruler when he ascended his throne.

the center of the rear wall of the apse, a location associated with paradise in the symbolism of church architecture. In later church architecture the episcopal throne is at the right of the altar, a location which, as has been noted, is also associated with paradise.[54] Positional symbolism thus reinforces the previously established identification of the bishop with the risen Christ. The "seating of the bishop" becomes a vision of the Ascension: "Then Christ ascended to heaven, to sit on the right hand of the Father. The bishop, who is the vicar of Christ in all ceremonies previously mentioned, should here enthrone in our memory the Ascension and throne of Christ. Therefore he ascends his throne after the labor of his ministry has been completed."[55]

Although the text is not entirely clear, Amalarius appears to have in mind the Roman Solemn Mass as celebrated in a basilican church with the episcopal throne placed in the apse. In the *Eclogae de officio missae* he states unambiguously that the bishop sits "facing the people and the presbyters with him."[56] This position is hard to reconcile with the Romanesque plan, according to which the episcopal throne is on the right of the altar facing the opposite (southern) wall rather than the congregation. The point is significant because in a basilican church the image on the dome of the apse has a close visual relation to the posture and gestures of the bishop seated immediately below. Moreover, the relation is probably intended to persist throughout the remainder of the service. In a Solemn Mass involving many members of the clergy, the bishop is not necessarily the celebrant. When he is not the celebrant, he remains at his throne in the sanctuary, his presbyters on either side, until the final benediction. From this position he may engage in concelebration, or he may act simply as an especially prominent clerical participant.[57] In either

---

[54] Above, n. 41.

[55] "Dein Christus ascendit in caelum, ut sedeat ad dexteram Patris. Episcopus, quia vicarius est Christi, in omnibus memoratis superius debet et hic ad memoriam nobis intronizare Christi ascensionem et sedem. Quapropter ascendit in sedem post opus et laborem ministrii commissi" (*PL*, CV, 1117ᵃ; H, III, 290).

[56] "Episcopus sedet versus ad populum, et presbyteri cum eo" (*Eclogae, PL*, CV, 1321ᵃ; H, III, 242).

[57] Amalarius is not entirely clear on this point. His confusion seems to stem from the awkwardness of adapting a Roman Stational Mass to non-Roman conditions (see Jungmann, *Mass*, I, 75). Amalarius uses the word *episcopus* to refer both to "bishop" in the formal sense and also as a loose equivalent for presbyter and *sacerdos*. Generally, *episcopus* predominates in his discussion of the Introit ceremonies and presbyter or *sacerdos* in what follows. A distinction between *episcopus* and celebrant is thus suggested, which alternates with a recognition that *episcopus* and celebrant are often one and the same person. When Amalarius states that the *episcopus* "ascendit in sedem post opus et laborem ministerii commissi" (*PL*, CV, 1117; H, II, 290), he seems to be coupling

case, a remarkable eschatological effect is produced. Instead of being limited to a single plane, the action of the Mass moves forward on two visible planes or stages. The first is the presbyterium. It is the plane of eternity, from which the ascended Christ looks down on suffering humanity. The second is the altar. It is the plane or stage of history upon which, amid the mobs of Jerusalem and the sorrowing disciples, the incarnate Christ is crucified and dies. These two planes intersect at the moment of sacrifice in a manner which transcends the normal limits of allegory. The interpretation devised by Alamarius fuses setting, characters, and action into a visible expression of the unseen realities of the Mass. The remainder of the Mass is focused on the sacrifice, but the sacrifice is firmly held *sub specie aeternitatis* by the symbolic drama extending from Introit to Gloria. Christ emerges from the timeless, dies, and ascends in the figure of the bishop. He re-emerges in the figure of the celebrant. At the end of the Mass, when the bishop rises to give his blessing, the celebrant is again enfolded in the world beyond time. In this interpretation we are close to the great abstractions of Byzantine art, and far indeed from the heavy emphasis on the Crucifixion that characterizes both the art and the Mass of the high Middle Ages.

---

rememorative allegory of the Ascension with the literal fact that after the Introit ceremonies the "labor" of the ministry of the *episcopus* is completed. Jungmann states that the emphatic transition in the early Mass between Introit ceremonies and readings resulted in "an abuse which the Roman Council of 743 had to denounce, namely, that many bishops and priests conducted only the procession and said the oration and left the rest of the Mass to another" (*Mass*, I, 388). Such a practice would be an abuse in a private Mass, but not in a Solemn Mass of the type used by Amalarius. In such a Mass, the presence of many *presbyteri* and (often) more than one *episcopus* makes it impossible for all to act as celebrants, although all may recite certain prayers of the Canon (concelebration). Those who did not "celebrate" heard the service from the presbyterium of the basilican church and the *sedes* in the chancel of later churches. The *episcopus* remained at his throne when he did not act as celebrant. Amalarius observes (*PL*, CV, 1117ᵉ; H, II, 291) that while some of the clergy are seated, others (presumably, the celebrant and his assistants, for whom the basilican church provides no seats if the presbyterium is filled) remain standing. The standing clergy represent the Church Militant (*in certarmine posita*). The *episcopus* and his group represent the *membra Christi in pace quiescentia*. The *episcopus* is also compared to the Lord watching over His City from His throne in heaven, an interpretation confirmed by the Greek etymology of *episcopus* ("overseer"). Further evidence that Amalarius differentiates between the *episcopus* of the Introit and the celebrant comes from his description of the distribution of Communion. The deacon is specifically instructed to bring the consecrated bread to the *episcopus* (or pontifex) at his throne. Since the celebrant would normally be at the altar, it is likely that *episcopus* and celebrant are, at this point, at least, two different persons. On the other hand, in the pontifical Mass of the seventh century, the *pontifex* conducted the service from his throne (Jungmann, *Mass*, I, 72; also below, p. 74 and n. 116).

2. From *Lectio* to Gospel

The major action of the sacred drama begins with the *Lectio* (Epistle). The selections from *Lectio* to Gospel are interpreted by Amalarius as an ascending series, culminating in the Gospel. Much of the ceremonial which fascinated later allegorists—the kisses, the genuflections, the crosses, and the procession to the Gospel ambo—are treated summarily by Amalarius. Nor does he place much stress here on positional symbolism, perhaps because the distinction between the "Gospel side" and the "Epistle side" of the altar did not become conventional until the high Middle Ages. Conversely, the mode of presentation of the *Lectio* is an essential clue to its significance. It is read (not chanted) by a subdeacon from either an Epistle ambo or a step on the Gospel ambo below that used for the Gospel. During the reading and until the Gospel is announced, the congregation remains seated. The *Lectio* is followed by chanted texts. First the gradual (responsory), and then the Alleluia or (on sorrowful occasions, of which Lent is the most important) the tract, which derives its name èither from the fact that it is sung straight through (*tractim*) or because it has a simple melody in contrast to the Alleluia.[58] The texts are clearly sequential, suggesting either increasing joy (gradual, Alleluia) or increasing gravity (gradual, tract). By the eighth century at the latest, the joyous connotations of the Alleluia were being indicated by melodic amplifications (melisma, jubilus) of constantly increasing length and complexity. By the ninth century the ascending or descending group of intermediate pieces was supplemented by a sequence (*sequentia*) that was usually related to the text of the Gospel for the day and a lyrical expression of the emotions appropriate to it. The reading of the Gospel is the climax of the series. Its importance is underscored by the blessing which the celebrant extends to the deacon before he leaves the altar, by the procession with thurible and candles from altar to ambo, by the melodic decorations of the reading itself, and by the fact that the congregation always stands when the reading is announced.[59]

The allegory of this phase of the Mass is chiefly rememorative. Although the interpretations in the *Liber officialis* at times seem strained, they are less so than those of the *Eclogae de officio missae*, where the *Lectio* is regarded as the teachings of the youthful Christ in the Temple and the intermediate chants as the *benevolentia* of the apostles. The *Lectio* is primarily didactic

---

[58] Jungmann, *Mass*, I, 430–31.

[59] For the melisma and sequences, see Frederick J. E. Raby, *History of Christian Latin Poetry from the Beginnings to the Close of the Middle Ages* (2d ed.; London, 1953), pp. 210–29; Jungmann, *Mass*, I, 435–40. For the Gospel ceremonial, see Jungmann, *Mass*, I, 442–55.

and hence associated with the law of the Old Testament. The subdeacon who reads must remove his casula (chasuble) in token of his labors for Christ. He is to treat his auditors "like neophytes in the school of the Lord." [60] Amalarius seems to have some sense here of the historical purpose of the *Lectio* as instruction for the catechumens. Since its function is teaching and since Old Testament readings are frequently used, the subdeacon is easily identified with the teachers of the Old Testament, especially Moses: "Thus the infancy of a devout man is instructed by the elements of the Old Testament so that he may arrive at the plenitude of the Gospel." [61]

The variations possible in the intermediate chants greatly complicate interpretation, but a few points are sufficiently independent of the proper of the Mass to be mentioned. The change from reading to chant is itself an indication of the rising pitch of excitement. The fact that the Gospel is sung leads Amalarius to associate the intermediate texts with it, rather than with the *Lectio*. If the *Lectio* is related to Moses and the other patriarchs, the intermediate texts must be related to the New Testament. Since the intermediate texts "lead to" the Gospel, they are preparatory, a notion which justifies associating them with the preparations and prophecies immediately preceding the appearance of Christ. By this admittedly devious reasoning, the intermediate texts are interpreted as the prophecies of John the Baptist. Whatever the merits of the identification, it was popular among later allegorists. The stress which it places on the anticipatory nature of the intermediate texts is, moreover, appropriate because as part of the proper of the Mass they were originally selected for their relevance to the liturgical occasion being commemorated. Perhaps the figure of the cantor, his hands extended over the congregation in the manner of a prophet, merged easily in the ninth-century mind with the figure of John crying in the wilderness, "Prepare ye the way of the Lord."

[60] "Lector legem Domini debet tradere auditoribus, quasi incipientibus in scola Domini exerceri. . . . Doctor et lector unum sunt" (*PL*, CV, 1118[b]; H, II, 294). The readings parallel readings from the Law and the Prophets of the synagogue; hence their association with the Old Testament rests on historical as well as allegorical grounds. In the Christian service the first reading consisted usually of a passage from the Law or the Prophets and a passage from the Acts or Epistles, hence the term Epistle applied (incorrectly) to the first reading as a unit. Gradually, the Epistle increased and the Old Testament selection diminished in importance, so that today on most Sundays the passage from the Acts or Epistles is the only one read (see Jungmann, *Mass*, I, 395–97). Clearly, Amalarius has in mind the older tradition.

[61] "Sic elementis veteris testamenti, ut ad evangelicam plenitudinem veniat, sancti vero eruditur infantia. Elementa lex Moysi et omne vetus instrumentum intellegendum est, quibus, quasi elementis et religionis exordiis, Deum discimus" (*PL*, CV, 1119[a]; H, II, 294–95).

It seems more likely, however, that the inadequacy of Amalarius' vocabulary has on this occasion led him astray. Recognizing the anticipatory nature of the *Lectio* and intermediate texts, he is forced by his method to relate them to Old and New Testament "preparations" for Christ's advent. The insight is valid, but the allegory is less closely related here than elsewhere to the texts and rubrics.[62]

With the ceremonies and prayers associated with the Gospel reading, the allegory once again becomes germane. The figure of the deacon, standing in full vestments in the tribunal, the "seat of magistrates" and the highest part of the ambo, merges easily with that of the Evangelist whose text he reads. The rising of the people renews their role in the drama. The reading begins with a procession from the left side of the altar to the Gospel ambo on the right. The thurible, the body of Christ "full of sweet odor," is filled by the celebrant, now identified with the living Christ whose deeds the Evangelist is to witness. The celebrant blesses the deacon with the familiar *Dominus sit in corde tuo*. The words give direct expression to the symbolism of inspiration—of Christ fixing himself "in the heart" of the reader—and their sense is reduplicated in the cross which the celebrant makes over the head of the deacon. The deacon removes the Gospel from the altar, identified by positional symbolism with Jerusalem, and carries it on his left arm, which represents "temporal life, in which the Gospel must be preached."[63] The congregation, now in the role of those who witnessed Christ's life and teaching, faces the deacon and, following the Gospel pericope, exclaims *Gloria tibi, Domine*.[64] When the reading begins, the congregation turns to the east, making the sign of the cross, for "what the celebrant fixed in the heart of the deacon by his prayer, each of the faithful should strive to fix in his own soul."[65] The prayers and crossings unite celebrant, reader, and congregation, again presenting a sharp con-

---

[62] This criticism does not take into account the possible emotional effect of the singing, to which Amalarius customarily ascribes great significance. Later interpretations regularly equate the Epistle (not the intervening chants, as in Amalarius) with the teachings of John the Baptist (Sicardus of Cremona, Hugh of St. Victor), as Amalarius had done in the *Eclogae*, or with the teaching of the apostles (Gonzalo de Berceo). This line of thinking made it necessary, for reasons of consistency, to interpret the intervening chants as the teaching of the youthful Christ. The interpretation in the *Liber officialis* seems preferable.

[63] "Portat evangelium in sinistro brachio, per quod significatur temporalis vita, ubi necesse est praedicare evangelium" (*PL*, CV, 1125 ᶜ; H, II, 309).

[64] *PL*, CV, 1125ᵈ–26ᵃ; H, II, 309. In the *Eclogae* (*PL*, CV, 1323; H, III, 247–48) the detail of the extinguishing of the candles after the Gospel is interpreted as a symbol that no learning (candles as symbols of wisdom) can surpass the Word of God.

[65] "Quod infixit sacerdos per suam deprecationem in corde diaconi, hoc unusquisque fidelis studeat infigere animo suo" (*PL*, CV, 1125ᵈ; H, II, 309).

trast to the Mass of the high Middle Ages. After the reading, the Gospel is returned to its place on the altar, and the tapers, here associated with the law and the prophets, are extinguished because the law and the prophets ceased with the ministry of Christ. Amalarius ends his discussion of the Gospel with the remark that the office as a whole "reveals the preaching of Christ up to the time of the Passion, and that of His preachers to the end of the world and beyond. The following offices reveal His Passion, Resurrection, and Ascension; and, likewise, the sacrifice or mortification and resurrection of His followers."[66]

3. From Offertory to Canon

The Offertory marks the beginning of the Mass of the Faithful. The catechumens have left, heightening the sense of unity of those who remain. The celebrant is increasingly isolated in the service from this point on. Consequently, he stands out more clearly as a dramatic figure, a focus of attention for clergy and congregation alike. Typological symbolism, according to which the altar is the *sanctum sanctorum* of the Temple and the oblation a Christian fulfillment of the holocaust offered by the High Priest on the Day of Atonement, intensifies the sense of the church as cosmic stage. The ninth-century Offertory, during which the people bring candles, oblation loaves, and wine to the deacon or celebrant, links them to the ceremony as participants rather than as passive witnesses.[67] The symbolism of the preparation of the bread and wine also emphasizes the idea of participation. The physical objects associated with the sacrifice—particularly the sindon (corporal), the sudarium (pall), the thurible, and the chalice—become components of the drama as their symbolic meanings are gradually revealed. The deployment of the celebrant, the deacons, and the subdeacons around the altar—one might almost speak of the choreography of the Mass—is profoundly symbolic and is repeatedly associated by Amalarius with the events of Holy Week. Finally, the Sanctus that introduces the Canon is both an emotional outburst praising Christ (*Benedictus qui venit in nomine Domini*) and an explicit echo of an appropriate New Testament text. It is the key to the interpretation of this phase of the Mass. Since it comes from the Gospel accounts of Palm Sunday

[66] "Praecedens officium praedicationem Christi usque ad oram passionis demonstrat, et suorum praedicatorum usque in finem mundi, et ultra. Sequens opus passionis Christi et resurrectionis atque ascensionis in caelos, similiter suorum vel sacrificium vel mortificationem, et resurrectionem per confessionem, atque suspirium in caelum" (*PL*, CV, 1126ᵉ; H, II, 311).

[67] For the ninth-century Offertory ceremonies, see Reichel, *Solemn Mass*, pp. 11–30; Jungmann, *Mass*, II, 4–17.

(Matt. 21:9; Mark 11:9), the Offertory becomes for Amalarius the joyful cries of the Hebrews welcoming Christ into Jerusalem during the period from Palm Sunday to Maundy Thursday.

Amalarius begins with an explanation of the way in which the Hebrew service was an adumbration of Christian sacrifice. The Temple foreshadows the Christian ecclesia; the tabernacle, the sanctuary; the High Priest, the *sacerdos;* the two altars of the old law, the double sacrifice of good works and of mortification of the new; the holocaust, the oblation; and so forth.[68] Although typological symbolism seems remote from the effect of the Mass today, it cannot be discounted. In allegorical interpretations of the high Middle Ages it is stressed even more heavily than in Amalarius, an indication of its perennial appeal to the medieval mind.[69] For Amalarius, however, it is a secondary element, whose chief interest lies in the fact that it links time past with time present: "All previous sacrifices prefigured Him, and all sacrifice is consummated in Him."[70]

Moving backward from the *Benedictus qui venit* of the Sanctus, Amalarius interprets the *Dominus vobiscum* which begins the Offertory as the greeting of Christ to the "great multitude" that met him as he "descended" from the Mount of Olives (Luke 19:29–38). Since the celebrant has already been identified with Christ, the salutation and response place the congregation in the role of the Hebrews. The *Oremus* immediately following the salutation has long been recognized as an anachronism because no prayer is prescribed.[71] Amalarius is not disturbed by it. Evidently private prayers or meditations were possible here during the ninth century. To Amalarius the *Oremus* represents Christ calming the overflowing joy of the Hebrew crowds: "by prayer the heart is made calm to prepare it for recognizing the Lord."[72] The Offertory hymn comes next. In the ninth century it was

---

[68] *PL*, CV, 1126[d]–28[a]; H, II, 311–14. Amalarius is quite definite concerning the fact that the congregation offers loaves and wine.

[69] See Goode, *Gonzalo de Berceo*, pp. 30–64, for comment and extensive documentation.

[70] "Omnis retro immolatio illum praefigurabat; in illo consummata est omnis immolatio" (*PL*, CV, 1128[a]; H, II, 314).

[71] In Eastern and early Western liturgies, the *Oremus* was followed by general prayers. By "retrogressive evolution" these were abandoned in the West, leaving the vestigial injunction without the means of carrying it out (Jungmann, *Mass*, I, 483–84). Amalarius' opinion is given as a commonplace observation in the *Praefatio altera* (*PL*, CV, 990[b]; H, II, 16): "Post salutationem sacerdotis, evangelio lecto, quando sacerdos dicit: 'Oremus,' et dein transit ad accipiendas oblationes, congruenter potest multitudo populi pro propriis conscientiis intercedere, ante quam transeat ad gratias agendas in praefatione. . . ." T. F. Simmons (*The Lay Folks Mass Book* [London: E.E.T.S., 1879], p. xxiii) suggests that the saying of private prayers here persisted in the thirteenth century.

[72] "Oratione enim serenatur cor ad cognoscendum Dominum" (*PL*, CV, 1128[c]; H, II, 315).

a lengthy affair similar to the Introit in form and composed of an antiphon and psalm verses. During the singing those who wish to receive Communion present their offerings to the deacon (or, alternately, the *sacerdos*), who then selects the loaves and wine to be consecrated. The dramatic quality of the Offertory procession is obvious. At the very least it reaffirms the importance of the role of the congregation in the unfolding drama.[73] To Amalarius the song and procession continue the motif of Christ's entry into Jerusalem. As long as the multitude praised him, Christ received its worship; and as long as the Offertory is sung, the celebrant will receive the physical symbols of the devotion of the people.

The return of the celebrant to the altar represents Christ's visit to the Temple, "in which there was an altar, and there he presented himself to himself and to God the Father as a future sacrifice."[74] Typological symbolism—the association of the altar with Jerusalem (see above, p. 50) and, in particular, with the Temple—reinforces the rememorative allegory. The *Secreta*, which Amalarius mentions next although this disturbs the normal sequence of events in the service, is a continuation of the visit to the Temple. The figure of the quietly praying celebrant fuses with the figure of Christ meditating on the sad events shortly to occur, which are still unknown to the people. Here, says Amalarius, the offering is called *hostia vel sacrificium* for the first time.[75] If the words of the *Secreta* were well known (perhaps they were said audibly[76]), its petition that the people be sealed to eternity through the paschal mysteries would seem an appropriate, even beautiful, equivalent to the prayers of Christ in the Temple.

Turning from the text of the Mass to the ceremony itself, Amalarius examines those acts which are performed during the Offertory procession. The sindon (corporal) is placed on the altar. It is a white linen cloth, here symbolizing purity of mind. The Communion loaves and wine are the

[73] Amalarius refers to "sacerdos . . . sive diaconus" (*PL*, 1128[d]; H, II, 315), although the deacon normally collected the offerings (Reichel, *Solemn Mass*, p. 16). Reichel and Simmons (*Lay Folks Mass Book*, pp. 234–35) agree that the clergy often performed the office. In any case a procession was necessary. The dramatic nature of the Offertory hymn is evident from a twelfth-century text from Limoges, in which the Offertory hymn has become a little play on the visit of the Magi (Young, *DMC*, II, 32–37).

[74] "Christus enim, post accepta vota cantantium, Hierusalem et templum Domini intravit, in quo erat altare, ibique se praesentavit sibi Deoque Patri ad immolationem futuram" (*PL*, CV, 1128[d]; H, II, 315).

[75] "In hac [secreta] primo nominatur hostia sive sacrificium, oblatio" (*PL*, CV, 1132[d]; H, II, 323). Obviously, the prayers currently used (*Suscipe, sancte pater*, etc.) were not employed by Amalarius.

[76] *Secrete* originally meant "in a low voice": "Secreta ideo nominatur, quia secreto dicitur" (*PL*, CV, 1132[d]; H, II, 323) therefore means that the prayer is to be said softly, not necessarily "in secret" or "silently" (see Jungmann, *Mass*, II, 90–91; Fortescue, *The Mass*, p. 312).

visible signs of the "invisible sacrifice" of the hearts and souls of the people. As the offerings are received, they are placed on the altar by the deacon in commemoration of the "seven first deacons."[77] The washing of hands (*Lavabo inter innocentes*) is, morally, a cleansing of the soul and is, in terms of rememorative symbolism, the tears wept by Christ for man before the Crucifixion. The theme of the unity of congregation and clergy is reinforced by the mixing of the wine with water performed by the deacon. Quoting Cyprian, Amalarius observes that "when water is mixed with wine in the chalice, the people are united with Christ, and the believers are joined and mingled with him whom they worship . . . if anyone offered wine only, the blood of Christ would be without us; and if water only were offered, the people would begin to be without Christ."[78] The eschatological concept of the incorporation of all Christians within the mystical body of Christ is prominent here in contrast to the more affecting, but perhaps narrower, emphasis of later times on the Crucifixion. It is repeated in reference to the Communion loaf in the idea that the individual grains of flour, representing the people, are united by the water of the Holy Spirit: "Thus in Christ, who is the celestial bread, we know that there is one body to which our number is joined and united."[79] Because the water used for the mingling was traditionally offered by the cantors, the mingling also suggests the unity of all "estates" in worship: "As wine and water are united in the chalice, so the people and the cantors in the body of Christ."[80] Following the mingling, the deacon places the chalice on the altar and the sudarium on the right. The sudarium will cover any uncleanness, permitting the celebrant to say the *Secreta* without being distracted by concern for the safety of the offering. Amalarius says that the celebrant now "prays for the remission of his own sins, that he may be

---

[77] *PL*, CV, 1130[a]; H, II, 318.

[78] "Quando autem in calice vino aqua miscetur, Christo populus adunatur, et credentium plebs et in quem credidit, copulatur et iungitur. . . . Unde ecclesiam, id est plebem in ecclesia constitutam . . . nulla res separare poterit a Christo. . . . Nam, si vinum tantum quis offerat, sanguis Christi incipit esse sine nobis, si vero aqua sit sola, plebs incipit esse sine Christo" (*PL*, CV, 1131[a]; H, II, 319–20). The quotation is from *Ad Caecilium de sacramento dominici calicis* (*PL*, IV, 384[a]). Compare the following (quoted by Reichel, *Solemn Mass*, pp. 12–13), from Cyprian's seventy-fifth epistle: "When the Lord calls bread combined out of many grains His body, He indicates our people whom He bore as being united; and when He calls the wine which is pressed from many grapes and clusters collected together His Blood, He also signifies our flock linked together by the mingling of a united multitude."

[79] "Sic in Christo, qui est panis caelestis, unum scimus esse corpus, cui coniunctus sit noster numerus et adunatus" (*PL*, 1131[b]; H, II, 320).

[80] "Omnis populus, intrans ecclesiam, debet sacrificium Deo offere. . . . Populus offert vinum, cantores aquam. Sicut vinum et aqua unum fiunt in calice, sic populus et cantores in corpore Christi" (*PL*, CV, 1131[c]; H, II, 320).

worthy to come to the altar to touch the oblation."[81] Evidently the ninth-century service employed a confessional text here, rather than the familiar *Suscipe, sancta Trinitas* of today's Mass, which was not generally used until the sixteenth century.[82] Next come the *Orate fratres* and the *Secreta*.

Structurally there is a major transition between the *Per omnia saecula saeculorum* that ends the Secret, and the Preface. Amalarius recognizes this division but does not stress it.[83] Rememorative allegory takes precedence over the formal division between Offertory and Canon. The celebrant's command *Sursum corda* is a call for alertness against the wiles of the "adversary" and also an injunction that the congregation "lift up its heart" with the celebrant as he prepares to enter the Holy of Holies for the coming sacrifice. The turning of the celebrant toward the oblation on the altar suggests a parallel between the ceremonial and the Last Supper as described by Matthew (26:20–29). The altar is now "the table of the Lord at which he feasted with His followers." The corporal is the "towel in which he girded himself" to wipe the feet of the apostles (John 13:4), and the sudarium, which from this point on is consistently a symbol of labor or suffering, is His sorrow for Judas, the traitor. The response of the auditors to the *Sursum corda* (*Habemus ad Dominum*) indicates that they, too, have "ascended to the banquet."[84] Their participation, either by direct response or vicariously, through the chorus, is again confirmed by their endorsement of the celebrant's *Gratias agamus*.

Further discussion of the Preface once more involves Amalarius in eschatology. The prayer *Vere dignum* is, he believes, the moment of an "angelic sacrifice" commemorated in the celebrant's reference to *angelis et archangelis* who join the participants in singing hymns of glory to Christ. Their voices rise like incense to God.[85] Apart from the notion of an angelic sacrifice, the idea that angels and archangels, thrones and domin-

---

[81] "Cantantibus adhuc cantoribus, vadit sacerdos ad altare, et orat. Quod ceteros praemonuit facere, agit. Orat pro suis propriis delictis remissionem, ut dignus sit accedere ad altare . . ." (*PL*, CV, 1130ᵉ; H, II, 318). See n. 75. Amalarius mentions that the *Per omnia saecula saeculorum* is said in a loud voice to end the *Secreta* in chap. xix (*PL*, CV, 1128ᵃ; H, II, 313–14).

[82] Fortescue, *The Mass*, p. 311. The prayer appears, however, in various forms in several early Sacramentaries (Jungmann, *Mass*, II, 46–52).

[83] *PL*, CV, 1128ᵃ; H, II, 313.

[84] *PL*, CV, 1133ᵇ; H, II, 324–25.

[85] *PL*, CV, 1133ᵈ; H, II, 325. The reference "altare nostrum aptatur altari thimi-amatum" is evidently purely figurative. In the *Praefatio altera* (*PL*, CV, 992ᵇ; H, II, 18) Amalarius remarks that the Romans "post evangelium non offerunt incensum super altare." For the angels, see J. Daniélou, "Les anges et les sacraments," *Les anges et leur mission* (Chenetogne, France, 1951), 76–92.

ions, and soldiers of the celestial army share in the celebration of the Mass is so clearly suggested by the text that it should be considered a gloss rather than an interpretation. But it leads directly to a striking interpretive comment. According to Amalarius, the Sanctus is more than a simple expression of praise in response to the Preface. It contains "two orders of voices," an observation which suggests that it may have been sung by two semichoruses. The first "order" extends to *Hosanna in excelsis*. It is the voice of the angels and archangels, who, having been invoked, now literally join the service. The invisible world impinges directly on the visible. By the same token, the *Benedictus qui venit*, which is a direct quotation of Matthew's description (21:9) of the reception of Jesus in Jerusalem, identifies the chorus (and, vicariously, the congregation) with the Hebrews.[86]

Meanwhile, the region of the altar itself is evolving toward a stage for the events of the Passion and Resurrection. The deacons and subdeacons are arranged around the celebrant in imitation of the words spoken to the apostles at the Last Supper: "He that is greatest among you, let him be as the younger; and he that is chief, as he that doth serve" (Luke 22:26). The subdeacons, the "least" of the servers, are in an especially prominent position at the altar. They stand before (*in facie*) the celebrant, while the deacons, the "greater," stand behind him.[87] There is dramatic significance in this arrangement, according to Amalarius. The subdeacons represent the faithful disciples and in particular "the women who persevered during the Passion of our Lord," whereas the deacons represent the apostles who fled in terror after Christ was betrayed. "The women, it is recorded, not only did not fear or take flight, but persevered even at the sepulcher."[88]

4. Consecration: From *Te igitur* to *Unde et memores*

During the high Middle Ages the Consecration and the elevation immediately following it formed the climax of the Mass. The rubrics instructing the celebrant to imitate the actions of Christ during the recital of the *Qui pridie* made the dramatic character of the *mysterium* and the identification of the celebrant with Christ supremely evident. The elevation, which unites the role of the celebrant with the symbolism of the Sacrament as *corpus Christi*, provided a focus for the emotions of the medieval congregation. During the elevation, the body of the Savior was

---

[86] *PL*, CV, 1134b-d; H, II, 326–27.

[87] *PL*, CV, 1134d; H, II, 327.

[88] "Mulieres autem non solum non timuisse, neque fugisse, sed etiam usque ad sepulchrum stetisse, memorantur" (*PL*, CV, 1135a; H, II, 328).

visibly suspended on the cross. By the beginning of the twelfth century, the Mass bell was being used to announce the elevation to those who could not follow the service or were too far away from the altar to witness it. Often, in defiance of regulations to the contrary, the elevation was performed several times to meet popular demand, and reports are common of lay Christians attending more than one service on the same day for the explicit purpose of seeing several elevations.[89] Lending still further drama to the moment, the celebrant stood with arms extended after the elevation. In the words of Bishop Durandus, "The celebrant therefore, representing this [crucifixion] while speaking of the blessed Passion, extends his hands in the manner of a cross, to represent the extension of the body and hands of Christ on the Cross."[90]

The importance of these events to Catholics of the high Middle Ages and early Renaissance was so great that the existence of an earlier and quite different attitude is often forgotten. Amalarius recognizes that the Consecration reproduces the events of the Crucifixion, but for him they do not form the climax of the service. He says nothing of the *repraesentatio Christi* during the *Qui pridie*, nor does he mention the *extensio manuum*. There is one comment which may refer to an elevation at the time of the Consecration, but if it does, no importance is attached to the ceremony. Amalarius is interested in a later elevation—the little elevation of today's Mass—during which the celebrant does not represent Christ at all. One reason for this approach is the difference in details between the ninth-century and the contemporary Mass. A more important one, however, is that the emphasis of the ninth-century Mass is eschatological. It is not the Crucifixion but the Resurrection which continually occupies Amalarius' thoughts.

Amalarius begins with ceremonial. At the *Te igitur* the deacons bow their heads. They will retain this position until the words *libera nos a malo* of the Lord's Prayer, which introduces the Communion. As during the Sanctus, they are the apostles who were "beset with great tribulation" during the Passion but "did not dare to rise and confess themselves

---

[89] For the history of the elevation, which took its present form around 1200, see Jungmann, *Mass*, II, 206–17. This ceremony evidently provided the impetus that led eventually to the establishment of the feast of Corpus Christi. For abuses of the elevation, see *ibid.*, I, 119–21.

[90] "Sacerdos igitur hoc repraesentans, dicendo tam beatae passionis, manus in modum crucis extendit, ut habitu corporis manuumque Christi extensionem in cruce repraesentet" (*Rationale*, IV, xliii, 3). The practice of forming a cross with the arms outstretched is not in the early Roman *Ordines* but is specified in the rubrics of the Ambrosian rite and was extremely popular in the northern countries (see Simmons, *Lay Folks Mass Book*, pp. 288–90).

Christ's followers."[91] The subdeacons, who stand facing the altar and (beyond the altar) the celebrant and the people, are the disciples and holy women who remained with Christ during the Passion. The identification of the subdeacons with the women who attended Christ is the more important of the two suggestions, and Amalarius refers to it continuously as the commentary proceeds. The secret tone of the prayers of consecration (i.e., in a low voice, but not necessarily silent) is in accord with Christ's injunction in the Sermon on the Mount: "But thou, when thou prayest, enter into thy closet . . . pray to thy Father in secret" (Matt. 4:6). It also suggests the isolation of Christ during the Passion.

There are three prayers in the *Te igitur* sequence. The first (*Te igitur*) is for the Church Universal. The second (*Memento, Domine*) is for particular individuals. The third (*Communicantes*) is for the communicants and celebrants. These prayers, Amalarius believes, echo the three prayers of Christ in the garden of the Mount of Olives before his betrayal. The interpretation, which seems awkward, depends on medieval Biblical exegesis.[92] From the point of view of the congregation, the content of the prayers is secondary to the visual parallel between Christ praying in the garden and the celebrant praying at the altar, with the deacons (the apostles) standing behind him, their bowed heads suggesting sleep. A curious and, in the opinion of the Synod of Quiercy, unauthorized doctrinal element is introduced by the suggestion that the *Te igitur* sequence is a "sacrifice of the elect."[93] This sequence is followed by the *Hanc igitur*. God is petitioned to accept the prayers and devotion of the faithful, and the uncertainties of temporal life are contrasted to the peace of heaven. The unity of congregation and celebrant is evident in both the text (*cunctae familiae tuae*) and the commentary. The end of the prayer parallels Christ's command to the apostles: "Rise, let us be going: behold, he is at hand that doth betray me" (Matt. 24:46). Appropriately, the sudarium recalls the drops of blood shed by Christ in His agony (Luke 22:44), and the sindon, His humility.

[91] "Ipsi stant inclinati, donec liberentur a malo. Hi enim sunt apostoli, qui magna tribulatione erant oppressi; ante quam audirent Domini resurrectionem, non se audebant erigere, ut confiterentur esse Christi discipulos" (*PL*, CV, 1136[a]; H, II, 330).

[92] "Primo vice Christi sacerdos tres orationes exercet, sicut Dominus fecit, postquam exivit in montem Oliveti ante traditionem suam, id est pro universali ecclesia, et pro specialibus fratribus, et pro coro sacerdotum" (*PL*, CV, 1137[d]; H, II, 333). Amalarius cites Jerome's commentary on Matthew (*PL*, XXVI, 199[b-e]). His interpretation seems based on the idea that Christ prayed (1) for the Jews, (2) for the Gentiles, (3) for the apostles. These prayers are paralleled by the Mass prayers for (1) the Church—the "chosen people"; (2) the "special brothers," who are not necessarily of the clergy; and (3) the saints, the true "followers of Christ." The sense, however, is obscure. In the triple blessing of the oblation (*haec dona, haec munera, haec sancta sacrificia*) Amalarius finds a parallel to the "triple sacrifice" demanded by the prophet Micah (Mic. 6:8).

[93] *PL*, CV, 1139[d]-40[a]; H, II, 337. For the controversy over this, see Cabaniss, *Amalarius*, pp. 61, 89.

The angelic sacrifice (Sanctus) and the sacrifice of the elect (*Te igitur*) having been accomplished, the "general sacrifice; that is, the sacrifice of Christ" is now performed. Amalarius includes the *Quam oblationem* with the prayers of the *Qui pridie* rather than those of the *Te igitur*, as is usually done today. It is a preface during which "the celebrant receives the bread in his hands after the example of Christ."[94] Amalarius does not offer an explanation of the series of crosses made between the *Te igitur* and the Consecration, although these fascinated later writers and he himself analyzed the ceremonial in detail in the *Eclogae*.[95] Here he merely observes that if the celebrant is to imitate Christ, he should either refrain from making the cross (Christ did not use the cross at the Last Supper because he was not yet crucified) or should make one or two crosses because Christ was crucified once, for two peoples.[96] The words *Haec . . . in mei memoriam facietis* "touch on the whole service of the Mass" and hence are a justification of rememorative allegory.[97] The sindon again suggests the towel in which the Lord bound himself and the sudarium, the labor of washing the apostles' feet.

Modern commentaries treat the *Unde et memores* as the response of faith to Christ's command, "Do these things in remembrance of me." The rememorative element is obvious in the text, which appears fully to support the allegory. Amalarius considers the prayer the celebrant's confirmation that Christ is now present in the memory as truly as he is in the consecrated elements. God, he believes, demands a sacrifice "of the heart" as well as the visible sacrifice of the oblation. The comment provides a clue to the deeper significance of the allegorical method. As it indicates, there are two concurrently developing patterns in the Mass. The first is the ritual, which, in spite of its highly stylized form, is a true and visible sequence of actions and texts. The ritual is timeless. It always occurs in the present and its central features are unchanging. It is not a representation but a re-creation. It is linked indissolubly with a second order of events which occurred in chronological time and which must therefore be re-created in the present by meditation—by an effort of the memory heightened through contact with ritual. The two elements cannot

[94] *PL*, CV, 1139ᵈ; H, II, 337.

[95] References in the *Liber officialis* in *PL*, CV, 1140ᵈ; H, II, 338–39; in the *Eclogae*, *PL*, CV, 1326–27, 1330–32; H, III, 256–58.

[96] *PL*, CV, 1140ᵈ; H, II, 338–39.

[97] "Hic concrepant verba dominicae mensae cum toto officio missae" (*PL*, CV, 1141ᵃ; H, II, 339). There is possibly an elevation here: "Canitur hic: *Accipiens panem . . .* quando suscipit oblatam in secreta missae, aut quando hic eam elevat." If so, it is the extremely restrained elevation which *preceded* the moment of Consecration before the thirteenth century (Jungmann, *Mass*, II, 206). On the other hand, Amalarius is probably referring to the elevation at the Pater Noster. See below, p. 70.

be separated. The ritual is not "pure" ritual (if such a thing can exist) but has explicitly rememorative parts, while the memory of the historical drama is colored and idealized in terms of the images furnished by ritual. As the tradition of the Mass of St. Gregory indicates, during moments of climactic intensity the vision in the memory can become indistinguishable from the reality of the ritual. Christ is literally present in the consecrated bread and wine, and, at the same time, His image burns in the consciousness of the participant. Is Dürer's woodcut an image of truth, a record of an hallucination, or a piece of late medieval didacticism? The question is irrelevant. It is asked from the point of view of the detached observer, and the detached observer is, by definition—by the very fact of his detachment—incapable of the experience against which the validity of the answer must be tested. To criticize the allegory or to explain it on grounds alien to Catholic faith is to eliminate all possibility of understanding the Mass as a cultural and historical institution. It is also, incidentally, to eliminate the possibility of understanding the relation of the Mass to liturgical drama.

Christ, says Amalarius, is now on the Cross. The *Supplices te rogamus* is the celebrant's echo of Christ's prayer: "Into thy hands I commend my spirit": "The celebrant bows, and he commends that to God the Father which is sacrificed in place of Christ." [98] The altar is the altar of the Cross. On it "we sinners" are reconciled to God. The sindon recalls the humility of Christ when commanded by God to die, and the sudarium, the suffering of the Passion. [99] The subdeacons, previously identified with the disciples and holy women, stand with bowed heads in token of their sorrow over Christ's suffering. Unlike the deacons, they do not remain bowed until the *libera nos a malo*. They raise their heads following the *Supplices te rogamus*, for after Christ's death, "knowing that His persecutors had no further way of venting their wrath on His body . . . they were in a sense consoled and drew themselves up, gazing on the adorable body while it hung on the Cross." [100] The ceremonial is sufficiently striking to underscore the idea of role-playing both among the subdeacons and among the members of the congregation.

[98] "Sacerdos inclinat se, et hoc quod vice Christi immolatum est, Deo Patri commendat" (*PL*, CV, 1142ᵉ; H, II, 342).

[99] *Ibid.*

[100] ". . . postquam emisit spiritum, scientes non iam habere persecutores unde rabiem suam amplius in Christi corpus expleant . . . consolantur aliquo modo, et erigunt se, aspicientes in dilectum sibi corpus, quousque pendet in cruce, maxime cum vident multa miracula fieri" (*PL*, CV, 1142ᵈ; H, II, 342–43). This explains why they lower their heads at the elevation. It is the Deposition. The "miracles" are paralleled in the Mass by the allegory of the centurion associated with the *Te igitur*.

Here, too, the deacons wash their hands. As Amalarius remarks, the awkwardness of washing one's hands while bowed in the attitude of sorrow or prayer makes it difficult to interpret the action simply as a cleansing. To Amalarius it is a dramatic symbol of the cleansing from sin which resulted from the Passion.[101]

The ensuing ceremonial is particularly impressive in the ninth-century form of the Mass. This fact itself places emphasis on the regenerative phase of the service. Amalarius is fully in sympathy with this emphasis. The allegory of the Passion is dealt with succinctly, whereas the movement from the *Nobis quoque peccatoribus* to the Lord's Prayer is examined in detail.[102] It represents the death of Christ (the moment when the sacrifice is completed), the Deposition, and the entombment. The clerical participants represent the Marys, the disciples, and the apostles. Because the *Nobis quoque* and the Lord's Prayer are in the first person plural and the latter is said by clergy and congregation concurrently, participation symbolism is prominent. This is recognized by Amalarius in the moral interpretation of the allegory, according to which the sacrifice is a "sacrifice of Penance" performed inwardly by all participants, and the subdeacons in their role of disciples represent the congregation as the "we sinners" of the celebrant's prayer. In other words, the subdeacons have a choral function. With them the congregation stands at the foot of the Cross, watches the Deposition, and mourns during the silence of Holy Saturday: "Morally, we can understand the subdeacons to be *nos peccatores*, who show our faces—that is, our awareness of our sins—to the celebrant as he offers our confession to God. This accomplished, . . . after the period of humiliation, the heart is enlarged as the devotion of the Holy Spirit grows within, becoming, as it were, a paten to receive the sacraments of the Church."[103]

At the beginning of the *Nobis quoque* Christ is "sleeping with head inclined" on the Cross. At the first word of the prayer, the spear of the centurion plunges into His side. Surprisingly, the celebrant is the cen-

---

[101] *PL*, CV, 1143ᵃ; H, II, 343.

[102] Amalarius devotes four chapters (26–29) to the subject. He does not mention the prayer of remembrance for the dead which in the contemporary service precedes the *Nobis quoque* (i.e., *Memento etiam, Domine*). It is quite possible that he considered this prayer a continuation of the *Supplices te rogamus*, which he does mention. However, Jungmann (*Mass*, II, 238–39) notes that it was associated with the Mass of the Dead during the early period and that its general use was "sporadic" during the eighth and ninth centuries.

[103] "Moraliter. Possumus subdiaconos nos peccatores intelligere, qui faciem, id est conscientiam peccatorum nostrorum, sacerdoti ostendimus, ut nostram confessionem offerat Deo. Quo peracto . . . fervore crescente Spiritus Sancti, dilatantur corda nostra, quasi patena, ad suscipienda sacramenta ecclesiae" (*PL*, CV, 1146ᵇ; H, II, 350).

turion of Matt. 27:54. He utters the first three words in a loud voice (a practice still observed in the modern Mass) because the centurion saw the earthquake following Christ's death and testified, "Truly this was the Son of God." During the prayer, miraculous blood and water flow from Christ's side into the chalice. That the reality of this event was deeply felt is indicated by the fact that in the Gallican service, as Amalarius notes in his Preface, the chalice is placed to the right of the paten to receive the Holy Blood.[104]

The role of the celebrant changes almost immediately. As the arch-deacon sees the celebrant make the third cross and begin to elevate the Host, he approaches, lifts the chalice from the altar, and holds it with the celebrant until the words *Per omnia saecula saeculorum*, which end the Consecration. Afterwards, he replaces the chalice on the altar and wraps it in the sudarium. The ceremony, which is suppressed in today's Mass, was the major elevation of the ninth century.[105] That it is performed with the assistance of the deacon is a reminder of the central part which he formerly played in the service. To Amalarius this elevation is a re-enact-ment not of the Crucifixion but of the Deposition and entombment. The archdeacon represents Joseph of Arimathea who "begged the body of Jesus. And he took it down, and wrapped it in linen, and laid it in a sepulchre" (Luke 23:52–53). The celebrant, who elevates the oblation and wraps it in the sindon, is the Nicodemus mentioned by John (19:39–40). The altar is the tomb. The two crosses which the celebrant makes over the chalice with the *oblata* complete the Deposition with a symbolic reminder that Christ died for two peoples, the Jews and Gentiles. The subdeacons, still close to the altar, are the holy women who assisted at the Deposition and burial. As the *Per omnia saecula saeculorum* is said in a loud voice, the entombment is enacted by the replacing of the chalice and paten—wrapped in their respective shrouds—on the altar.[106]

A secondary ceremony accompanies the drama involving celebrant and archdeacon. According to the Roman *Ordo* used by Amalarius, at the beginning of the Canon (i.e., during the *Sursum corda*) an acolyte ap-proaches the altar from the right, holding the paten before his breast

---

[104] *PL*, CV, 1143[d]; H, II, 344–45.

[105] For discussion, see Jungmann, *Mass*, II, 266–67. This is the so-called "little elevation" of today's service.

[106] *PL*, CV, 1144[c]–45[a]; H, II, 346–47. The details of ceremonial are clarified by reference to the *Eclogae* (*PL*, CV, 1327; H, III, 248–49, 252–55). The *Eclogae* also specifies that the three prayers said while the oblation remains on the altar (prologue, Pater Noster, embolism) symbolize the three days during which the Lord "rested" in the tomb. With the *Pax* and the commingling, the body of the Lord is taken from the altar, since on the third day His spirit, which had liberated the Just from hell, returned.

wrapped in a sindon. During the Canon (at the *Te igitur*) a subdeacon receives it, holding it in the fold of his planeta, a predecessor of the modern chasuble. He carries it before the altar. At the end of the Canon, it is received by the "regionary subdeacon," who stands behind the archdeacon. At the words *ab omni perturbatione securi* of the embolism, he presents the paten to the archdeacon, who kisses it and gives it to a second deacon. Amalarius remarks, "It seems to me that the time when the paten is presented is the time when the disciples or women were busy with the burial of the Lord."[107] Since the paten is here associated with the entombment, the fact that the subdeacon turns from the celebrant to receive it becomes dramatically significant. It is also significant that Amalarius finds a parallel between the paten and the ointment box carried by Mary to anoint the Lord's body (Mark 16:1).[108]

5. Communion: From Pater Noster to *Ite, missa est*

Mention of the ointment box makes it clear that the Mass has entered a phase closely associated with the events commemorated in the earliest liturgical plays. When the words *Per omnia saecula saeculorum* are pronounced, the regionary subdeacon receives the paten. This action signifies the fact that "the women first heard the joyous news of the Resurrection."[109] The joy is temporarily muted. The subdeacons have raised their heads following the *Supplices te rogamus* in imitation of the holy women contemplating Christ on the Cross. They bow again during the Pater Noster. Then, at the *libera nos a malo*, deacons and subdeacons raise their heads. The transition from the *tristia* of the Passion to the *gaudium* of the Resurrection is, for Amalarius, the turning point of the Mass. It is hinted at in the presentation of the paten, and the hint becomes more overt at the general raising of heads.

It now remains for Amalarius to relate the prayers and ceremonies of the beginning of the Communion to historical events. The seven petitions of the Pater Noster—already a traditional scheme of analysis by the ninth century—commemorate the seventh day (Holy Saturday), "when Christ rested in the sepulcher."[110] During Holy Saturday the apostles and

---

[107] "Videtur mihi ut ea ora praesentanda sit patena, qua circa sepulturam Domini satagebant discipuli vel mulieres" (*PL*, CV, 1146[d]). H, II, 351, has "qua circa mysteria passionis," which is clearly an inferior reading.

[108] *PL*, CV, 1147[e]; H, II, 352.

[109] "Subdiaconus regionarius accipit patenam, finito canone, quia laetitiam dominicae resurrectionis mulieres primo audierunt" (*PL*, CV, 1147[d]; H, II, 353).

[110] *PL*, CV, 1149[d]; H, II, 357.

disciples were beset with sorrow and fear and prayed to be "liberated from evil." By the same token, "the Holy Church now prays, as it were, on the seventh day . . . lest it be separated by the perils of this world from the hope of celestial joys."[111] The embolism, says Amalarius, is a continuation of the Pater Noster. The Harrowing of Hell is not mentioned, although from a reference in the *Eclogae* it is apparent that Amalarius knew the tradition. Evidently, the subject did not have the same fascination for him that it did for later allegorists.

The interpretation of the ceremonies which accompany the beginning of Communion is of great importance for the history of drama. The sub-deacons present themselves at the altar to receive the *corpus Domini*. They must wait, however, for the commingling and Fraction. While they wait, the transition from *tristia* to *gaudium* occurs. They are the Marys who visit the sepulcher and are informed by the angels, "He is risen; He is not here" (Mark 16:6): "When the holy women presented themselves at the sepulcher of the Lord, they found that the spirit had returned to the body, and there was the vision of the angels at the tomb, and they announced to the apostles what they had seen."[112] The reading specifies scene, characters, and events which were to be the basis of the *Quem quaeritis* play and which remained central in medieval drama until the fifteenth century. Interestingly, Amalarius can claim support for his interpretation from no less an authority than Bede, who, in his commentary on Luke, had already associated angels, women, and sepulcher with the ceremonies of the Mass.[113] The subdeacon who brings the paten and the subdeacon who receives it are two of the holy women. The fact that they are joined by a deacon is explained (somewhat awkwardly) by Paul's injunction concerning deacons, "Even so must their wives be grave" (I Tim. 3:10–12).

As the celebrant says the *Pax Domini*, he places the Host on the paten. "After Christ by His salutation made happy the hearts of the disciples, the prayers of the women were fulfilled, and the joy of the Resurrection was perceived."[114] Amalarius considers the commingling a visual rein-

---

[111] "Orat et nunc sancta ecclesia, quasi in septima die, quando, iam quiescentibus animabus sanctorum, instat ieiunando, vigilando, orando, certando in caritate, ne abrumpatur periculis huius mundi a spe caelestium gaudiorum" (*PL*, 1149ᵈ–50ª; H, II, 357). Amalarius draws for his interpretations of the Lord's Prayer on Cyprian, *Liber de oratione dominica* (*PL*, IV, 537–38).

[112] "Praesentantibus se sanctis mulieribus ad sepulchrum Domini, inveniunt spiritum redisse ad corpus, et angelorum visionem circa sepulchrum, ac adnuntiant apostolis quae viderant" (*PL*, CV, 1151ª; H, II, 359).

[113] Bede, *In Lucae evangelium expositio*, *PL*, XCII, 623ᶜ–24ª.

[114] "Postquam enim Christus sua salutatione laetificavit corda discipulorum, vota feminarum completa sunt percepto gaudio resurrectionis" (*PL*, CV, 1151ᵈ; H, II, 361). For the *Pax Domini*, see Jungmann, *Mass*, II, 294–95.

forcement of the drama enacted by the subdeacons and deacon. Interpretation is made difficult by the fact that practice varies. Sometimes the commingling occurs before and sometimes after the *Pax Domini*.[115] Amalarius prefers the first alternative because it is more consistent with the Mass drama. The commingling precedes the Fraction. The *Liber officialis* states that the preconsecrated sancta is to be used in this ceremony.[116] As has been noted, the sancta is a symbol of the unity of each Solemn Mass with all Masses previously celebrated. It is also the body of Christ, and the wine is His blood. The commingling reunites body and blood; hence, it literally re-creates the miracle of the Resurrection: "The cross which is formed over the chalice with a particle of the *oblata* brings the body itself before our eyes for whom it was crucified."[117] The congre-

---

[115] *PL*, CV, 1152[a-c]; H, II, 362–64. That the confusion of Amalarius was shared by his contemporaries is indicated by Jungmann, *Mass*, II, 311–12. Jungmann mentions the sancta here. Amalarius appears to describe the ceremony correctly, but see Jungmann, II, 213–14 and 310. Jungmann believes that the ceremony had largely disappeared by the ninth century "even in Rome itself." Evidently, either the *libellus Romanus* used by Amalarius described the rite, or Amalarius was familiar with it from Gallican practice. One thing is clear: his service includes a double commingling of which the first is the major one.

[116] "Estimo, secundum hunc sensum, quod non erret, si quis primo *sancta* ponat in calicem, et dein dixerit: 'Pax Domini . . .' salvo magisterio didasculorum" (*PL*, CV, 1152[c]; H, II, 362; italics mine). In the following paragraph Amalarius explicitly says that in the triple Fraction the "pontifex" "rumpit oblatam ex latere dextro [positional symbolism], et particulam quam rumpit, super altare relinquit, reliquas vero oblationes ponit in patenam. . . ." Later, the deacon carries the paten "ad sedem, ut communicet pontifex; qui dum communicaverit, de ipsa quam momorderat, ponit inter manus archdiaconi in calicem." This betrays none of the confusion which Jungmann attributes to the Gallican Church, nor is there any suggestion of the "multiple commingling" by the deacons mentioned by Jungmann (*Mass*, II, 313). What Amalarius is obviously and consciously describing is the sancta ceremony. Since the Mass begins, according to the *Liber officialis*, with an adoration of the sancta by the bishop at the altar, the first particle of the Fraction, *ex latere dextro*, may be intended as the sancta of the next Solemn Mass. At any rate, Amalarius equates it with the body of Christ "sleeping" in the sepulcher and does not refer to its consumption at a later point in the ceremony.

[117] "Crux quae formatur super calicem particula oblatae, ipsum corpus nobis ante oculos proscribit, quod pro nobis crucifixum est" (*PL*, CV, 1152[a]; H, II, 362). The removal of the chalice and oblation from the altar after the Fraction is, in the *Eclogae* (*PL*, CV, 1328; H, III, 258), the restoration of Jesus in living form to man. The *Pax* is both the peace of the Just released from hell and the peace brought to the disciples by the Resurrection. The symbolism of the chalice is elaborate. In the *Eclogae* it represents Christ's head (wine is associated with the soul which in turn is related to the intellect, vision, etc., hence the appropriateness of covering the chalice with the sudarium—the "sweatcloth" and later the model for the Veronica). The Host, by the same token, represents the body ("This is my flesh"). The crossing of the chalice with the Host just prior to the first commingling is thus a symbol of the reuniting of the head with the body. The four sides of the chalice represent (as in the *Liber officialis*) the four quarters of the earth to which news of the Resurrection will penetrate. A parallel is discerned by Amalarius between the commingling and the breathing of the

gation has listened with the Marys while the angels announced the miracle; now, in its role of disciples and apostles, it sees Christ appear in bodily form. Corporate symbolism, enfolding the congregation in the drama, is stressed: "He [the celebrant] touches the four sides of the chalice because by it the human race of the four corners of the earth achieves the unity of a single body and the peace of the Catholic Church."[118] The celebrant's prayer *Haec commixtio* (*Fiat commixtio*, according to the older wording used by Amalarius) is a petition that the sacrifice be acceptable. Then comes the *Pax Domini*, an expression of the peace brought to man by the Resurrection. It is followed immediately by the Kiss of Peace, an impressive act in which the congregation visibly and physically affirms the celebrant's words. The celebrant receives the kiss from the altar. It passes from him to the archdeacon, then to the clergy *per ordinem*, and then to the chorus and congregation. The people exchange embraces, although Amalarius sternly warns against men embracing women and vice versa because indiscriminate embraces might lead to thoughts less than holy.

Because the kiss is given by Christ and passes among all participants, it is a powerful symbol of unity, as well as a striking instance of role-playing during which the boundary between the visible and invisible again tends to disappear as it did during the Sanctus. After (or perhaps, during) the kiss, the oblation loaf is broken (the Fraction) and carried to the communicants, beginning with the celebrant and clergy. The paten is carried to the episcopal chair. There the bishop or pontifex, associated, it will be recalled, with the ascended Christ, partakes of the Host and drops a

---

"breath of life" into man in Genesis 2:7. During the Renaissance Neoplatonic critics like Tasso were fond of comparing the artist to God. Here we see the priest compared to God. As the Creator breathed life into Adam in the beginning, so the celebrant breathes life into the second Adam at each Mass. There is an important meaning in the parallel. The "creation motif" completes the effect of the typological symbolism of the Mass. The creation of man is reduplicated in the act of consecration. A "new life" is literally created both for Christ and for the participants: "In isto officio monstratur sanguinem fusum pro nostra anima, et carnem mortuam pro nostro corpore redire ad propriam substantiam, atque spiritu vivificante vegetari hominem novum, ut ultra non moriatur qui pro nobis mortuus fuit et resurrexit" (*Liber officialis*, PL, CV, 1152ᵃ; H, II, 361–62). Note especially the vocabulary: *spiritu vivificante, vegetari,* etc. The "sliding time" of the service now includes not only events of early history (the law and the prophets), but the very first event of all, from the human point of view' Since the Mass is oriented toward the eschatological world of the Ascension, *Per omnia saecula saeculorum,* it ends by passing beyond the further limit of chronological time. This treatment of time will be familiar to students of primitive religion. It also has significance for the development of religious drama in the Middle Ages.

[118] "Ideo tangit quattuor latera calicis, quia per illum hominum genus quattuor climatum ad unitatem unius corporis accessit et ad pacem catholicae ecclesiae" (*PL*, CV, 1152ᵇ; H, II, 362).

particle (a second commingling) into the chalice held by the archdeacon, an act which Amalarius does not attempt to explain.[119] During the ceremony of the Fraction, the Agnus Dei is sung antiphonally. Corporate symbolism and role-playing are sustained because the Fraction, says Amalarius, represents Christ's breaking of bread for the two at Emmaus (Luke 24:30), and the Agnus Dei recalls that they "sang an antiphon narrating in turn the Resurrection of the Lord."[120]

The discussion of the Eucharist involved Amalarius in serious difficulties. His general concept was orthodox enough. By it we are incorporated into the mystical body: "By the Eucharist Christ remains in us and we in him through His human incarnation."[121] His explanation of the Fraction practiced by the Roman Church was, however, condemned by the Synod of Quiercy. According to Amalarius, Christ has a triform body — the immaculate body which he received from the Virgin, the body which lives on earth, and the body of the Resurrection. These three bodies are revealed in the three parts of the Host. The one placed in the chalice is the body of the Resurrection. The one consumed by the faithful is the body which "still walks the earth." And the particle left on the altar (probably the sancta) is the body which slept in the sepulcher.[122] Doctrinal issues may, for present purposes, be discounted. What is significant in the interpretation is the evidence it provides that Amalarius associated the Fraction with life rather than death. He follows the Roman idea— as against the Mozarabic and Byzantine traditions— that the breaking of

---

[119] "Si hoc ita agitur in Romana ecclesia, ab illis potest addisci quid significet bis positus panis in calicem; non enim vacat a mysterio quicquid in eo officio agitur iuxta constitutionem patrum" (*PL*, CV, 1152[d]; H, II, 363). The ceremony of the Kiss of Peace includes the prayer "Domine Jesu Christi, qui dixisti apostolis tuis: pacem relinquo vobis." The prayer obviously accords with the identification with the apostles of all who exchange kisses. After the prayer in the modern service the celebrant kisses the altar (here, obviously, Christ) and then the deacon at his right, saying *Pax tecum.* The *libellus Romanus*, which Amalarius quotes, does not mention the details of the prayer and the kissing of the altar. The prayer is late, and probably no prayer was used in the early ninth century. The archdeacon transfers his kiss to the assistant bishop and then to the rest of the clergy *per ordinem.*

[120] "Antiphona sequens, id est vox reciproca, iura fraternitatis custodit. . . . Quem typum gesserunt illi duo, qui Dominum cognoverunt in fratione panis. . . . Illi nempe cantaverunt antiphonam vicissim narrando de resurrectione Domini" (*PL*, CV, 1153[e]; H, II, 365). Is it possible that Amalarius is here describing the trope *Qui resurrexisti, Agnus Dei consecratus et vivificatus* mentioned in the commentary *Missa pro multis*, based on his work? See Jungmann, *Mass*, II, 339–40.

[121] "Per eucharistiam Christus in nobis manet, et nos in illo per assumptum hominem. Ipse est Deus pacis, per quem pacata sunt caelestia et terrestria" (*PL*, CV, 1153[d]; H, II, 365).

[122] *PL*, CV, 1154[d]-55[a]; H, II, 367–68; Cabaniss, *Amalarius*, pp. 86–87, 89; Jungmann, *Mass*, II, 310–11.

the Host is a symbol of the risen Christ, and that while it occurs, Christ is a living presence at the service.[123]

Amalarius does not comment on the celebrant's Communion prayers, the ablution, or the *communio*. These prayers sustain the sense of joyful liberation which has already been adequately described in his comments on the ceremonial.[124]

At the end of the Mass, Amalarius writes, the celebrant "blesses the people and gives his salutation [i.e., the *Dominus vobiscum* and prayer]. Then he turns to the east to commit himself to the Ascension of the Lord. And the deacon says *Ite, missa est.*"[125] The tableau which is formed opens into eternity. Amalarius exclaims, "O, would that when we have heard the *Ite, missa est* our mind would rise to that country where our Lord has preceded us so that by our desire we would be there where the Desired of all nations awaits us with His emblem of victory."[126] According to the orthodox interpretation, the sacrifice is now being carried on the wings of angels to the celestial throne. The last benediction (especially important in Lent) completes the service, and with it, the sacred drama. The celebrant is Christ at the moment before the Ascension, blessing His disciples: "And he led them out as far as to Bethany, and he lifted up his hands and blessed them" (Luke 24:50). Morally, the congregation is the army of Christian soldiers armed by the blessing against the wiles of the devil. As it exclaims *Deo gratias*, it is also the group of witnesses who, according

---

[123] Reichel, *Solemn Mass*, pp. 28–29; Duchesne, *Christian Worship*, pp. 219f.; and Jungmann, *Mass*, II, 302–3. The Gallican ritual called for a Fraction in five parts, which were laid out "upon the corporal in some fanciful picture of the Lord's body" (Reichel). The Mozarabic Fraction was in nine parts. The Irish Fraction was the most complex, requiring up to 65 particles on the feasts of Christmas, Easter, and Pentecost. The pattern of the Mozarabic Fraction illustrates the tendency which this rite shared with the Greek Church (see Jungmann, *Mass*, II, 301) to regard the Fraction as an image of the Crucifixion. Seven of the nine particles are placed on the altar in the shape of a cross. The particle at the head is called *corporatio* (i.e., the Incarnation), and the one at the foot, *passio*. The one at the end of the right arm is *mors*, and on the left, *resurrectio*. The two remaining particles (*gloria, regnum*) are immediately below the left arm. These two particles are for the celebrant's Communion and the commingling.

[124] The *Pascha nostrum* of Easter was, for example, a lengthy choral piece ending with a triple alleluia, and was sung during the distribution of Communion.

[125] "Etenim Dominus ante ascensionem in caelos duxit discipulos in Bethaniam, ibique benedixit eos, et ascendit in caelum. Hunc morem tenet sacerdos, ut, post omnia sacramenta consummata, benedicat populo et salutet. Dein revertitur ad orientem, ut se commendet Domini ascensioni" (*PL*, CV, 1155[b]; H, II, 368). *Post omnia sacramenta consummata* may include the particle of the Host on the altar. On the other hand, it may refer merely to the *sacramenta* used in the Communion.

[126] "O utinam quando audimus a diacono: 'Ite missa est,' mens nostra ad illam patriam tendat, quo caput nostrum praecessit, ut ibi simus desiderio, ubi desideratus cunctis gentibus nos expectat cum suo tropheo . . ." (*PL*, CV, 1156[a]; H, II, 370).

to Luke, "returned to Jerusalem with great joy: and were continually in the temple, praising and blessing God."[127]

III

That the service which has just been described is dramatic cannot be doubted. The nature and, as it might be called, the tonality of the drama is another matter. It has a configuration which may be experienced but which cannot be fully communicated. The problems confronting the would-be critic are not unlike those posed by the analysis of a poem. The history, genre, ideas, social background, and rhetoric of the poem can be described, but its *raison d'être*, its mode of existence in the mind at the moment of full aesthetic response, eludes definition for the very simple reason that the only adequate expression of the poem's meaning is the experience of the poem itself.

Of course, the problems posed by an attempt to reconstruct the ninth-century Mass are more numerous than those posed by the analysis of a poem. There is the matter of belief, which for many scholars has proved an insurmountable barrier. "Willing suspension of disbelief" can, for those willing to practice it, permit a partial recovery of the experience. But, in fact, the Mass has never been a matter of willing suspension of disbelief. This approach leads off in the direction of *fin-de-siècle* "appreciations" of the Mass because of its picturesqueness. In spirit such appreciations are directly opposed to the attitudes of the ninth century. The service described by Amalarius has a very important aesthetic dimension, but it is essentially not a matter of appreciation but of passionate affirmation. It remained for later times—the high Middle Ages—to make the Mystery of the Mass mysterious by changing the Offertory ceremony, reserving the chalice to the clergy, reducing lay participation to a minimum, and drawing the veil of the rood screen between the congregation and the altar.

Sister Teresa Goode remarks concerning Gonzalo de Berceo's thirteenth-century allegory of the Mass that it is "elaborate enough, perhaps, for the uninitiated, but for those for whom he was writing, evidently quite simple."[128] If one considers the service outlined by Amalarius, there are moments, even for the non-Catholic, when the drama lives in the imagina-

---

[127] The parallel between the faithful and the Christian soldiers is drawn in the *Liber officialis* (*PL*, 1156[d]; H, II, 372). The parallel between the people and the witnesses mentioned by Luke (24:53) is cited in *Eclogae* (*PL*, CV, 1330; H, III, 264).

[128] P. 32.

tion with something like its original intensity. The effort of imagination is difficult. Considering the span of time which must be bridged, the differences of ceremonial, and the intricacy of the symbolism, at best the effort can be only partially successful. Some reconstructions are highly reliable, particularly where the text of Amalarius provides detailed guidance. Others must remain speculative.

Among the speculative issues is the question of how far the allegorical interpretation fused with the ceremony for the ninth-century Catholic. Did the congregation sense its role-playing function continually, or only during those ceremonies and prayers when it was assigned definite actions and speeches—the Introit procession, the reading of the Gospel, the Offertory, the Kiss of Peace, the Communion? To what degree did the subdeacons and deacons suggest by the use of physical objects and gestures their roles as the holy women and the apostles? How far did the celebrant carry his role as *repraesentatio Christi*?

From the anthropological point of view such questions are unnecessary. The Mass is a ritual drama no matter how it is performed. To students of the history of drama, however, they are important. They are a way of asking how far representational drama based on history, rather than psychologically determined patterns of ritual, emerged during the Mass itself.

According to the testimony of Deacon Florus of Lyons, Amalarius' interpretation "corrupted" churches throughout France, appealing especially to the *simpliciores*. What other basis could there be for this appeal than the fact that it renewed the sense of community participation in divine worship? And how else could this sense have been stimulated among the *simpliciores* than by emphasis during the celebration of the Mass on its dramatic elements? Clearly, what Deacon Florus means by his reference to the corruption of the French churches is that the works of Amalarius strongly and visibly influenced the way that the ceremonies were performed and the texts read. Amalarius remarks that the Offertory *Vir erat in terra* alludes to Job oppressed with sickness and that the "author of the office, to make the words vividly recall the suffering Job to our memory, repeated them often, in the manner of people who are sick."[129] Another ninth-century author, Bishop Agobard of Lyons, complains of "theatrical mannerisms and stage music" encouraged by Amalarius.[130] By the twelfth century Aelred, Abbot of Rievaulx, was complaining in his *Speculum*

---

[129] "Officii auctor, ut affecter nobis ad memoriam reduceret aegrotantem Iob, repetivit saepius verba more aegrotantium" (*PL*, CV, 1157ᵈ; H, II, 373).

[130] ". . . theatralibus sonis et scenicis modulationibus . . ." (Agobard, *De correctione antiphonarii*, *PL*, CIV, 334ᵉ). The translation is that of Cabaniss, *Amalarius*, p. 85.

charitatis of singing suggestive of feminine voices, sighs, sudden dramatic silences, vocal imitation of the agonies of the dying and the suffering, and priests who "contort the whole body with histrionic gestures." These practices, he observes, "amaze the common people" but are proper "to the theater, not the oratory."[131] Later evidence fully confirms the view that the clergy frequently translated Mass allegory into histrionic action. The elevation of the Host and its extravagant adoration during the high Middle Ages is a striking instance of the compulsion felt by all participants, including the clergy, to express invisible mysteries in visible dramatic form. The celebrant's imitation of Christ during the *Qui pridie* was already a venerable tradition when Amalarius wrote the *Liber officialis* and remains in the rubrics of today's Mass. The extension of the celebrant's arms during the *Unde et memores*, the elaborate Fractions of the Mozarabic and Gallican churches, the proliferating genuflections, kisses, and embracings, the veneration of the Gospel, the widening use of crucifixes, and the popularity of images of the saints directly behind the altar are all expressions of the mimetic tendency. And, returning to Dürer's woodcut of the Mass of St. Gregory, the art of the fifteenth and sixteenth centuries adds visual testimony to the evidence that the dramatic tradition survived intact until the Reformation.

Should church vestments then, with their elaborate symbolic meanings, be considered costumes? Should the paten, chalice, sindon, sudarium, candles, and thurible be considered stage properties? Should the nave, chancel, presbyterium, and altar of the church be considered a stage, and its windows, statues, images, and ornaments a "setting"? As long as there is clear recognition that these elements are hallowed, that they are the sacred phase of parallel elements turned to secular use on the profane stage, it is possible to answer yes. Just as the Mass is a sacred drama encompassing all history and embodying in its structure the central pattern of Christian life on which all Christian drama must draw, the celebration of the Mass contains all elements necessary to secular performances. The Mass is the general case—for Christian culture, the archetype. Individual dramas are shaped in its mold. As theologians have long known and anthropologists have recently discovered, man does not make God in his image. Rather, he makes himself in the image of his gods.

---

[131] ". . . quid illa vocis contractio et infractio? . . . aliquando virili vigore deposito, in femineae vocis gracilitates acuitur. . . . Videas aliquando hominem aperto ore quasi intercluso halitu exspirare, non cantare, ac ridiculosa quadam vocis interceptione quasi minitari silentium; nunc agones morientium, vel extasim patientium imitari. Interim histrionicis quibusdam gestibus totum corpus agitatur. . . . Stans interea vulgus . . . attonitusque miratur . . . eos non ad oratorium, sed ad theatrum, nec ad orandum, sed ad spectandum aestimes convenisse" (*PL*, CXCV, 571; cf. Chambers, *MS*, I, 81; Young, *DMC*, I, 548).

ESSAY III

The Lenten Agon:
From Septuagesima to Good Friday

I

THE EFFORTS OF an aging monarch to consolidate his empire and the appearance a century later of a drama about Christ's Resurrection would seem, offhand, to have no possible connection. History, however, is no respecter of probabilities. Throughout his long reign Charlemagne strove to bring cultural as well as political unity to his territories. The Roman Church was both ally and tool in this endeavor. In place of regional centers of power, it offered the ideal of a revived and Christianized Roman Empire. In place of the Babel of emerging European vernacular languages, it offered the universal tongue of Latin with its inexhaustible heritage of culture. In place of diverse and divisive religious traditions—pagan, Jewish, Mozarabic, Ambrosian, Gallican, Greek, and others—it offered the majestic forms of worship evolved by Pope Gregory and his immediate successors. Having received the imperial crown from Rome, Charlemagne had every reason to support the Roman claim of supremacy in religious matters—Roman authority, Roman theology, and Roman liturgy. Alcuin's schools at Aachen and Tours contributed to this end. In the ninth century, when the dream of political unity had faded into the reality of internecine warfare, Amalarius of Metz, Paschasius Radbertus, Rabanus Maurus, Walafrid Strabo, and Hincmar of Reims, to mention only a few of the most prominent scholars, carried on the work of cultural unification. As far as Roman supremacy was concerned, they were destined to succeed beyond their fondest hopes.

The dramatic interpretations of the Roman Mass by Amalarius of Metz are one link between Carolingian interests and later European drama. Another less obvious connection may be found in Carolingian discussions of baptism. Interest in this subject must have been in part political. During much of his reign Charlemagne was actively engaged in attempts to pacify and convert the Saxons. Heresy and apostasy were also a problem. Agobardus of Lyons managed to convince himself that conversions to Judaism were a serious threat to the Empire; the icono-

80

clasts battled with the iconodules; the Adoptionist, Filioque, and various other heresies and controversies threatened orthodoxy; and by the middle of the century the first Eucharistic controversy had taken shape in the conflicting essays by Radbertus and Remigius of Corbie. A proper initiation into the Church would not solve all problems, but it might at least reduce dissent and apostasy. Carolingian interest in baptism is evident as early as 789, when a decree was issued commanding the Frankish bishops to follow the Roman order. In 812 an imperial *interrogatio* was circulated among them requesting clarification of the baptismal rite. Replies survive by such luminaries as Jesse of Amiens, Leidrad of Lyons, Magnus of Sens, Maxentius of Aquileia, and Theodulphus of Orleans. Amalarius contributed *De scrutinio et baptismo*, which, while undistinguished, is his earliest surviving work. The upshot of this burst of scholarship was that in 813 the Council of Mayence decreed that the full Roman rite, now opened to all, should be observed throughout the Empire.[1]

In the ninth century a close relation existed between baptism and the liturgy of Easter. The Church was allowed to baptize at only two seasons of the year, Easter and Pentecost, and of these Easter was by far the more important. From the early days of the Church the Easter vigil service had been organized around a ceremony of mass baptism. On the authority of Paul to the Romans, baptism was considered a death and rebirth. It was considered only fitting that the regeneration of the individual Christian should occur at the same time as the celebration of Christ's Resurrection. Interest in baptism therefore meant renewed interest in the history, ceremonial, and symbolism of the Easter liturgy—and, inevitably, in the events depicted in the *Quem quaeritis* play.

For several reasons the liturgical forms adopted by the Carolingian bishops were particularly dramatic. Gustaf Aulén has shown in his *Christus Victor* that from the early Fathers until the *Cur Deus homo?* of

---

[1] The *Interrogatio Karoli imperatoris* is reprinted in Hanssens' edition of Amalarius, I, 235–36, and in *PL*, XCIX, 892. The replies are reprinted in the *Patrologia Latina* as follows: Jesse of Amiens, *De baptismo* (*PL*, CV, 781–96); Leidrad of Lyons, *De sacramento baptismi* (*PL*, XCIX, 853–72); Magnus of Sens, *De mysterio baptismatis* (*PL*, CII, 981–94); Maxentius, *De significatu rituum baptismi* (*PL*, CVI, 51–54); Theodulphus, *De ordine baptismi* (*PL*, CV, 223–40); Amalarius, *De scrutinio et baptismo* (*PL*, XCIX, 893–901; H, I, 236–51). Carolingian interest in baptism and the archaic quality of the rites proposed by the bishops is discussed by Pierre de Puniet, "Catéchuménat," in F. Cabrol and H. Leclercq (eds.), *Dictionnaire d'archéologie chrétienne et de liturgie* (hereafter cited as *DACL*) (Paris, 1907 *et seq.*), II, 2, 2612–16. Puniet writes: "Malgré les prescriptions du sacramentaire grégorien [on] continua donc au IXe siècle d'observer la discipline des scrutins. Elle se perpétua dans les siècles suivants, au moins dans certaines églises en France, en Germanie et en Italie." See also Puniet's article "Baptême" in *DACL*, II, 1, 251–346.

Anselm of Canterbury (1033–1109) a dramatic concept of the atonement prevailed in the Western Church. According to this view, the atonement is understood as an agon—a dramatic conflict between Christ and Satan culminating in the triumph of the Resurrection. The view was incorporated into the early liturgy and emphasized by Pope Gregory, who "outdoes all his predecessors" in his dramatic images of the atonement.[2]

The shape of the Easter liturgy powerfully reflects this dramatic view, but in ninth-century Rome the drama already had begun to fade. The liturgy of the fifth and sixth centuries depended heavily for its effectiveness on the presence at church services of adult candidates for baptism and reached a well-defined climax during the baptism-Communion sequence of Easter Eve. In Rome, infant baptism had gradually become more important than adult baptism, and tendencies toward anticipation—performance of the first Mass of Easter on Saturday evening or afternoon—were already appearing.

On the other hand, Charlemagne's bishops did not follow contemporary Roman practice. They relied perforce on documents rather than direct observation, and the documents preserved usages that were already somewhat archaic. Works like the *De ordine baptismi* of Theodulphus and the *Liber officialis* of Amalarius preserve the dramatic structure of fifth-century liturgy. Emphasis is placed on adult baptism, and it is assumed that the vigil Mass will come after midnight on Easter Eve at a time coincident with the historical Resurrection. If there is any relation between such works and Carolingian practice, the churches of the Empire, particularly of France and Germany, retained in their Easter liturgy a drama of extraordinary dimensions and subtlety. This drama is significant in its own right as one of the more remarkable creations of medieval culture. It is also the precondition for the emergence of what is usually called liturgical drama.

II

In one sense, at least, the Easter liturgy is a transitional phase between the sacred drama of the Mass and liturgical drama. As an isolated ceremony the Mass is static. It exists outside of time in what may be called the absolute present. Whenever it is celebrated, the original sacrifice is made present again (not commemorated) in all its original efficacy. At the same time each Mass is related to every other Mass through its connections with

[2] Gustaf Aulén, *Christus Victor: An Historical Study of the Three Main Types of the Idea of Atonement*, trans. A. G. Hebert (New York, 1951), chap. viii, pp. 4–7, 16–60.

the larger structure of the Church year. Thus each Mass is an episode in a cycle that repeats itself every 365 days. The ordinary of the Mass, which is its constant factor, relates it to the original sacrifice and hence to absolute time. The proper, which changes with the season, the day, and even the hour, relates it to the annual cycle. The dramatic significance of each Mass must therefore be considered a convergence of two distinct kinds of meaning. Its denotation, one might say, remains constant, but its connotation changes. This explains why the same ritual can be ecstatically joyful, as at Christmas, and somber, even tragic, as on Passion Sunday.

Once the difference between absolute and cyclical time is recognized, the Mass and the Easter liturgy may be seen to have important dramatic features in common. The Mass is comic in structure, having a descending action, a crisis, a reversal-recognition, and a joyful resolution. In terms of emotion this represents a movement from *tristia* to *gaudium*. In terms of allegory it is a presentation of the central events of Christian history—the Crucifixion, entombment, and Resurrection. The Easter liturgy has the same structure, emotional pattern, and historical associations. Its descending action begins with Lent. The point of crisis is reached on Good Friday, and Holy Saturday and Easter Sunday are devoted to the entombment and Resurrection, respectively. The reversal-recognition occurs early on Easter morning and is followed by a week of ceremonial rejoicing known in the ninth century as *octava in albis*, "the octave of white robes." As during Communion, this *gaudium* is more than simple joy over a happy ending. Something fundamental has happened to the participants as well as to the protagonist. During the *octava in albis* they share in the life of the Heavenly Jerusalem; their joy is that of saints dwelling in God. The transformation of the participants as a result of the peripeteia is essential to both the Mass and the cyclical drama. It has implications for the whole subject of dramatic catharsis.

Evidently the Mass and the Easter liturgy are restatements of the same drama in terms of two varieties of time. Since the Mass assumed what was essentially a modern shape long before the Church year, it might seem reasonable to suppose that absolute time precedes cyclical time in the growth of Christian drama or even that it *must* precede it. The matter, however, is not so simple. The Mass and the Easter liturgy have different proximate sources in the Gospel accounts of the Last Supper and the Resurrection, but they also have a common precedent (source is the wrong word here) in spring renewal ceremonies that are as old as organized society. It seems probable that the Mass and the Easter liturgy are not sequential developments but alternate, equally valid, ritual expressions of the renewal motif. The Mass assumed definitive shape before the Easter liturgy, simply because it is shorter and celebrated with much greater frequency.

During Holy Week a third kind of time becomes prominent in ninth-century forms of worship. A cluster of ceremonies appears which cannot be explained in terms of absolute or cyclical time. These ceremonies involve representation of events, figures, and scenes from the Gospels. Their common element is their use of linear time. Past time is not absolutely present, as during the Mass, nor is it eternally recurrent, as in the annual cycle. Instead, each event is a unique point on a line constantly moving forward into the future. An event occurs once and is forever and irrevocably past. This is historical time, and the representational ceremonies that use it are germinal history plays. Because they are concerned with events that cannot be recovered in the present, they use the devices of verisimilitude, in the exact sense of that word. The event is what is "true"; the representation can only be "similar" to truth. It is made similar in two ways, by copying the historical source and by illusion. Under the first heading come such common features of representational ceremonies as the use of dialogue taken from the Bible, pantomime, multiple actors for multiple roles, imitative voice inflection, costume elements, and props or arrangements of setting to suggest an historical locale. Under the second heading, illusion, come audience-stimulation devices, including responses and gestures that give the congregation a choral function; lyric stimuli, both poetic and musical; direct labeling; and anachronism, the dramatic equivalent of the *argumentum ad hominem*.

In spite of its importance, the Easter liturgy has never been examined as a dramatic structure by literary historians. Individual ceremonies like the *Elevatio Crucis* and the *Visitatio Sepulchri* have been studied in meticulous detail but always apart from their dramatic context. They have been classified rather than analyzed in terms of function, and the problem of variant forms has been solved by fiat. The assumption has prevailed that simple forms necessarily precede complex ones, and on this basis the chronological order of extant manuscripts has been neglected or dismissed. Equally misleading is the fact that the marked differences between the ninth-century Easter liturgy and modern or even high medieval forms have been ignored in the belief that they could be of interest to no one except liturgical scholars.

To progress beyond this point literary history needs first and foremost an understanding of the dramatic elements in the ninth-century Easter liturgy. It also needs to consider the relation between the liturgy proper and the representational ceremonies of Holy Week. Where do they occur, under what conditions, and what is their significance in the history of the

Quem quaeritis drama and its cognates? Variations within the same usage, differences between monastic and secular practice, local traditions, the diversity of Gallican, Roman, Mozarabic, and other rites, not to mention faulty manuscripts, careless scribes, and tired eyes, make it certain that the best one can hope for from a brief, nontechnical discussion of the ninth-century Easter liturgy is a consideration of a typical sequence, differing in details from the usage of any specific ninth-century church or region. Occasionally, even this modest objective is overly ambitious because ninth-century records are ambiguous or nonexistent. Reconstructions are sometimes possible on the basis of manuscripts much earlier or later than the ninth century, but these are dubious. The most reliable documents are the works of the Carolingian scholars themselves, particularly the first book of the *Liber officialis*, with the sources on which these scholars relied— the Gregorian *Liber sacramentorum, Liber antiphonarius,* and *Liber responsalis,* and the first of the *Ordines Romani*.[3]

The following discussion refers to a typical order followed in a Roman-influenced secular church of the ninth century. Three points will be useful for orientation. The first is that the ninth-century Easter liturgy has a striking degree of unity. Among the elements which contribute to unity are a clear beginning and end, internal progression, and a center of interest (normally, a climax) controlling the structure and tone of the whole. The ninth-century Easter liturgy meets all of these requirements. It is framed emphatically by ceremonies that announce its beginning and end. If its Masses are considered episodes, they develop sequentially, with Easter as their structural and emotional focus. Repeated images and themes provide tonal continuity and are fulfilled in the great inversions of the Easter vigil. Among them are those of alienation, tears, darkness, bondage, spiritual warfare, and wasteland. They are familiar to students of literature as well as of religion. If not archetypes, they have their roots in archetypal experience.

The second point is that the Easter drama is sustained by the liturgy and not by extraliturgical ceremonies. The Easter drama *is* the liturgy. The representational ceremonies are embellishments; that they are neces-

---

[3] These liturgical works are collected in Vol. LXXVIII of the *Patrologia Latina* in the edition of Hugo Ménard. To avoid needless repetition, the *Patrologia* volume number will be omitted in subsequent citations and the following abbreviations will be used: *Liber sacramentorum, LS; Liber antiphonarius, LA; Liber responsalis, LR; Ordo Romanus* I, *OR* I; *Ordo Romanus* II, *OR* II; etc. Ménard's notes to *LS* will be cited as *Notae,* and the *Commentarius praevius* to the *Ordines* as *Commentarius.* In this and later chapters I have referred to the *Patrologia* edition of the *Ordines* because of its accessibility to students of literature. The definitive edition of the *Ordines* is that by Michel Andrieu, *Les Ordines Romani du haut Moyen Age* (5 vols.; Louvain, 1931–61).

sary at all suggests in the participants a degree of psychic alienation from the events of Christ's life. The subordination of such material in ninth-century worship indicates that the alienation was limited and gives the liturgy of that period an almost classical severity in comparison to the baroque proliferation of extraliturgical forms in high medieval worship, a contrast also observable in the differences between Romanesque and High Gothic church architecture. In the ninth century the parts still retained an organic relation to the whole. Liturgical embellishments were, in general, regarded as distractions and admitted only under special circumstances, an attitude that persisted as long as lay participation in the Mass was encouraged.

A third point, a by-product of the first two, is that the appearance of extraliturgical forms in ninth-century ritual is governed with surprising regularity by two principles, the principle of articulation and the principle of coincidence. Liturgical articulation serves the same function as do punctuation marks. It is necessary throughout Lent and Eastertide to give dramatic shape to the succession of Masses. The "Farewell to the Alleluia," the "Dismissal of Penitents," and the "Laying Aside of Albs" are examples. Such articulation ceremonies are prominent at the beginning of Septuagesima, the beginning of Lent, the beginning of Passiontide, Good Friday, Easter Sunday, and Sunday after Easter. They mark the phases of the Easter cycle much as the rings of a tree mark its periods of annual growth. In effect, they divide the Easter liturgy into five distinct phases analogous to the acts of a play. Because their function is structural definition, they need have no historical referents and they are mostly nonrepresentational.

On the other hand, when an historical event of major importance—the Last Supper, for example—coincides with a regular liturgical service, a representational ceremony is likely. This is the principle of coincidence. It indicates that representational form is not fortuitous. When it first appears in the liturgy, it is an aberration, a momentary departure from the norm. There is a distinct feeling that it can only be used at points when events in the annual cycle coincide with events in linear time, so that, for example, the Adoration of the Cross, commemorating the Crucifixion, can only be performed on Good Friday when the historical Crucifixion took place. At least one important Holy Week ceremony suggests that the principle of coincidence is a compromise for what is basically a desire for literal identification. In Jerusalem it was customary to re-enact Christ's entry in its original locations, beginning with His descent from the Mount of Olives. The re-enactment included strongly representational elements. In addition to "entering" Jerusalem, the people carried palms and uttered the "hosanna" of the Hebrew crowds. These elements evidently were first suggested by the coincidence of historical and liturgical space as well as the coincidence of time. When the rite was transferred to the West as the Palm Sunday procession, the coincidence of time was retained but the space necessarily became symbolic. For obvious reasons, representational ceremonies are most frequent and most striking during Holy Week and least so between Pentecost and Advent.

III

Lent began during the ninth century with Wednesday before Quadragesima Sunday, today's Ash Wednesday. Since the sixth century, however, Lenten observances had been extended backward to Septuagesima Sunday.[4] From then until Easter continence was enjoined, worldly vanities were to be eschewed, and monks began light fasting by giving up fats. Although severe fasting, entailing abstinence from meat, eggs, and dairy products, nominally began in Lent, the more zealous often began two or three weeks earlier.[5] The resulting Septuagesimal period fascinated commentators, who drew on a rich body of patristic material for their interpretations. The Gospel texts, chants, and prayers for the Masses and hours services of Septuagesima accord closely with early interpretations and were evidently chosen for their symbolic appeal.

According to a tradition as old as Jerome, the number seventy associated with Septuagesima has a threefold meaning involving what will be called "recapitulation symbolism." Typologically, it is the seventy-year period of the Babylonian captivity, a time of suffering and alienation brought on by man's sinfulness. This point is made in Augustine's commentary on Psalm 129 (*De profundis clamavi*), the source of the tract for Septuagesima

---

[4] L. A. Molien, *La prière de l'Eglise* (Paris, 1924), II, 220–23; Francis X. Weiser, *Handbook of Christian Feasts and Customs* (New York, 1958), pp. 154–57; Abbot Guéranger, *The Liturgical Year*, Vol. IV: *Septuagesima* (London, 1923), pp. 1–6; Leclercq, "Septuagésime," *DACL*, XV, 1, 1262–66. For comment from the ninth-century point of view, see Amalarius, "De septuagesima," in *Liber officialis* (*PL*, CV, 996[b-d]; H, II, 32–36).

[5] Weiser, *Handbook*, pp. 156–57. Early monastic practice is illustrated by the *Regularis concordia*, ed. Dom Thomas Symons (London, 1953), p. 32, where fat (*pinguedum*) is dropped from the diet on Septuagesima, meat on Quinquagesima. The Mozarabic *Missale mixtum* calls Sexagesima "Dominica ante carnes tollendas" (*PL*, LXXXV, 282[d]). Peter of Blois summarized the twelfth-century view of the matter by saying that religious orders began fasting on Septuagesima, the clergy on Quinquagesima, and the laity on Ash Wednesday. This, however, represents a degree of standardization not yet attained in the ninth century. See Guéranger, *Liturgical Year*, IV, 3; and for a more scholarly treatment, E. Vacandard, "Carême," *DACL*, II, 2, 2139–58; esp. 2146.

Sunday. At the same time, Septuagesima is associated with the seven days of creation and the seven ages of the world foreshadowed in them. The idea is embodied in the choice of matins readings throughout Septuagesima and Lent. The reading for Septuagesima Sunday relates the Fall and expulsion from Paradise, the initial breach between God and man; that of Sexagesima tells of the Deluge; that of Quinquagesima, the sacrifice of Abraham; and so on, until the eighth, enduring age of the New Jerusalem symbolized by the Easter octave.[6] Finally, by implication and

[6] This comment touches on an extremely important layer of symbolism current throughout Septuagesima and Lent, which will be mentioned where appropriate but which cannot be treated fully here, since it is expressed most fully not in the Mass liturgy but in the readings and chants of the canonical hours. According to this tradition, the Septuagesimal period recapitulates the whole history (i.e., the seven ages) of the world. The concept is introduced into the Lenten liturgy in the reading of the parable of the husbandman, and most obviously sustained by the readings and responses for nocturns (the modern matins). It rests on traditions as old as Jerome and Augustine, summarized emphatically in St. Gregory's homily on the parable, which is read during the matins of Septuagesima Sunday. Gregory writes:

The householder, then, for the cultivation of his vineyard goeth out early in the morning, and at the third hour, and at the sixth hour, and the eleventh hour, to hire labourers into his vineyard. Thus the Lord, from the beginning to the end of the world, ceaseth not to gather together preachers for the instruction of His faithful people. The early morning of the world was from Adam until Noah; the third hour from Noah until Abraham; the sixth hour from Abraham until Moses; the ninth hour from Moses until the coming of the Lord; the eleventh hour from the coming of the Lord until the end of the world. At this eleventh hour are sent forth as preachers the Holy Apostles, who have received full wages, albeit they come in late.

Translation from *The Roman Breviary*, trans. John, Marquess of Bute, Vol. I: *Winter* (London, 1908), p. 417. Although Gregory, accommodating his interpretation to the Gospel passage, finds only five ages in the history of the world, Augustine and others agreed that there were seven, parallel to the years of the Babylonian captivity, and when Lenten observances were extended backwards to Septuagesima, the parallel was, perhaps, inevitable. The ages are, in the form most often encountered, (1) Adam to Noah, (2) Noah to Abraham, (3) Abraham to Moses, (4) Moses to David, (5) David to the return from captivity, (6) the return from captivity to Christ, and (7) Christ to the Last Judgment. The eighth age would then be the eternal age of the New Jerusalem: "Nam quod etiam post septuaginta annos secundum ejusdem Hiermiae prophetiam reditur ex captivitate et templum renovatur, quid fidelis Christianus non intelligat post evoluta tempora, quae septenarii dierum numeri repetitione transcurrunt, etiam nobis, id est ecclesiae Dei, ad illam coelestem ex hujus saeculi peregrinatione redendum" (Augustine, *Contra Faustum, PL*, XLII, 723; cf. *De doctrina Christiana*, III, 35 [*PL*, XXIV, 86]). The "ages" are clearly reflected in the readings of the matins office. Septuagesima (Sexagesima in *LR*) records the creation, Fall, and expulsion from Paradise—a motif to be reiterated powerfully during the dismissal of penitents on Ash Wednesday. The reading for Sexagesima tells the story of Noah; of Quinquagesima, Abraham; of the third Sunday in Quadragesima, Joseph; of Laetare Sunday, Moses; and of Passion Sunday, the captivity (through the lamentations of Jeremiah). On *Coena Domini* (Maundy Thursday) the "New Law" is instituted, followed by the Crucifixion. Finally, the octave of Easter celebrates Augustine's "second age," particularly through the ceremonies involving the neophytes (see below, pp. 167–70). For the matins responses which reinforce the readings, see *LR*, 748ff; and for the hours

in several instances by explicit identification in prayers and chants, individual Christians recapitulate in their own lives the whole span of history from the Fall to the Last Judgment and beyond. In his commentary on Psalm 148 Augustine wrote: "There are two times, one which is *now*, and is spent in the temptations and tribulations of this life; and the other which shall be *then*, and shall be spent in eternal security and joy. In figure of these, we celebrate two periods: the time before Easter and the time after Easter. That which is before Easter signifies the sorrow of this life; that which is after, the blessedness of our future state." Echoing this sentiment, Amalarius taught that Septuagesima symbolizes "the whole of the present age during which we are separated from the Heavenly Jerusalem" and urged his readers to "live . . . that the sorrow [*luctus*] of penance may be changed to the joy [*gaudium*] of the Resurrection of the Lord which returns us to the Heavenly Jerusalem."[7] The observation has the eschatological bias evident in Amalarius' interpretation of the Mass. It is also a statement about the unity of the Easter liturgy, whose beginning is not an isolated episode and must be interpreted in terms of the event which is the climax of the drama.

The beginning of the Easter cycle is announced by two changes in the Mass ordinary. The Gloria in Excelsis (though not the Gloria Patri) and Alleluia are henceforth omitted.[8] The basic symbolism is quite simple.

---

services, see *The Roman Breviary*, Vol. I: *Winter*, pp. 414–59; and Vol. II: *Spring*, pp. 213–414.

In respect to recapitulation symbolism the modern breviary is not markedly different from that used during the Carolingian era (see Pierre Batiffol, *History of the Roman Breviary*, trans. A. M. Y. Baylay [London, 1912], pp. 67–119; esp. pp. 90–92). For an important comment on the relation of the recapitulation symbolism of Lent to the form and content of medieval Biblical epic and cyclical drama, see Adelina M. Jenney, "A Further Word as to the Origin of the Old Testament Plays," *MP*, XIII (1915), 59–64.

[7] Augustine, "Commentary on Psalm 148," *PL*, XXXVII, 1037; Amalarius, *Liber officialis*, *PL*, CV, 994 c-d; H, II, 30. Cf. *ibid.*, 993 a; H, II, 26–27: "Populi Dei tempus captivitatis significat, qui peccando recessit a Deo, et per misericordiam eius revertitur ad requiem. Populus Dei in Babilonia detentus est captivus sub numero septuagenario; suo numero completo reversus est in Hierusalem." See also Guéranger, *Liturgical Year*, IV, 7–9; Molien, *Prière*, II, 228–29.

[8] The Gloria in Excelsis is allowed on saints' days and on Maundy Thursday. Other changes in the liturgy may be mentioned. The *Ite, missa est* is dropped, and *Benedicamus Domino* is said in its place. The *Te Deum* is dropped from lauds. By far the most striking visual change today is in the Lenten vestments. Beginning on Septuagesima in the contemporary church the normal color changes to violet for penance. Exceptions are Laetare Sunday (rose), Maundy Thursday (white), Good Friday (black), and Holy Saturday (part white) (Adrian Fortescue, *The Ceremonies of the Roman Rite Described* [London, 1930], p. 284). Changes in vestments were far less strictly observed in the ninth century. The only two liturgical colors regularly stressed are white and black. The latter color may have been common during Lent and was certainly customary for

Both are conventionally interpreted as angelic songs (*cantica coelestia*). To omit them is to announce that an alienation has occurred between man and the inhabitants of the Heavenly Jerusalem. Because both are songs of joy, their absence gives a somber tone to the service, which is intensified by the tracts which replace the Alleluia from now until the first Mass of Easter. Of the two chants, the Alleluia is the more significant. On Septuagesima Sunday or during vespers of the preceding Saturday, the departure of the Alleluia was commemorated with a formal valediction. The antiphonary of St. Cornelius (IX C.), for example, calls for a quiet "Farewell" that already looks forward to the Easter "Return": *Angelus Domini bonus comitetur tecum, Alleluia, et bene disponat itineri tuo, ut iterum cum gaudio reverteris ad nos.* [9] The hymn *Alleluia dulce carmen* is a much more ambitious piece. It identifies the Alleluia with the choir of the Heavenly Jerusalem and the congregation with the Israelites weeping "by the waters of Babylon." By extension, the "Return" of the Alleluia will signal the healing of the breach between man and God. Although dated by Weiser in the tenth century, the hymn perfectly expresses the interpretation of Septuagesima found in Augustine and Amalarius:

Good Friday: ". . . tempore quadragesimae, et diebus jejunii, vestes sacrae et pallia altaris nigri erant, quae modo sunt violacei" (*Missale mixtum, PL,* LXXXV, 469 [d]). Modern scholars agree that the present elaborate color symbolism was not observed before the thirteenth century. See Herbert Norris, *Church Vestments: Their Origin and Development* (New York, 1950), p. 70; Patrick Morrisroe, "Colours," in *Catholic Encyclopedia,* IV, 135.

[9] Ninth-century Alleluia antiphons for Septuagesima are reprinted in *LR,* pp. 747–48; "Gothic Breviary," *PL,* LXXXVI, 259–60; Guéranger, *Liturgical Year,* IV, 110 (from the antiphonary of St. Cornelius), etc. The dropping of the Alleluia is discussed and the symbolism of the breach between man and the heavenly hosts is explored by Amalarius, *Liber officialis, PL,* CV, 997 [a–b]; H, II, 32–33. For modern comment, see Weiser, *Handbook,* pp. 157–60; Guéranger, *Liturgical Year,* IV, 5–6, 106–15; Leclercq, "Le depart de l'Alleluia," *DACL,* XV, 2, 2178. The suspension of the Alleluia at vespers on Saturday before Septuagesima Sunday dates from Leo IX (XI C.). The Mozarabic "Farewell" opens with a lovely hymn stressing the relation between the Alleluia and the heavenly choir. It begins, *Alleluia piis edite laudibus / Cives aetherei.*

By the later Middle Ages the dramatic and symbolic meanings of the "Farewell" were obscured by mock "Burials," perhaps absorbed from folk custom. In these the symbolism of a "return" of the Alleluia to its heavenly home is almost literally inverted by the connotations of death surrounding a burial. The Alleluia has become simply a "joyous song" and its interment simply a symbol for the putting off of joy during Lent. The "Burial" ceremony reflects high-medieval modes of thought in two ways. First, it reflects the general loss of the eschatological bias of the earlier liturgy, accompanied by a compensating stress on the penitential aspects of Lent and its associated death imagery. Second, it is a rather pointless bit of representational drama apparently included principally for its own mildly sensational effect. A fifteenth-century *ordo* for the "Burial" is printed in Du Cange, *Glossarium,* s.v. "Alleluia," and reprinted by Young, *DMC,* I, 552–53.

The sweet Alleluia-song, the word of endless joy, is the melody of heaven's choir, chanted by those who dwell for ever in the house of God.

O joyful mother, O Jerusalem our city, Alleluia is the language of thy happy citizens. The rivers of Babylon, where we poor exiles live, force us to weep.

We are unworthy to sing a ceaseless Alleluia. Our sins bid us interrupt our Alleluia. The time is at hand when it behooves us to bewail our crimes.[10]

The most important use of the Alleluia in the liturgy is during Mass. Its absence is first apparent in the Mass of Septuagesima Sunday. The emotional keynote of this Mass is sounded by the Introit references to groans of death and the pains of hell: *Circumdederunt me gemitus mortis, dolores inferni circumdederunt me, et in tribulatione mea invocavi Dominum, et exaudivit de templo sancto suo vocem meam.* The torments of the soul in the dark night of sin, its fear of spiritual death, and its horror of the Day of Wrath are all brought vividly before the congregation. The same imagery will recur with increasing vividness until the final, brutal moments of the Crucifixion. It forms what will be called the alienation theme of Lent. Lacking the Gloria, Mass proceeds swiftly to the Epistle, which introduces two more themes that are sustained throughout Lent. The first counters the alienation theme with the idea of spiritual struggle, or "agon" (to use the word in the Latin text itself). In this case the agon is symbolized by athletic contests: "They which run in a race run all, but one receiveth the prize. So run that ye may obtain" (I Cor. 9:24).[11] The second theme is that

---

[10] Dated by Weiser, *Handbook*, p. 159; text in Guéranger, *Liturgical Year*, IV, 114–15

[11] For the relation of the agon to the idea of the atonement, see Aulén, *Christus Victor*, pp. 16–60. Aulén points out: "In Gregory the Great the classic idea of the Atonement finds vigorous expression. He pictures the drama of the redemption in lurid colors. Many realistic and even grotesque images had been employed in the previous centuries to illustrate this theme, but Gregory outdoes all his predecessors" (pp. 40–41). The question arises, is the agon motif of the liturgy a reflection of the theology of the atonement or vice versa? Given the relation of the Christian agon to primitive forms of worship, the answer seems to be that the agon comes first and the theology is a rationalization of it. By the same token, the loss of a sense of agon from the liturgy during the tenth and eleventh centuries—a loss having little to do with formal theology—is reflected by the eleventh century in the ultimately triumphant view of Anselm and his scholastic successors. The agon was, however, recognized and stressed in the ninth century. Amalarius mentions it frequently, as, for example, in his comment on Quinquagesima: "[Jesum] precamur ducem militiae nostrae dicendo: *Et propter nomen tuum dux mihi eris, et enutries me.* Iam in patria sumus. Advenit doctissimus athleta, solito more hortans nos. Docet quibus munimentis muniri nos oporteat. . . . De quibus dicit in alia epistola: *In omnibus sumentes scutum fidei.* . . . Triumphator militiae nostrae Deus est" (*Liber officialis, PL*, CV, 999°; H, II, 40). Another ninth-century discussion emphasizing agon is that by Rabanus Maurus. The third book of the *De disciplina ecclesiae* (*PL*, CXII, 1193ff.) is devoted to the struggle between the Christian soldier and the forces

of Exodus. It foreshadows the part to be played by baptism in the Easter liturgy: "I would not that ye be ignorant how that all our fathers . . . passed through the sea; and all were baptised unto Moses in the cloud and in the sea" (10:1). The crossing of the Red Sea is a standard type of baptism, well known to Augustine. It is mentioned frequently in the next few weeks, most emphatically during the vigil service. It forms another link between the Mass of Septuagesima Sunday and the climactic moments of Easter.

The tract returns to the tone of the Introit with increased urgency. God is invoked "from the depths," both of hell and of mortal sin: *De profundis clamavi ad te, Domine; Domine exaudi vocem meam.* The Gospel (Matt. 20) presents God's answer to this cry. It has special relevance for converts and penitents. The parable of the workers in the vineyard makes the point that the master pays full wages to those summoned at the eleventh hour, as well as to those summoned in the early morning, i.e., those who turn to God late in life will receive the same reward as those faithful from birth. Allegorically, it was also considered a parable of the ages of the world.[12] The service ends on a note of calm. The Communion antiphon petitions God for illumination: *Illumina faciem tuam super servum tuum.* It is followed by the psalm *In te, Domine, speravi,* and final prayers.

The generally penitential tone of the Septuagesima Mass needs no explanation. Several features of the service, however, will be lost to the reader familiar only with contemporary usage. The concept of spiritual agon, for example, has a specific application to the medieval practice of public penance. In the ninth century those accused of particularly heinous crimes against God or the Church were forced to undergo a rigorous discipline as the price of being readmitted to the ranks of the faithful.[13] Ash Wednesday was the normal time for their initial arraignment. Early in

---

of paganism. Modern interpretations continue to take note of the agon element in Lenten imagery: Molien, *Prière*, II, 227; Guéranger, *Liturgical Year*, Vol. V: *Lent*, pp. 21–22; Dom Camille Leduc and Dom Jules Léon Baudot, *The Liturgy of the Roman Missal* (New York, n.d.), p. 125.

[12] For St. Gregory's homily explaining this parable as an allegory of the ages of the world, see n. 6.

[13] Jungmann, *Early Liturgy, to the Time of Gregory the Great* (trans. Francis A. Brunner [Notre Dame, Ind., 1959], pp. 240–48), discusses the origins and early forms of public penance, pointing out that private penance was relatively late. The numerous early medieval handbooks of penance are surveyed and several reprinted in John McNeill and Helen Garner, *Medieval Handbooks of Penance* (New York, 1938). For Gregorian practice, see *LS*, pp. 212–14 (prayers) and *LS Notae*, pp. 437–66 (includes selections from contemporary manuals of penance); also Halitgarius, *De poenitentia, PL*, CV, 651–710. For more general comment, see Weiser, *Handbook*, pp. 174–76; Molien, *Prière*, II, 257–60; Vacandard, "Carême," pp. 2153–58, etc.

the morning they assembled before the church, barefoot and dressed in sackcloth. They were marked with ashes (the origin of today's general distribution of ashes) and made the subject of special prayers by the bishop. When they had abased themselves, given evidence of sincere contrition, and offered humble petitions for forgiveness, they were assigned penance and dismissed. They were forbidden to re-enter the church until Maundy Thursday (the word "quarantine," a forty-day isolation, origi- nates in this practice), when the solemn rite of reconciliation could be performed.[14] For them the notion of Lent as an agon had special meaning. Penance was extremely harsh, involving abstinence from such creature comforts as bathing and shaving, isolation from family and friends, physical mortification, rigorous fasting, and constant prayer. Punitive fines were uncommon, but the scourge, the hair shirt, the pallet of boards, the penitential pilgrimage, the loneliness of the hermitage, and the even less tolerable supervision of monastic brothers sufficed to make Lent a harrowing experience for those seriously at odds with the Church. On Septuagesima Sunday the *poenitentes* and their well-wishers hear the first warning of the trial which they must endure before receiving the prize spoken of by Paul.

Still more important than the *poenitentes* in the eyes of the Church were the catechumens.[15] Adult baptism existed side by side with infant baptism in the ninth century. The Roman *Ordines* provide for both, but their wording indicates that the number of adult converts had dwindled and that infant baptism was the normal procedure. Old-fashioned documents, an expanding empire, and a plentiful supply of heathens, particularly Saxons, made adult baptism a much more serious business in Roman- influenced churches of the Carolingian empire.[16] If the penitents were

14 The full ceremony is preserved in the Gelasian Sacramentary (VI and VIII C.), in *PL*, LXXIV, 1064 a-d. Most authorities agree that the penitents were rigorously excluded from worship, but Duchesne (*Christian Worship*, p. 436) says that the peni- tents could attend Mass but were dismissed with the catechumens. This mitigation would appear to be later than the ninth century.

15 Scholarly treatment in Pierre de Puniet, "Baptême" and "Catéchuménat," pp. 251–346 and 2579–2621; and Duchesne, *Christian Worship*, pp. 292–341. For the early forms, see Jungmann, *Early Liturgy*, pp. 248–65, and, for a useful summary, Weiser, *Handbook*, pp. 172–73. A large amount of relevant information, together with the most important early texts bearing on baptism, is brought together by Philip T. Weller, *The Easter Sermons of St. Augustine* ("Catholic University Studies in Sacred Theology," Second Series, No. 87; Washington, D.C., 1955), pp. 32–73.

16 The question of whether or not a given *ordo* is intended primarily for adults is greatly complicated by the fact that the catechumens were, from earliest times, re- garded as "children" in the process of being "reborn." Hence adults and children alike are referred to in early times as *infantes*. By and large, the Gregorian documents—along

engaged in a private agon, the catechumens were the center of a public one. Between Ash Wednesday and Easter they were repeatedly exorcized before the entire congregation. A minister—eventually the bishop himself—raised his hands over them and announced, "I command you, unclean spirit, to depart." The gradual freeing of the catechumens from Satan was both the release from bondage foreshadowed by Exodus and the hard-won victory of the forces of Christ over those of His great enemy. When they "received" the Creed, they were advised, "Let the devil . . . find you ever armed with this Creed. Thus, having conquered the adversary whom you have renounced, may you have Divine Grace."[17]

Arrangements for preparing the catechumens differ widely. All sources call for a number of preparatory ceremonies, called scrutinies, which are incorporated into specified Lenten Masses. The number, timing, and content of the scrutinies varies. According to the most common procedure, that found as late as the *Ordo Romanus* VII, there should be seven. The third and seventh are the most important. The third usually occurs during the week after Laetare Sunday. It includes the transmission (*traditio*) of the Creed and the Pater Noster to the catechumens by the clergy. The seventh is usually held on the morning of Holy Saturday, but is sometimes combined with the Easter vigil. It provides for the return (*redditio*) of the Creed and Pater Noster by the catechumens.[18]

As the allusion to the Red Sea in the Epistle for Septuagesima Sunday indicates, the catechumens are important throughout Lent. The ordinary members of the congregation, the faithful, function alternately as spectators and chorus. The catechumens, on the other hand, are star performers. Readings, chants, prayers, and sermons all remind them of their

---

with the bulk of scholarly testimony—confirm the view that adults continued to be baptized along with children throughout the period from the sixth to the tenth century but that their number dwindled, while infant baptism came to be accepted as the norm. In ninth-century Gaul *infantes* refers equally to children and adults. Pseudo-Alcuin explains the term by saying, "Renati per baptismum, sint, quasi recens editi infantes" (*PL*, CII, 569d). The term appears in the *Missale mixtum* and is explained as follows: "Neophyti omnes, etsi aetate senes, infantes appelabantur. Hinc octavae Paschae, apud Sanctum Augustinum octavae infantium appellantur, quotquot enim baptizati erant, utpote regenerati, novam vitam ingressi erant" (*PL*, LXXXV, 467d).

[17] From the Gelasian Sacramentary, *PL*, LXXIV, 1091b-c: "Invicta est enim semper talium animorum potestas contra omnes insidias inimici ad bonam Christi militiam profituris. Diabolus, qui hominem tentare non desinit, munitos vos hoc Symbolo semper inveniat. Ut, devicto adversario, cui renuntiatis, gratiam Domini . . . servetis."

[18] The form of the scrutinies given here is based on the rite in the Gelasian Sacramentary (*PL*, LXXIV, 1084a–93b, 1105–6); the seventh *Ordo Romanus* (*OR* VII, pp. 994–1000); the *De ordine baptismi* of Theodulphus (*PL*, CV, 223–40, esp. 225–30); and Amalarius, *De scrutinio et baptismo* (H, I, esp. 240–47). The *traditio* frequently occurs on Palm Sunday and sometimes on Maundy Thursday. I have followed *OR* VII here.

role. Before Holy Saturday they are spiritually dead. The *plebs sancta*, which includes the human community of Christians in a state of grace as well as the saintly inhabitants of the Heavenly Jerusalem, yearns for their fellowship and encourages their progress with hymns. To enter the Heavenly Jerusalem, they must be buried and reborn in Christ through baptism. As Paul wrote to the Romans, "Know ye not, that so many of us as were baptized into Jesus Christ were baptized into His death? Therefore we are buried with him by baptism into death: that like as Christ was raised up from the dead by the glory of the Father, even so we also should walk in newness of life. For if we have been planted together in the likeness of his death, we shall be also in the likeness of his resurrection" (Rom. 6:3–5). The redemption theme has numerous ramifications in the imagery (e.g., rebirth, purification, liberation) and tone (e.g., outbursts of joy) of the liturgy. It is the antithesis of the alienation theme associated with penance, and it culminates in the regeneration of the catechumens through baptism on Holy Saturday. Clothed in white garments, radiant with newness of spirit, they are visible analogues to the invisible mystery of the Resurrection. The familiar Easter hymn *Ad coenam agni* was originally intended for the catechumens. Its first stanza beautifully fuses the images of Exodus, redemption, and white garments:

> Prepared for the supper of the Lamb,
> Radiant in our white robes,
> Having passed through the Red Sea,
> Let us sing to Christ the Lord.[19]

As long as the catechumens played an important role in the services of Lent, these elements retained something of their original dramatic meaning. By the tenth century the increasing importance of monastic churches, the decrease in adult converts, widespread infant baptism, and changes in fasting regulations all conspired to reduce the importance of the catechumens. For example, the *Regularis concordia*, composed for monastic use around 970, omits the baptismal parts of the Easter vigil altogether and combines the first Mass of Easter with vespers of Holy Saturday.[20] In consequence, much of the drama of the liturgy is obscured.

[19] The text is here taken from the tenth-century version in the *Analecta hymnica*, II, 46. The hymn is, however, Ambrosian, if not by Ambrose himself. John Mason Neale (*A Short Commentary on the Hymnal* [London, 1853]) identifies the hymn correctly as one just before or during the Mass of the Easter vigil. Asserting that it is sung by the catechumens, he says, "These newly baptized persons were now for the first time about to take holy communion" (quoted by John Julian in *A Dictionary of Hymnology* [London, 1925], s.v. *Ad coenam agni*).

[20] *Regularis concordia*, ed. Symons, pp. 47–49.

Without the catechumens the redemption theme has no immediate referent. Eventually, the very *raison d'être* of the joyful parts of the Lenten services was forgotten. Only the penitential phase continued to have direct relevance to the experience of high medieval congregations, and the resulting exclusive emphasis on sorrow was in itself a distortion. If we are to understand the shape and import of the liturgy in the period immediately preceding the appearance of the *Quem quaeritis* play, we must remember that while the penitents were conspicuous by their absence, the catechumens participated in Lenten services up to the reading of the Gospel. The result is that in the older liturgy a tension is sustained between the theme of alienation and that of redemption, a tension which is correlative to the concept of Lent as an agon. Amalarius sums up the roles of penitents and catechumens in the Easter drama as follows: "The catechumens who, in addition to sins of commission, are in bondage to Original Sin, are washed in the Resurrection by the water of baptism, and we by penance. And they and we continue in the Resurrection until the full Septuagesimal period. . . . And after we are spiritually reborn in the Resurrection through penance or baptism we should celebrate until the day of rest which is the Sabbath after this life." [21]

The tone of the liturgy from Septuagesima to Lent is one of sorrow, moderated by growing confidence that the trial will, with God's help, be successfully endured. Amalarius considers the Masses of Sexagesima and Quinquagesima to be commemorations of spiritual preparation and commitment, respectively. [22] The Introit of the first urges *Exsurge,* and of the second, *Esto mihi in Deum protectorem.* The dominant themes of Sexagesima are spiritual agon, conveyed by Paul's description of the persecution and humiliation he has suffered for Christ (II Cor. 11:24–30), and anticipation, suggested by the parable of the sower (Luke 8:4–15). The themes of Quinquagesima are charity (I Cor. 13) and divine grace. The Gospel selection (Luke 18:31–43) touches on the latter theme in two ways. It begins with Christ's prediction that the words of the prophets are to be fulfilled, for the Gentiles "shall scourge him, and put him to death: and the third day he shall rise again." The idea of redemption is again linked with the climactic events of the Easter liturgy, the Crucifixion and the Resurrection. The second part of the Gospel selection describes the curing of the blind man of great faith. The theme of miraculous salvation through faith has obvious relevance for the penitents and catechumens. Its expression in terms of blindness and sight answers the Communion prayer of

---

[21] *Liber officialis, PL,* CV, 994d–95e; H, II, 30–33. For earlier expressions of this idea, see, for example, Philip Weller, *Easter Sermons of St. Augustine,* pp. 14–23.

[22] *Liber officialis, PL,* CV, 998d–99d; H, II, 36–44.

Septuagesima (*Illumina faciem tuam super servum tuum*). It also decisively establishes light imagery as a major Lenten symbol, with Christ as its source. The final prayers and chants of the Mass of Quinquagesima are confident, almost joyful. The terrors of death have faded. God will provide: *Manducaverunt, et saturati sunt nimis, et desiderium eorum attulit eis Dominus.*

IV

Wednesday before Quadragesima, the modern Ash Wednesday, is the beginning of the second phase of the Easter drama. Originally, Lent began on Quadragesima Sunday. Because Sundays are feast days, it was extended back to Wednesday at about the time of Pope Gregory in order to permit a full forty days of fasting.[23] The tenor of Lent is indicated by the Biblical associations of the number forty. From the time of Jerome forty was associated with suffering and affliction. It is the number of days of the deluge that destroyed all men except Noah, it is the number of years that the Hebrew people were condemned to spend in the wilderness, and it is the number of days of the fasts of Moses and Elias before they approached the Lord on Mount Sinai and Mount Horab. Finally, it is the number of days spent by Christ in the desert and the number of hours between the Crucifixion and the Resurrection, a point stressed in the Preface for the day in the Ambrosian missal.[24]

In accordance with the principle of articulation, several events demarcate Lent from the preceding liturgical period. The defining Old Testament symbol during Septuagesima is that of Babylonian captivity. Although this symbol is never abandoned (it recurs powerfully in allusions to the New Jerusalem and readings from Jeremiah during Holy Week matins), it is displaced during Lent by imagery from Exodus chosen because of its application to the catechumens. The scrutinies were regarded as a "journey toward baptism," and the passage of the Israelites through the Red Sea was considered a type of baptism. In addition, the agon motif is renewed at the beginning of Lent. General fasting begins on Wednesday,

---

[23] E.g., Duchesne, *Christian Worship*, pp. 243–44; Molien, *Prière*, II, 250–52; Guéranger, *Liturgical Year*, IV, 4–5. Cf. Amalarius, *Liber officialis*, PL, CV, 1003ᵃ; H, II, 47–48.

[24] For early speculation on the significance of the number forty, see Augustine, *De doctrina Christiana*, II, xvi (*PL*, XXIV, 48); *De consensu evangelistarum* (*PL*, XXXIV, 1074–75); Leduc and Baudot, *Liturgy*, pp. 133–34; Guéranger, *Liturgical Year*, V, 20–28. The Ambrosian Preface is reprinted by Guéranger, V, 140–41. See also St. Gregory's hymn, *ibid.*, 147–48.

hence its ninth-century title, *Caput jejunii*. The collect for Wednesday makes the connection between fasting and Christian warfare explicit: *Concede nobis, Domine, praesidia militiae Christianae sanctis incohare jejuniis.* Not surprisingly, Amalarius picks up this idea. Lent is "a time of labors when we struggle under the discipline of Christ the King against the devil." On Wednesday "we commit ourselves to battle," and by their references to fasting the Epistle and Gospel "show us the arms with which we should fight."[25]

Liturgically, the most striking articulation ceremony is the dismissal of public sinners. This took place on Wednesday between tierce and sext. Weiser gives a colorful description of its typical features:

> Public sinners approached their priests shortly before Lent to accuse themselves of their misdeeds, and were presented by the priests on Ash Wednesday to the bishop of the place. Outside the cathedral, poor and noble alike stood barefoot, dressed in sackcloth, heads bowed in humble contrition. The bishop, assisted by his canons, assigned to each one particular acts of penance according to the nature and gravity of his crimes. Thereupon they entered the church, the bishop leading one of them by the hand, the others following in single file, holding each other's hands. Before the altar, not only the penitents but also the bishop and all his clergy recited the seven penitential psalms. Then as each sinner approached, the bishop imposed his hands on him, sprinkled him with holy water, threw blessed water on his head, and invested him with the tunic of sackcloth.
>
> After this ceremony the penitents were led out of the church and forbidden to re-enter until Holy Thursday (for the solemn rites of reconciliation). Meanwhile, they would spend Lent apart from their families in a monastery or some other place of voluntary confinement, where they occupied themselves with prayer, manual labor, and works of charity. Among other things they had to go barefoot all through Lent, were forbidden to converse with others, were made to sleep on the ground on a bedding of straw, and were not allowed to cut their hair.[26]

---

[25] Amalarius, *Liber officialis, PL,* CV, 1001[b]-2[d]; H, II, 44, 47. The reference to struggling against the devil is quoted by Amalarius from Augustine, *De consensu evangelistarum, PL,* XXXIV, 1075. Other traditions made Lent an occasion of general social significance. During the early centuries and evidently as late as the ninth century litigation was suppressed, trials were suspended, executions were forbidden, and minor offenders were pardoned. As today, alms-giving, extra prayers, and frequent Communion were enjoined. For Lenten customs other than fasting, see Weiser, *Handbook,* pp. 169–73; Vacandard, "Carême," pp. 2139–58.

[26] *Handbook,* p. 175; Duchesne, *Christian Worship,* p. 436. The exclusion of penitents from the church during Lent apparently continued into or through the fourteenth century. See *Registrum Johannis de Trillek, Episcopi Herefordensis,* transcribed and edited by Joseph Henry Parry ("Canterbury and York Society Series," Vol. VIII; London, 1910), p. 61 (*anno* 1346).

To Weiser's account may be added the fact that the texts used in the dismissal define with precision the role of the penitents in the Lenten drama. They are to be representatives par excellence of the alienation theme. As in today's Ash Wednesday service, the dismissal begins with the chant *Exaudi nos, Domine*.[27] Four prayers, dating from the eighth century, are said, and the ashes are imposed on the foreheads of the penitents in the form of a cross.[28] They are symbols of death. During their imposition the priest says, *Memento homo, quia pulvis es, et in pulverem reverteris*.[29] During this rite the chorus expresses the feelings of the penitents: *Immutemur habitu in cinere et cilicio; jejunemus et ploremus ante Dominum*. The dismissal itself is a repetition of the original expulsion from Paradise—a striking instance of the recapitulation symbolism first encountered in the readings of Septuagesima: "With groans and sighs [the priest] announces to them that as Adam was driven from Paradise, so they are to be expelled from the church for their sins. After this let him order the ministers to drive the sinners from the church doors. But let a cleric follow them singing the responsory *In sudore vultus tui vesceris pane tuo*."[30]

---

[27] The original antiphons in *LA*, p. 657[a]. This is the origin of the Ash Wednesday service, which did not involve a general distribution of ashes until the Council of Benvenuto in 1091. The modern ceremony does not appear in the Roman *Ordines* until the twelfth century. The shift from an imposition of ashes on penitents to an imposition on the whole congregation illustrates perfectly the larger shift from the ninth-century conception of Lent as an agon to the later conception of Lent solely as a penitential season requiring general and unrelieved mortification. Discussion in Cabrol, "*Caput Jejunii*" and "Mercredi des Cendres," *DACL*, II, 2, 2134–37 and 3040–43; Molien, *Prière*, II, 255–62.

[28] I have accepted Weiser's dating (*Handbook*, p. 174). The prayers are given in Guéranger, *Liturgical Year*, V, 206–8; compare Gelasian Sacramentary, *PL*, LXXIV, 1064, and *LS*, pp. 212–13.

[29] The association between ashes and penance is Biblical. It is mentioned by Tertullian, *De poenitentia*, *PL*, I, 1354. The early existence of a ceremony for imposing ashes is attested by Isidore, *De ecclesiasticis officiis*, XVI (*PL*, LXXXIII, 802[c]), and it is mentioned in the ninth century by Rabanus Maurus, *De clericorum institutione*, *PL*, CVII, 341[c]. For discussion, see Cabrol, "Les cendres dans l'antiquité," *DACL*, II, 2, 3037–40.

[30] "Et cum gemitu et crebris suspiriis eis denuntiet quod sicut Adam projectus est de Paradiso, ita et ipsi ab ecclesia pro peccatis abjiciantur. Post haec jubeat ministris ut reos extra januas ecclesiae expellant. Clerus vero prosequatur eos cum Responsorio *In sudore vultus tui vesceris pane tuo*" (*LS Notae*, p. 439[b]). The responsory is given in the *Liber responsalis* (p. 748[d]) for Sexagesima matins. The concept of Christ as the second Adam provides for one of the standard image inversions of Easter: "Fratres, diximus iam, nisi fallor, hesterno die Adam unum hominem fuisse, et ipsum esse totum genus humanum. . . . Et gemit unus pauper, modo ipse Adam, sed in Christo innovatur, quia sine peccato venit Adam, ut peccatum Adae solveret in carne sua, et ut redintegraret sibi Adam in imaginem Dei. [De] Adam ergo caro Christi, de Adam ergo templum quod destruxerunt Iudaei et resuscitavit Dominus triduo" (quoted by Amalarius [*Liber officialis*, *PL*, CV, 1004[a]; H, II, 49–50] from Augustine's commentary on John, *PL*, XXXV, 1472–74).

Because the practice of beginning Lent on Wednesday is relatively late, the Wednesday Mass is more recent than the Mass for Sunday. Its texts have a certain obviousness which betrays their origin. The chants and prayers ask for divine mercy, while the readings instruct the congregation in Lenten practices. The Introit recalls the dismissal of the penitents: *Miserere omnium, Domine . . . : dissimulans peccata hominum propter poenitentiam, et parcens illis.* The reading (Joel 2:12–19) is almost naïvely direct: "Therefore also now, saith the Lord, turn ye even to me with all your heart, and with fasting, and with weeping, and with mourning: And rend your hearts and not your garments, and turn unto the Lord your God." It combines the theme of penance with that of conversion ("turn ye even to me") and the promise of divine succor. The gradual (*Miserere mei, Deus*) and tract (*Domine, non secundum peccata nostra quae fecimus nos*) repeat the petition of the Introit. The Gospel (Matt. 6:16–21) is, like the selection from Joel, direct to the point of bluntness. It is Christ's advice in the Sermon on the Mount about fasting: ". . . when ye fast, be not, as the hypocrites, of a sad countenance: for they disfigure their heads that they may appear unto men to fast. . . . Lay not up for yourselves treasure upon earth. . . . But lay up for yourselves treasures in heaven." Mass ends with a final injunction from the deacon, *Humiliate capita vestra*, which will be repeated on ferial Masses until Easter.[31] After a special prayer for God's blessing, the people depart.

Because it originally marked the beginning of Lent, the Mass of Quadragesima Sunday resembles Wednesday's Mass in tone and orientation. As it is the older service, it is oriented more strongly toward redemption and shows less preoccupation with penance and fasting per se. Its station is St. John Lateran, the station of the Easter vigil. This station not only links it with the climax of the Resurrection drama but also indicates that it has special reference to the catechumens, John being associated above all with baptism.

Mass begins on a positive note. In place of petitions for mercy, the Introit announces confidently, *Invocabit me, et ego exaudiam eum.* The collect refers explicitly to Lent, but the tone is again confident and the negative values of abstinence are balanced against the positive ones of good works: *Deus, qui Ecclesiam tuam annua quadragesimali observatione purificas: praesta familia tua; ut quod a te obtinere abstinendo nitatur, hoc bonis operibus exsequatur.* Like the Wednesday reading from Joel, the Sunday reading (II Cor. 6:1–10) refers to tribulation, but the context is much broader than Joel's

---

[31] *OR* I, p. 949 ᵉ. The phrase, which is preserved in today's liturgy, was evidently assimilated from the dismissal of public penitents. For the agon motif in the collect of this Mass, see text above, p. 98.

"fasting, weeping, and mourning." The tribulations mentioned by Paul are "stripes, imprisonments, tumults, and labors" as well as "watchings and fastings." They are, in fact, the trials of the Christian soldier. Mention of them renews the motif of spiritual agon, now projected in the imagery of warfare. Difficulties are overcome, says Paul, "by the word of truth, by the power of God, by the armour of righteousness on the right hand and on the left." Accordingly, the gradual refers to guardian angels sent by God *ut custodiant te in omnibus viis tuis;* and it is succeeded by the tract *Qui habitat in adjutorio,* with its majestic images of spiritual combat: *Scuto circumdabit te veritas ejus, non timebis a timore nocturno. A sagitta volante per diem, a negotio perambulante in tenebris, a ruina et daemonio merediano. Cadent a latere tuo mille, et decem millia a dextris tuis: tibi autem non appropinquabit.*[32] In the Gospel the imagery of conflict is subsumed in Matthew's account (4:1–11) of Christ's own agon in the wilderness, which has been a favorite symbol of heroic endurance from Prudentius to Milton. It is dramatically significant that while the emphasis of the Gospel readings from Septuagesima to Quinquagesima is on Christ's teaching and miracles, the emphasis at the beginning of Lent shifts to Christ's life. With the account of the temptation in the desert, the figure of the divine protagonist of the Lenten agon emerges for the first time. The identification between the fasting Savior and the fasting members of the congregation can only intensify the dramatic effect. Like the chorus of Greek tragedy, the congregation shares in some measure in the fate of the hero.

The second and third Sundays of Lent balance consciousness of unworthiness against faith in salvation. The Introit of the second Sunday is a petition, *Reminiscere miserationum tuarum, Domine.* The sorrow of the gradual (*Tribulationes cordis mei dilatatae sunt*) leads directly to the assurance of the tract, *Confitemini Domino, quoniam bonus.* The Epistle (I Thess. 4:1–7)

---

[32] *LS*, p. 58[b]. Amalarius remarks concerning this Mass, "In quadragesima aliqua pars pugnae peracta est. Dicit nobis quem in quinquagesima protectorem invocavimus, *Invocabit me, et ego exaudiam eum.* . . . In responsorio angeli Domini custodiunt nos. In tractu scuto veritatis circumdati sumus. In evangelio ad triumphum tendimus, ut dicamus inimico: *Vade, Satana,* in interitum" (*Liber officialis, PL,* CV, 1001[b]; H, II, 44). The Mozarabic Preface neatly fuses the Old-New Adam image with the imagery of the victory of Christ, related to the "classical" idea of the atonement: "Aggreditur itaque diabolus Virginis Filium: Dei quoque nesciens unigenitum. Et licet veternosa calliditate eisdem machinis quibus Adam primum dejecerat, etiam secundum seducere obtineret: tamen hoc non valuit, nec fortissimum bellatorem in ulla potuit omnino fraude subripere. . . . Hic est qui virtute propria fretus, cum diabolo tenebrarum principe dimicavit: et eo prostrato victoriae tropheaum ad coelos magnifice portavit" (*Missale mixtum, PL,* LXXXV, 369). Useful surveys of the concept of Christ as epic hero are found in M. Y. Hughes, "The Christ of *Paradise Regained* and the Renaissance Heroic Tradition," *SP,* XXXV (1938), 254–77; Elizabeth Pope, *Paradise Regained: The Tradition and the Poem* (Baltimore, 1947).

restates the theme of self-denial with special warnings against lust (perhaps a reminder of the continence enjoined during Lent by the medieval Church). The Gospel (Matt. 17:1–9) describes the Transfiguration, interpreting it as a means of strengthening the faith of Christ's followers (hence, the congregation) prior to the trials of Holy Week.[33]

The third Sunday elaborates the themes of contrition and conflict. There appear to be several allusions to the catechumens whose scrutinies will begin in the coming week.[34] The station is St. Lawrence. Prudentius had written of this saint, "Rome triumphs over her barbarous religion, giving herself to Christ through the victory of Lawrence her guide."[35] The illustrious archdeacon, alleged to have played such a large part in the conversion of the Romans, provided an excellent type of the clergyman— especially of the deacon—who would guide the catechumens to safety. The Introit is a prayer for purification: *Oculi mei semper ad Dominum . . . unicus et pauper sum ego.* The collect reiterates the petition using the imagery of spiritual agon: *ad defensionem nostram dextram tuae Majestatis extende.* While urging the imitation of Christ, the Epistle (Col. 5:1–8) specifies the defilements of secular man—fornication, covetousness, filthiness, foolish talking, idolatry—and contrasts heathen and Christian in terms of light imagery: "For ye were sometimes darkness, but now are ye light in the Lord: walk as children of light." The contrast between darkness and light is itself suggestive of the transformation resulting from baptism, but the text is more than a general allusion. We have noticed the importance of light-darkness imagery as early as Septuagesima. It recurs in the account of curing the blind (Quinquagesima) and in the references of the second Sunday of Lent to the glory of the Transfiguration, when "his face did shine as the sun, and his raiment was white as the light." The special association of illumination with baptism is exceedingly ancient; in fact the

---

[33] Cf. Leduc and Baudot, *Liturgy*, p. 159. *LA*, pp. 662ᶜ–63ᵈ, has *Dominica vacat*, reflecting the tradition of omitting Mass on Sundays following a vigil (Saturday is labeled *Sabbato in XII lectionibus*). After this rubric a Mass is given for *Dominica secunda Quadragesimae*, which, however, has a different tract, apparently reflecting a different reading.

[34] Originally, the scrutinies were held not on Wednesdays and Saturdays but on the third, fourth, and fifth Sundays of Lent (Leclercq, "Scrutin," *DACL*, XV, 1, 1049; de Puniet, "Catéchuménat," pp. 2605–10); hence the prominence of allusions to the catechumens on the first two of these Sundays. The third (Passion Sunday) is almost wholly preoccupied with the Passion. See also Molien, *Prière*, II, 289; Leduc and Baudot, *Liturgy*, pp. 168–69; Guéranger, *Liturgical Year*, V, 252–53.

[35] Quoted by Molien, *Prière*, II, 289, from Prudentius' poem *Laurentius Archilevita*, ll. 3–5, in *Peristephanon*, *PL*, LX, 295ᵃ.

Greeks referred to baptism as *photismos*, an "enlightening."[36] And during the Easter vigil the light-darkness imagery finds physical embodiment in various candle ceremonies such as the blessing of the new fire and the plunging of the paschal candle into the baptismal font.[37]

If the Epistle encourages the catechumens to become "children of light," the gradual and tract remind them that spiritual warfare continues. The chants begin with *Exsurge, Domine, non praevaleat homo* and ends with *Miserere nobis, Domine, miserere nobis.* The Gospel (Luke 11:14-28) both answers these petitions and completes the earlier allusions to the catechumens. The theme of purification is carried forward in the story of Christ's exorcism of the demon from the dumb man. The act is a type of the exorcism ceremonies which are repeatedly performed on the catechumens during the scrutinies. As Father Molien observes, "the demon represents humanity . . . which does not recognize Christ . . . the soul is delivered from bondage to the demon through baptism; from ignorance through the Gospels; and from sins committed after baptism through penance."[38] Finally, the narrative repeats the imagery of conflict. "When a strong man armed keepeth his palace, his goods are in peace: But when a stronger . . . shall come . . . he taketh from him all his armor . . . and divideth his spoils." The emphasis throughout the Mass on texts and motifs relating to the catechumens is explained shortly. Either today or after Monday's Mass the deacon announces the first scrutiny of the year, through which Satan will ultimately be defeated: *Ut coeleste mysterium, quo diabolus cum sua pompa destruetur . . . peragere valeamus.*[39]

In the early Church, candidacy for baptism normally took three years, and preparations for the ceremony were so rigorous that it was fairly common to remain a candidate until shortly before death, the most famous case of deferred baptism being the Emperor Constantine.[40] By the ninth century conversion was far easier, but the framework of the earlier system survived. During their candidacy the catechumens stood at the

[36] For baptism as *photismos*, see Jungmann, *Early Liturgy*, p. 259. The light imagery applies to the function of the clergy during the scrutinies. They are "accensores . . . luminum, et ideo . . . in scrutineo . . . dicimus: *Ut digneris eos inluminare lumine intelligentiae suae*" (Amalarius, *De scrutinio et baptismo*; H, I, 240).

[37] For these ceremonies, see below, pp. 145-54.

[38] *Prière*, II, 290.

[39] Gelasian Sacramentary, *PL*, LXXIV, 1084ᵃ. Here and in the *Ordo Romanus* VII the announcement comes after Monday's Mass; but the earlier order required the scrutinies on Sunday, i.e., at one time, apparently, Laetare Sunday was itself the day of the *Apertio Aurium*. The scrutinies could evidently be at sext as well as tierce. See *OR* VII, pp. 993ᵈ and 940. For early practice, see Duchesne, *Christian Worship*, p. 576; Lecercq, "Scrutin," pp. 1037-52.

[40] Jungmann, *Early Liturgy*, p. 248.

rear of the church (originally called the interior narthex) but departed before the reading of the Gospel. According to the *Ordo Romanus* VII, which is a reliable guide to ninth-century Carolingian usage, the names of the catechumens seeking baptism were taken before Mass on the Wednesday after the third Sunday in Lent.[41] They were then summoned to church by public roll call. The men stood on the right, the women on the left, with the sponsors behind. The priest crossed each with his thumb, blessed them, and placed a pinch of salt, the "sacrament of the catechumens," in their mouths, saying, *Accipe sal sapientiae propitiatus in vitam aeternam.* They then returned to the rear of the church. From this point on, they were known as the *electi* or the *competenti.* The Introit of the Wednesday Mass given in the seventh *Ordo* (different from those in the Gregorian and contemporary missal) refers to them. The Introit mentions both purification by water and the gift of the Holy Spirit: *Cum sanctificatus fuero in vobis, congregabo vos de universis terris; et effundam super vos aquam mundam . . . et dabo vobis spiritum novum.* The collect speaks not for the congregation at large but for the *electi*: *Da, quaesimus, Domine, electis nobis. . . .*

Before the lesson the deacon loudly calls, *Catechumeni procedant.* When assembled before the altar, the candidates are commanded, *Orate electi.* They kneel for the Pater Noster, and at the command *Levate* they rise, say the *Amen* in unison, and cross themselves. The major exorcisms now begin. The sponsors trace the sign of the cross on the candidates' foreheads, and three acolytes—originally exorcists—pronounce the ancient formulas, *Audi, maledicite Satanas* and *Exorcizo te, immunde spiritus.*[42] Finally the priest makes the sign of the cross over the *electi* and the regular order of Mass is resumed. The reading (Ezek. 36:25–29) foreshadows baptism with the promise, "I will sprinkle clean water upon you and ye shall be clean." After the gradual and tract the deacon dismisses the *electi* with the formula *Catechumeni recedant. Si quis catechumenus es, recedat. Omnes catechumeni exeant foras.* The remaining parts of the Mass (the *Missa fidelium*) form what is essentially a votive Mass for the catechumens and their sponsors. The offering is made directly by the sponsors or vicariously by the catechumens themselves. During the Consecration prayer (*Memento Domine*) the celebrant recites the names of the sponsors. After the *Hanc igitur* the names of the *electi* are mentioned. The prayer concludes with the petition *Hos, Domine, fonte baptismatis innovandos,* an overt joining of baptism and rebirth. Mass ends with an announcement of the next scrutiny: *Die Sabbati venite, collegite vos temporarious ad ecclesiam.*

---

41 P. 995ª. This *ordo* is dated as sixth- to seventh-century by Andrieu, *Ordines Romani,* II, 409–13.

42 The prayers are given in full in the Gelasian Sacramentary, *PL,* LXXIV, 1084ᵃ– 93ᵇ. See esp. the exorcisms, 1085ᵃ–86ᵈ, for the agon motif.

Saturday's scrutiny is a duplicate of Wednesday's. The Introit, *Verba mea auribus percipe*, and the readings, both of which deal with lust, appear to refer to the penitents as much as to the catechumens, but the general theme of purification through divine grace is clear enough.

The sequence of scrutinies is now broken by the Mass of Laetare Sunday, a festive Mass of great importance for the drama which is unfolding. The death imagery associated with penance is momentarily overwhelmed by the life imagery associated with baptism. Music may be played, the altar decorated, and the violet or black vestments of the clergy put aside for rose-colored ones. In the later Middle Ages, when the catechumenate had been all but forgotten, the day was regarded simply as a moment of relief from the severities of the season: "On this Sunday . . . a measure of comforting relaxation is permitted so that the faithful may not break down under the severe strain. . . ."[43] In the ninth century, on the other hand, the original reason for the festivity was clearly understood. On Wednesday of this week the major scrutiny of the catechumens, the *Apertio Aurium*, is to be held. Sunday's Mass expresses the joy of the congregation and, more generally, of the entire communion of saints at the progress of the elect. The service is dominated by allusions to Jerusalem, fusing the present moment with sacred history on the one hand and eternity on the other. Typologically, the catechumens are repeating the journey of the Chosen People from Egyptian bondage to the Promised Land and, hence, to the historical Jerusalem. Mystically, they are also seeking the Heavenly Jerusalem of Augustine. It is as inhabitants of the Heavenly City that the congregation, the *plebs sancta*, is asked to rejoice: *Laetare Jerusalem; et conventum facite omnes qui diligitis eam. . . . In domum Domini ibimus.*[44] The reading (Gal. 4:22–31) also combines Old Testament

---

[43] This is the conventional modern view; e.g., Guéranger, *Liturgical Year*, V, 313: "The Church's motive for introducing this expression of joy into today's liturgy is to encourage her children to persevere fervently to the end of this holy season." The true motive—the third scrutiny—is identified by de Puniet, "Catéchuménat," p. 2605; Weiser, *Handbook*, p. 177. The subtlety of the ramifications of the Jerusalem image is further indicated by the fact that the station is Santa Croce in Jerusalem (called simply *Hierusalem* in the older liturgical books). The Mass thus refers simultaneously to the past, the present, and the future: to the past, in that the type of Septuagesima is the Babylonian captivity which will end with the return to Jerusalem; to the present, in that the congregation of the faithful, who are already participants in the mystical body, gathers in a literal Jerusalem to celebrate Mass, joining its voice to the chorus of the saints rejoicing over the progress of the *electi*; to the future, in that the *electi* will be united with the mystical body at their first Communion on Easter Eve. Note how the motif is reinforced by the idea that the Alleluia is carried to the Heavenly Jerusalem on Septuagesima Sunday (above, p. 91) and "returns" on Easter Eve.

[44] Cf. Molien, *Prière*, II, 303: "Les testes s'expliquent ainsi, ils sont visiblement choisis en vue des catéchumènes. Jerusalem leur apparaît dans l'introit comme un ville puissant . . . , " etc.

history with Christian eschatology. In Paul's words, the two sons of Abraham are an "allegory" of bondage to the old law versus freedom in the Spirit. He assures his readers, "Jerusalem which is above is free, which is the mother of us all." The chants reiterate the theme of journeying (*In domum Domini ibimus*) and the idea of the Heavenly City (. . . *non commovebitur in aeternum qui habitat in Jerusalem*). Since the goal has not been reached, a tension is suggested. Its resolution is foreshadowed in the Gospel account (John 6:1–15) of the feeding of the five thousand. Christ is shown in His role of pastor (literally, "feeder"), for it is through the *panis coelestis* of His body that the catechumens will ultimately be incorporated into the communion symbolized by Jerusalem.

In view of the dramatic contrast of the liturgy of the day with that of Lent in general, it is not surprising that an extraliturgical ceremony was associated with it at least as early as the eleventh century. On this day it was customary for the Pope to bless a rose. The rose was carried from the Lateran to Santa Croce, the station for the day, where the Pope delivered a sermon on its beauty and symbolism. It was then presented to the Roman Emperor or to a great Christian prince. After Pope Leo IX, an exquisitely wrought golden rose was substituted for the natural one.[45] The blessing may be a survival of pagan spring celebrations. Whatever its origin, it has no structural or rememorative function and must be considered to be a lyric amplification of the joyful mood of the day.

The most important event of the week is the third scrutiny.[46] In its common form this ceremony involved an "opening of the ears" (*apertio aurium*) to receive the Word of Scripture and a "transmission" (*traditio*) of the Creed and Pater Noster.

The ceremony begins with the usual public summons and group prayer. Two lessons are then read. Like those of the first scrutiny, they differ from the readings in the Gregorian (and contemporary) service. The Gregorian selections stress penance, while those of the *Ordo Romanus*

---

[45] Molien (*Prière*, II, 304–5) traces this to 1049 at the Abbey of the Holy Cross of Wolffenheim and suggests that the service may be a relic of the presentation of golden keys of the city to great rulers. More recently, Weiser suggests that the ceremony originally involved a natural rose and was derived from pagan spring celebrations. This would, of course, imply a date much earlier than the eleventh century.

[46] Amalarius, *Liber officialis*, PL, CV, 1005ᵇ; H, II, 52: "Memorata quarta feria apud cultores ecclesiae in apertione aurium dicitur. Eadem die agitur scrutinium tertium, quod maximum est inter septem scrutinia. Eadem die tanguntur aures et nares catechuminorum . . . instruuntur de auctoribus et initiis quatuor evangeliorum . . . percipiunt orationem dominicam et symbolum, ad reddendum in sabbato sancto paschae." The ceremony is repeated on Holy Saturday: ". . . dicit eis: *Effeta*. Istud officium praelibatum est in memorata quarta feria, sed fors ideo repetitur quia aliqui nondum venerant" (*ibid.*, p. 1040ᵈ; H, II, 126).

VII are directed toward the catechumens and stress redemption. In the first (Isa. 55:2–7) the idea of hearing predominates: "Hearken diligently unto me" (*Audite, audientes me*). The foreshadowing of the *Apertio Aurium* is obvious. The gradual, *Venite filii, audite me* . . . *et illuminamini*, has survived in the contemporary service, where it seems slightly incongruous. Originally it was an invitation to the catechumens. The word *audite* echoes the reading from Isaiah, and the *illuminamini* reiterates the idea of baptism as *photismos*. The second reading, Paul's epistle to the Colossians (3:9–17), is equally plain in its advice to "put off the old man with his deeds; and . . . put on the new man, which is renewed in knowledge." The second gradual (*Beata gens*) repeats the theme of the communion of saints from Laetare Sunday. After it, four deacons preceded by candles and thurible station themselves at the four corners of the altar. Each holds one of the Gospels. In some orders, such as the Gallican, the celebrant touched the ears and nose of each candidate, murmuring *ephpheta* ("Be thou opened"). The ceremony, recalling Christ's healing of the deaf man (Mark 7:32 34), seems an appropriate preparation for the reading of the Gospels, but the seventh Roman *Ordo* defers it until Holy Saturday.[47]

With or without the *ephpheta*, the Gospels are now "exposed." Since the catechumens heretofore have had to leave the service before the Gospel lesson, this is an impressive occasion. The priest first explains their content, form, and symbols: a man for Matthew, a lion for Mark, an ox for Luke, and an eagle for John. A deacon then ascends the Gospel ambo, reads the first chapter (1–21) of Matthew, and explains its content in a brief, formalized speech (*Filii carissimi, ne diutius vos teneamus*). When this is over, the first Gospel is placed on a linen cloth and carried reverently to the sacristy by a subdeacon. The process is repeated for the Gospels according to Mark, Luke, and John, with the emphasis of the final "explanation" falling on rebirth: ". . . the Church that has begotten you and still bears you in her womb exults at the thought of the new increase to be given to the Christian law when, on the venerable day of Easter, you are to be born again in the waters of baptism."[48]

When the *Apertio* is over, the "transmission" part of the scrutiny begins. A prayer (*Dilectissimi nobis*) informs the catechumens of their need to understand the mysteries of the Apostles' Creed (*Symbolum*). A male

[47] This is evidently the meaning of the remark "eadem die tanguntur aures et nares." For the more common Roman practice, see *OR* VII, p. 998[d]; Gelasian Sacramentary, *PL*, LXXIV, 1106[b]. See comment by de Puniet, "Catéchuménat," p. 2614; Duchesne, *Christian Worship*, pp. 317–18.

[48] Gelasian Sacramentary, *PL*, LXXVI, 1087[a-e]; Guéranger, *Liturgical Year*, V, 344–52.

catechumen is chosen to stand before the celebrant while an acolyte recites the Creed to him in Greek. The recitation is repeated with a female catechumen, and then twice more in Latin. A short exposition (*Hic summa est fidei nostrae, dilectissimi*) follows in which, among other things, the link between baptism and the Resurrection is strongly reaffirmed: "Believe with firm and unshaken faith that the Resurrection which was accomplished in Christ will likewise be accomplished in you. . . . The sacrament of baptism, which you are soon to receive, is the visible expression of this hope; for in it is represented both a death and a resurrection. . . ." The dramatic continuity between the scrutinies and the events of Easter Eve could hardly be more explicitly set before the participants. As the prayer continues, the imagery of spiritual conflict, the Lenten agon, is introduced. The Creed is a kind of "armor." It is "invincible against all attacks of the enemy; it should be worn by the true soldiers of Christ. Let the devil . . . find you ever armed with this Creed. Triumph over the adversary whom you have just renounced."[49] Finally, the Pater Noster is recited, together with a rather lengthy line-by-line exposition. When it is completed, the catechumens are dismissed with the usual formula and Mass concludes as on the previous scrutiny days. The major scrutiny is over. The next three resemble the first. Presumably, the catechumens now study and memorize the Creed and Pater Noster in preparation for the scrutiny of Holy Saturday.

The second phase of the Easter drama ends on the Saturday after Laetare Sunday. It has opened on the theme of alienation, objectified in action by the dismissal of penitents and in text by the imagery of death: *Memento homo quia pulvis es et in pulverem reverteris.* Reinforcing elements include allusions to darkness, yearning, sickness, and wasteland. At the opposite extreme is the theme of redemption, objectified in the scrutinies and expressed poetically by the imagery of rebirth: *Hos, Domine, fonte baptismatis innovandos.* Here the reinforcing elements are allusions to light (baptism as *photismos*), fulfillment, purification, healing, and the Heavenly

---

[49] The translation is a free rendering by Guéranger, *Liturgical Year*, V, 348–49. The Latin text is no less vivid (Gelasian Sacramentary, *PL*, LXXIV, 1091 b-e):

Secura et constanti fide credite resurrectionem, quae facta est in Christo, etiam in nobis omnibus esse complendam. . . . Quoniam et ipsum quod percepturi estis baptismi sacramentum, hujus spei esprimat formam ibi. Quaedam enim ibi mors, et quaedam resurrectio celebratur. Vetus homo deponitur, novus sumitur. . . . Ille abjicitur, qui traxit ad mortem, et suscipitur ille qui reduxit ad vitam. . . . Invicta est enim semper talium armorum potestas contra omnes insidias inimici ad bonum Christi militiam profuturis. Diabolis, qui hominem tentare non desinit, munitos vos hoc Symbolo semper inveniat. Ut, devicto adversario, cui renuntiatis, gratiam Domini . . . servetis, ut in quo peccatorum remissionem accipitis, in eo gloriam resurrectionis habeatis.

Jerusalem. The tension between these two opposing themes is also expressed, most directly in the imagery of agon. References to warfare, armor, and various kinds of struggle recur in the liturgy. At first the agon is generalized; that is, it is projected as a conflict between two factions best identified as "the forces of darkness" and "the forces of light," rather than as a specific antagonist and protagonist. With the exception of the Gospel of Quadragesima Sunday, Christ remains above the action rather than in it. As Passion Sunday approaches, a sharpening of dramatic focus is evident. Two groups are isolated from the body of the congregation. The alienation theme attaches to the penitents, who are expelled from the church as Adam from the original Paradise, while the redemption theme is centered on the *electi*, who are formally labeled "Christian soldiers" as they receive the Creed. The *electi* are not, however, entirely pure. If they are Christian soldiers, they are also in a real sense the battleground for the war between the forces of darkness and light. At each scrutiny they are exorcized with the repeated commands *Audi, maledicite Satanas* and *Exorcizo te, immunde spiritus,* while the faithful look on as spectators or participate as chorus. The heightening of the drama continues between Passion Sunday and Maundy Thursday. During Passiontide Christ assumes the role of protagonist. The mediator and pastor descends to the plane of history to oppose the *adversarius* in person.

V

Historically, Lent seems to have spread outward from the Vigils service of Easter Eve. It was first expanded to include the sacred triduum from Good Friday to Easter Sunday, which became for the Greeks the period of *xerophagia*, the "dry" or total fast. The next expansion was to the two-week period preceding Easter and beginning on Passion Sunday. Not until the fourth century did the forty-day Quadragesimal fast become general, and, as we have noted, the extension of Lenten practices to Septuagesima Sunday is later still. The process appears to have been a natural one. It helps explain the organic quality of the Lenten drama. Ultimately, all developments move outward from the moment of the Resurrection. Each reaches completion and, in turn, serves as the basis for the next.

Passion Sunday initiates the third phase of the Lenten drama. The mood of sorrow abruptly returns, and the focus of the liturgy shifts from the congregation to the historical Christ. As Weiser observes, "the Mass texts are dominated by the image of the Just One, persecuted by His enemies, as He approaches the supreme sacrifice of Golgotha."[50] The agon begins to resemble the conflict of representational drama. It is localized in setting and time by readings from the Gospel accounts of the last two weeks of Christ's life, and especially by repeated readings of the Passion narrative. Not surprisingly, liturgical embellishments place a sympathetic emphasis on the devices of historical representation.

The Mass of Passion Sunday begins with the image of persecution: *Judica me, Deus . . . ab homine iniquo et doloso eripe me.* At other times of the year this Introit is recited by the celebrant during preparation for Mass. The one occasion on which it is normally not recited by the celebrant is the service for the dead.[51] That it is sung by the chorus and not by the celebrant on Passion Sunday gives the Mass for this day some of the connotations (though not the form) of a requiem. Passiontide thus opens with a subtle allusion to death. In consonance with this allusion, the Gloria Patri is now dropped except in Masses commemorating a saint's feast. The last regular text connoting joy has been eliminated. The liturgy is as bare as the altar itself after it has been stripped on Maundy Thursday.

The Epistle (Heb. 9:11–15) carries forward the somber tone of the service. It is a warning that redemption cannot be purchased except by the blood of the Savior: "Neither by the blood of goats and calves, but by his own blood he entered in once into the holy place, having retained eternal redemption for us." The gradual repeats the petition of the Introit, *Eripe me, Domine, ab inimicis meis,* and the tract sustains the tone: *Saepe expugnaverunt me a juventute mea.* The Gospel (John 8:46–59) provides the historical setting for the chants. For the first time Christ is shown persecuted by his human adversaries. In return for his proclamation, "Before Abraham was, I am," "they took up stones to cast at him: but Jesus hid himself, and went out of the temple." The first representational ceremony of Passiontide is associated with this reading. It was customary at the Papal Chapel in Rome to shroud the cross and holy images as the deacon read ". . . Jesus hid himself." The action is a simple and obvious instance of copying. It was imitated throughout Europe and was often anticipated in the high Middle Ages by its performance on vespers of the preceding Saturday.[52] The clergy has worn the vestments of mourning since Septua-

---

[50] *Handbook*, p. 179. Weiser adds, "During the first four weeks of Lent the spirit of personal penance prevailed, but these last fourteen days are devoted entirely to the meditation of Christ's Passion."

[51] Leduc and Baudot, *Liturgy*, p. 208.

[52] Weiser, *Handbook*, p. 179; Molien, *Prière*, II, 325–28. The suggestion is that the ceremony originated in the ninth century from the more general rite of stripping the altars.

gesima. Now the church itself symbolizes grief. It may be added that two highly charged observances of the high Middle Ages were unknown during the ninth century. These are the so-called "Feast of the Seven Sorrows," celebrated on Friday after Passion Sunday, and the stations of the cross, introduced at the time of the crusades.[53]

On Saturday before Palm Sunday no station is mentioned in the Gregorian service books, which leads Amalarius to conclude that no service is held. Although some sources give the Lateran or St. Peter's, all agree that the day is to be devoted to works of charity in commemoration of Mary's anointing of Christ's feet. "The house," writes Amalarius, "is filled with sweet odor; the world is filled with the good fame of the woman. The Pope follows this most precious example, and would that we would follow it too."[54] The act of giving alms in imitation of Mary Magdalene is a step toward representational expression of Gospel history. Many churches carried the impulse further and held a Maundy service on this day.

The Palm Sunday procession is one of the outstanding liturgical events of Holy Week and a striking instance of the principle of coincidence. It originated in Jerusalem and became popular in the West during the eighth century.[55] Its form and popularity during the ninth century are disputed, but Amalarius was familiar with the basic elements: "In memory of Christ's entry," he says, "we carry branches and cry hosanna."[56]

---

[53] Weiser, *Handbook*, pp. 179–80.

[54] *Liber officialis*, PL, CV, 1008[b]; H, II, 58. Cf. Pseudo-Alcuin, *De divinis officiis*, PL, CI, 1200–2; and see Molien, *Prière*, II, 337; Guéranger, *Liturgical Year*, VI, 66–68, 227–28; Leduc and Baudot, *Liturgy*, p. 222. The anointing of Christ's feet is described in John 12. This would normally be the Gospel for Saturday, but because of the lack of a Mass (no station is given) it is deferred until Monday. The fact does not prevent the commemorative ceremony based on the Gospel text. Various special practices are described in the *Commentarius praevius* of the Roman *Ordines*, p. 886[b-c]. For the consecration of the *fermentum* see Guéranger, *Liturgical Year*, VI, 167, and below, p. 122. The ceremony explains the mention of a station in *LS*, p. 75[d].

[55] Aldhelm, *De laudibus virginitatis* (*PL*, LXXXIX, 122–23) testifies to the custom. See *LS Notae*, pp. 310[a]–12[a]. Holy Week ceremonies are treated from an historical point of view by Leclercq, "Semaine sainte," *DACL*, XV, 1, 1151–85 ("Dimanche des rameaux," pp. 1154–56; "Jeudi saint," pp. 1156–67; "Vendredi saint," pp. 1167–75; "Samedi saint," pp. 1175–85). Popular treatments abound. John Feasey, *Ancient English Holy Week Ceremonial* (London, 1897), has been used frequently because of its colorful descriptions, but it ignores the liturgy and the "ceremonial" is mostly of the twelfth to fifteenth centuries. For the modern rite, see Fortescue, "Triduum," in *Ceremonies of the Roman Rite*, pp. 302–63. Weiser, Molien, Guéranger, and Leduc and Baudot also have useful summaries.

[56] *Liber officialis*, PL, CV, 1008[b-d]; H, II, 58–59. The procession antiphons are found in the *Liber responsalis*, pp. 762[d]–63[b], where they are given as matins (i.e., lauds) antiphons. Cf. Rabanus Maurus, *De clericorum institutione*, PL, CVII, 347[a-b]; Isidore, *De ecclesiasticis officiis*, PL, LXXVIII, 763[b-c].

Since there is no detailed ninth-century description, two accounts bracketing the period may be cited. Toward the end of the fourth century the Roman lady Etheria visited Jerusalem and described the liturgical ceremonies of the Holy Land in her much-read *Peregrinatio* (i.e., travel memoirs). The Palm Sunday ceremonies that she witnessed were highly developed. At about the seventh hour, she observes, the bishop and the people proceed from Jerusalem to the Mount of Olives, where hymns and antiphons are sung. At the eleventh hour the Gospel account of Palm Sunday (Matt. 21:1–11) is read. The bishop and his flock then return to Jerusalem singing *Benedictus qui venit* and bearing olive branches or palm fronds.[57] The ceremony was a popular one. The people were not only acting out the welcome of the Hebrews to Christ at the time of year when it had historically occurred, but they were doing so at the original sites themselves.

In the West a greater degree of symbolism was necessary. The procession could, and frequently did, leave the gates of the town and re-enter them, but it was also common for the precincts of the church or the cloister to stand for the Mount of Olives, and the church itself, for Jerusalem. The ninth-century ceremony begins with a formal blessing of palms or olive branches at the altar.[58] After they are distributed, a procession leaves the church, proceeds to whatever spot symbolizes the Mount of Olives, and returns. When it reaches the church, the doors are closed. The priest must strike the doors three times. They are then opened, and the procession enters to the responsory *Ingrediente Domino*. From later practice it appears likely that the procession included a Christ symbol. This would normally be a cross, but could be the Gospels, carried on a bier (*feretrum*), or some other sacred object—a phylactery, reliquary, and/or a consecrated Host in a capsa.[59] According to pious (and probably false) legend, the hymn *Gloria, laus, et honor* attributed to Theodulphus (d. 821) was first sung on Palm Sunday by the saint himself when he was a prisoner in Angers around 818.[60] Whatever the details, however, the essential representational elements—symbolic space, stylized costume, and dialogue based on

---

[57] As reprinted in Duchesne, *Christian Worship*, pp. 505, 553–54.

[58] Cf. Molien, *Prière*, II, 343. The modern service (prior to the reforms of 1955), which resembles an incomplete Mass, is given in Guéranger, *Liturgical Year*, VI, 189–95. The Palm Sunday rite is considered from a dramatic point of view by Young, *DMC*, I, 90–98. This treatment is vitiated by Young's unwillingness to differentiate between forms of the rite contemporary with the earliest liturgical plays and forms of the high Middle Ages.

[59] *Ibid.*, and *Commentarius*, p. 887[b-d]. The *feretrum* is a feature of the procession described by Pseudo-Alcuin.

[60] Raby, *Christian Latin Poetry*, pp. 174–75.

Gospel history—are as old as the procession itself. Later amplifications simply elaborated one or more of these. The version in the *Regularis concordia* (*ca.* 970) illustrates the process. It is not known whether this account describes ninth-century practice, but there is no reason for rejecting the possibility:

> On Palm Sunday [before the Mass of the day] ... the brethren, vested in albs, if this can be done and the weather permits, shall go to the church where the palms are, silently, in the order of procession and occupied with psalmody. On reaching the church they shall say the prayer of the saint to whom the church is dedicated. . . . When the prayer is finished, the gospel *Turba multa* (John 12:12–19) shall be read by the deacon as far as the words *Ecce mundus totus post ipsum abiit:* the blessing of the palms shall follow. After the blessing the palms shall be sprinkled with holy water and incensed. While the children begin the antiphons *Pueri Hebraeorum* the palms shall be distributed. Then the greater antiphons (e.g., *Cum appropinquaret, Cum audisset,* etc.) shall be intoned and the procession shall go forth. As soon as the Mother church is reached the procession shall wait while the children, who shall have gone before, sing *Gloria laus* with its verses, to which all shall answer *Gloria laus,* as the custom is. When this is finished the cantor shall intone the respond *Ingrediente Domino* and the doors shall be opened. When all have entered and the respond is finished they shall do as has been said before, holding their palms in their hands until the Offertory has been sung, and then offering them to the priest. [61]

A still more elaborate form of the ceremony is found in the Mozarabic *Missale mixtum,* where the entry into the church is expanded by a dialogue also associated with the Harrowing of Hell. The *Missale mixtum* was compiled at the beginning of the sixteenth century from a variety of sources, some of them dating back to the seventh century. Its Palm Sunday procession cannot be earlier than the ninth century and gives every evidence of being much later. Some features, however, may be very ancient in view of the fact that Isidore of Seville seems to refer to the Palm Sunday procession in his seventh-century *De officiis ecclesiasticis.* [62] Its date aside, the Mozarabic rite merits citation as an illustration of secular—in contrast to monastic—practice. First palms are blessed and asperged. A procession forms and leaves the church singing antiphons (*Dum appropinquaret Dominus; Veniente Domino*). Then, say the rubrics,

> let the boys' choir stand by the church door and sing the hymn *Gloria, laus, et honor.* When they are finished, let the bishop [*pontifex*] or priest

---

[61] *Regularis concordia,* ed. Symons, pp. 34–36.

[62] I, XXVIII (*PL,* LXXXIII, 763b).

ascend to the west portal [*januam indulgentiarum*]: and striking it with a staff or the wood of the cross, let him say in a loud voice, *Attollite portas principes vestras: et elevimini portas eternales: et introibit Rex gloriae.* Then two canons standing within the church should reply in the same tone, *Quis est iste Rex gloriae.* And the bishop should say, *Dominus fortis et potens.* Again let the bishop or priest strike the door and say in a still louder voice, *Attollite portas.* And those within the church reply as before but louder, *Quis est iste Rex gloriae.* Then the bishop or priest should say, *Dominus potens in proelio.* And again the priest should strike the door and say in a still louder voice, *Attollite portas.* And those within reply still more loudly, *Quis est iste Rex gloriae.* And the priest replies, *Dominus virtutum ipse est Rex gloriae.* This completed, the doors should be opened and the cantor should begin the respond *Ingrediente Domino.* And when the priest has approached the altar of St. Mary at the station made for him in the chorus, the antiphon *Ave Rex noster* is to be chanted by a singer with a scepter in his hands, bending his knee three times and raising his voice each time while the choir replies, *Filius David Redemptor mundi.*[63]

The representational elements in this ceremony are quite advanced. Among the identifiable "characters" are Christ, Satan, the Hebrews, and the *plebs beata*, represented by the cantor with the scepter. Evidently the space represents not only the historical Jerusalem, as in the original Palm Sunday procession, but also the Heavenly Jerusalem into which the triumphant Christ is welcomed.

Whatever the precise form of Palm Sunday rites in the ninth century, they existed to complement the Mass of the day, not as separate, detachable ceremonies. The Mass of Palm Sunday carries forward the dramatic agon. The procession has been exultant; the hosannas and palm fronds suggest the victory of the *Rex gloriae* over his *adversarius.* As Mass begins, the mood of triumph gives way to reminders of the trial to come. The Introit that follows the procession is in the somber key of the Lenten petitions. Still more ominous, it foreshadows the words of Christ on the Cross: *Domine, ne longe facias auxilium tuum a me. . . . Deus, Deus meus, respice in me: quare me dereliquisti?* The theme of alienation, of loss of divine favor, dominates the long tract for the day.[64] It leads to the first of the Holy Week accounts of the Passion, that of Matthew 26–27. The reading is given special emphasis by the omission of the customary preparatory rites,

[63] *Missale mixtum, PL,* LXXV, 390[b]–91[o]. Compare the example in Young, *DMC,* I, 92–93. It is worth noting that the Mozarabic ceremony repeats literally the story of Christ's visit to the Temple after His entry.

[64] *LA,* p. 673[b-o].

especially the celebrant's benediction and the lights of the procession to the ambo. What is more striking is the fact that the reading is delivered in three distinct tones. The medieval rubrics were once thought to indicate the use of three readers for the occasion and, consequently, to specify a form of presentation akin to stage dialogue. Karl Young demonstrated that they refer to different tones of voice to be used by one reader—low for the speeches of Christ, medium for the narrative sections, and high for the speeches of the crowds, priests, and judges.[65] His evidence put an end to the speculation that liturgical drama evolved from the reading of the Gospel as dialogue, but it does not alter the fact that throughout Holy Week the Gospel is read in a manner which anticipates representational technique. The principle of articulation encourages a distinctive method of reading during Holy Week, and the principle of coincidence encourages choosing the one that will make the history most vivid to the congregation.

According to the first *Ordo Romanus*, "all priests in the city and suburbs" gathered at St. Mary Major on Wednesday at tierce for solemn prayers led by the Pope.[66] Similar gatherings were held at episcopal sees throughout Europe. The prayers said are the same ones recited today on Good Friday. They ask divine aid and mercy for the Church, the Pope, the Emperor, the clergy, the catechumens,[67] and the afflicted, and for heretics, Jews, and pagans. Before each prayer the deacon cries *Flectamus genua*, and afterwards, *Levate*. All sources agree that because the Jews mockingly bowed to Christ, calling him "King of the Jews," the Christian congregation should disregard the deacon's command during the prayer for the Jews, a unique instance in the Easter liturgy of dramatic impulse overcoming regard for history.[68] In spite of this qualification the prayers carry forward the motifs of love and regeneration while they increase the dramatic reality of the *adversarius* for the congregation. The reduplication on Good Friday of Wednesday's prayers (since abandoned) was explained as rememorative symbolism. Wednesday, observes Amalarius, is the day when the Jews devised their plan to slay the Lord, and Friday is the day when they carried it out. That the Church selects Wednesday and Friday to pray for her enemies demonstrates her ability to forgive them at the very time when they are harming her most.[69] Repeated responses to the deacon's commands—including refusal to bow for the Jews—confirm the

[65] "Observations on the Origin of the Mediaeval Passion-Play," pp. 309–33.

[66] *OR* I, p. 961[b-c]; Molien, *Prière*, II, 365.

[67] This was the week of the sixth scrutiny (Guéranger, *Liturgical Year*, VI, 251).

[68] E.g., *LS*, p. 79[b]; *OR* I, p. 961[c]; Amalarius, *Liber officialis*, *PL*, CV, 1027[c]; H, II, 98.

[69] *PL*, CV, p. 1027[c-d]; H, II, 98. The Kiss of Peace is also omitted on the basis of coincidence: it would recall the kiss given Jesus at the betrayal.

congregation's sense of participation at least as a chorus, in the developing action.

Mass begins with the antiphon *In nomine Domini omne genu flectatur*, which recalls the Epistle of Palm Sunday (Phil. 2:10) as well as the prayers. If the prayers are illustrations of heroic charity, as Amalarius believed, this forgiving mood is soon tempered by readings in which death imagery recurs with great vehemence. The fluctuation here between joy and sorrow, life and death, parallels the change in emotion from procession to Mass of Palm Sunday and, like it, is a symbolic expression of the Lenten agon. The first reading (Isa. 63:1–7) depicts a Savior who comes for vengeance rather than forgiveness: "I will tread them in mine anger, and trample them in my fury; and their blood shall be sprinkled upon my garments, and I will stain all my raiment. For the day of vengeance is in mine heart." The tone softens somewhat with the collect, which asks for life (*ut resurrectionis gratiam consequamur*), but the second reading (Isa. 53:1–12) remains heavy with death imagery. The Savior is described as "a root out of a dry ground"; one "despised and rejected of men; a man of sorrows"; "wounded for our transgressions"; and, finally, "brought as a lamb to the slaughter." These allusions, which define Christ's role in the agon as that of sacrificial victim rather than heroic conqueror, lead directly to the historical narrative illustrating them, the Passion according to Luke. That the sequence of readings was intensely moving to the congregation cannot be doubted. Etheria recorded that during Wednesday's Gospel "there was such a moaning and groaning of all the people that no one can help being moved to tears."[70] There is no reason to suppose that the attitude of the ninth-century congregation would be different from the fourth-century one on this occasion. Groans, weeping, and other expressions of direct involvement in the action may be assumed throughout Holy Week, reaching a crescendo on Good Friday.

Maundy Thursday is the third major event of Holy Week. It commemorates the institution of the Lord's Supper and is therefore called *Coena Domini* in the *Ordines*. There are provisions in the early *Ordines* for three Masses, each with a special function. In addition, liturgical embellishments are found from dawn until evening. In general, the mood of the day is positive, with an emphasis on conciliation and acts of charity. It obviously reflects the operation of the principle of coincidence. Christ's institution of the Eucharist is commemorated with joy, if not with exuberant rejoicing. To Amalarius it marks the beginning of history under

---

[70] *Peregrinatio*, in Duchesne, *Christian Worship*, p. 555.

the new law, although the new law does not actually take effect until the Resurrection.[71]

Practice varied during the ninth century, but according to the Roman usage the Tenebrae service was first performed during the early hours of Maundy Thursday. Tenebrae is essentially a gradual extinguishing of lights during the celebration of the night service between midnight and dawn. In the ninth century this service was simply called nocturns, but today it is called matins, and the ninth-century matins has been renamed lauds. A total extinction of lights could be performed three times (Maundy Thursday, Good Friday, Holy Saturday) or once, on the evening of Good Friday, or the morning of Holy Saturday.[72] During his trip to Rome, Amalarius was surprised to learn that the latter practice was followed in the Holy City. In any case, Tenebrae is a death ceremony. It commemorates the extinguishing of the Light of the World and is coincident with the period of the year when the Passion is uppermost in the mind of the Church. The chants are mournful, and the readings (Jeremiah, Augustine, Paul) stress death. Today Tenebrae concludes with a general striking of benches, occasionally taken by allegorists to symbolize the scourging of Christ, but the practice may postdate the ninth century.[73] In addition to symbolizing death, Tenebrae prepares for the complementary illumination ceremonies of the Easter vigil. Hence it contributes to both continuity and dramatic contrast. Amalarius brings these points together in his explanation of Tenebrae:

That the lights of the church are extinguished on these nights seems to me to be in commemoration of the Sun of Justice Himself, who is buried for three days and three nights. Christ illuminated His Church day and night like a sun, that in the prosperity of the day she might rejoice with moderation, and in the adversity of night she might endure with equanimity. . . . Our church is illuminated with twenty-four candles and at each song—where we might otherwise rejoice—we choose sadness because our true Sun has set; and thus during the individual

---

[71] *Liber officialis* (*PL*, CV, 1023[a]; H, II, 88), based on Bede, *De temporum ratione* (*PL*, XC, 334[a]).

[72] For early descriptions, see *OR* I, pp. 959[c]–61[b]; Amalarius, *Liber officialis*, *PL*, CV, 1202[b-d]; H, II, 472–73; *De ordine antiphonarii*, *PL*, CV, 1292[c-d]; H, III, 79–81. Historical details in Molien, *Prière*, pp. 357–63; Guéranger, *Liturgical Year*, VI, 274–316; Fortescue, *Ceremonies of the Roman Rite*, pp. 302–5.

[73] Leduc and Baudot, *Liturgy*, p. 248; Molien, *Prière*, II, 360. The practice derives from the method used in the synagogue to announce the end of prayer, but in the Christian context it takes on the connotation of an expression of mourning. The reference is to the service prior to the liturgical reforms of 1955.

hours the lack of the sun is increased until complete extinction.[74] This happens three times because it recalls the three-day burial of the Lord. During the day the fire is renewed.[75] . . . It is rekindled because of our infirmity, for we cannot perform our offices in the church without light. Otherwise, it would be proper that, after the first extinction, it should remain unkindled until the glory of the Resurrection and the renewal of the New Testament.[76]

In keeping with the rhythmic alternation between moods of exultation and extreme grief which is so pronounced during Holy Week, Maundy Thursday now takes on a positive note, countering death with forgiveness, darkness with light. The first Mass of the day (at prime) was known as the Mass of Remission because it included the reconciliation of penitents.[77] Early in the morning the penitents, barefoot, unwashed, unshaven, weak from fasting, and gaunt from the rigors of penitential discipline, prostrated themselves before the church doors. Meanwhile the bishop recited the seven penitential psalms and the Litany of the Saints in the sanctuary. One imagines that the recitation was unhurried. While it was in progress, two subdeacons came twice before the penitents to announce the possibility of reconciliation: *Nolo mortem peccatoris* . . . , and *Poenitentiam agite*. A deacon then commanded *Levate capita vestra*, and the penitents were allowed to enter the nave of the church.[78] Meanwhile the bishop, who had seated himself on a throne at the head of the nave, arose and approached them. The following choral dialogue ensued:

SACERDOS: *Averte faciem tuam a peccatis meis.*
RESP.:   *Et omnes iniquitates meas dele.*
VERS.:   *Cor mundum crea in me, Deus.*
RESP.:   *Et spiritum rectum innova in visceribus meis.*
VERS.:   *Domine exaudi orationem meam.*
RESP.:   *Et clamor meus ad te veniat.*[79]

[74] Symons notes several variations of the ritual in his edition of the *Regularis concordia*, p. 36.

[75] In Rome the new fire was originally kindled on Thursday and sequestered until used on Friday and Saturday for lighting the candles extinguished at Tenebrae (*OR* I, p. 961 ᵉ). Later, it was kindled on Good Friday, and finally the Gallican practice of kindling it on Holy Saturday was assimilated. See below, Essay IV, n. 13.

[76] *Liber officialis*, *PL*, CV, 1202 ᵇ⁻ᵈ; H, II, 472–73.

[77] Molien, *Prière*, II, 365–67.

[78] See Gelasian Sacramentary (*PL*, LXXIV, 1095 ᵇ–97 ᵉ) and *LS Notae* (pp. 445–50) for reconciliation ceremonies. Amalarius discusses the reconciliation of penitents (*Liber officialis*, *PL*, CV, 1020 ᵇ; H, II, 83–84) but is far more interested in the consecration of holy oils.

[79] This exchange is first found in the *Ordo Romanus* X, *PL*, LXXVIII, 1019 ᵇ.

After a leisurely set of prayers and exhortations, the penitents, now joined by congregation and clergy, prostrated themselves again. In a formal inversion of the dismissal rite of Ash Wednesday, they were blessed, censed, and sprinkled with holy water. When allowed to rise, they filed hand in hand to the bishop's throne, where the reconciliation was completed. They then departed to change into normal garb, shave, and (one hopes) bathe prior to receiving Holy Communion. According to the tenth Roman *Ordo*, written about 1100 but preserving many ancient usages, the church bells are rung following the reconciliation.[80] They then remain silent until Easter Eve.

The second Mass of the day intensifies the joyful mood introduced by the reconciliation of penitents. It is the *Missa chrismalis*, celebrated at tierce or sext.[81] As far as ninth-century liturgists are concerned, it is the most important Mass of the day. Even now it is one of the most splendid services of the Church year, requiring the participation of a bishop, no less than twelve priests, seven deacons, and seven subdeacons, all in white vestments. During the *Missa chrismalis* three kinds of holy oil are blessed— oil of the sick, oil of the catechumens, and chrism, a mixture of oil and balsam used at the Easter vigil in blessing the font, in baptism, and in confirmation. The *Ordines* and Sacramentaries refer to the blessing as a consecration, and it involves what appears to be a survival of concelebration. It is symbolically associated with Maundy Thursday through the ideas of healing and cleansing, and it is a necessary preparation for ceremonies of Holy Saturday. It thus has both a rememorative and a liturgical function. Above all, it repeats the previously established connection between the imagery and mood of redemption and the catechumens.

Details of the service are provided in the Gregorian *Liber sacramentorum* and the early *Ordines*.[82] It begins with a joyous salute to the cross and includes the Gloria in Excelsis. In Rome flasks of oil and chrism were originally prepared at the church of St. Thomas and St. George. The Pope mixed the oil and balsam himself before going to the Lateran to celebrate Mass. The flasks were brought later in solemn procession. A cardinal deacon accepted the chrism, and subdeacons accepted the oil of the sick and the oil of catechumens. The *Ordines Romani* omit the procession and call for the preparation of the chrism just prior to Mass. Before the words of the Canon, *Per quem haec omnia*, the subdeacon presents the flask

---

[80] *Ibid.*, p. 1009ᵇ and note.

[81] Molien, *Prière*, II, 369–76; Guéranger, *Liturgical Year*, VI, 323–30; Leduc and Baudot, *Liturgy*, pp. 352–54.

[82] Gelasian Sacramentary, *PL*, LXXIV, 1099ᶜ–1102ᵃ; *LS*, pp. 81ᵈ–85ᵃ; *LS Notae*, pp. 327ᵈ–31ᵇ; *OR* I, pp. 951ᵉ, 962ᵃ⁻ᵈ.

containing the oil of the sick to the celebrant. It is exorcised with a prayer said *plena voce* by all ministers of sacerdotal rank, then blessed. The celebrant next completes the Canon. When he has received Holy Communion, he places the chalice and paten on the altar, covering them with a clean linen cloth (sindon). Immediately the flasks containing the oil of catechumens and chrism are brought forward.

The manner in which they are to be carried is symbolic and must have been considered quite important by the early Church because the rubrics are unusually detailed on this point. The flasks are to be held in the left hand, partially wrapped in a sindon but in such a way as to be visible to the congregation. The chrism is received first. An archdeacon offers it to the celebrant who, with the twelve assisting priests, breathes on it three times, exorcizes it, and consecrates it, using the *Sursum corda* formula of the Mass Preface said *excelsa voce*. The Consecration prayer is said *tacite*. The flask is now exposed while the bishop and priests bow before it, saying *Ave sanctum Chrisma*, and kissing it. It is then covered with a white cloth. A similar ceremony without the Consecration is performed for the oil of catechumens, which is covered with a violet cloth. A solemn procession transports all three flasks to the sacristy, where the oil of the sick will be distributed to the faithful throughout the year. The Communion service then resumes. It is possible that the hymn of Fortunatus, *O Redemptor sume carnem*, was sung.

As may be imagined, the *Missa chrismalis* is impressive in its own right. The ritual covering and display of the flasks intensifies the sense of solemn mystery. Whatever its early significance, it was interpreted in the ninth century as rememorative drama. The dual nature of chrism—part oil and part aromatic balsam—led it to be identified with Christ; hence the flask containing it is "in a sense the body of the Lord received from the Virgin Mary."[83] The initial partial concealment of the flask is a symbol of Christ before His active ministry, and the white veil is a symbol of His purity. The moment of full disclosure on the altar unites this symbolism with the Mass interpretation associating the Consecration with the Crucifixion. The exposed flask symbolizes Christ on the Cross, fully revealed to man. The subsequent veiling of the flask becomes an image of the Ascension, when Christ is withdrawn from human vision.[84]

Three additional ceremonies dramatize the liturgy of Maundy Thursday. In them the joyful tone of the morning Masses is gradually modulated to one of sadness, which leads inevitably to Tenebrae. If the reconcili-

---

[83] *Liber officialis, PL,* CV, 1017ᵃ; H, II, 76. The tradition goes back to Dionysius the Pseudo-Areopagite, *De ecclesiastica hierarchia,* trans. B. Corderio, IV, 4 (*PG,* III, 478–79).

[84] *Liber officialis, PL,* CV, 1017ᵃ⁻ᵈ; H, II, 76–77.

ation of penitents and the *Missa chrismalis* reveal the principle of coincidence operating in a general way, these later ceremonies are more specific. They occur at times of day associated with the events commemorated, and because of this they are strikingly representational. They are, in order, the reservation of the Host, the Maundy service, and the stripping of the altars. At least the first and third are associated with death. In addition to them, two local Roman ceremonies are mentioned in the early *Ordines*. For lack of better names, these may be called the "Manifestation of the Blood" and the "Renewal of the Altar." Both of them involve burial symbolism.[85] Purely liturgical innovations which reinforce the death motif include the substitution of wooden clappers for bells and the elimination of the Kiss of Peace.

[85] These two ceremonies must be understood in terms of the following description of the altar of the Lateran: "In Coena Domini hora sexta celebratur Missa ad Lateranis. Sic incipiens Pontifex dicit *Oremus*. Tunc ponuntur in altare Sancta, et altare est cavum. Omnibus rite in altare compositis, oblata est libamenta, paucaque per ecclesiam luminaria accensa. . . . Sic intrat in Missam" (*Commentarius*, p. 888ᵇ). From this description we learn (1) that the Lateran altar is hollow; and (2) that before the *Missa chrismalis* of Maundy Thursday one or more Hosts are placed in the hollow. Both "Manifestation" and "Renewal" ceremonies involve the use of this altar and (presumably) the Host. The "Manifestation" and "Renewal" are described in OR X, p. 1011ᵇ⁻ᶜ:

> Levatur mensa de altari, pallis desuper complicatis, et cum reverentia et omni devotione ab eisdem reportetur in capella sancti Pancratii juxta claustrum canonicorum, quia ibi est locus reservationis, et cum omni cautela usque in diem Sabbati custodiatur.
>
> Deinde Pontifex venit ad altare, accipiens ampullam vitreum, quae intus se continet quoddam vasculum aureum, et in illo vasculo est lapis pretiosus concavus, et in illa concavitate lapidis est diligenter pretiosus Christi sanguis inclusus, qui dicitur miraculose de quaedam imagine Christi percussa profluxisse, qui annualiter extrahitur, et reponitur in concavitate arcae; et tunc levatur a pontifice, et ostenditur, ut tota turba populi valeat cum timore et reverentia et omni devotione cum videre. Postea traditur custodienda priori et canonicis ejusdem ecclesiae usque in die Sabbati. Tunc Pontifex ad sacrificandum intrat solus infra arcam, ut significetur quod in Veteri Testamento scriptum est, quia solus pontifex intrabat semel in anno in sancta sanctorum.

Evidently the hollow top of the altar (or a portion of the altar) containing the sancta is carried reverently into the chapel of St. Pancratius and kept there ("buried"?) from Maundy Thursday until Holy Saturday. How it was "deposed" and "returned" is not said. The "Manifestation" involves displaying a vial of blood supposedly from an image of Christ. The vial is then given to the presiding canon of St. Pancratius and also kept until Holy Saturday. Following this, the pontiff enters the sanctuary alone in imitation of the High Priest entering the Holy of Holies on the Day of Atonement. When the sacrifice is completed, the pontiff apparently takes Communion and then the *Missa chrismalis* proceeds in normal fashion. These ceremonies are extremely suggestive, but their full significance is not clear. The one emphatic point is that the "reservation" spans the time from Maundy Thursday to Holy Saturday. It thus preserves what must have been the shape of the liturgy before the widespread celebration of the Mass of the Presanctified.

The reservation of the Host occurred during the second or third Mass of the day. The origin and significance of this rite occasioned much speculation in the Middle Ages, beginning with Amalarius, and is still imperfectly understood. As Reichel indicates and as the *Liber officialis* makes clear, some kind of reservation ceremony was a regular part of Solemn Mass in the ninth century. Amalarius assumes that Mass will begin with the celebrant's adoration of the reserved Host, or sancta.[86] It is probably significant that the *Liber sacramentorum* and the early *Ordines* refer to the reserved Host of Maundy Thursday as a sancta. The situation is complicated, however, by the existence of related but distinct rites involving what was called a "fermentum." As a result of Jungmann's careful investigation of the term, it is clear that the fermentum has a symbolism parallel to that of the sancta but is more ancient and has particularly close associations with Roman stational Mass.[87] According to the *Codex Ratisponensis* the term usually refers to the particles reserved on Maundy Thursday, Holy Saturday (i.e., the Easter vigil Mass), Easter Day, Pentecost, and Christmas, whereas "sancta" refers to reservations occurring every Sunday.[88] We learn from Leduc and Baudot that on Saturday in Passion Week

it was the custom for the Pope to send by acolytes to the various churches in Rome a particle of consecrated bread to be consumed by the priests belonging to these churches at the same time as the sacred Host consecrated at the Mass celebrated by them. The custom . . . explains the words *datur fermentum* which we find in the old records. A similar distribution is said to have taken place every Sunday. . . . The distribution on this Saturday was exceptional; no doubt the functions of Palm Sunday would not allow of it being easily accomplished on that day. The distribution of the *fermentum* at the beginning of Holy Week had its importance on account of the Paschal Communion, for which it is sometimes called *fermentum paschale*.[89]

---

[86] *Eclogae* (*PL*, CV, 317ᵈ; H, III, 234): "Primo episcopus adorat sancta."

[87] For the texts, see *LS*, p. 85ᵉ; *OR* I, p. 952ᵉ; *OR* X, p. 1011ᵈ. For several variations, see *LS Notae*, pp. 324ᵈ–25ᵉ; *Commentarius*, pp. 869ᵇ–72ᵇ, 888ᵈ–93ᵉ; and esp. Jungmann, "*Fermentum:* Ein Symbol kirchlicher Einheit," *Texte und Arbeiten: Colligere Fragmenta* (Beuron, Germany, 1952), pp. 185–90; Leclercq, "Réserve eucharistique," *DACL*, XIV, 2, 2385–90. Leclercq points out that the Greek Church reserves the Hosts of the week's Masses on Sundays throughout Lent. Thus every ferial Mass is a Mass of the Presanctified.

[88] *Commentarius*, pp. 870ᵈ–71ᵃ.

[89] Leduc and Baudot, *Liturgy*, pp. 222–23; cf. Guéranger, *Liturgical Year*, VI, 167. For sources, see *Commentarius*, pp. 886ᵉ–87ᵃ.

Evidently, this fermentum was reserved not for Palm Sunday but for the first Mass of Easter. We thus have two reservation ceremonies during Holy Week prior to, and/or in addition to, the reservation of Maundy Thursday. The first is the sancta ceremony and the second, the fermentum; in both cases the reserved Host is used for the first Mass of Easter rather than on Good Friday. The *Codex Ratisponensis* explicitly warns: "On Easter vigil [*Sabbato sancto Paschae*] no priest at the baptismal churches may offer communion to anyone before he has commingled that *sancta* which the Lord Pope offered." [90]

There is no detailed information concerning the form of the reservation ceremonies, but three bits of evidence indicate that they took on connotations of a burial. First, the reserved Hosts were kept in what the first *Ordo Romanus* calls a *conditorium*, i.e., a resting place for bodies. Second, they were transported to the altar in a capsa, which during the early centuries was regularly made in the shape of a tower (hence it is also called a *turris*) in imitation of the supposed shape of Christ's tomb. [91] Third, Amalarius refers to the particle of the Host which is to be reserved as "the body of the Savior that sleeps in the tomb." [92]

Whatever reservation ceremonies may have been practiced in the eighth and ninth centuries, the reservation of Maundy Thursday is the only one which survived into the high Middle Ages. The decline of the solemn form of the Mass accounts for the disappearance of the fermentum and sancta, while the survival of the Maundy Thursday reservation is evidently a consequence of the interaction of monastic piety with rememorative symbolism. [93] Good Friday is the nadir of the Easter drama. The principle of coincidence requires particularly striking liturgical ceremonies to commemorate the death of Christ, and the most striking ceremony possible is a suspension of the daily sacrifice. Because the Lord is dead, there can be no Consecration. At the same time, many Christians of the eighth and ninth centuries, particularly monks and nuns, were in the

---

[90] *Ibid.*, p. 871 [a]: "Tamen Sabbato sancto Paschae nullus presbyter per ecclesias baptismales neminem communicat, antequam mittatur ei de ipsa sancta, quam obtulit dominus papa." See also the *ordo* of St. Amand, in Duchesne, *Christian Worship*, p. 471.

[91] For the rubrics, see *OR* I, p. 941 [b]. The shape and symbolism of the capsa is discussed by Neil C. Brooks, *The Sepulchre of Christ in Art and Liturgy* ("University of Illinois Studies in Language and Literature," VII; Urbana, Ill., 1921), pp. 20–22; Leclercq, "Cassette," *DACL*, II, 2, 2340–48.

[92] *Liber officialis* (*PL*, CV, 115 [d]; H, II, 367–68): "Per particulam oblatae . . . relictam in altari, [Christus] iacens in sepulcris."

[93] Jungmann, *"Fermentum,"* pp. 185–90, traces the decay to the rise of parish churches. See also above, Essay II, p. 42. The Maundy reservation appears to be a result of the desire, especially among monks, for daily Communion.

habit of receiving daily Communion. The Church provided for them by reserving a Host on Thursday for use in Friday's service, which was a Communion service only and was called "the Mass of the Presanctified." The Mass of the Presanctified was apparently being celebrated in Rome by the seventh century but did not become common in Gaul and Spain until later. Amalarius, writing in the ninth century, is still vague about the reservation and puzzled by the theological significance of the Mass itself. In fact, when he visited Rome he discovered that papal practice apparently violated the rubrics of the *Ordines*. He was informed that "at the station where the Pope adores the cross [on Good Friday] no one may communicate."[94] He thoroughly approved of this on the grounds of rememorative symbolism: "The order considers that we should wait until the Lord consecrates the sacrament of His blood and body on the Cross and renews them through His Resurrection. . . . And in this order, after the adoration of the cross, individuals should return home without Communion."[95] On the other hand, to compound our difficulties, Amalarius returns to the reserved Host in the fourth book of the *Liber officialis*, this time remarking that it and the abbreviated Friday Mass are normal and proper.[96]

These details of liturgical history are worth bearing in mind because the reservation of the Host on Maundy Thursday generated a secondary phenomenon with implications for the *Quem quaeritis* play. A ceremony developed for removing the Host to the place of repose. In the high Middle Ages the receptacle was often called a *monumentum* or *sepulcrum*. The most

---

[94] *Liber officialis* (*PL*, CV, 1032ᵇ; H, II, 107): "In ea statione ubi apostolicus salutat crucem, nemo ibi communicat." The whole complex matter is reviewed in *Commentarius*, pp. 892ᵃ–93ᵉ, with the conclusion that Roman acceptance of the Mass of the Presanctified cannot be positively dated before Pope Gregory: "Verum ritus ille apud Latinos non videtur fuisse universalis ante Gregorii pontificatum." At this time the Mozarabic Church practiced only the Adoration of the Cross and—in some instances—shut its doors entirely on Good Friday (*Commentarius*, p. 892ᵉ). The *Regula magistri* shows that the Mass of the Presanctified was practiced in Gallican monasteries in the eighth century, but other evidence indicates that it was not general: "in antiquissimis libris liturgicis, qui ante receptum Romanum Ordinem apud nostrates Gallos in usu erant, nihil hac de re praescriptum legatur" (*ibid.*, p. 893ᵃ). Modern research has, if anything, increased doubts about the general practice of the Mass of the Presanctified. Dom Pierre Salmon, ed., *Le lectionnaire de Luxeuil* ([Rome, 1944], I, 88), remarks, "A Rome, jusqu'au VIIe siècle, on ne célébrat aucun office le vendredi; à plus forte raison ignorait-on cette messe des présanctifiés, qui, absente des vieux sacramentaires gallicans, n'a pas d'avantage trouvé place dans les livres ambrosiens ou wisigothiques."

[95] *Liber officialis* (*PL*, CV, 1032ᵉ; H, II, 108): "Ratus ordo est ut expectemus, usque dum Dominus noster consecret sacramenta corporis et sanguinis sui in cruce, et nova ea faciat per resurrectionem suam. Et isto ordine, post salutationem crucis oportet singulos remeare ad sua."

[96] *Ibid.*, p. 1200ᵇ⁻ᶜ; H, II, 468–89.

important single stage property of the *Quem quaeritis* play, a place symbolizing Christ's tomb, thus appears for the first time in the Easter liturgy
on Maundy Thursday. What is equally important, if the Host is "buried"
on Maundy Thursday, it must be "revived" at some later time. The idea
of resurrection from the sepulcher is implicit in this revival.

The early *Ordines* are somewhat vague in their treatment of the reservation ceremony. The first, for example, merely states that after the
consecration of oils the pontiff washes his hands, serves Communion, and
servat de sancta usque in crastinum. To this curt rubric may be added the
testimony of an eighth- or ninth-century *ordo* of Corbie, according to
which at the Fraction the third particle of the Host is placed on the altar
and covered by two deacons with a corporal (*sindone munda*). This particle,
"which remains covered on the altar," is reserved for Good Friday.[97] In
another early account the Sacrament is transported from the altar at
vespers to the place of repose: "Let it be carried with veneration by a
priest and deacon with the other ministers holding a white cloth [*linteamen
mundissimum*] over it. And let this be done without consecrated wine, and
with thurible and light preceding, until it is in the place of repose; and
never let it be without a light."[98] The ceremony resembles that of the
eleventh-century *Ordo Romanus* X. It has no obvious burial connotations.
By contrast, the elaborate reservation of the *Missale mixtum* is dominated
by the idea of burial. The details are high medieval, but the form is
similar to that of the ceremonies previously cited:

> After the priest has taken Communion let him receive a clean chalice.
> And he should place in the chalice the pall with which it is covered.
> Let him reverently receive the *Corpus Christi* and place it in the chalice
> on the pall. Then let him receive another pall to cover the chalice, and
> place the paten over the chalice and a fair veil over both which should
> entirely cover the chalice. And he should hold it above his shoulders
> and thus reverently carry the Eucharist to the tomb [*monumentum*].

[97] *OR* I, p. 952[d]. The *Codex Corbiensis*, dated "before the ninth century," asserts
(*Commentarius*, p. 889[e-d]): "Sacerdos vero cum fregerit Sancta, mittat . . . tertiam in
altare . . . illud, quod remanet super altare, cooperietur a duobus diaconibus, ut-
rumque sindone munda. . . . Ipsa vero oblata, quae super altare cooperat remanserant,
serventur in crastinum juxta consuetudinem."

[98] *Ibid.*, p. 890[a] (from a missal of the bishop of Rieux, dated before the seventh
century): "diaconus cooperit Sancta de sindone super altare. . . . Et corpus Domini in
crastinum diligentissime reservetur, et dum chorus Vesperas dixerit, ubi reservari
debet, veneranter deportetur a sacerdote et diacono cum reliquis ministris linteamen
mundissimum desuper tenentibus; et hoc sine sanguine, et thuribulo [et] luminaribus
praecedentibus, usquequo reponatur ubi reponendum est, et nunquam sine lumine
remaneat." Cf. *OR* X, pp. 1012[d]-13[a].

Meanwhile the whole chorus sings *Hoc corpus quod nobis traditur* . . . , walking before the Eucharist and preceded by candles and incense. And let one boy ring a little bell. And let a veil or pall be reverently carried over the *Corpus Domini* by four or six lords from among the more noble citizens. Let one of the ministers of the church stand at the exit of the chorus throwing green branches under the feet of those carrying the *Corpus Domini*, as should happen on the next day on the return of the *Corpus Domini* from the tomb to the altar. And when the tomb is reached, let the bishop or priest ascend vested in superhumerals. . . . And when the Eucharist is placed in the tomb the bishop or priest should uncover the chalice and humbly show the consecrated Host to two of the lords. When the chalice is covered as before, it should be placed in the tomb with a cross and missal or Bible, and an unkindled thurible with incense boat and bell. Let the tomb be censed reverently with another thurible and most carefully closed with two keys and double-sealed with red sealing-wax. The lords should keep the keys and seals. And there should be a light always before the tomb [here, *sepulchro*]. When the Lord has been buried [*sepulto*] and the tomb shut, as the priest and ministers return to the altar, vespers is sounded with wooden clappers.[99]

There can be no question about this being a burial ceremony. Much of it, particularly the locking and sealing of the *monumentum*, is probably quite late. Other features—the procession, the canopy, the cross, candles, and thurible—are akin to the rite described in the tenth *Ordo*. Still others —the use of wooden clappers instead of bells, the participation of laymen, and the use of the chalice as a repository for the Host—are of uncertain date but have parallels in eighth- and ninth-century practice. The death symbolism could be early or late. It is significant, however, that the reservation of the Host is followed immediately in most *Ordines* by an act of liturgical mourning. The cross and images have been shrouded since Passion Sunday. Now the church and altar are stripped bare. Reciting the Twenty-first Psalm with its antiphon *Diviserunt sibi vestimenta mea*, the ministers remove linen, candles, veils, and ornaments.[100] The desolation of the church is now complete.

If Maundy Thursday includes ceremonies foreshadowing the death of Christ, it also commemorates the institution of the Holy Eucharist.[101] The

---

[99] *Missale mixtum*, *PL*, LXXXV, 418ᵇ–19ᵃ; *Liber officialis*, *PL*, CV, 1201ᵇ; H, II, 468–69.

[100] *OR* I, pp. 953ᵃ–62ᵈ; *Liber officialis*, *PL*, CV, 1023ᵉ; H, II, 89. For the modern service and the recitation of the Twenty-first Psalm with the antiphon *Diviserunt sibi vestimenta mea*, see Guéranger, *Liturgical Year*, VI, 353–56; Weiser, *Handbook*, p. 195.

[101] See, e.g., *Liber officialis*, *PL*, CV, 1023ᵇ; H, II, 89.

reservation ceremony, in fact, clashes with the generally positive tone of the liturgy. The alternation of joy and grief, death and the sense of new beginnings, may be intentional because it projects the agon pattern of the Easter liturgy. On the other hand, it breaks into the larger rhythm of the day, which is a movement from joy to expiation to the death symbolism of Tenebrae. Originally, there were three Masses on Maundy Thursday, devoted to the penitents, the blessing of oils, and the Mandatum, respectively.[102] By the ninth century the *Missa chrismalis* and the third Mass were often combined. Whether or not this happened, the central reading of the day is John's account of the Last Supper (13:1–15), ending with Christ's injunction, "I have given you an example, that ye should do as I have done unto you." The command (*mandatum*) gave rise to one of the most directly representational ceremonies of Holy Week, the Maundy service.

The Maundy service began with general washing of the church pavement, the altar, and the sacred vessels.[103] The Mandatum proper occurred later in the day, after the *Missa chrismalis* or (most often) in the early evening. In the latter case it followed the third Mass or was incorporated into the vesper services. It is one of the most ancient ceremonies of the Church. Pope Gregory is reputed to have performed it daily, but by the ninth century it was usually restricted to the Easter season. Originally, twelve pilgrims or poor men, arbitrarily selected, were brought to church. The priest removed his chasuble, wrapped himself in a linen cloth (sindon) or towel, and washed and kissed their feet while antiphons were sung.[104] Occasionally a meal had already begun which was interrupted for the Mandatum,[105] but usually the twelve were asked to dine with the priest in the refectory after the washing. The ceremony has penitential over-tones, but it is first and foremost an expression of Christian love. Its most famous antiphon is one of the most moving expressions in the Easter

---

[102] The three Masses do not survive in the *Liber sacramentorum* or the *Ordines Romani*, but they are preserved in the Gelasian Sacramentary, *PL*, LXXIV, 1095ᵃ–1103ᵃ.

[103] See Guéranger (*Liturgical Year*, VI, 356), who traces this part of the Mandatum to the time of Isidore.

[104] The antiphons of the Mandatum are given at the end of the *Liber responsalis*, pp. 848–50. The number of "poor men" whose feet were washed varied between twelve and thirteen. The story goes that Pope Gregory performed the Mandatum daily for twelve poor men. One day he found that he was washing the feet of thirteen men: the thirteenth was an angel. Since then the papal Mandatum has included thirteen men. In the Gallican and Milanese Churches the feet of the *electi* were washed in preparation for their baptism. It is, above all, an expression of Christian charity. For these and other curious details, see Molien, *Prière*, II, 382–85.

[105] Amalarius, *Liber officialis*, *PL*, CV, 1019ᵃ; H, II, 80.

liturgy of the idea of charity: *Ubi est caritas et dilectio, ibi sancta est congregatio, ibi nec ira est nec indignatio, sed firma caritas in perpetuum.*[106]

A circumstantial account of the Mandatum as performed in the tenth century is given in the *Regularis concordia.* There is no reason to think that the ceremony was much different one hundred years earlier, although in a secular church it would have been performed for lay folk and in public. In the *Regularis concordia* the Mandatum begins with the washing of the feet of an unspecified number of paupers by the brethren of the monastery. This act precedes the *Missa chrismalis.* After Mass the abbot performs the full ceremony for the brothers, and two senior brothers, in turn, perform it for him. A deacon then begins reading the Gospel according to John (13:1-15). Before it is completed, he is interrupted by a small bell, which is the signal for all to move to the refectory. There the Gospel reading is resumed. While it continues, the abbot drinks the health of each brother, shakes his hand, and kisses his head. After supper all repair to compline.[107]

The Mandatum may be considered the concluding ceremony of the third phase of the Easter drama. This phase begins with the sorrow of Passion Sunday and ends on the note of Christian charity. The final mood is on the whole positive. The prominence of the representational element contributes to it while bringing the events and protagonist of the Easter drama vividly before the eyes of the participants. It also separates the third phase of the liturgy from the climactic triduum beginning on Good Friday. In the Mozarabic church the rite was immediately followed by the extinction of all lights except the one burning before the *monumentum.* Amalarius indicates that his church also extinguished all candles after the Mandatum, not relighting them until the Easter vigil. Elsewhere the Tenebrae service was followed.[108]

VI

The most important expression of sorrow on Good Friday is the cessation of the daily sacrifice. It appears that this hiatus was both awesome and frightening to Christians of the ninth century. It is above all a representation of death: "The Shepherd is struck down, the sheep are scattered. The shepherds, who are the clergy, represent by their refusal of

---

[106] *LS,* pp. 849-50; Molien, *Prière,* II, 383. Amalarius also stresses the symbolism of regeneration rather than that of penance.

[107] *Regularis concordia,* ed. Symons, pp. 38-39.

[108] *Missale mixtum, PL,* LXXXV, 420ᵇ-21ᵇ; Amalarius, *De ordine antiphonarii, PL,* CV, 1292ᵉ; H, III, 79-80.

their office the quality of this period as experienced by the disciples of Christ."[109] By extension, the congregation feels the emotions of the original disciples. Etheria remarked that during the observance of Good Friday in Jerusalem "the emotion shown and the mourning by all the people . . . is wonderful; for there is none, either great or small, who, on that day, during those hours, does not lament more than can be conceived that the Lord had suffered those things for us."[110]

Christians of the ninth century were equally moved. All of the resources of the liturgy are used to inculcate the proper mood. The church is desolate, its altar bare, its images shrouded, its lights extinguished. The clergy is vested in black. As Mass begins, they lie prostrate before the altar while the members of the choir kneel with heads bowed. The bishop (or pontiff) then rises and moves silently to the episcopal throne. Without preamble a subdeacon begins reading from the Epistle ambo: "In their affliction they will seek me early. Come, and let us return unto the Lord; for he hath torn, and he will heal us" (Hos. 6:1–6).[111] Although somber, the lesson is not without hope. The imagery is that of creative suffering: the torn will be healed and the dead raised up on the third day. Its function appears to be to relate the death and Resurrection directly to the lives of the participants. Amalarius stresses this relation with a quotation from Jerome: "Today, that is, Good Friday, we commemorate the Passion in order to imitate it ourselves. . . . He not only heals but revives after two days, and, rising from Hell on the third, He revives all human kind with Him."[112] The tract, *Domine, audivi,* affirms the participation of the congregation. Its reference to the Lord *in medio duorum animalium* suggests the Crucifixion between two thieves, while the tract contrasts Judas with the thief who was saved. The second reading (Exod. 12:1–11) carries the congregation still closer to the great events of the day. It is the Lord's institution of the first Passover, the great type of Christ's sacrifice in the Old Testament. Its long tract is an almost frenzied petition for deliverance from "evil men and the unjust," who are the contemporary equivalents of the Egyptian overlord.

The reading of the Passion according to John was—and continues to be—a deeply moving experience. It resumes the motif of the earlier

---

[109] *Liber officialis, PL,* CV, 1032[b]; H, II, 107–8.

[110] *Peregrinatio,* in Duchesne, *Christian Worship,* p. 560.

[111] This is the second, not the first, according to Amalarius. A quite different effect is created by the "hours service" preserved in the *Lectionnaire de Luxeuil,* ed. Salmon, pp. 89–96.

[112] *Liber officialis, PL,* CV, 1025[a-c]; H, II, 92–93. From Jerome's commentary on Isaiah, *PL,* XXV, 867[a-b].

readings of the week, interrupted by the Maundy Thursday account of the Last Supper. Young has suggested that Christ's question in the Garden of Olives, *Quem quaeritis*, may have influenced the author of the *Quem quaeritis* play.[113] It seems more pertinent that the reading is one of the high points in the Easter drama. In it Christ emerges as the supreme instance of the Divine Victim, the "lamb led to the slaughter" of the original Passover. The agon of the preceding weeks leads with ritual inevitability to abuse, defilement, torture, and destruction, the Christian embodiment of the *spargamos* of pagan religion.[114] The historical setting of the narrative gives it a unique kind of vividness, and coincidence and dramatized chanting intensify the effect. Not surprisingly, an impulse toward representational elaboration was associated with the reading itself as early as the eighth century. The first Roman *Ordo* requires that immediately after the Gospel "two deacons remove the cloth [*sindon*] from the altar which had earlier been placed under the Gospel book. They should do this in a furtive manner."[115] Amalarius interprets this action as a commemoration of the flight of the apostles: "When the Gospel is removed, that which is under it is snatched away, because when our Lord was given over into the hands of evil men, the apostles fled and hid like thieves."[116] A more elaborate, though probably contemporary, ceremony is preserved in the *De divinis officiis* falsely attributed to Alcuin. In this ceremony two additional deacons hold sindons before the altar until the words *partiti sunt vestimenta mea* (John 19:24). They then divide them and carry them furtively away in a pantomime of the soldiers who crucified Christ.[117]

The solemn prayers of Wednesday are now repeated. Again the congregation refuses to genuflect at the prayer for the Jews. The prayers completed, all silently leave the church.

Although some ninth-century churches doubtless combined the solemn prayers with the Adoration of the Cross in a single long service resembling that of the contemporary church, the *Ordines* assume a substantial time lapse between the readings and prayers and the later devotions. The first service took place at a cathedral church and was a corporate function

---

[113] *DMC*, I, 204.

[114] For this term in relation to drama, see Gilbert Murray, "Excursus on Ritual Forms Preserved in Greek Tragedy," in Jane Harrison, *Themis* (London, 1912), pp. 342–43.

[115] *OR* I, pp. 953ᶜ–63ᵃ. Cf. *LS*, p. 86ᵇ.

[116] *Liber officialis*, PL, CV, 1026ᶜ; H, II, 96.

[117] *PL*, CI, 1208ᶜ⁻ᵈ. Whether there was a pause and prostration after the *tradidit spiritum*, and a silent prayer at the altar after *Videbunt in quem transfixerunt*, as in the contemporary service, is not clear. The two actions involving the sindon appear conflated in *Regularis concordia*, ed. Symons, p. 42.

presided over by a bishop. The second took place in the evening at parish churches and was private in the sense that it did not require the participation of all ranks of the clergy. It began with a repetition of the solemn prayers and ended with the Adoration of the Cross. The evening service appears to have had both a cathartic and a didactic function. It allowed for expression of the climax of doubt, fear, and mortification reached on Good Friday, and by placing the *simpliciores* at the foot of the Cross with the Jews and holy women, it acquainted them with the brutal realities of the Crucifixion. Amalarius stresses the usefulness of this physical imitation: "On the day when the cross is kissed, Christ humbled himself for us to the Father, even unto death. If we would be imitators of His death, we should also endure His humiliation. Therefore we prostrate ourselves before the cross that our fixed humility of mind may be shown through physical gesture. We cannot better express humiliation than by prostrating the whole body on the ground."[118]

The adoration rite, imported from Jerusalem, was well developed by the fourth century, as the circumstantial account in the *Peregrinatio Etheriae* demonstrates.[119] By the seventh century it was a regular part of Roman usage.[120] The station for the day, Santa Croce in Gerusalemme, is chosen explicitly for the ceremony—a reminder of the tendency of the principle of coincidence to operate in terms of space as well as time. In the course of the Adoration marked representational elements appear. The cross ceases to be a simple object of meditation. It is treated as the original Cross, and two deacons, standing in the darkness behind it, supply reproaches (*improperia*) understood to be spoken by Christ himself. Meanwhile priest and choir reply in the manner of a tragic chorus.

The *improperia* are extremely ancient. They came into general use between the ninth and tenth centuries.[121] Following the order of Abbot Ratold of Corbie, we learn that in the evening after solemn prayers two deacons enter the sanctuary or conceal themselves behind the altar. They begin with a bitter refrain which introduces each of Christ's speeches:

---

[118] *Liber officialis, PL*, CV, 1028[d]; H, II, 100. Cf. Rabanus Maurus, *De clericorum institutione, PL*, CVII, 349[e]. The German ceremony of "creeping the cross" (*zum Kreuze kriechen*) is cited by Weiser, *Handbook*, p. 108. The almost hysterical prayers for indulgence of the Mozarabic rite give a good idea of the emotional effect of the day's events. See *Missale mixtum, PL*, LXXV, 428[d]-30[a].

[119] Text given in Duchesne, *Christian Worship*, pp. 558–59.

[120] The antiphon and the *Pange lingua* are in the *Liber antiphonarius*, pp. 676[c]–77[b]. See also *LS*, p. 86[b-c]; *OR* I, p. 954[a]; etc.

[121] Molien, *Prière*, II, 392–98, summarizes the whole rite. See esp. p. 397; also, Guéranger, *Liturgical Year*, VI, 438–46. The *improperia* are part of the *Regularis concordia* service (*ca.* 970) (*Regularis concordia*, ed. Symons, p. 42).

Popule meus, quid feci tibi? The lament continues with a reference to Christ's deliverance of the Hebrews: . . . *Quia eduxi te de terra Aegypti, parasti crucem Salvatori tuo.* Meanwhile two priests stand by the altar holding the shrouded cross. When the first *improperium* is completed, they reply with the holiest of all Greek prayers, the Trisagion:

> PRESBYTER: *Agios o Theos.*
> CHORUS: *Sanctus Deus.*
> PRESBYTER: *Agios ischyros.*
> CHORUS: *Sanctus fortis.*
> PRESBYTER: *Agios athanatos, eleison imas.*
> CHORUS: *Sanctus immortalis, miserere nobis.*

The cross is now carried forward and the second *improperium*, also an allusion to Exodus, is begun: *Quia eduxi te per desertum quadraginta annis.* . . . Again the Trisagion is chanted in reply and the cross advanced. After the third *improperium*, the cross is advanced again, its shroud is removed, and it is elevated while the *Ecce lignum crucis* is sung. Although the *Codex Ratoldus* is not specific, the remaining *improperia* must have followed. During this time the pontiff or bishop and the priests come forward individually, abase themselves three times before the cross, and kiss it.[122]

The first part of the Adoration is extremely somber. The reproaches of the dying Christ are directed to clergy and congregation alike. The dramatic setting makes the death motif extremely powerful—for many, perhaps, close to unbearable.

The second part of the Adoration, which is older than the first, provides some relief. If the *improperia* are not sung, in fact, the major emphasis falls not on death but on victory. The *Liber antiphonarius* shows that essentially the same texts were used in the ninth century as today. First the cross is placed before the altar on a table or other support by two acolytes.[123] An antiphon glorifying the cross is begun: *Crucem tuam adoremus, Domine, et sanctam resurrectionem tuam laudamus.* It is chanted with Psalm 66, *Deus misereatur nostri.* Only then does the chorus sing the invitation, *Ecce lignum crucis, in quo salus mundi perpendit. Venite adoremus.* Evidently the congregation began to come forward at this point. The antiphons that follow interpolate an extremely realistic word picture of the Crucifixion between the introductory chant and the concluding *Pange lingua.* They appear designed to assist the imagination and thus to intensify the people's sense of being present at the historical event. While he moved forward in the

---

[122] *LS Notae*, p. 332[d], quoted from the *ordo* of Abbot Ratold of Corbie.
[123] *LS*, p. 86[b] and note: *OR* I, p. 963[b].

darkened church to kiss the wood which supported his Savior, the ninth-century Christian heard the following chants:

ANTIPHON: While the Creator of the world was suffering death on the Cross, crying in a loud voice He gave up the spirit: and the veil of the temple was sundered, the tombs were opened, and there was a great earthquake, for the world cried that it could not endure the death of the Son of God.

VERSICLE: And when the lance of the soldier opened the side of the crucified Lord, blood and water flowed to redeem our health.

VERSICLE: O wonderful ransom, by whose weight the captivity of the world has been redeemed, the infernal prisons of hell broken open, and the doors of the Kingdom opened to us.[124]

In the last versicle of this chant there is a further lightening of tone. It leads to the last text of the adoration ceremony, the *Pange lingua* of Fortunatus.[125] Here the agon is described as an heroic victory:

> Sing, my tongue, the strife
> Of the glorious conflict;
> And over the trophy of the Cross,
> Sing a noble song of triumph:
> How the Redeemer of the world
> Conquered through death.

The sequence which began on the theme of mortification culminates in one of the great paradoxes of Christian victory: the emblem of shame has become a symbol of glory; defeat has become triumph; the helpless Victim has become a conqueror by dying. The hymn plays on these subjects, returning to them, weaving them into a pattern of contrasts:

> Here the vinegar, the gall,
> The spittle, the nails, the spear:
> His tender body is pierced;
> Water and blood flow forth.
> With this river are cleansed
> The earth, the sea, the stars, the world.

---

[124] *LA*, p. 676ᵉ.

[125] *Ibid.*, pp. 676ᵈ–77ᵇ. The refrain stanzas (*Crux fidelis*) are not included; evidently they were not sung at this time. For a survey of the question of whether the hymn should be ascribed to Fortunatus or Claudianus Mamertus, see Raby, *Christian Latin Poetry*, pp. 90–91. The modern text is given by Raby and in the *Analecta hymnica*, L, 73.

Bend your branches, lofty tree;
Relax your fibers . . .

Everywhere be glory and honor
To God, the Most High:
Equally to the Father and Son
And glorious Paraclete—
To whom praise and honor
Through everlasting ages.

In Roman usage the Mass of the Presanctified follows without interruption. While the Adoration is still in progress, two priests enter the sacristy where the Host has been reserved. They place it on a paten which is carried, together with a chalice of unconsecrated wine, to the bare altar. Because of the mournfulness of the occasion, glass vessels are used. The Pater Noster and embolism are recited, the Host is commingled with the wine, and all (in later times, the priest only) communicate.[126] In the words of the Gregorian Sacramentary, *expleta sunt omnia.* The year has reached nadir.

VII

Two embellishments of the Mass of the Presanctified are of interest to students of the drama. The first is the procession to the altar with the presanctified Host. There is not much information from the ninth century about this procession. For one thing, the Mass was not celebrated everywhere. For another, the procession that restores the Host to the altar has connotations which harmonize poorly with the events commemorated on Good Friday. This may be illustrated by the elaborate procession called for by the *Missale mixtum:*

while the clergy and the people adore the cross, let the priest with his ministers descend to the sacristy and put on their shoes. The priest should take a black chasuble and the deacon and subdeacon black dalmatics. Let them come to the entrance of the great choir preceded by candles and a thurible. When the cross has been adored by the chorus and the people, the two priests who held the cross should reverently take it from the table with its cloth and carry it to the middle of the altar singing the antiphon *Super omnia ligna cedorum tu sola excel-*

---

[126] These and other details in Molien, *Prière*, II, 400–2; Weiser, *Handbook*, pp. 199–200; Guéranger, *Liturgical Year*, VI, 447–51. Also, *LS Notae*, pp. 890 c–903 b. The detail of the glass vessel is found in the *Regula magistri, PL*, LXXXVIII, 1016 a: "Sacramenta vero in altaris in patena majore vitrea finiantur."

sior. . . . At the end they should place it reverently on the altar. Then
priests and ministers, chorus and people form in a silent procession.
Let the priests go first with a second black [covered?] cross and a candle
and a burning thurible. Let them proceed to the tomb [*monumentum*],
and on arrival let the priest ascend with the two lords who kept the keys
and seals . . . and when the tomb [*sepulcro*] is opened, let the priest take
some of the incense from within and place it in the thurible and
immediately cense the *Corpus Domini*. Then let him uncover the cup and
show the consecrated Host secretly and humbly to the aforesaid lords
with its veil, as he carried it the day before. And with the ministers—
that is, the deacon and subdeacon—assisting and the others supporting
him, let him proceed gently and carefully with the *Corpus Domini*. And
the aforementioned silk veil is carried by four or six noble lords of the
city over the *Corpus Domini*, always preceded by the cross, candles,
thurible, and incense, while green branches are strewn before as
mentioned earlier [in the Maundy Thursday rite]. And let a sexton
dressed in a white superhumeral carry a black banner in the middle of
the procession; that is, between the canons and sextons. And in this
order let them proceed to the high altar. On arrival let the deacon
expand his corporal over the altar and the priest with extreme reverence
place the Corpus Christi with its chalice on the altar. This done, let him
descend to the steps of the altar and there make confession. Then let
him reascend and wash his hands. Next let him take the Corpus Christi
reverently from the chalice. . . . The Pater Noster is to be said and at
the words *panem nostrum quotidianum* let him show the people the Corpus
Christi in its place on the altar.[127]

In this mélange of details, some of them patently late and others,
perhaps, quite early, a general outline of the "Return of the Host" in a
secular service can be discerned. The silent procession, the use of simple
liturgical objects (chalice, cross, thurible, etc.), and the lay participation
are all compatible with ninth-century practice. The black banner is a
curiosity, probably undatable, while the suggestion of many altars, the
elaborate *monumentum*, and the use of keys and seals to protect the host are
high medieval, the latter probably a by-product of the obsessive fear of
Jewish desecration of the Sacrament. More interesting are the inconsistencies between the imagery of death dominating Good Friday as a
whole and the rebirth symbolism of any return from a *sepulcrum*, especially
a return preceded by green branches and involving a minister in white
vestments. Whether emphasized or not, some sort of return ceremony is

---

[127] *Missale mixtum, PL,* LXXXV, 432 ᶜ–35 ᵃ. Also, *LS Notae,* pp. 431–34. Compare the
ordo from the monastery of Prüfening, reprinted by Young, *DMC,* I, 159–60. The
symbolism is identical, but the *ordo* is for Easter, not Good Friday.

necessitated by the Mass of the Presanctified. On the other hand, the Mass of the Presanctified was a relatively late institution and was not universal even in the ninth century. Earlier practice would require reservation of the Host as fermentum or sancta on Saturday, Palm Sunday, or Maundy Thursday, and its "return" at the first Mass of Easter, the vigil Mass. In this case, the rebirth connotations of the ceremony would obviously be appropriate.

Testimony from the middle of the tenth century indicates the existence of a second, less incongruous ceremony deriving from the day's liturgy. This is a burial service involving the Host, the cross, or both. It may be indigenous to Good Friday, since it coincides with the death of Christ. On the other hand, it is something of a liturgical anomaly. In its earliest form it requires that the Host be reserved on Maundy Thursday, returned on Good Friday, reserved again after the Mass of the Presanctified, and finally returned on Easter. This is neither efficient nor particularly elegant. When we recall the late origin and irregular diffusion of the Mass of the Presanctified, the possibility occurs that the return and burial of Good Friday are makeshifts, and that in its pure form the sequence required one burial on Maundy Thursday and one return during the first Mass of Easter. At any rate, the earliest description of the Good Friday burial is found in a tenth-century life of St. Ulrich. It describes what was apparently a traditional practice of the Cathedral of Augsburg around 950:

On Good Friday . . . early in the morning, he hastened to complete the Psalm service; and, when the holy mystery of God was completed, the people fed with the holy Corpus Christi, and the remainder buried [sepulto] in the customary manner, he finished the Psalm service while walking from church to church. . . . When the most delectable day of Easter arrived, he entered the church of St. Ambrose after prime, where he had placed the Corpus Christi on Good Friday, covering it with a stone. And there with a few clerks he celebrated the Mass of the Holy Trinity. When the Mass was completed, he took the Corpus Christi and the Gospels with him, along with candles and incense. And, with an appropriate chant of greeting sung at the porch by the boys' choir, he proceeded to the church of St. John the Baptist.[128]

Apart from its duplication of the Maundy Thursday reservation, the Augsburg ceremony is quite appropriate. It is emphatically a burial, and

[128] Translated from the version in Young, *DMC*, I, 553. See also Brooks, *The Sepulchre of Christ*, pp. 32–33. J. N. Dalton (*The Collegiate Church of Ottery St. Mary* [Cambridge, 1917], pp. 252–53) expresses the belief that the *Depositio* was practiced as early as the seventh century.

it follows the Mass representing the death of Christ. The phrase "customary manner" (*consuetudinario more*) indicates that the ceremony was traditional, which probably means that it had been followed for at least fifty years. Furthermore, it is rather elaborate, with highly developed representational elements. The Host is interred in a receptacle with a rock covering it in imitation of the tomb of Christ. Quite possibly, the Gospels and a thurible are also interred, in the manner of the Mozarabic Maundy Thursday reservation. On Easter there is a quite splendid procession to the church of St. John (the Roman station for the Easter vigil) with some sort of welcoming chant (*congrua salutatione versuum*) at the church door. This could be the Easter Introit (*Resurrexi et adhuc tecum*); it could even be something like the *Quem quaeritis* play. Most probably, however, it would be the *Tollite portas* dialogue or an antiphon such as the *Cum rex gloriae*, since these are associated in later medieval texts with the "Elevation of the Host."[129]

Another deposition ceremony, perhaps a variant, occurs between the Adoration and the Mass of the Presanctified. Like the "Burial of the Host" the "Deposition of the Cross" commemorates the entombment. Its genesis is obvious. The congregation has stood at the foot of the Cross, listened to Christ's *improperia*, and kissed its base. It now assists at the last rites. Later, usually before matins on Easter morning, the cross is "elevated" in a Resurrection ceremony. The earliest circumstantial account of such a "deposition" is that in the *Regularis concordia*, where it is adapted to monastic use. Its alternate use of *sacerdos* and *abbas* to refer to the celebrant and its allusion to neophytes suggest that it derives from a secular *ordo:*

> since on [Good Friday] we solemnize the burial of the body of our Savior, if anyone should care or think it fit to follow in a becoming manner certain religious men in a practice worthy to be imitated for the strengthening of the faith of unlearned common persons and neophytes, we have decreed this only: on that part of the altar where there is space for it there shall be a representation, as it were, of a sepulchre, hung about with a curtain, in which the Holy Cross, when it has been venerated, shall be placed in the following manner: the deacons who carried the cross shall come forward and, having wrapped the cross in a napkin [sindon] there where it was venerated, they shall bear it thence, singing the antiphons *Habebit* and *Caro mea requiescat in spe*, to the place of the sepulchre. When they have laid the cross therein, in imitation as it were of the burial of the Body of our Lord Jesus Christ, they shall sing the antiphon *Sepulto Domino, signatum est monumentum, ponentes milites qui custodirent eum*. In that same place the Holy Cross shall

[129] Brooks, *The Sepulchre of Christ*, pp. 42–43.

be guarded with all reverence until the night of the Lord's Resurrection [*usque dominicam noctem Resurrectionis*]. And during the night let brethren be chosen by twos and threes, if the community be large enough, who shall keep faithful watch, chanting psalms.

When this has been done the deacon and subdeacon shall come forth from the sacristy with the Body of the Lord, left over from the previous day, and a chalice with unconsecrated wine, which they shall place on the altar. Then the Priest [*sacerdos*] shall come before the altar and shall sing in a clear voice *Oremus. Praeceptis salutaribus moniti*, the *Pater noster* and *Libera nos quaesimus, Domine* up to *Per omnia saecula saeculorum. Amen.* And the abbot [*abbas*] shall take a portion of the holy sacrifice and shall place it in the chalice saying nothing; and all shall communicate in silence.[130]

This harmonizes well with the historical associations and tone of Good Friday. Nothing is said of a procession for the return of the presanctified Host to the altar. The task is performed unobtrusively by a deacon and subdeacon while the Adoration is still in progress. The omission of the Host from the burial is explained by the fact that it takes place before Communion has been celebrated. The existence of ceremonies involving cross and Host together can be explained in two ways. There may have been two independent ceremonies which merged because of their common burial symbolism and the fact that both cross and Host are surrogates for Christ. On the other hand, the Burial of the Host may have been the original and the Deposition of the Cross a construction by analogy or a substitute designed to meet complaints that the consecrated Host, being the living Christ, cannot be "buried."[131]

The first day of the triduum ends shortly after the burial-deposition. In many cases the ninth-century church would already be dark, bare, and deserted. In others, Tenebrae would follow. The extinction of lights completes the death symbolism. For the moment, and despite the *Pange lingua*, the *adversarius* appears to have triumphed. The literal agony of the Crucifixion is replaced by a mood of quiet mourning, almost a suspension of feeling. A peculiar stasis prevails while the Church waits for the turning point—the peripeteia—of the Easter drama.

---

130 *Regularis concordia*, ed. Symons, pp. 44–45.
131 See Young, *DMC*, I, 131–32.

ESSAY IV

Christus Victor:
From Holy Saturday to Low Sunday

I

THE LAST AND most crucial phase of the Easter drama occurred during the ninth century on Easter Eve. It commemorates the Resurrection, which is also commemorated, according to the allegorists, at every Mass at the commingling of the Host and wine. Structurally, it is a peripeteia, a reversal causing the action "to veer around in the opposite direction," to use the definition in the *Poetics*. Such reversals are characteristic of religious ritual. They are always miraculously generated, for if they were explained causally, they would no longer be manifestations of divine but of human or natural agency. Frazer and his followers have shown that they are closely related to the cycle of the seasons, and most often to the seasonal transition from winter to spring. They involve rebirth or resurrection and tend to symbolize the renewal not merely of the god but of the whole of creation. Without exception they involve an emotional transition from *tristia* to *gaudium*, or, to use Gilbert Murray's term, "theophany." The latter is dominated by a sense of fulfillment projected in action through reaffirmation of community and in imagery through emphasis on natural and human fertility and the emotion of love, features that are dimly echoed in the convention of ending comedies with reconciliations and marriages. The Christian drama of renewal utilizes these elements. Because early theologians regarded the atonement as a dramatic victory of Christ over Satan, its emphasis on heroic imagery is particularly strong. The fact helps explain the prominence given by the liturgy to the apocryphal legend of the Harrowing of Hell.

What is most unique, however, about the Christian drama of renewal is the richness and brilliance of its articulation. A dramatic reversal is an instantaneous event. It is made effective by what precedes and what follows. The mode of presentation of what may be called the agon and theophany phases of the drama determines whether the peripeteia will be experienced as an event of cosmic significance or merely accepted as the repetition of a necessary but personally irrelevant form.

The Christian liturgy extends the agon phase of the drama backward from its peripeteia some nine weeks to Septuagesima Sunday. One way of solving the problem of making a peripeteia effective, the simple way, is by straightforward contrast. One emotional tone is established before the moment of reversal, and the opposite tone follows it. In fact, modern Catholic practice is based on the method of contrast. Lent is regarded as a time of penance. The faithful must devote themselves to fasting, self-examination, and contrition, and the penitential elements of the liturgy—alienation, defilement, lamentation, and death—are stressed. On Easter Sunday the Lenten mood is abruptly and somewhat arbitrarily replaced by personal and liturgical rejoicing.

The ninth-century solution, which still exists in vestigial form in the modern liturgy, is more dramatic. Penitential themes are prominent and even gain in intensity during Lent, but they are juxtaposed with the theme of redemption associated with the catechumens. The two elements clash with one another, creating antitheses which are the analogues of spiritual agon. At first the agon is generalized; later, as the climax approaches, it attaches itself to the quasi-historical figures of the *adversarius* and the Divine Victim. Additional articulation is provided by the rhythmic ebb and flow of the agon. Septuagesima begins with *gemitus mortis* (groans of death) and ends with a feeling of confidence in God's protection. Quadragesima begins with the dismissal of penitents—*memento homo quia pulvis es et in pulveri reverteris*—and ends with the joyous mood of Laetare Sunday. Passiontide begins with anticipations of the Passion and an act of liturgical mourning—the shrouding of the images—and ends with the reconciliation of penitents, the festive blessing of holy oils, and the Maundy service.

The triduum repeats the pattern of movement from death to life, sorrow to rejoicing, and leads naturally to the theophany of the Easter octave. Good Friday is the culminating liturgical expression of the death theme. Christ's torn and bleeding body hangs from the Cross, while the Christian community lies prostrate before it. Now the chief object of the liturgy must be to express rebirth as effectively as death. This is extremely difficult. Death is a universal and deeply felt phenomenon. It can be dramatized by the use of any number of techniques—action and pantomime, narrative, lyric, changes of setting, repeated images, and the like. On the other hand, resurrection is entirely outside the normal pattern of history. Pantomime and physical images in which Christ is shown literally rising from the tomb are awkward and risk cheapening the event. Although the later Middle Ages used such devices, the earlier solution was to imply rather than state directly. Early pictures of the Resurrection, as well as the *Quem quaeritis* play itself, symbolize the Resurrection in terms of the visit to the tomb by the holy women. It is the emptiness of the tomb rather than the animated body of the Savior which conveys the idea of resurrection.

Placing major emphasis on nonrepresentational modes, the early Christian liturgy solved the problem of making the Resurrection as vivid as the Crucifixion through the ceremonies of Holy Saturday. These form an ordered sequence foreshadowing the Resurrection. In them the emotion of joy becomes increasingly pronounced, and images of "death changed to life" are increasingly prominent. The office of lauds initiates the sequence. It hints of a victory already gained in the eschatological world—the Harrowing of Hell—and contrasts this victory with continued sorrow in the human world. Lauds is followed by the seventh and final scrutiny of the catechumens. Later in the day the vigil service begins with the lighting of the new fire and continues with the blessing of the paschal candle, baptism, and the illumination of the church. In each of these ceremonies physical symbols and actions reinforce the liturgical texts. The vigil service culminates some time after midnight with the celebration of Mass. During Mass, symbol gives way to reality: the real presence of Christ returns again to the altar. The peripeteia of the ninth-century Easter drama has been completed.

In the tenth century and later, coincidence between the vigil Mass and the historical Resurrection was gradually lost. The vigil Mass was celebrated on Saturday evening, then in the afternoon, and eventually at the unlikely time of Saturday morning. When this occurred the dramatic emphasis shifted from the Mass to the only other ceremony that could be thought coincident with the Resurrection—Easter matins. The arrangement remained, however, an awkward compromise. It was based on symbolic commemoration rather than the action (praxis) which occurs at the commingling of consecrated bread and wine. That dramatic form is not relative—that it exists independent of cultural conditioning—is strikingly illustrated by the fact that in 1955 the Church decreed the restoration of the vigil Mass to its original position.

II

Lauds begins on Holy Saturday with the chant *Miserere* (Ps. 50). The Psalm lament is modified by the antiphon, *O mors ero mors tua: morsus tuus ero inferne.* The words prophesy the Harrowing of Hell. Their word play is serious and reflects the paradox of Christian peripeteia. The Easter Resurrection antiphon *Christus resurgens* will repeat them: *Christus resurgens ex mortuis iam non moritur: mors illi ultra non dominabitur.* Their force persists undiminished in Donne's familiar line, "Death shall be no more; death, thou shalt die." The reading which follows (Isa. 58) presents, according to allegorical exegesis, "a figure of Christ in his tomb, beseeching his Father to give him a speedy resurrection to life."[1] It also touches again on the theme of the Harrowing of Hell. The *Canticum triumphale*, a favorite antiphon of Easter, will return to this theme: *Cum rex gloriae Christus infernum debellaturus intraret.*[2] Still more pertinent, the Gregorian texts for Easter stress it. The Offertory for the Easter Mass celebrates the peace established in Sion by the "breaking" of powers, forts, shields, swords, and wars: *Et factus est in pace locus ejus. . . . Ideo confregit potentias, arcum, scutum, gladium, et bellum; illuminans tu mirabiliter a montibus aeternis, alleluia.*[3]

Although these heroic ideas are not elaborated in the lauds service, there is a noticeably positive tone in the chants following the passage from Isaiah. The antiphon of the reading is a prayer for deliverance from hell: *A porta inferii, erue, Domine, animam meam.* There follows a joyous hymn of praise, *Laudate Dominum* (Ps. 150). The mood now changes as the office turns from the triumph of Christ over the kingdom of hell to the sorrow of the holy women still keeping vigil before the tomb: *Mulieres sedentem ad monumentum lamentabantur, flentes Dominum.*

It does not seem fanciful to read into this sequence a contrast between eschatological and human history. In terms of the former, Christ has

---

[1] Guéranger, *Liturgical Year*, VI, 489.

[2] Reprinted in Young, *DMC*, I, 151. For Augustine's sermon, see *PL*, XXXIX, 2059–61. For additional discussion of the Harrowing of Hell, see Cabrol and Leclercq, "Descente du Christ aux enfers," *DACL*, IV, 1, 690–91; Young, *DMC*, I, 149–77; and Young's monograph, "The Harrowing of Hell in Liturgical Drama," in *Transactions of the Wisconsin Academy of Sciences, Arts, and Letters*, XVI (1909), 889–947.

[3] *LA*, p. 678[c]. For other allusions to the Harrowing of Hell, see *LR*, p. 768[b], and the Gregorian Preface for the vigil Mass.

Compare the Easter hymn, *Ad coenam agni:*

> O vere digna Hostia
> per quem fracta sunt tartara,
> redempta plebs captivata
> redit ad vitae praemia.
>
> Cum surgit Christus tumulo
> victor redit de barathro,
> tyrannum trudens vinculo,
> et reserans paradisum.

Text in *Analecta hymnica*, II, 46. The hymn appears to be a Communion hymn for the vigil service. See Essay III, n. 19. The passages in the hymn derived from Paul, I Cor. 5 (*Fratres, expurgate vetus fermentum*, etc.), would appear at first to associate it with the Mass of Easter Day, when the passage from Paul is read as the Epistle. However, the passage was also associated with the vigil service. It is used, for example, in the Preface to the vigil Mass in the Gelasian Sacramentary.

already achieved His victory over the *adversarius*. The souls released from hell sing *Laudate Dominum*. In terms of earthly history, however, Christ is still dead. The holy women remain bowed in sorrow before the tomb: *lamentabantur, flentes Dominum*. The office ends with a prayer for human salvation.

The hint of joy in the lauds service carries over into two other morning ceremonies. The seventh scrutiny of the catechumens was usually held on Saturday after *hora tertia*. The candidates and sponsors are assembled by roll call, as on previous scrutiny days. The bishop or priest signs them with a cross and again exorcises them. If the ceremony has not already been performed during the third scrutiny, he touches their ears and noses with spittle, commanding, *Ephpheta* ("Be opened!"), and adding the exorcism *Tu autem effugare, diabole, appropinquabit enim judicium Dei*. The familiar renunciation of Satan and all his works comes next. After each interrogation the priest (not the acolyte or deacon as on previous exorcisms) signs the chest and back of the catechumen with a cross of baptismal oil as a protection against evil. These rites completed, the formal "return" (*redditio*) of the Creed and Lord's Prayer occurs. With the priest's hand on his head, each catechumen gives a public recitation of both texts. The catechumens are now ready for baptism. As they are dismissed, the deacon proclaims *Filii charissimi, revertimini in locis vestris, expectantes horam qua possit circa vos Dei gratia baptismum operari*.[4]

The progress of the catechumens toward their own regeneration hints of the larger regeneration to follow. The exorcism and rejection of the devil, the protective crossings with baptismal oil (the shield of the Christian soldier) invert the imagery of defeat at the hands of the *adversarius*. A second morning ceremony, peculiar to Rome, has the effect of bringing Christ himself before the eyes of the people. The archdeacon of Rome customarily prepared "paschal lambs" (*agni paschali*) from oil, wax, and incense. The lambs were blessed and reserved for distribution to the faithful on the Sunday after Easter. Like the crosses of baptismal oil, they represented the benign powers of Christ, for they were used to purify houses and cure the sick. Both iconographic tradition and the uses to

---

[4] This sequence is reconstructed chiefly on the basis of the Gelasian Sacramentary, *PL*, LXXIV, 1105[d]–6[e], and the seventh Roman *Ordo*, *PL*, LXXVIII, 998[e-d], 999[a]. See also *OR* I, pp. 954[e]–55[b]. In several instances the seventh scrutiny is found combined with the vigil service. This was evidently the custom of the Spanish Church and the Church of Milan (Duchesne, *Christian Worship*, p. 318). Amalarius regarded the seventh scrutiny as part of the vigil service: *Liber officialis* (*PL*, CV, 1040[e]–41[d]; H, II, 125–28) and *OR* X (p. 1015[b]) employ this form, evidently because the increase in infant candidates for baptism made the morning scrutiny unnecessary. For comment, see Molien, *Prière*, II, 403–4.

which the lambs were put show that they were emblems of creative sacrifice. The death symbolism of the mangled body of Good Friday is transformed in the image of the Agnus Dei, whose fragrance wards off evil and whose touch can heal the sick. It is, Amalarius comments, "the immaculate Lamb made for us. . . . When we see the lamb of wax, we recall the lamb of prophecy sacrificed [for us] on Easter."[5]

The Easter vigil, "mother of all holy vigils" according to Augustine,[6] is the most splendid and one of the oldest services of the Church year. Originally it began at midnight and continued until dawn on Easter.[7] Early Christians believed that the Second Coming would occur at midnight on Holy Saturday to coincide with the early hours of Easter.[8] The possibility of the Second Coming made watching until after midnight imperative. After midnight the sense of reprieve combined with the desire to celebrate the Resurrection to produce the vigil Mass. As we have noticed, after the fifth century parts of the vigil service began to be performed in the early evening (or even the afternoon) of Holy Saturday. A comparison of the *Ordines Romani*, the *Liber sacramentorum*, and the *Liber officialis* indicates that in the Carolingian Empire during the ninth century the vigil began in the afternoon after *hora nona* and continued until midnight or shortly thereafter, when the vigil Mass was celebrated. Amalarius notes that Pope Innocent explicitly forbade Mass on Holy Saturday. He goes on to quote both Augustine and Jerome to show that the vigil should extend beyond midnight, and he appears to consider this arrangement the conventional one.[9]

[5] For the ceremony see *OR* I, p. 960[d], and *LS Notae*, p. 338[a-b]. For Amalarius' observations, see *Liber officialis*, *PL*, CV, 1033[c]; H, II, 110.

[6] Sermon 219, *PL*, XXXVIII, 1088.

[7] Weller, *The Easter Sermons of St. Augustine*, pp. 39–73, summarizes the early rite in detail.

[8] The practice of beginning at midnight persisted until the sixth century; e.g., *Lectionnaire de Luxeuil*, ed. Salmon, p. 97. The *Liber sacramentorum* has "hora octava" and the early *Ordines Romani*, "hora nona."

Jerome, "Commentary on Matthew," IV, xxv (*PL*, XXVI, 184): "Traditio judaeorum est Christum media nocte venturum in similitudinem Aegyptii temporis, quando pascha celebratum est et exterminator venit et dominus super tabernacula transiit et sanguine agni postes nostrarum frontium conservati sunt. Unde reor et traditionem apostolicam permansisse ut in die vigiliarum paschae ante noctis dimidium populos dimittere non liceat expectantes adventum Christi. Et postquam illud tempus transierit, securitate praesumpta festum cuncti agunt diem." Also Lactantius, *Divinarum institutionum*, VII, xix (*CSEL*, XIX, 644): "Haec est nox, quae a nobis propter adventum regis ac dei nostri pervigilio celebratur: cujus noctis duplex ratio est, quod in ea et vitam tum recepit, cum passus est, et postea regnum orbis terrae recepturus est."

[9] Ninth-century thought is best reflected in Amalarius' insistence that Mass must follow the vigil service but cannot be on Holy Saturday. *Liber officialis* (*PL*, CV, 1032[d]; H, II, 108–9) asserts that on Holy Saturday "hodie non celebrari missam," and con-

Light is the most important physical symbol of the Easter vigil. In the fourth century a brilliant illumination of houses, streets, and churches occurred at nightfall and lasted until dawn. In Milan in the year 331 this "transformed the night of the sacred vigil into the brilliance of day," according to Eusebius.[10] The collect of the Easter Mass addresses God as One "who makes the night radiant" (*qui hanc sacratissimam noctem gloria dominicae Resurrectionis illustras*), and the light theme recurs in the final benediction. Likewise the *Exsultet*, dated around the eighth century, refers to Easter as "holy service of light" (*sacrum lucinarium*), "night of radiance" (*irradiata fulgoribus*), and "this luminous night" (*luminosa haec nox*).[11] Folk custom contributed something to this symbolism; during the ninth century in Ireland and France bonfires blazed on the hillsides from dusk until dawn.[12]

The uses of light in the ninth-century liturgy are more complex than they appear to have been in, say, the fourth century. Most forms of the vigil service begin with the new fire. Archdeacon Theodore informed Amalarius that in Rome the new fire was kindled on Good Friday and brought from a place of seclusion on the afternoon of Holy Saturday.[13] More commonly, it was rekindled on Maundy Thursday, Good Friday, and Holy Saturday, each time with more solemnity, or, alternatively, kindled for the first time just before the vigil service began. In either case the kindling was performed outside of the church or in the sacristy and

---

tinues, "Vigiliae agendae sunt in nocte, ex auctoritate Patrum recolimus. . . . Quod die tertio resurrexit a mortuis Dominus Christus, nullus ambigit Christianis. Haec autem nocte hoc factum esse, sanctum evangelium contestatur." The comment cites the decretals of Pope Innocent I for confirmation (*PL*, LXVII, 239 ᶜ–40 ᵃ). Since Amalarius follows the *Ordines Romani* in assuming that the vigil will begin around *hora nona*—i.e., 3:00 P.M.—we may accept Guéranger's schedule of the events of the day (*Liturgical Year*, VI, 569): "The Vigil began about the hour of None and continued, as we have seen, till early on Sunday morning."

[10] *Life of Constantine, PL*, VIII, 75.

[11] Text in Guéranger, *Liturgical Year*, VI, 506–10.

[12] Weiser, *Handbook*, p. 216. These are Christian adaptations of pagan rituals.

[13] The usual explanation of the discrepancies between the practice followed by Amalarius and that followed in Rome is that at the time of Pope Gregory the new fire was kindled on Maundy Thursday and used on Good Friday and Holy Saturday to light the candles extinguished at Tenebrae. Then, in the middle of the ninth century, "the custom of procuring new fire every day from a flint was extended also to Holy Saturday" (Guéranger, *Liturgical Year*, VI, 499). However, Amalarius discovered from Archdeacon Theodore of Rome that new fire was kindled on Good Friday: "In feria sexta nullum lumen habetur lampadum sive cereorum. . . . sed tamen in ipsa die novus ignis accenditur, de quo reservatur usque ad nocturnale officium" (Amalarius, *De ordine antiphonarii, PL*, CV, 1292 ᶜ; H, III, 79–80).

by a bishop.[14] A hint of creation symbolism is conveyed by the fact that it must be created by "natural" means, by the rubbing of flint on stone or by using a burning glass.[15] The blessing identifies the flame with both Christ and the "heavenly desires" (*coelestibus desideriis*) kindled in man by the paschal feast. This is followed by the first of several references to Exodus, the Old Testament type of baptism: *sicut illuminasti Moysen exeuntem de Aegypto, ita illumines corda et sensus nostros; ut ad vitam et lucem aeternam pervenire mereamur.*[16]

The new fire is used immediately to light a candle. The Roman *Ordines* require a procession into the church, where a second candle is lighted. In the sixth century the service continued with readings and the baptismal ceremonies. By the ninth century, however, Rome had thoroughly assimilated the texts and rites associated with the paschal candle. The first candle was thereafter regarded as a means of transporting the new fire from the church door to the paschal candle proper. This is in keeping with the fact that the paschal candle was, even in the eighth century, extremely large. The early *Ordines* describe it as "of human stature," and during the high Middle Ages it grew to enormous dimensions, sometimes standing as high as thirty feet.[17] As the words of the blessing make plain, the paschal candle is a Christ symbol. Amalarius accepts the symbolism but regards the first candle as the paschal candle and the second as "the light of the apostles, derived from Christ," a view based less on intrinsic symbolism than on the differing ceremonies of the Roman and Gallican Churches.[18]

[14] Described in the *Regularis concordia*, ed. Symons, p. 39. The kindling is performed on three days, first by the sacrist (*aeditus*), next by the dean (*decano*), and finally by the provost (*praepositus*). In secular churches the ceremony was often performed successively by subdeacon, deacon, and priest, or deacon, priest, and bishop.

[15] *OR* X, p. 1014[b]: "de crystallo sive de lapide." The curious detail that the fire is to be carried on a staff in the form of a serpent or dragon is found in the Mozarabic rubric (*Missale mixtum, PL*, LXXXV, 470[a]) and the *Regularis concordia*, ed. Symons, p. 93, among other places. Could this be an assimilation from one of the mystery cults?

[16] Guéranger, *Liturgical Year*, VI, 501. The long Gelasian *Benedictio cerei* may be examined in *PL*, LXXXIV, 1106[d-7e].

[17] Feasey, *Ancient English Holy Week Ceremonial*, pp. 189–202. However, the candles must have already been extremely large in the ninth century. *OR* VII, p. 999[a], describes them as "staturam hominis in altum."

[18] *Liber officialis* (*PL*, CV, 1038[e-d]; H, II, 121–22): "Sit cereus consecratus in Christi persona, sit alter cereus, inluminatus a primo cereo, chorus apostolorum; utrique sint in ecclesia, utrique praecedant catecumenos nostros ad baptismum, praecedant nos ad terram promissionis." The *Exsultet* form of the service was originally distinct from the Roman form. In the former, the illumination takes place at the beginning of the service; in the latter, it takes place at the end of the vigil and just before Mass. The Roman form seems symbolically and dramatically more effective, but it lacks the magnificent text provided for the *Exsultet*. Evidently, at some time before the ninth century the two were combined, with the result that the ninth-century form (and the modern one) involves two illuminations—one at the blessing of the paschal candle, and the second at the beginning of the vigil Mass.

The essential parts of the modern ceremony of blessing the paschal candle were present in the ninth century. A statement by the Venerable Bede indicates that the candle was inscribed with the date, and the Gelasian Sacramentary provides for the imposition of a cross and the blessing of grains of incense, which, however, may not have been inserted into the wax.[19] The practice of blessing five grains, commemorating the five wounds of Christ, is fully in harmony with the vivid realization of the candle symbolism in the ritual, but it is later than the ninth century.[20]

If we accept as standard the Roman order rather than Amalarius, it is the fire rather than the candle which represents Christ. As early as the fifth century the choir greeted its entrance with the cry *Lumen Christi*, to which the congregation replied, as in the modern service, with *Deo gratias*.[21] A deacon in white vestments then ascended the gospel ambo, where the paschal candle stood, as yet unlit.[22] While the *Lumen Christi* flickered by his side, he began the *Exsultet*. The text of this chant, one of the most beautiful of the Church year, dates from the seventh or eighth century. In the tenth century it was read from "*Exsultet* rolls," which contained pictures inverted with respect to the text. As the deacon read, the scroll unwound over the ambo, revealing its illuminations to the congregation. The device, a sort of medieval equivalent of the illustrated slide lecture, may be much older than the tenth century. Whatever its age, however, it is merely for emphasis. The words on which the illustrations depend are the important elements in the ritual. They constitute a lyric definition of the meaning of the Easter vigil. The chant begins with acclaim for the victorious Champion:

> Let now the heavenly throngs of angels rejoice: let the divine mysteries exult: and let salvation's trumpet proclaim the victory of so great a King.

[19] Feasey, *Ancient English Holy Week Ceremonial*, pp. 204–32; Molien, *Prière*, II, 411–20; Duchesne, *Christian Worship*, pp. 251–52. The Gelasian prayer is in *PL*, LXXIV, 1106[d]–7[a]; also *Commentarius*, *PL*, LXXVIII, 908[b-d].

[20] Molien, *Prière*, II, 414, places it in the tenth century.

[21] Leclercq, "*Praeconium paschale*," *DACL*, XIII, 2, 1567. This is part of the *Exsultet* form of the ceremony and is not native to Rome. *OR* I, p. 955[b], for example, requires that the entry into the church be in silence: "procedunt simul omnes de sacrario cum ipso cereo in ecclesiam cum silentio, nihil canentes; et ponitur candelabro ante altare." On the other hand, Amalarius refers to the paschal candle as *Lumen Christi* and echoes phrases in the *Exsultet;* he was apparently familiar with something like the modern form of the service with its introductory procession, cries of *Lumen Christi*, reading of the *Exsultet* text, and blessing. See *Liber officialis*, *PL*, CV, 1034[b-e]; H, II, 112–13; also Molien, *Prière*, II, 414–20.

[22] See Leclercq, "*Praeconium paschale*," pp. 1559–71, for discussion.

Light, naturally, is a dominant image:

> Let the earth also be filled with joy, aglow with so great a glory: and let her know that the darkness which overspread the whole world is chased away by the splendor of our eternal King. Let too our mother the Church be glad, finding herself adorned in the radiance of so great a light. . . .

The chant then takes the form of the Mass Preface, beginning with the *Sursum corda*. In it the two Lenten themes of baptism and penance are linked to the victory of the Resurrection. Baptism is introduced through allusions to the deliverance of Adam and the passage of the Hebrews through the Red Sea:

> [Christ] paid for us, to His eternal Father, the debt of Adam, and by His dear blood canceled the penalty due to that primeval crime. For this is the paschal feast, in which the true Lamb was slain, with whose blood the doors of the faithful are consecrated.

> This is the night wherein of old thou didst bring forth our forefathers the children of Israel from Egypt, leading them dry-shod through the Red Sea. This is the night which cleansed away the darkness of sin, by the pillar of fire. This is the night which now delivers, throughout the world, the faithful of Christ from the wickedness of the world and the darkness of sin, restores them to grace, and to the fellowship of sanctity. This is the night in which Christ snapped the chains of death, and rose conqueror from hell. For it availed us nothing to be born, had it not prevailed that we should be redeemed. . . .

It has been shown that the modern practice of inserting incense at the phrase *incensi huius sacrificium* is based on a confusion of the participle (i.e., *incensi cerei*) for the noun *incensum*. However, a fairly early *ordo*, that of Abbot Ratold of Corbie, agrees with modern usage in requiring the illumination of the paschal candle at the words *ignis ascendit*. A general illumination of the tapers of the congregation may have followed. The chant beautifully fuses praise of the bee, the source of the wax, with allusions to the mystic union of human and divine which occurs on Easter Eve:

> Because it is fed by the melted wax which the mother bee made for the substance of the precious torch.

O truly blessed night, which despoiled the Egyptians, and enriched the Hebrews! A night, in which things heavenly are wedded to those of earth, and divine to human.[23]

The *Exsultet* is a fitting introduction to the Easter vigil. Light, baptism, and Resurrection mingle in its imagery, moving outward as the ceremony proceeds to physical realization in the lighting of tapers. During the ninth century, in fact, this ceremony established the dominant tone for the whole Easter octave. Throughout the octave, the candle preceded the bishop and the white-robed neophytes in processions to the churches where stational services were held. Drawing on the text of the *Exsultet*, Amalarius makes the obvious interpretation: "The Paschal candle has the same meaning as the pillar of fire that illuminated the people of Israel at night. . . . That column of fire preceded the Hebrews before they crossed the Red Sea; our column, that is, the candle, precedes the catechumens. Its light signifies the light of Christ by which the present night is illuminated through the Resurrection, and also the catechumens who are coming to baptism. . . . The candle precedes the Pontiff, who is the head of the people, because the column of fire preceded the people [of Israel] even to the Promised Land."[24]

After the *Exsultet* the deacon revests. The twelve prophetic readings of the Easter vigil follow. The number, order, and choice of these readings have changed several times in the history of the vigil service, although almost all versions require the inclusion of the creation, the Flood,

---

[23] I have quoted the translation in Guéranger, *Liturgical Year*, VI, 506–10. This text has been shortened by the omission of several lines in praise of bees. The lines were originally dropped because of what was regarded as an unseemly dependence on Virgil's *Georgics*, iv. The omitted passage is, however, of particular interest to the student of the relation between the Christian liturgy and drama on the one hand, and liturgy and pagan influences on the other. For this reason, and for its almost humanistic expressiveness, it is quoted here in the version from the *Codex* of Abbot Ratold of Corbie (*PL*, LXXVIII, 335[b]):

Apes caeteris quae subjecta sunt homini animantibus antecellit: cum sit minima corporis parvitate, ingentes animos angusto versat in pectore; viribus imbecillis, sed fortis ingenio. Haec explorata temporum vice, cum canitiem pruinosa hiberna posuerunt, et glaciale senium verni temporis moderata deterserint, statim prodeundi ad laborem cura succedit, dispersoeque per agros, libratis paululum pennis, cruribus suspensis insidunt, partim ore legere flosculos, partim oneratae victualibus suis ad castra remeant; ibique aliae inaestimbaili arte cellulas tenaci glutino instruunt, aliae liquentia mella stipant, aliae vertunt flores in ceram aliae ore natos fingunt, aliae collectis e foliis nectar includunt. O vere beata, et amabilis apes, cujus nec sexum masculi violant, fetus non quassant, nec filii destruunt castitatem; sicut sancta concepit virgo Maria virgo peperit, virgo permansit. . . . O vere beata nox, quae exspoliavit Aegyptios. . . .

[24] *Liber officialis, PL*, CV, 1034[c-d]; H, II, 113.

Abraham and Isaac, and Daniel, which may be considered the most fundamental Old Testament texts for the exposition of the history of God's ways to men. Consistency ends, however, with these four. The Gelasian Sacramentary calls for ten selections with intervening prayers and four tracts. The Gregorian *Liber sacramentorum* stipulates eight, while the first *Ordo Romanus* appears to stipulate four but requires that they be read in Greek and Latin. Amalarius refers to six readings in Greek and Latin and attributes the practice to "the ancient Romans" who served mixed congregations. The tenth *Ordo Romanus* calls for the canonical twelve readings, but requires that they be presented in Greek and Latin, making twenty-four in all: Since both Jungmann and Molien agree that the sequence of twelve readings is as ancient as other variations, we may take this as the norm.[25] It is, as Molien remarks, "an immense tableau of all of God's works for the good of man since the creation."[26] The readings are, in order: Gen. 1-2, Gen. 5-8, Gen. 22, Exod. 14-15, Isa. 54-55, Bar. 3, Ezek. 37, Isa. 4, Exod. 12, Jonah 3, Deut. 31, and Dan. 3. Each is followed by a prayer, and tracts are sung after the fourth, eighth, eleventh, and twelfth. The readings are not announced, as they are during the Mass. According to Amalarius, the effort would be wasted on the catechumens because they are as yet too ignorant to appreciate the authority of the books selected.[27]

If the explanation is fanciful, it calls attention to the dramatic beginning of the readings. As the deacon ascends the ambo, the church is entirely silent. Two candles—one the paschal candle—burn beside him. Without preamble he begins: *In principio creavit Deus coelum et terram.*

The reading is intended in part to acquaint the catechumens with the primitive innocence which they will recover through baptism.[28] This point is underscored by the collect, which associates creation with redemption: *mirabiliter creasti hominem, et mirabilius redemisti.* As valuable as this lesson may be, the choice of the creation as the first reading of the Easter vigil is also influenced by motives more basic than the desire to instruct. It is one of the common features of primitive ritual that rebirth is not simply a renewal or resurrection of the deity. It is in some sense a repetition of

---

[25] *Prière*, II, 421, 424; Jungmann, *Early Liturgy*, p. 263; *Lectionnaire de Luxeuil*, ed. Salmon, 97-98, note.

[26] Molien, *Prière*, II, 421. These readings appear to parallel—even to recapitulate—the readings for matins from Septuagesima to Easter. See above, Essay III, n. 6.

[27] *Liber officialis*, PL, CV, 1039[b-d]; H, II, 122-24. Based on *OR* I, p. 955e.

[28] Molien, *Prière*, II, 421.

original creation.[29] The idea is subsumed in the rhythms and language of one of the most impressive passages in Scripture. Within this context the Resurrection assumes a cosmic dimension, or, to put the matter more accurately, cosmic events are brought within the context of the Resurrection. The words are the more effective for their close relation to the light rituals preceding them: *Terra autem erat inanis et vacua, et tenebrae erant super faciem abyssi, et Spiritus Dei ferebatur super aquas. Dixitque Deus: Fiat lux. Et facta est lux.*

The stories of Noah and of Abraham and Isaac come next. Both have extremely rich typological significance, and both set before the catechumens examples of heroic faith. Noah is the new man, saved by the Church (the ark was a common type of the Church), and the rainbow is God's first covenant and a foreshadowing of redemption. In the same way, Abraham's sacrifice is a type of the sacrifice of the Lamb of God, and Isaac is mankind redeemed from death by Christ. The collect which follows the story of the Flood points the lesson: *Totusque mundus experiatur et videat, dejecta erigi, inveterata renovari, et per ipsum redire omnia in integrum.*

The fourth reading is the climax of the series, and a tract provides articulation between it and the fifth. It begins with a reference to the column of fire in which the Lord concealed himself at the time of the destruction of the Egyptians and continues with a description of the passage through the Red Sea. Like earlier references to Exodus the reading is a typological reference to baptism. It ends with the canticle of Moses celebrating the escape of the Hebrews: *Tunc cecinit Moyses et filii Israel carmen hoc Domino, et dixerunt:* [Tractus] *Cantemus Domino.* . . . In case the allusion escapes any of the listeners, it is again emphasized in the collect. The reference to the catechumens in the Gregorian version is far more pointed than in the text currently used: *Deus cujus antiqua miracula in praesenti quoque saeculo coruscare sentimus, praesta, quaesumus, ut sicut priorem populum ab Aegyptiis liberasti, hoc ad salutem gentium per aquas baptismatis opereris.*[30]

If the first group of prophecies ends with heavy emphasis on baptism, the second unit carries this emphasis forward. The fifth reading begins with the invitation *Omnes sitientes, venite ad aquas,* and ends with the image of the wasteland restored: ". . . as the rain cometh down, and the snow

---

[29] See, for example, Henri Frankfort, "Myth and Reality," in *Before Philosophy* (Harmondsworth, England, 1949), pp. 32–36; Mircea Eliade, *The Sacred and the Profane* (New York, 1959), pp. 68–113. Vilhelm Grönbech (*The Culture of the Teutons* [London, 1931], II, 222) calls attention to this feature of Germanic ritual: "In order to do justice to the plot, we must say that it not only condenses and renews the past, but in true earnest creates it over and over again."

[30] *LS,* p. 87°.

from heaven and . . . watereth the earth, and maketh it bring forth and bud, that it give seed to the sower, and bread to the eater: So shall my word be that goeth forth out of my mouth." Again the Gregorian collect points the lesson: *concede propitius ut quos aqua baptismatis abluis, continua protectione tuearis.*[31]

The next three readings balance warnings against sin with promises of divine aid for the faithful. Baruch dwells on the God who "prepared the earth and filled it with cattle"; while Ezekiel tells of the dry bones that live in the Lord: "Behold, I will open your graves, and we will bring you to the land of Israel." The strong emphasis of this selection on burial and rebirth anticipates the ritual burial and resurrection of the baptism ceremony. It is followed by Isaiah's prophecy of the seven women charged with defilement. The tabernacle of safety formed by the Lord is a foretaste of salvation, which is reiterated in images of natural fertility in the tract and collect:

> TRACTUS: *Vinea facta est dilecta in cornu, in loco uberi.* . . .
> ORATIO: *Deus qui . . . manifestasti . . . satorem te bonorum seminum, et electorum palmitum esse cultorem: tribue populis tuis . . . ut, spinarum et tribulorum squalore resecato, digna efficiantur fruge fecundi.*

Having touched on God's creative love for man and man's search for God, the readings now turn to issues directly related to Easter. The ninth (Exod. 12) tells the story of the original Passover. The tenth and eleventh refer to the divine mandate of the Church to "go to Nineva, the great city, and preach in it" and to her obligation, illustrated by the warning of Moses to the Hebrews, to remind men of the ways of righteousness, an idea stressed again in the tract: *Attende coelum et loquar.* Finally, the selection from Daniel is a warning against apostasy. The faith of the children in the lion's den is offered as a warning and stimulus to those about to take baptismal vows. It is followed by a prayer for divine inspiration because *in nullo fidelium, nisi ex tua inspiratione, proveniunt quarumlibet incrementa virtutum.*

During the readings the catechumens are passive spectators along with the rest of the congregation. Now they become actors in the drama. Their role is defined by Paul's words to the Romans (6:4): "Therefore we are buried with him by baptism into death: that like as Christ was raised up from the dead by the glory of the Father, even so we also should walk in

---

[31] *Ibid.*, p. 87[d]. This collect follows the reading from Baruch in more recent forms of the service.

newness of life."[32] The terms actor and role are inexact, however. It is of the essence of baptism that it is not a symbol but an event. Amalarius insists, "[Paul] does not say we symbolize burial but we *are* buried . . . through the symbol of the burial of the Lord which we receive in baptism, we experience the thing itself."[33] The catechumens are thus living witnesses to the reality of the Resurrection: "Christ arose for our justification. The Holy Spirit raised him from the dead. Likewise the Spirit will raise, or will vivify, our mortal bodies."[34]

The chant *Sicut cervus desiderat ad fontes aquarum*, responsible for the common iconographic motif of the stag's head on medieval baptismal fonts, serves as a transition from the readings to the blessing of the font. According to the first Roman *Ordo*, it is sung both in Greek and Latin. While the celebrant prays with the congregation, a priest with flasks of oil and chrism stands at the right of the altar. A procession forms. The paschal candle leads, followed by incense-bearers, the catechumens, the priest with holy oils, and the celebrant. The effect must have been quite remarkable. The catechumens, worn and perhaps near collapse from the rigors of the final three-day fast, file out to the singing of the *Sicut cervus*. As they approach the baptistery they hear a new chant, the Litany of the Saints. The whole heavenly hierarchy is invoked for their benefit.

The almost hypnotic invocations of the Litany end with the Agnus Dei after which the celebrant begins the solemn rite of blessing the baptismal water. To do this he divides the water with his hand, exorcises it, and crosses it. The words accompanying these actions are, like the *Exsultet*, deeply impressive. The idea of cosmic creation is reiterated in the invocation of the Holy Spirit as the force which *super aquas inter ipsa mundi primordia ferebatur*. The font is not only a grave but a womb (*utero*) from which "new creatures" are "born": *in novam renata creaturam progenies coelestis emergat*. Remarkably, it is also the source of the waters which nourished Eden and renewed the wasteland: [*Deus*] *te de paradiso manare in quatuor fluminibus totam terram rigare praecipit, . . . te in deserto amaram suavitate rudita fecit esse potabilem, et sitienti populo de petro produxit.*[35] By extension it is also referred to as the waters of Jordan, the waters changed into wine at Cana, and the water mixed with blood that flowed from Christ's side.[36] In sum, just as the rebirth of Christ is a cosmic renewal and the kindling of

[32] This is, in fact, the reading in the Mozarabic rite (*Missale mixtum, PL*, LXXXV, 470°; also, *Lectionnaire de Luxeuil*, ed. Salmon, p. 115; and the Bobbio missal).

[33] *Liber officialis, PL*, CV, 1043ᵈ; H, II, 132.

[34] *Ibid.*, 148ᵈ; H, II, 141–42; cf. *City of God*, XXI, 27, 3 (*PL*, LXI, 748).

[35] Text in *LS*, pp. 88ᵈ–89°.

[36] *Ibid.*, p. 89°.

the new fire a repetition of the original *Fiat lux*, the baptismal font is associated with the source of all waters of the earth.[37]

After blessing the font, the celebrant breathes upon the water and dips the paschal candle into it three times. The third time he plunges it to the bottom of the font, extinguishing it, and in the Roman service the tapers of the participants are also extinguished. Like many other features of the Easter vigil, the ceremony is a literal representation. The paschal candle has been identified with Christ since its first appearance. The liturgy and allegorical interpretation agree that the extinction of the candle expresses the union of Christ and the Holy Spirit in the waters of the font.[38] While it is extinguished, Christ is "buried" in the font. When it is relighted just before Mass, He has "returned" to the altar.[39]

The celebrant now pours chrism on the water *in modum crucis*, spreading it over the entire font. He asperges the people, who, in turn, may collect vials of it "to sprinkle their homes, their vineyards, their fields, and their crops."[40] The waters of the font, having first watered Paradise, are thus returned to the spring fields.

Formal baptism follows. The texts are similar to those used today, but the setting and ceremony are quite different. The rite was performed in a baptistery separate from the church. The building was large, and there was usually only one in each city; in Rome, where Saturday's station is St. John Lateran, it was the Baptistery of Constantine.[41] The center of the baptistery is occupied by a large sunken basin, octagonal or round, with three steps on either side, and a dove symbolizing the Holy Spirit sus-

---

[37] Compare with the discussion of primitive water symbolism in Frankfort, *Before Philosophy*, pp. 32, 59–62, 159–61, 170–74, etc.

[38] Amalarius, *Liber officialis* (*PL*, CV, 1046ᵇ; H, II, 137): "Ut enim per partem inluminatum ad memoriam reducimus columnam ignis, quae figurabat Christum . . . ita per cereos extinctos . . . Spiritus sancti persona designatur." The prayer makes this clear enough. The candles are immersed as the priest says *Descendat, Domine, in hanc plenitudinem fontis. Virtus Spiritus tui, totamque hujus aquae substantiam, regenerandi fecundet effectu* (*LS*, p. 89ᵈ).

[39] *Liber officialis* (*PL*, CV, 1046ᵉ; H, II, 137–38): "Sine lumine sunt cerei neophytorum usque ad tempus quo ceteri cerei ecclesiae inluminantur: tempore quo ceteri cerei inluminantur, inluminantur et neophytorum. . . . Solemus differre officium inluminandorum cereorum usque ad missae officium: sive propter causam ut prius accipiant neophyti impositionem manus episcopi, et sic eos credamus inluminari Spiritu Sancto; seu propter noctem . . . ut, sicut gloria resurrectionis inlustrata est, ita inlustretur lumine nostrorum cereorum."

[40] Not in *LS*, but included in *OR* I (p. 956ᵉ) and appendix (p. 964ᵇ).

[41] Plans and discussion of architectural features in Fletcher, *A History of Architecture on the Comparative Method*, pp. 221–22, 230. A beautiful description of the service as performed at the Lateran around the time of Pope Gregory is given by Molien, *Prière*, II, 424–25.

pended above it. In early centuries, prior to baptism adult catechumens were led to pavilions where they removed their clothes.[42] They emerged naked before their fellow catechumens, sponsors, clergy, and members of the congregation, and stood awaiting baptism on a rough cloth or garment of sackcloth.[43] They then descended three steps into the font, were immersed or had water poured on their heads three times, were crossed, and ascended the three steps on the other side. The entire sequence of actions is—and was understood as—a representation of rebirth. The sackcloth is the "old man" put off in baptism. The descent is death; the immersion (by virtue of the extinction of the paschal candle), a burial in Christ; and the ascent, regeneration. The seven steps represent the seven gifts of the Holy Spirit. Standing naked before sponsors, clergy, and congregation, the neophytes, as they are henceforth called, are infants reborn in the innocence of Adam. They are anointed by a priest with chrism and receive linen robes from their sponsors to be worn until confirmation.[44]

Such, at least, is the ceremony in its early form. By the ninth century there had been several modifications. Although explicit provision is made for adults in the *Liber sacramentorum* and early *Ordines*, the emphasis falls on infant baptism. Moreover, the symbolism of nudity was probably discarded in favor of a token removal of clothes. On the other hand, the Carolingian treatises on baptism retain many features of the older order. The work of converting pagans, a work requiring adult baptism, was still going forward on the borders of the Empire, and there is some evidence that even within the Empire infant baptism was regarded as theologically dubious. Jesse, Theoduphus, Amalarius, Pseudo-Alcuin, and others assume in their discussions of the vigil and the Easter octave that adult candidates will participate, and Amalarius felt that infant baptism was sufficiently novel to require defense in a long, rather murky chapter of the

---

[42] Copious details in Weller, *The Easter Sermons of St. Augustine*, pp. 46–56.

[43] *Ibid.*, p. 51. The authors cited by Weller point out that the neophytes now resemble Adam *before* the Fall—another example of recapitulation symbolism. See also Molien, *Prière*, II, 429.

[44] For the symbolism of the font as sepulcher and the interpretation of the seven steps, see, e.g., Theodulphus of Orleans, *De ordine baptismi*, PL, CV, 233ᵃ: "Fons quoque baptismi similitudinem gerit sepulchri Christi. . . . Cujus fontis septem gradus, tres in sescensu tres noctes, et tres in ascensu tres dies significare videntur . . . ," etc. This identification is the basis for the use of the baptismal font rather than the altar as the "sepulcher" in the *Visitatio Sepulchri* ceremony and its performance during vespers throughout Easter Week. See below, pp. 173–75. For the high symbolic value placed on the baptismal robe, see Molien, *Prière*, II, 432n., and Jesse of Amiens, *De baptismo*, PL, CV, 789ᵈ–90ᵉ.

Liber officialis.[45] We may assume, then, that the typical Carolingian service of the ninth century included adults as well as infants and that the ceremonies of adult baptism were both understood and practiced. Although they disappeared from the regular services of most European churches in the tenth and eleventh centuries, their practice has continued at St. John Lateran down to the present day.[46]

Confirmation immediately follows baptism so that the neophytes can receive first Communion at the vigil Mass. The pontiff or bishop usually baptizes two or three individuals and then retires to the sacristy or to a section of the baptistery called the *chrismarium*.[47] The chorus meanwhile resumes the Litany of the Saints, repeating each invocation seven, then five, then three times. While it is chanting, the neophytes enter the *chrismarium* in the order in which their names are inscribed on the scrutiny roll.

They first receive white robes, or albs, to be worn throughout the ensuing week. When they appear before the bishop, he delivers ten light buffets (*siliquae*) on the cheek, a reminiscence of the ancient Roman ceremony for freeing a slave. Infants are held by their sponsors, while each adult stands with his foot on the foot of his sponsor to symbolize the child-parent relationship.[48] The bishop invokes the sevenfold gifts of the Holy Spirit, imposes his hands on each neophyte and crosses their foreheads with chrism. This second anointing was regarded as a protection against defilement, and a band or veil is presented to each neophyte to protect the area during the coming week.[49] The Kiss of Peace is given, and all are dismissed. The neophytes return to the now darkened church, where the chorus, which precedes them, continues to chant the rhythmic invocations of the Litany of the Saints.

[45] *PL*, CV, 1042–43; H, II, 128–34. The defense of infant baptism does not indicate a reluctance on the part of the Carolingian clergy to baptize infants, but it does show that infant baptism still raised questions and (perhaps) occasional opposition.

[46] Guéranger, *Liturgical Year*, VI, 498; Leduc and Baudot, *Liturgy*, p. 266.

[47] *OR* VII, p. 999[b]; *Commentarius*, p. 905[a]; Guéranger, *Liturgical Year*, VI, 557.

[48] *LS*, p. 90[e]: "Infantes quidem in brachiis dextris tenentur, majores vero pedem ponunt super pedem patrini sui." The confirmation service and the list of items given or bestowed—including the *siliquae*—is outlined in *OR* I, p. 957[b]: ". . . dat singulis stolam, casulam, et chrismale, et X siliquas; et vestiantur." The chrismale was a band or veil to be worn over the forehead to protect the cross of chrism made during confirmation (see Guéranger, *Liturgical Year*, VI, 558).

[49] This is the chrismale referred to in n. 48. It was also called a veil (*velamen*). See, e.g., Jesse of Amiens, *De baptismo*, PL, CV, 790[b]; Theodulphus, *ibid.*, p. 235[b]: ". . . mens renatorum . . . habeat tegamentum ut et contra vitia sacerdotale velamine muniantur . . . et unctione sacrosancta chrismatis liniatur." The veil was also compared to a royal diadem, and was said to symbolize the priesthood of all believers in Christ.

The striking nature of the vigil service is self-evident. The time elapsed from its beginning at *hora nona* to the chanting of the final litany was evidently sufficient in the ninth century to require the beginning of the Mass around (or even after) midnight. What needs to be stressed is that baptism is an integral part of the sequence that reaches its climax during the vigil Mass. St. Theodulphus (d. 821) linked baptism with both the Resurrection and the historical incidents which later became the subject matter of the *Quem quaeritis* play. "We die to sin," he wrote, "when we renounce the devil and all his works. We are buried with Christ when, during the invocation of the Holy Spirit, we are immersed three times in the cleansing font, descending as into a sepulcher. We arise with Christ when, cleansed of all sins, we emerge from the font as from a sepulcher." The cleansing of the catechumens before baptism (they were allowed to bathe on Holy Saturday) is parallel to the preparation of Christ's body for the tomb "with clean wrappings and fragrant ointments" (*mundissima linteamina et aromata*). Finally, the albs of the neophytes are associated with the angels who announce the Resurrection: ". . . it is most appropriate that the angel who announced the Resurrection is described as seated in white garments; and those who announce His return to the apostles appear in white garments; and we, too, are dressed in white garments after baptism that we may retain that purity in our works which we have received in our regeneration, preserving both our own renewal and the beauty of angelic splendor."[50] The comment is more than a fanciful analogy. The neophytes bear witness to the invisible reality of the Resurrection through their visible emergence from the font and through the albs that proclaim them "new men." After baptism they continue in their role as witnesses. The Introit of Laetare Sunday has informed them that they are about to enter the New Jerusalem. During the octave in albs, their white robes proclaim their uniquely close relation to the inhabitants of that heavenly community.

An illumination ceremony separated the vigil service from the Mass that followed. The *Liber sacramentorum* requires that when the chorus has sung the Agnus Dei after the last (threefold) litany, the *magister scholae* should announce *Accendite*. Thereupon the church is illuminated and the celebrant emerges from the sacristy, preceded by the paschal candle.[51] Occurring as it did in a darkened church at an advanced hour of the night, the ceremony must have been impressive even where it duplicated the

---

[50] Theodulphus, *De ordine baptismi*, PL, CV, 232ᵈ–33ᵈ.
[51] *LS*, p. 91ᵃ; *OR* I, p. 957ᵈ, and Appendix, p. 964ᵉ.

paschal candle rite.[52] The revelation of the clergy in white vestments, of the newly unveiled images, and of the altar once more decorated as for a festive Mass strongly suggests resurrection. An early Spanish *ordo* indicates that the illumination could at times develop further toward a resurrection ceremony. Here, candles are concealed behind veils on the altar. A clerk must stealthily (*occulte*) enter the sanctuary without permitting a glimpse of light to be seen from the front. The illumination proceeds in the usual fashion until all tapers are burning. Then the veil on the altar is suddenly raised, revealing the candles behind it, and the bishop intones *Deo gratias*.[53] Whatever the details of the action, the symbolism is apparent:

> On the night of the Lord's Resurrection all the lights are rekindled. On account of the sacrament of the Lord's death and Resurrection on Easter night, the order provides that when we reach the office that pertains to Christ's Resurrection, a new and enduring fire should arise which will illuminate the whole church. This is the fire that I mentioned being reserved on the sixth day to light the [paschal] candle. . . . The other lights are extinguished until the last Litany, which leads to the office of the Mass of the Resurrection of the Lord. At this moment the lights of the church and the neophytes are kindled to symbolize the illumination of the world by the Resurrection of Christ from the earth.[54]

Another ceremony must have occurred at the beginning of the vigil Mass in many churches throughout Europe up to—and perhaps after— the ninth century. In the various *Ordines* and descriptions of early ceremony there are no less than four occasions when a particle of the Host was reserved for the Easter services. In Rome on Saturday before Palm Sunday there was a reservation of the fermentum for the vigil Mass. On Palm Sunday the weekly reservation of the sancta would have occurred in many cities as part of the normal rite of Solemn Mass. In those churches that did not offer Communion on Good Friday, the Host reserved on Maundy Thursday would normally have served as the sancta for the vigil Mass, while in many of the variants of the *Depositio Crucis* a Host is reserved on

---

[52] In the rite followed by Amalarius it was the first general illumination. See above, n. 38.

[53] Leclercq, "Pasques," *DACL*, XIII, 2, 1567. Compare the *Ordo* of St. Amand, reprinted in Duchesne, *Christian Worship*, pp. 469–70. Presumably the deacons are concealed and emerge at the *accendite* which begins Mass. Cf. also *Missale mixtum*, *PL*, LXXXV, 470ª. The church bells, silent since Maundy Thursday, are rung here or during the Gloria in Excelsis.

[54] Amalarius, *De ordine antiphonarii*, *PL*, CV, 1293ᵇ⁻ᵉ; H, III, 80–81. Also *Liber officialis*, p. 1056ᵇ; H, II, 157.

Good Friday and "returned" some time after midnight on Easter.[55] According to the *Codex Ratisponensis*, cited by Hugo Ménard, there were special reservations on the great feast days of the Church, and Maundy Thursday is the first of these: "Concerning the fermentum . . . the Roman custom is to reserve the sancta for the whole year during the Masses sung on *Coena Domini*, Holy Saturday, Easter Day, Pentecost, and Christmas; and during stational Masses, if the pontiff is not present, the sancta is placed in the cup when the *Pax Domini* is said."[56] The same source indicates that mingling of the fermentum during the vigil Mass received special emphasis. It warns that "on Holy Saturday [i.e., during the vigil] no priest at the baptismal churches may communicate anyone before he receives the sancta which the pontiff offered."[57] Since we know from Amalarius and other sources that the sancta ceremony was adopted for episcopal use and persisted irregularly throughout the ninth century, it is clear that a return of the sancta to the altar must have been a feature of many ninth-century vigil services. While there are no instructions for the "return" given in connection with the vigil Mass, the first *Ordo Romanus* describes the procedure regularly used. It can be assumed that the Holy Saturday return was closely related to the standard one. This ceremony is part of the Introit procession. After the pontiff has vested, a subdeacon standing in the sacristy cries *Accendite* to the chorus. The chorus then begins the Introit, and the pontiff advances to the altar with the usual contingent of acolytes, incense-bearers, subdeacons, and deacons. At this point the return of the sancta occurs: "Before they reach the altar, let two acolytes [approach] holding open caskets [*capsas*] containing the sancta,

---

[55] See the discussion of the reservation ceremonies in Essay III above, pp. 122–26. Brooks, *The Sepulchre of Christ*, pp. 34–36, lists the reservations involving a Host.

[56] Quoted, *Commentarius*, pp. 870ᵈ–71ᵃ: "De fermento quod dicit, mos est Romanis, ut de Missa quae cantatur in Coena Domini, et in Sabbato sancto, et in die sancto Paschae, et in Pentecosten, et in Natali Domini, de Sancta . . . per totum annum servetur; et ubicunque per stationes, si ipsi papa ad Missam praesens non fuerit, de ipsa Missa . . . mittitur in calicem, cum dicitur *Pax Domini sit semper vobiscum*."

[57] *Ibid.*, p. 871ᵃ: ". . . Sabbato sancto Paschae nullus presbyter per ecclesias baptismales neminem communicat, antequam mittatur ei de ipsa sancta, quam obtulit dominus papa." A different symbolism is suggested by the (unfortunately ambiguous) comment in the *Regula magistri*, which gives monastic usage. The *Regula* seems to indicate that a point was made of finishing all of the Sacrament *before* Holy Saturday in order that the Consecration during the vigil Mass might be a genuine renewal. If this is, indeed, a proper interpretation of the *Regula*, we have an interesting situation where the *emptiness* of the repository for the preconsecrated Hosts becomes symbolic of the Resurrection (*Regula*, *PL*, LXXXVIII, 1016 [*ordo* for Maundy Thursday]): "Sacramenta vero altaris in patena majore vitrea finiantur: Ut cum sexta feria Judei ad passionem Christum quaesierunt, sit ipso die mentibus nostris reclusus, ut sabbato nobis per resurrectionem in novo sacramento appareat."

and followed by a subdeacon holding his hand over the top of the casket. And let him show the sancta to the pontiff or the deacon who has gone before. Then, bowing his head, let the pontiff or deacon venerate the sancta; and let him examine it so that if there is more than necessary he may order it placed in its receptacle [conditorio]."[58] This rubric raises several questions, but its general sense is clear. The procession to the altar is interrupted by a second procession bearing a receptacle with preconsecrated Hosts. At least one is venerated, then placed on the altar for use in the later commingling, while the rest are returned to some sort of repository called a conditorium. Two observations are pertinent. First, the cry Accendite, which begins the procession, is also the cry which initiates the illumination ceremony at the beginning of the vigil Mass. Second, the word conditorium is a technical term referring to the place where a corpse or its ashes are kept, hence, a sepulcher. The return of the sancta would therefore seem to be essentially a resurrection ceremony.

The vigil Mass is both shorter and more closely related to the historical event commemorated than is usual at other times of the year. It was sometimes labeled the "Mass of the Resurrection."[59] There is no Introit, and the Offertory, the osculum pacis, the Agnus Dei, and the Communion hymn are omitted. Details concerning the positive features of the service are lacking, but two curious customs dating from the early Church were still recalled and irregularly observed in the ninth century. First, a lamb was frequently blessed during or just after the vigil service. In some German and French churches the blessing apparently took the form of a consecration. The lamb was used for the bishop's supper following the service. In Rome the lamb was never blessed during the service, and

[58] OR I, p. 947[b]: ". . . prius quam veniant ante altare, diacones in presbyterio exuuntur planetis . . . et tunc duo acolythi tenentes capsas cum Sanctis apertas, et subdiaconus sequens cum ipsis tenens manum suam in ore capsae, ostendit Sancta pontifici, vel diacono qui praecesserit. Tunc inclinato capite pontifex vel diaconus salutat Sancta, et contemplatur, ut si fuerit superabundans, praecipiat ut ponatur in conditorio." The ordo of St. Amand confirms the fact that the sancta was employed in the vigil Mass during the ninth century (Duchesne, Christian Worship, p. 471): "Ipsa nocte omnes presbiteri cardinales non ibi stant, sed unusquisque per titulum suum facit missa. . . . Et transmittit unusquisque presbiter mansionarium de titulo suo ad ecclesiam Salvatoris, et expectant ibi usque dum frangitur sancta, habentes secum corporales. Et venit oblationarius subdiaconus, et dat eis de sancta quod pontifex consecravit, et recipiunt ea in corporales, et revertitur unusquisque ad titulum suum et tradit sancta presbitero. Et de ipsa facit crucem super calicem et ponit in eo et dicit Dominus vobiscum. Et communicant omnes."

[59] Among the names are Missa in nocte paschatis, Missa ad noctem, Missa (or Festum) Dominicae resurrectionis, Missa in sabbato sancto, Missa in nocte sabbati sancti, Missa in vigilias paschae, Sacrificium neophytii, etc.

elsewhere the ceremony was made nonliturgical.[60] Its existence, however, illustrates the degree to which coincidence encouraged literal representation at the climax of the Easter drama. The hymn *Ad coenam agni*, which has been attributed to Ambrose, reflects the same tendency, if not the rite itself. A second, equally representational, ceremony is the custom of offering infants and neophytes milk and honey after Communion. The milk and honey had their own blessing. They symbolize both the newborn state of the recently baptized and the completion of their Exodus-like journey. Having passed through the Red Sea, they can enter the Heavenly Jerusalem flowing with milk and honey.[61]

The blessing of the lamb and the offering of milk and honey, while highly representational, are subordinate to the liturgy itself. The effect of the shortened form of the vigil Mass is to stress those joyful texts which have been omitted during the previous weeks. The Kyrie is followed immediately by the Gloria in Excelsis, which, as Amalarius teaches in his discussion of the Mass ordinary, is a song of the angels.[62] At the vigil Mass it announces the healing of the breach between man and the divine which opened at Septuagesima. To communicate further the joy of the moment, the church bells, silent since Maundy Thursday, are tolled.[63] The glory

---

[60] Formulas in the *Missale mixtum*, the Bobbio missal, and several of the *Ordines Romani*. A typical blessing is given in the *Missale mixtum* (*PL*, LXXXV, 447 ᶜ–78 ᵇ), where it follows the Mass. Micrologus observes "juxta Romanum auctoritatem agnus in Pascha benedicitur, non ad altare, sed ad communem mensam." The Greek Church accused the Romans of blessing the lamb along with the Sacrament. That the lamb was, in fact, blessed during the Canon in some Western churches during the ninth century is proved by Walafrid Strabo, *De rebus ecclesiasticis*, xviii (*PL*, CXIV, 939), who attacks those who "agni carnes in Pascha, juxta vel sub altari eas ponentes, benedictione propria consecrabant, et in ipsa Resurrectionis die ante ceteros corporales cibos de ipsius carnibus percipiebant." For discussion, see Weiser, *Handbook*, pp. 232–53.

[61] ". . . baptizatis hoc sacrificii genus offerri, et intelligant quia non alii, sed ipsi qui participes fiunt corporis et sanguinis Domini terram repromissionis accipient, cujus iter incohantes, tanquam parvuli lacte nutriuntur et melle" (John the Deacon, quoted in *Commentarius*, pp. 906 ᵈ–7 ᵃ; see also *LS Notae*, p. 380 ᵃ). The Introit of Easter Monday recalls the practice: "Introduxit vos Dominus in terram fluentem lac et mel, alleluia." See also the Offertory of Thursday in Easter Week. The blessing and administration of the milk and honey could occur during Mass or after the service proper (Molien, *Prière*, II, 437–38). Sources cited by Ménard indicate that the milk and honey were still offered occasionally during the ninth century, but the practice was definitely on the decline.

[62] *Liber officialis* (*PL*, CV, 996 ᵃ–ᵇ; H, II, 32–33): "Alleluia et *Gloria in excelsis Deo* cantica caelestia sunt. . . . De *Gloria in excelsis Deo* nulli dubium quin Angelorum cantus sit."

[63] Amalarius does not explicitly mention the bells, but he does mention the three-day suspension of bell-ringing beginning on Maundy Thursday (*Liber officialis*, *PL*, CV, 1201 ᵇ; H, II, 470). The Mozarabic rubric may be taken as the norm: "[Post *Gloriam*] . . . statim pulsentur omnes campane tam majores quam minores. Et discooperiantur

of the moment is emphasized in the collect, where it is expressed in terms of light symbolism: *Deus qui hanc sacratissimam noctem gloria dominicae Resurrectionis illustras, conserva in nova . . . progenie . . . ut corpore et mente renovati, puram tibi exhibeant servitutem.*

The allusion to the neophytes (*nova progenie*) reminds us that the Mass is the dramatic consummation of the sequence that began with the first scrutiny. "The voice of the ministers," says Amalarius, "is directed to the neophytes up to the Gospel."[64] It is to them that the ringing words of Paul to the Colossians are addressed: "Brethren: If ye then be risen with Christ, seek those things which are above. . . . For ye are dead, and your life is hid with Christ in God."[65]

A second wave of lyricism, perhaps more intense than that associated with the Gloria, sweeps over the congregation after the Epistle. The Alleluia was sorrowfully abandoned on Septuagesima. Now, at last, it is restored. The celebrant breaks into the lovely Easter Alleluia, and the chorus replies. The exchange is repeated three times, each time with more confidence, and followed by the choral affirmation, *Confitemini Domino, quoniam bonus, quoniam in saeculum misericordia ejus.* This is followed immediately by the equally joyous tract: *Laudate Dominum, omnes gentes: et collaudate eum, omnes populi.* The dramatic significance of the return of the Alleluia for the ninth-century Christian is expressed by Amalarius: "The Alleluia and the following tract are based on a single theme; that is, that the neophytes should offer a sacrifice of praise of God. . . . The neophytes in attendance have made their journey to enter the Kingdom of Heaven: the door is open to them, which we, who are stained with worldly sins committed after baptism, must seek to open by good works. . . . And now the sacrifice of the neophytes is over."[66]

For students of the history of drama the intense liturgical stress on resurrection and rebirth, reinforced by rememorative ceremonies, by light symbolism, church vestments, and decoration, is significant in itself. The *Quem quaeritis* is above all a resurrection play, and recognition of its context in Church ceremonial serves to dispel any notion that it originated by accident or through haphazard "mutation." The Church recognized

---

altares frontalibus nigris: et retabula aurea: et omnia appareant solemniter. Et finito hymno angelorum Diachonus dicat. *Pro competentibus. Flectamur genua. Levate*" (*Missale mixtum, PL,* LXXXV, 470ª). A similar ceremonial is called for by Pseudo-Alcuin, *De divinis officiis, PL,* CI, 1221ᵇ; Reims *ordo* in *LS Notae,* p. 336ᵇ; *Regularis concordia,* ed. Symons, p. 48.

[64] *Liber officialis, PL,* CV, 1056ᵉ; H, II, 157.

[65] The other common choice is Romans 6:1–12, as in *Missale mixtum* and *Lectionnaire de Luxeuil.* Bobbio missal has I Cor. 5:6–9.

[66] *Liber officialis, PL,* CV, 1057ᵇ⁻ᵈ; H, II, 159–60.

the climactic nature of the vigil Mass and placed it in the most splendid of all liturgical settings. Extraliturgical, representational, rememorative, and purely mimetic ceremonies are also used in greater profusion for this occasion than for any other of the year. Almost all of them involve death-rebirth symbolism, and several have associations linking them to the *Quem quaeritis* play—white robes, burial, and tomb symbols, to name the most obvious.

The Gospel (Mark 16 or Matt. 28) supplies historical details and parts of the dialogue of the Resurrection play. The reading begins with a solemn procession to the Gospel ambo. The deacon is preceded by a thurifer, but the customary candles are omitted. The allusion to the visit to the tomb is unmistakable. Amalarius wrote: "Next the Resurrection of the Lord is recalled and the speech of the angel to the women and the emotions of the women. The Gospel tells of the manner of coming of the women according to Mark. . . . In my opinion the Roman *Ordo* says that nothing is to be carried before the Gospel on this night except the censer, to imitate the women; or because, doubting whether the Lord had restored His body to its full splendor after the descent into hell, the women bore themselves in this way."[67] The author of the *De divinis officiis* adds the note that the thurible represents "the *aromata* which the women brought to anoint the Lord."[68]

The procession to the Gospel ambo is dramatic but definitely not climactic. The omission of tapers connotes sorrow. The deacon and his assistants represent the Marys *before* they have learned of the Resurrection. The Gospel text, because it announces the Resurrection, might be considered climactic, but such an interpretation ignores the ordinary of the Mass. Not only Amalarius but the Church Fathers themselves equated the Consecration with the Crucifixion. The reading of the Gospel was to recall the words and acts of Christ, but during the Canon a transition occurred from commemoration to action. Hence even after the reading of the Gospel, the mood of the vigil service is restrained. The absence of an Offertory hymn suggests a continuation of the mood of sorrow: "At the time of the sacrifice the cantors are silent, recalling the silence and the sacrifice of the women, which was that they bore ointment for anointing the body of the Lord."[69]

A suggestion of movement toward climax is found in the Gregorian Preface. Christ is here invoked as the champion of the Easter agon, the

[67] *Ibid.*, pp. 1057ᵈ–58ᵃ; H, II, 160.

[68] Pseudo-Alcuin, *De divinis officiis*, *PL*, CI, 1222ᵃ.

[69] *Liber officialis*, *PL*, CV, 1058ᵇ; H, II, 161.

victor over His *adversarius: inferorum claustra disrumpens, victoriae suae clara vexilla suscepit, et triumphato diabolo, victor a mortuis resurrexit.* The mood is immediately reinforced by the Sanctus, which is sung, says Amalarius, "because it is the song of the angels, and the angels were not silent concerning the Resurrection—neither the one who is mentioned by St. Mark, nor the two described by John as sitting, one at the head and one at the feet." [70] In other words, the liturgy is now moving swiftly into the eschatological dimension so prominent in ninth-century thought and in the vigil service in particular. The neophytes have almost reached their goal. The eschatological world has already touched the historical one in the Gloria and Alleluia. Like Adam in Paradise, the reborn neophytes can hear the music of the angels as they welcome Christ. The sense of mystery is heightened by the Consecration, which includes a special prayer for the catechumens, *quos regenerare dignatus es ex aqua et Spiritu sancto.* The climax occurs at the commingling. It is this moment of the Mass ordinary that Amalarius and later allegorists equated with the Resurrection, and the vigil Mass is the one service of the year when the commingling coincides with the historical event it symbolizes. There has been no sacrifice since Maundy Thursday. Now the Divine Victim is reborn on the altar. The idea of the Real Presence makes it clear that this is not a symbol but a praxis—an action, a literal resurrection. Amalarius writes, "Christ himself through His glorious presence makes himself manifest to whoever wishes to see him." [71]

Although the comments of Amalarius on the vigil Mass do not constitute an Easter play, they touch on several key elements of the *Quem quaeritis.* The deacons, the thurible as *aromata*, the albs, the tomb motif, and above all the resurrection symbolism are examples. An important additional element may have entered the service because of the omission of the Agnus Dei and the Communion antiphon. Perhaps at one time in the history of the vigil Mass the sense of completion following the commingling was best expressed by Communion in silence. However, the *Codex Ratoldus* and the *Regularis concordia* (among many other texts) indicate that it was common to chant a shortened form of vespers while the congregation was receiving Communion. How early this practice began and how widespread it was

---

[70] *Ibid.*

[71] *Ibid.*, p. 1058 °; H, II, 161: "Sacerdos, vicarius Christi, implet officium suum. Dubitantibus apostolis de sua resurrectione, timentibus mulieribus et nihil dicentibus, angelorum concentus clamat Christum resurrexisse a mortuis. Christus ipse per suam gloriosam apparitionem manifestum se facit quibuscumque vult." The effect would be all the more impressive if the Consecration were the prelude to the first Communion since Maundy Thursday. For a possible description of such a sequence, see the rubric in the *Regula magistri* quoted above, n. 57.

is unclear, but the need for texts to occupy the time required in a crowded church for Communion in both species must have made itself felt long before the tenth century.[72] The common form required the singing of Psalm 116 (*Laudate Dominum*) with a triple alleluia as its antiphon. This was followed by the Magnificat and its antiphon, *Vespere autem Sabbati*. Of these selections the antiphon is by far the most interesting. Its repeated alleluias suggest that it was written for use with the vigil Mass rather than for vespers of Holy Saturday, when the Alleluia had not yet been restored. It also includes many of the phrases found in the *Quem quaeritis* play and has dialogue-like characteristics:

ANT.: *Vespere autem Sabbati, quae lucescit in prima Sabbati, venit Maria, Magdalene et altera Maria videre sepulchrum, alleluia.*

ANT.: *Et ecce terrae motus factus est magnus. Angelus enim Domini descendit de coelo, alleluia.*

ANT.: *Angelus enim Domini descendit de coelo, et accedens revolvit lapidem, et sedebat super eum, alleluia, alleluia.*

ANT.: *Erat autem aspectus ejus sicut fulgur, et vestimenta ejus sicut nix, alleluia, alleluia.*

ANT.: *Prae timore autem ejus exterriti sunt custodes, et facti sunt velut mortui, alleluia.*

ANT.: *Respondens autem angelus dixit mulieribus: Nolite timere; scio quod Jesum quem quaeritis crucifixum; surrexit, alleluia.*

ANT.: *Jesum quem quaeritis non est hic, sed surrexit; recordare qualiter locutus sit vobis, dum adhuc in Galilaea esset, alleluia.*

ANT.: *Venite et videte locum ubi positus erat Dominus, alleluia.*

ANT.: *Cito euntes, dicite discipulis, quia surrexit Dominus, alleluia.*[73]

(See Appendix)

When we recall that Bede and Amalarius interpreted the deployment of the ministers during the Fraction and commingling as a representation

---

[72] We may assume crowded services. Not only was the rite extremely impressive and coincident with the Resurrection itself; there was some feeling that attendance was a Christian obligation. That this feeling persisted in the ninth century is indicated by the remark of Rabanus Maurus that a Christian who did not receive Communion during the vigil Mass hardly deserves to be called *Christian* (*De clericorum institutione*, PL, CVII, 350ᵉ): ". . . cujus participatione quicunque fidelium se hac nocte abstinuerit, nescio quomodo dicam illum Christianum." Also *Codex Ratoldus*, in *LS Notae*, p. 380; and *Regularis concordia*, ed. Symons, p. 48. It seems possible from the formulation in the *Liber sacramentorum* that the antiphon was first used during the vigil Mass and then transferred to vespers, rather than the reverse. At any rate, the hymn *Ad coenam agni* demonstrates that the vigil Mass included texts supplementing the Gregorian ones at a time prior to the Gregorian formulation. The Mozarabic Mass for the Easter vigil confirms this view. It includes Offertory and Communion chants.

[73] *LR*, p. 769ᵇ. Note that the celebrant censes the altar during the *Magnificat* (Guéranger, *Liturgical Year*, VI, 570).

of the visit of the Marys to the tomb, the likelihood of a more overt representation, associated with the *Vespere autem* antiphon, becomes intriguing matter for speculation. Unfortunately, there is no evidence within the Mass *ordines*. On the other hand, it is clear that at the climax of the Easter drama liturgy and allegorical comment both stress the visit to Christ's tomb, which was, in fact, the accepted and traditional symbol for the Resurrection. As Brooks has pointed out, it was not until the twelfth century that artists depicted the Resurrection by showing Christ himself.[74]

The Fraction and commingling ceremonies of the Mozarabic vigil Mass have the same Resurrection symbolism found in the *Liber officialis*. At the Fraction the celebrant elevates the *Regnum* particle of the Host before the congregation and exclaims: *Vicit Leo de tribu Juda radix David, alleluia;* to which the chorus replies, *Qui sedes super cherubin Radix David, alleluia.* This is repeated three times. Then, placing the particle in the cup, the celebrant says *Humiliate vos benedictioni,* and delivers his blessing. The following piece is chanted during the Communion:

> PRESBYTER: *Gaudite populi et letamini: Angelus sedit super lapidem Domini: ipse vobis evangelizavit. Christus surrexit a mortuis Salvator mundi: et explevit omnia suavitate: gaudete populi et letamini.*
>
> CHORUS: *Erat autem aspectus ejus sicut fulgur: et vestimenta ejus sicut nix: et dixit.*
>
> PRESBYTER: *Christus surrexit a mortuis.*
>
> CHORUS: *Et exierunt mulieres cito de monumento cum timore et gaudio magno: currentes nunciare discipulis ejus quia surrexit.*
>
> PRESBYTER: *Christus.*
>
> CHORUS: *Gloria et honor Patri Filio et Spiritui Sancto in saecula saeculorum. Amen.*
>
> PRESBYTER: *Gaudete populi et letamini.*
>
> COMMUNIO: *Refecti Christi corpore et sanguine: te laudamus Domine. Alleluia. Alleluia. Alleluia.*[75]   (See Appendix)

The vigil Mass ends with a variant of the normal dismissal and the final benediction. The deacon announces *Ite, missa est, alleluia, alleluia,* and the people reply *Deo gratias, alleluia, alleluia.* The repeated exclamations

---

[74] Brooks, *The Sepulchre of Christ*, p. 13. This date is, perhaps, late. The "crucifixion" mentioned by Brooks as usually appearing *above* the tomb is not the Crucifixion at all, but the standard iconographic emblem for Christ Triumphant—a fact indicated by the arm and hand positions. See the illustrations, pp. 14, 16, 18. Thus the "process" of the Resurrection is not shown in these scenes. Rather, they show two different moments— the Resurrection and the "Return of Christ" to heaven following the Ascension.

[75] *Missale mixtum*, PL, LXXXV, 476 ᵃ⁻ᵇ. Compare to the rite in the Gothic breviary, PL, LXXXVI, 614ᵃ–16ᵃ; esp. the *Lauda*, p. 616ᵃ.

effectively sustain the joyous mood of the Communion. The Gregorian benediction completes the Mass and, in a sense, the whole enormous drama which began on Septuagesima. After the major action—the triumph of Christ—has occurred, secondary actions are completed. The theme of sterility and death is reversed in images of fecundity. The neophytes are infants "reborn" from the "emboldened womb" of the Church: *Deus, qui Ecclesiae suae intemerato utero novos populos producens, eam virginitate manente nova semper prole foecundat, fidei, spei et charitatis vos munere repleat, et suae in vos benedictionis dona infundat.* Likewise, the themes of darkness and defilement are reversed in images of light and purifying flame. The imagery of rebirth links the neophytes with the conclusion of the Easter drama. The imagery of darkness turned to light refers to them and also to the second group that stands out from the congregation during Lent, the penitents, who are now freed from the "shadow of sin": *Et qui hanc sacratissimam noctem Redemptoris nostri Resurrectione voluit illustrare, mentes vestras peccatorum tenebris mundatas virtutum copiis faciat coruscare.* The prayer ends with a lovely allusion to the marriage of the soul to Christ. The congregation is the five wise virgins united in Christ, the bridegroom. Christ is their beginning through the baptism, and their end through the Resurrection: *Quo eorum qui modo renati sunt innocentiam imitari certetis, et vascula mentium vestrarum exemplo praesentium luminum illustretis, et cum bonorum operum lumpadibus ad ejus sponsi thalamum cujus Resurrectionem celebratis, cum prudentibus virginibus intrare possitis. Amen.*[76]

III

The interval between the vigil Mass and Low Sunday is the theophany of the Easter drama. It expresses an almost otherworldly joy and is dominated by the theme of union in Christ. The idea of union is projected in two complementary ways. The lyric texts of the Mass sustain the festive mood with allusions to Christ's victory and to the Heavenly Jerusalem, while the readings commemorate Christ's appearances to the holy women and the disciples.

The Introit of Easter Day triumphantly announces the accomplishment of prophecy: *Resurrexi et adhuc tecum sum, alleluia . . . mirabilis facta est scientia*

---

[76] *LS*, pp. 91ᵈ–92ᵃ. The Song of Songs is related to the Easter vigil service by Augustine in one of his longest sermons (No. 138, in *PL*, XXXVIII, 763ff.), and by Cyril of Jerusalem and Ambrose. See Weller, *The Easter Sermons of St. Augustine*, pp. 21–23. Compare the *Charagan* of the Armenian Church, in Guéranger, *Liturgical Year*, VII, 267–69.

tua. The collect speaks of the Resurrection in terms of victory over death: *aeternitatis nobis aditum, devicta morte, reserasti . . . ;* while the Gregorian Preface contrasts "days of fast" with present and future joys: *. . . expletis jejuniorum sive passionis Dominicae diebus, paschales festi gaudia celebratis, ad ea festa, quae non sunt annua, sed continua . . . exsultantibus animis veniatis.*[77] The motif of otherworldliness was sometimes further stressed by the omission of the response *Et cum spiritu tuo* following the celebrant's *Pax Domini* at the Fraction. According to legend, once when Pope Gregory was celebrating Easter Mass a choir of angels responded with such a sweet melody that the earthly choir feared to join their voices. The *Et cum spiritu tuo* was omitted in commemoration of this miracle.

In the later Masses of the week allusions to the neophytes are frequent. On Monday the Exodus motif is recalled, along with the rite of administering milk and honey during the vigil service: *Introduxit vos Dominus in terram fluentem lac et mel, alleluia.* On Tuesday the reference is to the waters of baptism: *Aqua sapientiae potavit eos, alleluia: firmabitur in illis, et non flectetur, alleluia;* the collect remembers that God "enlarges thy Church through continual increase" (*Ecclesiam tuam novo semper foetu multiplicas*). The motif of victory recurs in the gradual, which commands the neophytes, "redeemed from the hands of the enemy," to testify to their new life: *Dicant nunc, qui redempti sunt a Domino, quos redemit de manu inimici, et de regionibus congregavit eos.* On Wednesday the neophytes are invited to share in the eternal kingdom (*Venite benedicti Patris mei; percipite regnum . . . quod vobis paratum est ab origine mundi*), while the Offertory summons them to the Communion feast (*et pluit illis manna, ut ederent: panem coeli dedit eis*). Today, the ceremony of blessing the Agnus Dei, formerly a part of the services of Holy Saturday, occurs on Wednesday. The fact is of some interest because Wednesdays of Lent are scrutiny days and the paschal "lambs" were originally blessed for distribution to the neophytes. Placing the ceremony on Wednesday appears to sustain the association. The blessing is, however, a papal rite and is now performed only once every seven years.[78]

There is little variation in the chants of the later Masses of the week. The Thursday Introit combines the theme of victory with an allusion to the new-found eloquence of the *infantes: Victricem manum tuam, Domine, laudaverunt pariter . . . quia Sapientia aperuit os mutum, et linguas infantium fecit disertas.* The collect reinforces the Introit, being a prayer for the faith of the newly baptized: *. . . da ut renatis fonte baptismatis una sit fides mentium, et pietas actionum.* Friday returns to the Exodus motif: *Eduxit eos Dominus in*

[77] *LS,* p. 92°. Still more emphatic in the Gelasian and Mozarabic rites.
[78] Text in Guéranger, *Liturgical Year,* VII, 226.

spe . . . et inimicos eorum operuit mare. Finally, Saturday opens with a reference to the salvation of the *electi: Eduxit Dominus populum suum in exsultatione . . . et electos suos in laetitia.*

When Mass was celebrated in the early hours of Easter Sunday, Low Sunday was the last day of the Easter octave. The Mass of Low Sunday retains the texts selected for this order. Its Introit refers to the neophytes as *infantes* and recalls the rite of administering milk and honey at the vigil Mass: *Quasi modo geniti infantes . . . rationabile sine dolo lac cupiscite.* The Epistle (I John 5) refers again to the paschal victory, again relating it to the rebirth achieved through baptism: "Whatsoever is born of God, overcometh the world: and this is the victory which overcometh the world, our faith." The Postcommunion antiphon concludes the Easter theophany with a prayer for grace to persevere in the faith. Two articulation ceremonies emphasize the close of the Easter drama. In Rome the Agnus Dei was distributed, and throughout Europe the neophytes removed their white robes on Low Sunday. The rite is the source of the common medieval title for Low Sunday, *Dominica in albis depositis.*

The second way in which the Masses of Easter Week express the idea of "union in Christ" is through the readings, particularly the Gospels. Each day commemorates an appearance of Christ after the Resurrection, and during the later Middle Ages representational dramas were performed on days associated with the appearances. The exceptions to this rule are the readings of Easter Sunday (Mark 16) and Low Saturday (John 20), which refer to the visit to the tomb and the announcement of the angels rather than to Christ's appearances. On Monday Christ's appearance at Emmaus (Luke 24), the basis of the *Peregrini* drama, is commemorated; on Tuesday, His later supper with the apostles (*ibid.*); and on Wednesday, the appearance by the Sea of Tiberius (John 21). Thursday's reading returns to the visit to the tomb, relating the appearance of Christ to Mary Magdalene (John 20), the basis of the so-called *Hortulanus* episode of later drama. On Friday the appearance by the Sea of Galilee (Matt. 23) is recalled, and on Saturday John's narrative is again read. Sunday's Mass continues the chapter from John. It tells the story of Christ's appearance to Thomas and is apparently intended as a last warning against doubt. Clearly, these readings are dominated by a single motive, the wish to present as emphatically as possible the fact of Christ's physical presence among men after the Resurrection. If the neophytes symbolize the possibility of a human approach to the divine, the readings emphasize God's willingness to humble himself to the condition of human existence. The two ideas are physically embodied during Easter Week in the processions of white-robed neophytes following the paschal candle—the *lumen Christi*—and the bishop to the stational churches.

The Easter octave, then, has a definite function in the Easter drama, to which texts, lyric chants, settings, and costumes are related. The general bent is eschatological and almost Dantesque in its mingling of things physical and spiritual. Doubtless in early Christian centuries it was intensely moving. Comments in the *Liber officialis* and other contemporary documents show that it had not lost its appeal in the ninth century. During the octave there are three services of special interest to the historian of drama. The first is the nocturns service on Easter morning. The second is the Mass of Easter Day. The third is the Roman vesper service for Easter Week.

IV

As long as the vigil service ended at or near sunrise, the nocturnal office was not said. When Mass began near midnight, however, a gap developed between the end of Mass and the beginning of the daytime services. The interval was initially too brief to permit the full office, but there was time for a shortened version consisting of the third of the conventional three nocturns. At the same time, certain monastic churches and churches without baptismal fonts appear to have omitted the vigil service, following the regular order of vespers (with or without Mass), compline, and a triple nocturn. Later, such churches adopted the Roman order for Easter, omitting the first two nocturns.[79] The details of this process are obscure. The point is that by the tenth century the shortened vigil service and the celebration of a single nocturn shortly before dawn on Easter had become quite general.

When the vigil Mass had been displaced, the Church was compelled to find another rite to mark the moment of the Resurrection. In tenth-century manuscripts two Resurrection ceremonies are found in association with the Easter nocturn. The first is the "Elevation" (*Elevatio*) of the cross "deposed" on Good Friday after the Adoration. It usually occurs just before the beginning of the Easter nocturn. Since the cross was restored along with ornaments and festive decorations for the vigil Mass, the tenth-century *Elevatio* can only be a makeshift necessitated by the displacement of this Mass. Perhaps for this reason it received less emphasis than a second ceremony performed at the end of the Easter nocturn and coinciding with Easter sunrise. This is the "Visit to the Sepulcher"

[79] See Young, *DMC*, I, 547, for discussion.

(*Visitatio Sepulchri*). The earliest surviving version of the *Visitatio*, that from the late tenth-century *Regularis concordia*, includes detailed rubrics and the dialogue of the *Quem quaeritis* play. The time of the *Visitatio* was explained during the later Middle Ages as coinciding with the moment of the Resurrection.[80] It became extremely popular, and occasionally it assimilated parts of the *Elevatio* rite.

Both the *Elevatio* and the *Visitatio* may have existed before the tenth century. Even if they did not, however, the Easter nocturn service is itself an emphatic commemoration of the Resurrection. The office begins with the glad tidings of the angels to the holy women, *Surrexit Dominus vere*, chanted with Psalm 94, *Venite, exsultemus Domino*. The lessons are of particular interest. They are from Pope Gregory's homily on Mark 16. In this homily Pope Gregory relates the visit to the tomb to the lives of the faithful. The holy women are symbols of devotion, and all Christians should imitate them: ". . . this that they did, teaches what we, the members of the Church, should do . . . if laden with the fragrance of virtue and the reputation of good works, we seek the Lord, we may truly be said to come to the sepulcher with sweet spices. Moreover, the women, who came with sweet spices, saw angels; and those souls come to the vision of the heavenly citizens, who, fragrant in virtue, tend to the Lord by their holy desires."[81] This interpretation is closely associated with a series of responses based on the passage being explained. Sung antiphonally, they come remarkably close to the form and wording of the *Quem quaeritis* play:

Resp.: *Angelus Domini descendit de caelo, et accedens revolvit lapidem; et super eum sedit, et dixit mulieribus: Nolite timere; scio enim quia crucifixum quaeritis. Jam surrexit. Venite et videte locum ubi positus erat Dominus, alleluia.*

Vers.: *Angelus Domini locutus est mulieribus dicens: Quem quaeritis, an Jesum quaeritis? Jam.*

Resp.: *Angelus Domini locutus est mulieribus dicens: Quem quaeritis, an Jesum quaeritis? Jam surrexit, venite et videte, alleluia, alleluia.*

Vers.: *Ecce praecedet vos in Galilaeam, ibi eum videbitis, sicut dixit vobis. Jam.*

Resp.: *Dum transisset Sabbitum, Maria Magdalene, et Maria Jacobi et Salome emerunt aromata, ut venientes ungerent Jesum, alleluia, alleluia.*

---

[80] Gregory's homily, in Guéranger, *Liturgical Year*, VII, 118–21, relates the visit in considerable detail. Gregory's interpretation, as well as the interpretations of Augustine, Bede, and other early writers, will be considered in connection with the *Quem quaeritis* play. For the tradition that the Resurrection coincides with the beginning of lauds, see Weiser, *Handbook*, p. 216; Young, *DMC*, I, 231–32. Compare Amalarius, *Liber officialis*, "De octo diebus neophytorum" (*PL*, CV, 1058 ᶜ–61 ᵉ; H, II, 161–67).

[81] Guéranger, *Liturgical Year*, VII, 119.

VERS.: *Et valde mane una Sabbatorum veniunt ad monumentum, orto jam sole. Ut venientes.*

RESP.: *Super lapidem monumenti sedebant angeli, et psallabant de resurrectione Domini; et ante sepulchrum Jesu stabat Maria dicens: Domine, si tu sustulisti eum, dic ubi posuisti eum, alleluia.*

VERS.: *At illa existimans, quod hortulanus esset, dicit ei, Domine, si.* [82]

(See Appendix)

One more text may be included here from the Easter office. This is the text of the antiphons for lauds (i.e., the Gregorian matins). Again form and wording are close to those of the *Quem quaeritis* play:

ANT.: *Et valde mane una Sabbatorum veniunt ad monumentum, orto jam sole, alleluia.*

ANT.: *Et dicebant ad invicem: Quis revolvet nobis lapidem ab ostio monumenti? Alleluia, alleluia.*

ANT.: *Et respicientes viderunt revolutum lapidem, erat quippe magnus valde, alleluia.*

ANT.: *Nolite expavescere, Jesum Nazarenum quaeritis crucifixum, non est hic; surrexit, alleluia.*

ANT.: *Praecedam vos in Galilaeam; ibi me videbitis sicut dixi vobis, alleluia.*

ANT.: *Cito euntes, dicite discipulis quia surrexit Dominus, alleluia, alleluia. Post passionem Domini factus est conventus, quia non est corpus in monumentum. Lapis sustinuit perpetuam vitam, monumentum reddidit coelestem margaritam, alleluia.*

ANT.: *Venerunt ad monumentum Maria Magdalene, et altera Maria videre sepulcrum, alleluia.* [83]

(See Appendix)

The heavy emphasis of both of the preceding texts on the visit to the tomb is explained by their timing. Gospel accounts place the Resurrection "early in the morning" or "at sunrise." The vigil Mass coincides with the former moment, and the nocturns-lauds sequence with the latter. Since Christ did not appear until after the initial visit, emphasis falls on the empty tomb and the testimony of the angels. In the next to last antiphon of lauds a shift in emphasis is observable. The reference to the completion of the covenant and the "heavenly pearl" lead from the event to its consequences.

The idea of "completion" carries over naturally into the Easter Mass. Aside from the Gospel (Matt. 16), there is no allusion to the visit to the tomb. This event is now past history. The Introit refers to it in the perfect tense: *Resurrexi et adhuc tecum sum*—"I *have* arisen and am as yet with you."

[82] *LR*, pp. 769d–70a.

[83] *Ibid.*, p. 770a-b.

The Epistle (I Cor. 5:7–8) follows suit: *Pascha nostrum immolatus est Christus.* This sentence is repeated in the gradual and Communion antiphon. The Mass prayers also stress completion. In the Preface the redemption is an accomplished fact: *Ipse enim verus est Agnus. . . . Qui mortem nostram moriendo destruxit, et vitam resurgendo reparavit.* Only one text of the ninth-century Easter Mass differs from that used today. The difference is as instructive as the similarities. Today's service employs an eleventh-century sequence, *Victimae Paschali laudes,* in place of the Gregorian tract. The *Victimae Paschali* is highly dramatic (in fact, it was often incorporated into Latin Resurrection plays), but it describes the visit to the tomb. For this reason it is slightly incongruous. Conversely, the Gregorian text stresses joy in the accomplishment of redemption: *Haec dies quam fecit Dominus, exsultemus et laetemur in ea. . . . Dicat nunc Israel quoniam bonus . . . dextra Domini exsultavit me. . . . Benedictus qui venit in nomine Domini. . . . Pascha nostrum immolatus est Christus, Epulemur in azymis sinceritatis et veritatis.*[84]

Since Amalarius stresses the visit to the tomb in his comment on the Easter vigil but does not mention it in his discussion of the *Resurrexi* Mass, we are safe in concluding that the Gregorian orientation persisted at least to the ninth century.[85] We may also regard with suspicion the tenth-century use of the *Quem quaeritis* dialogue as an Easter Introit trope. Whatever the origin of the *Quem quaeritis,* it was not composed to be used in conjunction with the *Resurrexi* antiphon.

One further Easter rite must be mentioned. Roman practice requires an especially elaborate vesper service throughout the week. The service involves a procession to the baptismal font accompanied by psalms and antiphons. It was originally composed for the neophytes, and it has all the elements of a resurrection ceremony. The font is treated as a sepulcher, several texts are derived from the story of the visit to the tomb, and the participants assume well-defined roles. The version in the *Liber responsalis* includes rubrics as well as texts:

Conveniente schola temperius cum episcopis et diaconibus in ecclesiam majorem ad locum crucifixi incipiunt *Kyrie eleison,* et veniunt usque

---

[84] *LS,* p. 91ᵇ (Preface), and *LA,* p. 678ᵇ (gradual). The *Haec dies* is a key text, repeated in all Masses of the octave.

[85] *Liber officialis (PL,* CV, 1061ᶜ–62ᵈ; H, II, 167–68): "Die sancto paschae in introitu per ora prophetarum praesentat se Christus ex resurrectione Patri suo. . . . Oratio prima demonstrat aditum esse apertum sanctae ecclesiae regni caelestis." There is no discussion of the visit of the holy women, who so preoccupy Amalarius in the discussion of the rites of Holy Saturday and the vigil Mass. We have now passed the moment of the Resurrection and are in "the new age of the Heavenly Jerusalem."

altare; et ascendentibus diaconibus in pogium . . . annuit archidiaconus primo scholae, et ille inclinans se incipiat *Alleluia* cum Psalmo *Dixit Dominus Domino meo*. . . . Hac expleta . . . incipiat archidiaconus.

ANT.: *Scio quod Jesum quaeritis crucifixum; surrexit, alleluia.*

ANT.: *Jesum quem quaeritis, non est hic; sed surrexit. Recordare qualiter locutus sit vobis dum adhuc in Galilaea esset, alleluia.*

Post hoc det sacerdos Orationem, et descendant ad fontes cum Antiph. *In die resurrectionis meae . . . effundam super vos aquam mundam, alleluia. . . .* Postea sequitur diaconi secundus in Evangelio.

ANT.: *Venite et videte locum ubi positus erat Dominus, alleluia.*

Deinde dicat sacerdos Orationem, et tunc vadunt ad sanctam Joannem ad vestem, canentes. . . . *A Domino factum est istud, et est mirabile in oculis nostris, alleluia, alleluia*. Deinde. . . . Psal. *In exitu Israel*. . . . Post hanc sequitur diaconus.

ANT.: *Cito euntes, dicite discipulis quia surrexit Dominus, alleluia, alleluia.*

Deinde oret semper sine *Kyrie eleison*. Et tunc vadunt ad sanctum Andream ad crucem, canentes: *Vidi aquam egredientem de templo a latere dextro, alleluia: et omnes ad quos pervenit aqua ista, salvi facti sunt, alleluia, alleluia*. . . . Quo finito primus scholae incipit *alleluia. Venite exsultemus*. . . .

ANT.: *Cito euntes dicite discipulis*. . . .

Deinde descendunt primates ecclesiae ad accubitum. . . .[86]

(See Appendix)

Unlike the *Visitatio Sepulchri*, which represents the event, Roman vespers is a commemoration. Two closely related moments are recalled— the Resurrection and the baptism of the catechumens—and each phase of the service alludes to both Gospel history and Holy Week liturgy. It begins with actions recalling the Crucifixion and the Adoration rite of Good Friday. At "the place of the cross" the chorus sings the Kyrie, a prayer for mercy, and proceeds to the altar, also a symbol of Christ. The vesper Psalms (109, 110, 111) follow. They are hymns of praise but do not refer explicitly to the Resurrection. The bishop, the chorus, and the neophytes are, in a sense, waiting. Then, as the Psalms are concluded, the archdeacon begins the angelic chant, informing them, "Jesus whom you seek is not here; he has arisen. . . . Remember what he said to you in Galilee." What makes the exchange striking is that, having been informed of the miracle, all present file out of the church. It is quite clear that they are "seeking" Jesus. As they leave they chant an antiphon in which Christ

---

[86] *LR*, pp. 770ᶜ–71ᵇ. See also the *ordo* of St. Amand, in Duchesne, *Christian Worship*, pp. 472–73. This most interesting service is discussed without reference to its resurrection symbolism by Young, *DMC*, I, 456–58. Guéranger, *Liturgical Year*, VII, 157–69, gives the service in its modern form.

promises to "pour out upon you clean water" on "the day of my Resurrection," and they proceed directly to the baptismal font, which contains the "clean water" referred to. When they are assembled, a second deacon invites them to "come and see the place where Christ was placed." The reference can only be to the font itself, where Christ was "buried" in the paschal candle ceremony of Holy Saturday. The Gospel dialogue identifies it with the original sepulcher. Originally, the neophytes crowded around the font and gazed into it during the chant. After the collect, all move from the baptistery to the Lateran vestry (*sanctum Johannem ad vestem*).[87] They have now "witnessed" the Resurrection. Therefore they praise the miracle accomplished "before our eyes." The symbolism of the procession is further enriched by Psalm 113, which recalls the time "when Israel went out of Egypt, the house of Jacob from a barbarous people." Again they are addressed by the deacon in words taken from the Gospel: "Go quickly, announce to the disciples that the Lord is risen." Like the original holy women, the participants are commanded to testify to the miracle. After the Kyrie they obey the command. Proceeding across Rome to Saint Andrea, they announce to all the city, "I saw living water flowing from the temple on the right side . . . and all who were touched by this water were saved." This is followed by the invitation *Venite exsultemus*. On arrival, the clergy enters the refectory, where a fraternal toast is offered in three varieties of wine, symbolizing the unity of all men in Christ.

Throughout the Roman vespers there is a close relation between text, setting, and action. The assigning of roles—the deacons as angels, the neophytes and chorus as the holy women—is unmistakable. The response of the "women" to the angelic commands is direct and emphatic. The ceremony is a Resurrection play centered around the font rather than the altar. Its length and elaboration make it a good deal more impressive than the earliest versions of the *Quem quaeritis* play. At the very least, its existence demonstrates that representations of the Resurrection were known before the tenth century.

V

On Sunday after Easter the neophytes remove their white robes. This act symbolizes both the final repose of the blessed and the entry of the neophytes into the ranks of the Church Militant. The deposition of albs marks the close of the Easter drama. It is a framing element as emphatic

[87] Or, perhaps, the oratory (see *LR*, 771ᵈ).

as the "Farewell to the Alleluia" which began the drama. Theoretically, the cycle will continue to the Ascension and even to Pentecost, but the mood of the Easter octave cannot be sustained over such a long period. The cycle ends as a unified composition on Low Sunday.

Like the Mass, the Easter cycle is dramatic in structure and nonrepresentational in mode. Unlike the Mass, it includes representational episodes. These are not essential; in fact, many of them are clearly nonliturgical. Their characteristic feature is their use of linear or chronological time. For this reason they have the quality of germinal history plays, and they employ devices of verisimilitude such as pantomime, stage props, costume, and dialogue taken from their historical source, i.e., the Gospels. Their occurrence is governed by coincidence between the time (and, as far as possible, the space) of the event commemorated and the liturgical rite. They are prominent throughout Holy Week. With one exception, each of the major events in Christ's life from Palm Sunday to Easter had its representational ceremony during the ninth century. The exception is, of course, the Resurrection, which is the climax of the entire drama. The vigil Mass coincides with this moment but is in the nonrepresentational mode of the liturgy proper. Not until the tenth century is there manuscript evidence of a representational ceremony marking the Resurrection. This is the *Quem quaeritis* play associated with the Easter nocturns or the first Mass of Easter. The situation is sufficiently incongruous to suggest the possibility of a Resurrection ceremony well before the tenth century and associated with the Easter vigil. Changes in the liturgy—particularly the shift of the vigil sequence—would explain the displacement of the ceremony, as well as the fact that tenth- and eleventh-century versions, while obviously related, differ among themselves in respect to text, rubrics, and time of presentation.

Here, before going too far afield, we may put a limit on conjecture. The drama of the Easter liturgy does not exist for the sake of future developments but for its own sake. Considered purely from the point of view of the literary critic, it is one of noblest monuments of medieval culture. It is a response to what the early Middle Ages considered its most imperative challenge: the need to achieve outward and visible expression of the forms of union between the human and the divine. The result is a product of collective effort, but it is not anonymous in the manner of folk literature. From apostolic times to the age of Pope Gregory the liturgy drew on the talents of men of exceptional learning and sensitivity. Their learning accounts for its rich complexity in structure, symbolism, theological concepts, uses of Scripture, and echoes of classical tradition. Their sensitivity, which is perhaps ultimately the more important factor, accounts for the universality of the forms subsumed in the liturgy and for the transcendence of their expression when compared to non-Christian ritual. A movement from agon to peripeteia to theophany characterizes rituals from earliest times to the present day, from cultures as diverse as Mayan, Hindu, Greek, and American Indian. It may, as Frazer believed, reflect conditions that occur in all societies as a necessary stage of development. It may, as Jung maintained, reflect a characteristic of the mind—categories or archetypes that are preconditions of cognition and transmitted by heredity. Or, as Father Rahner appears to argue, it may reflect a sense of kinship with God existing in all men as a kind of blurred recollection of their divine origin. The first two assumptions lead to the conclusion that the Christian liturgy is qualitatively like the other rites studied by comparative religion; the third, to the hypothesis that it is qualitatively different from them in the way that truth differs from all of its approximations and adumbrations.

We need not attempt to arbitrate between these differing points of view. Apart from the fact that the effort would be presumptuous, the conclusions to be reached evidently depend on assumptions that are beyond the purview of scholarship. What is indisputable is that in articulation and language, in all those elements that distinguish a living creation from an archetype, the Easter liturgy is an unique achievement.

ESSAY V

The Early History of the
Quem quaeritis

I

THE DIALOGUE CALLED *Quem quaeritis* enjoys a position unique in the history of literature. Although it is obviously related to many extraliturgical embellishments observable in religious ceremony of the eighth, ninth, and tenth centuries, it became, quite literally, the bridge whereby medieval culture made the transition from ritual to representational drama. But it was more than a transitional form, to be discarded as soon as the dramatic methods to which it pointed had been mastered. The central event of world history, from the point of view of medieval Christianity, is the Resurrection. The climax of the Mass commemorates this event; it is the pivot around which the cyclical drama of the liturgical year is organized; and it remained the decisive moment for the religious drama of the high Middle Ages.

In Aristotelian terms the Resurrection is both the peripeteia and the anagnorisis of the Christian mythos. It is the point at which the action of history "veers around in the opposite direction," and it is the moment when humanity, represented by the holy women visiting the tomb of Christ, first recognizes the full significance of the Incarnation. The *Quem quaeritis* dramatizes this moment. It is not a tentative and blurred effort to express a felt experience in representational form but a decisive realization of experience in terms of the history that the Middle Ages regarded as its basis. The *Quem quaeritis* not only persisted in recognizable form from its first appearance in the tenth century to the enormous vernacular dramas of the fifteenth century, but it also served as a model for early liturgical pieces dramatizing the Nativity and the Ascension. The dialogue in the earliest manuscript consists of a question, an answer, and a reply:

> *Quem queritis in sepulchro, o Christicole?*
> *Ihesum Nazarenum crucifixum, o celicole.*
> *Non est hic, surrexit sicut ipse dixit; ite nunciate quia surrexit.*[1]

[1] Text given in Young, *DMC*, I, 210.

(Whom seek you in the tomb, O followers of Christ?
Jesus of Nazareth who was crucified, O Heaven-Dwellers.
He is not here, he has arisen as he said; go announce that he has arisen.)

Some four hundred years later, the same exchange appears in the Wakefield *Resurrection:*

I Angelus:	Ye mowrnyng women in youre thought,
	Here in this place whome have ye soght?
Maria Magdalene:	Ihesu that vnto ded was broght,
	Oure Lord so fre.
II Angelus:	Certys, women, here is he noght;
	Com nere and se.
I Angelus:	He is not here, the sothe to say;
	The place is voyde ther in he lay;
	The sudary here se ye may
	Was on hym layde.
	He is rysen and gone his way,
	As he you sayde.[2]

The use of the *Quem quaeritis* as a model may be observed in two early dialogues on the Nativity and the Ascension:

> *Quem quaeritis in praesepe, pastores, dicite?*
> *Salvatorem Christum Dominum, infantem pannis involutum,*
> *secundum sermonem angelicum.*
> *Adest hic parvulus cum Maria, matre sua. . . .*

And:

> *Quem cernitis ascendisse super astra, o Christicolae?*
> *Ihesum qui surrexit de sepulchro, o caelicolae.*
> *Iam ascendit, ut praedixit. . . .*[3]   (See Appendix)

That there were other, apparently similar, extraliturgical embellishments during the ninth and tenth centuries is a matter of record; that there also existed pagan ceremonies, quasi-dramatic folk rituals, and performances by minstrels, scops, and other popular entertainers, all classified under the term "ludi," may be inferred, although their nature

---

[2] Text given in *Chief Pre-Shakespearean Dramas*, ed. Joseph Q. Adams (Boston, 1924), p. 195.

[3] Both tropes are given in Chambers, *MS*, II, 11.

and extent is disputed.⁴ Whatever may be said about them, they never became central to the development of liturgical drama as it can be known from existing documents. Their influence, when it can be traced, remains tangential. One must agree with M. H. Marshall that "the tradition of the liturgical drama established certain basic modes of dramatizing the materials of sacred history which persisted through the course of medieval religious drama."⁵

II

Since Chambers' *Mediaeval Stage* was published, the accepted position regarding the origin of the *Quem quaeritis* has consisted of five points:

1. The simplest form of the *Quem quaeritis* is the earliest form.
2. The *Quem quaeritis* is an original composition stemming from the monastery of St. Gall.
3. In its original form the *Quem quaeritis* is an example of the type of liturgical embellishment called a trope.
4. The first version of the *Quem quaeritis* was written around 900 A.D., probably by the monk Tutilo of St. Gall, a predecessor and mentor of Notker Balbalus.
5. It was originally intended as a trope of the Introit of the Mass of Easter Day, but was later expanded and transferred to the end of the matins service on Easter Morning.⁶

These five points have occasionally been questioned. Perhaps the most direct challenge was made in 1926 by Professor Joseph Klapper. On the basis of manuscript rubrics, Professor Klapper concluded that the Breslau

---

⁴ The basic study of folk drama, mimes, and other quasi-dramatic entertainments of the Middle Ages is the first volume of Chambers' *Mediaeval Stage*. The strongest claim for the influence of folk drama on medieval drama is that made by Stumpfl, *Kultspiele der Germanen als Ursprung des mittelalterlichen Dramas*, and more recently (but no more persuasively) by Benjamin Hunningher, *The Origin of the Theater* (New York, 1961). For a recent review of the evidence for dramatic performances in the early Middle Ages, see J. D. A. Ogilvy, "*Mimi, Scurrae, Histriones:* Entertainers of the Early Middle Ages," *Speculum*, XXXVIII (1963), 603–19.

⁵ "The Dramatic Tradition Established by the Liturgical Plays," *PMLA*, LVI (1941), 991. The same conclusion is reached by Sister John Sullivan, *Themes of the Sacred Passion in the Medieval Cycle Plays* (Washington, D.C., 1943).

⁶ Chambers, *MS*, II, 2–28; Young, *DMC*, I, 202–306. The classification, though not the theoretical justification, originated with Carl Lange, *Die lateinischen Osterfeiern* (Munich, 1887), pp. 17, 167–71. It persists unchanged in such recent studies as those by Hardin Craig and Grace Frank.

Visitatio Sepulchri preserved a form of the *Quem quaeritis* in use in Jerusalem at the Church of the Holy Sepulchre between the sixth and eighth centuries. He therefore asserted that the Jerusalem version was the original and that it was transferred to the West in the same way as the Palm Sunday and Good Friday ceremonies. From this it followed that extant Western manuscripts are simplified or "degenerate" versions.[7] Klapper's hypothesis concerning the Breslau manuscript has been decisively disproved; in fact, it has been shown that the Jerusalem *Visitatio* was imported from the West between 1099 and 1160 by crusaders.[8] On the other hand, Klapper's basic point—that extant manuscripts may be simplified versions of an original—and several of his subsidiary arguments are still worth consideration.

Other, and more particular, objections are numerous. Edith Wright feels that France, rather than Switzerland, is the most probable country of origin for the *Quem quaeritis*.[9] The theory that the *Quem quaeritis* was an original composition in the form of a trope is questioned by Paul Kretzmann, who prefers to regard it as a collection of antiphons and antiphon fragments.[10] All of the preceding views carry with them the implication that the *Quem quaeritis* may have originated at a considerably earlier date than 900. Paul Weber and others argue for an earlier date on the basis of manuscript illuminations from the ninth century that seem to depict the visit to the sepulcher in dramatic form.[11] Finally, the attachment of the original *Quem quaeritis* to the Mass of Easter was questioned by Walter

[7] Klapper, "Der Ursprung der lateinischen Osterfeiern," *Zeitschrift fur deutsche Philologie*, L (1923), 46–58.

[8] *DMC*, I, 262, 591.

[9] *The Dissemination of the Liturgical Drama in France* (Bryn Mawr, Pa., 1936), pp. 31, 41. Also Frank, *Medieval French Drama* (Oxford, 1954), pp. 66–67: "It seems probable . . . that both the Easter and Christmas plays arise in France, the former in the tenth, the latter in the eleventh century. . . . The Abbey of St. Martin in Limoges was the earliest exponent of the liturgical drama and created in embryonic form most of the important plays adopted elsewhere." The likelihood of a French origin for the *Quem quaeritis* has been increased by the emphasis placed by scholars since Gautier on the extensive history of the trope in France before its arrival at St. Gall. See, e.g., Clemens Blume, *Analecta hymnica medii aevi* (Leipzig, 1905), XLVII, 10–17; Raby, *Christian Latin Poetry*, pp. 220–21; H. F. Muller, "Pre-History of the Medieval Drama," *Zeitschrift fur romanische Philologie*, XLVI (1924), 544–75.

[10] *The Liturgical Element in the Earliest Form of Medieval Drama* ("University of Minnesota Studies in Language and Literature," No. 4; Minneapolis, Minn., 1916), pp. 135–36. Like Klapper, Kretzmann assumes that the "original" form of the dialogue was the "abbreviated form" considered below, p. 197.

[11] Weber, *Geistliches Schauspiel und kirkliche Kunst* (Stuttgart, 1894), p. 32. An early date is also suggested by the existence of a version of the ceremony in a manuscript of the *Liber officialis* of Amalarius edited by A. Wilmert, which Wilmert believes may be as early as the ninth century. See *Revue benedictine*, XXXIV (1922), 161–62.

Frere in his edition of the Winchester troper. In the tenth-century manuscript of the Winchester troper the *Quem quaeritis* precedes the blessing of the paschal candle on Easter Eve. Frere therefore inferred that the piece was originally "independent" but "came to be used as a trope of the Introit of Easter."[12] Although none of these arguments have made much headway, they all reflect dissatisfaction with the orthodox position.

The first of the five points of the orthodox position may be called the "simplest version" hypothesis. If it is true that the simplest version of the *Quem quaeritis* is necessarily the earliest, the other points follow as corollaries.

Yet the "simplest version" hypothesis is neither deductively inevitable nor empirically verifiable. Whereas in evolution simpler forms usually precede more complex ones, in literary history the reverse is often true. Complex forms are often simplified or changed radically in the process of being adapted to changed conditions. Moreover, although some parallels to biological evolution may occur in the history of the most primitive forms of literature, in all cultures sufficiently sophisticated to have a literary tradition preserved in written form, influences, sources, and conscious manipulation by individual authors are demonstrably more significant than a hypothetical impulse or instinct toward gradually increasing complexity. Does the epic become more complex after Homer? The lyric after Sappho? The drama after Aeschylus? The Mass after Pope Gregory? The answer is obviously no. There are changes (often for the worse), but there is no pattern of steadily increasing complexity. These observations do not disprove the "simplest version" hypothesis as applied to the *Quem quaeritis*, but they do indicate that it is only one of several equally possible alternatives and that it should not be accepted until its liabilities have been thoroughly examined.

If the "simplest version" hypothesis were supported by empirical evidence, it would have to be accepted no matter what its liabilities. Contrary to the impression given by Chambers and Young, however, it is contradicted, rather than supported, by the small amount of evidence that is available. The earliest manuscript of the *Quem quaeritis* gives the dialogue in an elaborated rather than a simple form and is from Limoges rather than St. Gall. The Limoges text is dated between 923 and 934, while the simple version generally accepted as the original cannot be dated before the middle of the tenth century. If the St. Gall text preserves the earliest version, we must assume (1) that it is a copy of a lost original; (2) that the manuscript from which it was copied was written before 923; (3) that the original manuscript or a copy of it was taken from St. Gall to Limoges

---

[12] *The Winchester Troper* (London, 1894), p. xvi.

and there improved for reasons as yet unexplained; and (4) that the monks of St. Gall either did not know of the improvement or preferred to continue using the simpler form. None of these assumptions are impossible. On the other hand, Edith Wright's suggestion that Limoges is the original and St. Gall a simplified copy both agrees with manuscript chronology and avoids postulating a lost St. Gall original.

The reason for the acceptance of the "simplest version" hypothesis has nothing to do with historical evidence. The hypothesis was attractive to Chambers, Manly, Young, and their followers because it accorded with the analogy between biological evolution and the development of literary forms. Varying interpretations of the mechanism of evolution also account for the differences between Chambers on the one hand and Manly and Young on the other. Accepting the idea that evolution proceeds by minute variations, Chambers suggested that the dramatic impulse begins with inarticulate expressions of joy formalized in the melisma of the ninth-century Alleluia, is articulated through the words attached to the melisma for mnemonic reasons, and eventually emerges as drama in the *Quem quaeritis*.[13] Manly and Young, as we have observed, regarded evolution as a discontinuous process in accordance with De Vries's theory of mutations.[14] While they did not openly reject Chambers' suggestions, they placed major stress on the originality of the *Quem quaeritis*—its qualitative difference from all that preceded it.

In either case, the "simplest version" hypothesis leads directly to the four corollary points of the orthodox position. Because the earliest manuscript containing a simplest version is from St. Gall, that monastery becomes the logical point of origin. Since the St. Gall version occurs among a series of tropes and is labeled *item*, it is natural to assume that the original was a trope. Because the more complex version from Limoges can be dated around 930, a date of around 910 becomes necessary for the original, and "the famous Tutilo, who was actively engaged in this sort of composition during the early years of the tenth century, and was still living in 912" is the most likely author.[15] Finally, because the St. Gall *Quem quaeritis* is evidently attached to the Introit of Easter Mass, the idea follows easily that it was first an Introit trope and was later transferred to the matins service.

To the "simplest version" hypothesis several objections may be made. In the first place, the simplest version is some thirty years later than the

---

[13] *MS*, II, 7–10. Chambers' chronology is distorted by the fact that he apparently (II, 8) regards the St. Gall manuscript as a ninth-century document.

[14] Above, Essay I, pp. 21–25.

[15] *DMC*, I, 205.

earliest version. If the evolutionary analogy is abandoned, at least two other hypotheses are equally possible. As has been noted, Limoges may be the source of the St. Gall version. Again, both Limoges and St. Gall may be derived from a common source. The first possibility cannot be rejected, but the second is, perhaps, the more immediately attractive. It does not require the assumption that any extant manuscript is original. Furthermore, it raises the possibility that the Limoges and St. Gall texts may both be modified versions of the original. If so, other texts, even quite late ones, may reproduce the original more faithfully. Without some idea of the shape and function of the original, there is no way to differentiate between "faithful," "expanded," and "degenerate" versions. The "simplest version" hypothesis solves this problem by fiat. Once it is questioned, the need for a fresh look at the manuscripts becomes imperative.

In the second place, the "simplest version" hypothesis assumes a process of gradual development by incremental addition between the St. Gall "original" and the more complex versions. Yet the evidence used to illustrate the process is entirely a posteriori. No early texts of the *Quem quaeritis* have been published since Karl Young's *Drama of the Medieval Church*. Young's collection may therefore be taken as complete. To test the theory of gradual development, we may restrict ourselves to manuscripts cited by Young to illustrate the period between the composition of the original and the emergence of a full dramatic text of the *Visitatio Sepulchri*, adapted for use at matins and including dialogue, supplementary liturgical pieces, and full rubrics. For simplicity, only manuscripts cited in Young's text will be listed. Those mentioned in the notes enlarge the pattern without changing it. In his chapter on the earliest versions of the *Quem quaeritis*, Young gives twenty examples ranging from simple to complex:

St. Gall	?950
Vercelli	XII C.
Ravenna	XI–XII C.
Bobbio	XI C.
Abruzzi	X–XI C.
Vercelli	XII C.
Monza	XI C.
Limoges	XI C.
Limoges	923–34
Mantua	XI C.
Limoges	988–96
Apt	X–XI C.
Limoges	XI C.

Ripoll	XII–XIII C.
Cassino	XI C.
Cassino	XII C.
Benevento	XII C.
Novalesa	XI C.
Piacenza	XI–XII C.
Brescia	XV C.

In the next chapter ("The Easter Introit Trope in Transition"), Young reproduces manuscripts showing that "in seeking dramatic freedom, the trope gradually detached itself from the Introit and the Mass altogether."[16] These manuscripts are intended to show that there was an intermediate stage between the trope used with the Mass Introit and its attachment to matins:

Ivrea, Italy	1001–11
St. Martin of Tours	Date uncertain
Heidenheim	XI C.
Monza	XII C.
St. Gall	XI C.
St. Gall	XI C.
Monza	XIII C.
Vienne	Date uncertain

The following chapter ("The Visit to the Sepulchre: First Stage") illustrates the attachment of the *Quem quaeritis* to matins and its gradual development as a part of the *Visitatio Sepulchri*. We need mention only the twelve manuscripts leading up to the first version that includes dialogue, supplementary antiphons, and highly developed stage directions:

Tours	Date uncertain
Place uncertain	XI–XII C.
Utrecht	XII C.
Fulda	XV C.
Minden	XI C.
Clermont-Ferrand	XIV C.
Senlis	Date uncertain
Arras	XI C.
St. Gall	XII C.
Speyer	XIV C.
Remiremont	XII C.
Regularis concordia	965–75

[16] *DMC*, I, 223.

The preceding list is, to say the least, a remarkable piece of historical scholarship. It is presented as a reconstruction of an evolutionary process that logically must have taken place in the sixty years between the alleged composition of the original (*ca.* 910) and the "transferred" and "elaborated" version found in the *Regularis concordia* (*ca.* 970). Forty manuscripts are cited, yet only three of these can be dated in the same century as the *Regularis*, whereas two are "X–XI C.," twelve are "XI C.," three are "XI–XII C.," and no less than fifteen are between the twelfth and the fifteenth century. Of Young's examples only two (Limoges and St. Gall) can definitely be dated before the *Regularis* version, which is presumably the end product of the process illustrated by all forty manuscripts, and, far from illustrating the process, these two contradict it. Equally striking, not a single "intermediate" manuscript illustrating the alleged detachment of the *Quem quaeritis* from the Mass can be dated in the tenth century.

One further point concerning the *Regularis concordia*. All authorities agree that the *Visitatio* of the *Regularis concordia* is derived from continental sources, most probably from a monastery related to Fleury.[17] Since the *Regularis* itself is dated 965–75, the source of the *Visitatio* cannot be later than 965, and *ca.* 950 would seem to be a reasonable guess as to its date. The source version, then, is approximately contemporary with the St. Gall "simplest version" and is only twenty years later than the Limoges text. Accepting 910 as the date for the composition of the St. Gall original, we have an outside limit of forty years (910–50) for the process of gradual evolution supposedly illustrated by the forty manuscripts. The point of this observation is simply that there is no reason to consider the *Regularis* version a development of the St. Gall version. It may equally well be a "less degenerate" or "more faithful" reproduction of a common source.

This observation raises questions about each of the four points stemming from the "simplest version" hypothesis.

1. The *Regularis* version is not a trope. It is an extraliturgical ceremony, including antiphons, chanted dialogue, and fairly elaborate use of liturgical stage props. It is more closely related to such ninth-century ceremonies as the Palm Sunday procession and the "Visitation of the Font" of Easter vespers than to the lyric embellishments of Mass texts found in tenth-century tropers. If it were closer to the original than the St. Gall or Limoges texts, the latter would have to be regarded as simplified versions stripped of their rubrics and adapted to processional singing. The inclusion of the simplified version in tropers of the tenth and eleventh centuries would prove only that in its simplified form the dialogue functioned as a trope, a point that no one questions.

---

[17] *Regularis concordia*, ed. Symons, pp. xlv–l.

2. If the *Regularis* version were close to the original, the claims of St. Gall and Tutilo would be weakened, and arguments for a French origin would be strengthened.

3. The date of 910 for the original depends entirely on the idea that the *Quem quaeritis* originated at St. Gall. According to Notker Balbulus the monks of Jumièges were writing tropes in the middle of the ninth century. If the *Quem quaeritis* began as a trope, a date between 850 and 900 would be quite possible. On the other hand, if it began as a ceremony with antiphons and dialogue, a still earlier date would be possible. While not decisive, the fact that Amalarius of Metz does not mention the ceremony suggests that a date earlier than 820 would be unlikely, though not, of course, impossible, because Amalarius ignores many features of ninth-century worship not found in the Roman *Ordines* that are the chief sources of the *Liber officialis*.

4. If the *Regularis* may be considered close to the original, there is no reason to assume that the *Quem quaeritis* was originally associated with the Easter Introit. It may have originated in connection with matins and then have been transferred to the Mass because of its popular appeal, or it may have been independent of both ceremonies. It is often forgotten that the earliest manuscript evidence of any sort of formal Resurrection ceremony on Easter morning is a reference in the tenth-century *Life* of St. Ulrich to an *Elevatio Hostiae* associated with the morrowmass of Easter and evidently performed in Augsburg around 950.[18] The earliest evidence of a *Visitatio* ceremony—with or without the *Quem quaeritis* dialogue—is none other than the *Regularis* itself. In other words, evidence that the *Quem quaeritis* was transferred from Easter Mass to a pre-existing *Visitatio* ceremony is totally lacking, as is evidence that the *Elevatio* and/or the *Visitatio* existed prior to the middle of the tenth century. On the other hand, we know that in the ninth century a whole series of vivid ceremonies was used to celebrate the Resurrection during the Easter vigil and that a well-developed commemorative ceremony was performed throughout the Easter octave at vespers. Although the evidence does not permit positive conclusions, it does show that there is no more reason to believe that the *Quem quaeritis* originated in connection with matins than in connection with the Easter Mass.

III

Three possibilities are now before us. (1) The *Quem quaeritis* was composed as a trope for the Easter Introit around 910. (2) It was composed

18 *DMC*, I, 121, 553.

some time before 930 as a matins ceremony and then simplified and adopted as a processional for Easter Mass. (3) It was composed some time before 930 as a ceremony commemorating the Resurrection for use at an unspecified occasion and later used for two different occasions, the first being matins and the second, Easter Mass.

There are, in all, fourteen versions of the *Quem quaeritis* that may be dated in the tenth century. All but one are cited in Young's text and notes. Five of the fourteen are dated X–XI C., while nine may be classified as unambiguous. Of the fourteen, six are associated by Young with Easter Mass, three have no clear liturgical associations, and five are related to the *Visitatio Sepulchri:*

St. Gall	?950	Mass
Bamberg troper	X C.	*Visitatio* (matins)
Bamberg gradual	X C.	Ambiguous
Paris MS	996–1024	Mass
Vienna MS	X C.	Ambiguous
Abruzzi	X–XI C.	Mass
Limoges	923–34	Mass
Limoges	988–96	Mass
Apt	X–XI C.	Mass
Regularis concordia	965–75	*Visitatio* (matins)
St. Vito	X C.	*Visitatio* (matins)
Paris MS	X–XI C.	*Visitatio* (matins)
Winchester troper	978–80	Ambiguous
Reichenau	X–XI C.	*Visitatio* (matins)

The manuscripts clearly assignable to the tenth century are, in the best chronological order possible:

1. St. Martial of Limoges	923–34	Mass
2. St. Gall	?950	Mass
3. *Regularis concordia*	965–75	*Visitatio* (matins)
4. Winchester troper	978–80	Ambiguous
5. St. Martial of Limoges	988–94	Mass
6. Bamberg troper	X C.	*Visitatio*
7. Bamberg gradual	X C.	Ambiguous
8. Vienna	X C.	Ambiguous
9. St. Vito	X C.	*Visitatio* (matins)[19]

[19] The texts of these plays are reprinted as follows: St. Martial, *DMC*, I, 210; St. Gall, *DMC*, I, 201; *Regularis*, *DMC*, I, 248; Winchester, *DMC*, I, 254; St. Martial, *DMC*, I, 211–12; Bamberg troper, Lange, *Lateinischen Osterfeiern*, p. 29; Bamberg

All of the latter nine manuscripts come from monastic rather than secular churches. Either the *Quem quaeritis* was not used in secular services or (more likely) the secular *ordines* have perished. Five versions (1, 2, 4, 5, 6) come from tropers, two (3, 9) come from collections of monastic rules, one (7) from a gradual, and one (8) from a "miscellany." Three (1, 2, 5) are evidently related to Easter Mass, three (3, 6, 9) to the *Visitatio Sepulchri*, and three (4, 7, 8) are ambiguous. In other words, there is not the slightest evidence that tenth-century liturgists favored the association of the *Quem quaeritis* with Easter Mass. If anything, the manuscripts suggest that the *Quem quaeritis* was regarded as an independent composition to be included wherever convenient. This in turn suggests that the original was not closely associated with any of the liturgical occasions where it later (in the eleventh and twelfth centuries) became conventional.

Closer examination of the texts permits some refinement on these observations. It shows that no tenth-century text can be considered entirely free of anomalies and that the anomalies are often significant.

Of the nine texts the most clearly labeled is the later Limoges text (5), which is titled *In die sancto pasche stacio ad sanctum Petrum*.[20] The first part of the title is clear enough, but the second raises a question. All documents, from the Gregorian *Liber sacramentorum* to the contemporary missal, agree that the station for Easter Day is not St. Peter's but St. Mary Major. St. Peter's is the station for Easter Monday.[21] The two halves of the title contradict one another. This in turn raises the possibility that at some point in its history before 980 the *Quem quaeritis* was associated with a liturgical occasion other than Easter matins or Easter Mass. In the absence of further evidence, it can only be conjectured that the occasion was the Mass of Easter Monday. Another anomaly in this text is its ending. The last word of the piece is *Resurrexit*, and it is followed not by the Easter Introit but by the rubric *item alius*. Young emends *Resurrexit* to *Resurrexi* on the assumption that the word is an erroneous transcription of the *incipit* of the Easter Introit. The emendation is doubtless justified in context because it is evident that the Limoges *Quem quaeritis* was, in fact, used at the beginning of the Mass. On the other hand, tenth- and eleventh-century versions of the *Quem quaeritis* regularly end with the antiphons *Resurrexit*

---

gradual, Brooks, "Osterfeiern aus bamberger und wolfenbuttel Handschriften," *Zeitschrift fur deutsche Philologie*, LV (1914), 52–61; Vienna, *DMC*, I, 569; St. Vito, *DMC*, I, 578. In the following discussion I have also used the Winchester text edited by Frere (*Winchester Troper*, p. 17) and the *Regularis* text edited by Symons (pp. 49–50). Young refers to all versions except that of the Bamberg troper in his text and notes.

[20] *DMC*, I, 211.

[21] E.g., *PL*, LXXVIII, 91[d], 93[d], 678[d], and *passim*.

Dominus and *Surrexit Dominus* even when they are a part of matins rather than Mass. It is therefore not at all clear that *Resurrexit* is a simple scribal error. It could equally well be a transcription of an antiphon *incipit* from a version not associated with Easter Mass. The relative frequency of the same error and the same emendation in later manuscripts strengthens this possibility.[22] If the original version ended with *Resurrexit* or *Surrexit*, it is easy to see how it could become associated with the Easter Introit and why the apparent error in transcription tends to recur.

The St. Gall trope (2) is more ambiguously labeled than the Limoges. It is called *Item de resurrectione Domini*. This title does not specify performance on Easter Day. In fact, it relates the St. Gall trope to the Winchester text (4), which is titled *Angelica de Christi resurrectione*, and which was definitely not a part of Easter Mass.[23] On the other hand the St. Gall trope ends with an unambiguous *Resurrexi*, and there is no doubt that, whatever its origin, the monks of St. Gall used it as with the Easter Introit.

The earliest Limoges version (1) also presents problems. It is titled *Trophi in pasche*, and Young's emendation to *Trophi in die pasche* is purely editorial.[24] The placement of the text in the Limoges manuscript is also curious. It does not end with *Resurrexi* but with *Deo gratias, dicite eia!*, followed by the standard trope of the Easter Introit, *Dormiui, Pater.* . . . Only after the first line of this trope is there an abbreviation (*Po.*) referring to the Easter Introit itself. We can assume that the first words of the Introit, *Resurrexi, et adhuc tecum sum*, preceded the trope, but there is no reference to them in the manuscript. The effect is that of two separate liturgical pieces, the *Quem quaeritis* and the Introit trope, run together. Evidently the *Quem quaeritis* was used at Limoges as part of the Easter Introit, but the manuscript does not justify the conclusion either that the Limoges version is original or that the original was part of the Introit. The evidence supports the idea of the conflation of two separate pieces equally well, if not better.

The most curious of all the early texts of the *Quem quaeritis* is that preserved in the Winchester troper (4). It appears in the manuscript after the Palm Sunday pieces and before the rubric *Sabbato sancto primum benedictio cerei*. Frere, the editor of the Winchester troper, considered it "a dramatic dialogue which came to be used as a trope of the Introit of Easter: but at Winchester it kept its independent place."[25] Although dis-

---

[22] E.g., *DMC*, I, 206, 208, 209 ("Resur." emended "Resurrexi"), 212, 221, 222.

[23] *Ibid.*, p. 254; Frere, *Winchester Troper*, p. 17.

[24] *Ibid.*, p. 210. There is a photograph of the manuscript itself on the facing page.

[25] *Winchester Troper*, p. xvi.

counted by Chambers and Young,[26] Frere's observation conforms to the evidence of the Winchester manuscript. The fact is that the Winchester *Quem quaeritis* is not where it should be if the piece had the sort of quasi-official relation to Easter Mass and matins postulated by orthodox scholarship. Three explanations are possible. First, the scribe may have been careless or may have inserted the *Quem quaeritis* before the vigil service simply because there was space for it at that point in the manuscript. Both of these suggestions may be rejected. The manuscript is careful, it was intended to give an accurate sequence of liturgical pieces to its users, and its spacing is not irregular. This being the case, we must conclude that there existed a tradition according to which the *Quem quaeritis* was performed on Easter Eve rather than Easter Day. The second explanation is that it was truly "independent" in Frere's sense and could therefore be included in any one of a number of places in the sequence of Easter services. This is possible but unlikely. If the *Quem quaeritis* were truly independent, we would expect to find a much wider variation in its placement than we do. The third possibility is that there still existed in 980 a tradition associating the *Quem quaeritis* with a specific liturgical occasion other than matins and Easter Mass. Chambers conjectured that at Winchester it may have been performed on Good Friday, an idea that Young rightly calls "inconceivable."[27] The obvious alternative is that it was performed at the time indicated in the Winchester manuscript, i.e., in conjunction with the services of Easter Eve. The Easter vigil was primarily a Resurrection service, and, as we have seen, in the ninth century it overshadowed the Mass of Easter Day. Consequently, there is no liturgical reason why the *Quem quaeritis* should not have been associated with the vigil. The likelihood of its association with the vigil is considerably increased by the existence of two mutually independent manuscripts from Madrid (XII C.) and Constance (1587) in which it is also associated with the *Benedictio cerei*.[28] The best conclusion seems to be that the Winchester troper preserves a version of the *Quem quaeritis* performed in connection with the Easter vigil as part of the candle ceremonies. The title of the piece, *Angelica de resurrectione Domini*, provides no obvious clue to its placement.

[26] Chambers, *MS*, II, 12–14, 15n.; Young, *DMC*, I, 587.

[27] *DMC*, I, 587.

[28] In the Madrid manuscript (*DMC*, I, 599) it immediately follows the *Benedictio cerei;* in the Constance version (*DMC*, I, 302), it precedes the *Benedictio*, as in the Winchester version. The existence of three manuscripts so disparate in time and location precludes mutual influence. Evidently, they are drawing independently on the same tradition.

Unexpected light is thrown on the early history of the *Quem quaeritis* by the eleventh-century revision of the Winchester troper preserved at Corpus Christi College.[29] Here the *Quem quaeritis* is preceded by Palm Sunday pieces and followed directly by *Tropi in die Christi resurrectione*. Comparison of the tenth- and eleventh-century manuscripts provides an example of conflation actually in progress. In the earlier manuscript, the Easter vigil service occurs in something like its original (sixth- to ninth-century) form and separates the *Quem quaeritis* from the pieces for Easter Day. By the eleventh century, however, the form of the vigil service has changed markedly. The result is that the *Quem quaeritis*, instead of being separated from the pieces appropriate for Easter Day, immediately precedes them. In the manuscript, therefore, it can be interpreted as the first piece in the series. The last antiphon in the Winchester *Quem quaeritis* is *Surrexit Dominus de sepulcro*. . . . If it were copied as an *incipit* and changed to *Resurrexit* or *Resurrexi*, the attachment of the piece to Easter Mass would be complete. In fact, Young assumes that the eleventh-century version was a part of the *Tropi in die*, in spite of the fact that it is still separated from them by the rubric.

The fullest and most attractive of all tenth-century texts of the *Quem quaeritis* is that preserved in the *Regularis concordia* (965–75). In the *Regularis* it is part of a sequence that begins with the Deposition of the Cross (*Depositio Crucis*) on Good Friday after the Adoration ceremonies. The instructions introducing the sequence indicate that it was optional and that it was considered particularly appropriate for popular instruction: ". . . if anyone should care or think fit to follow in a becoming manner certain religious men in a practice worthy to be imitated for the strengthening of the faith of unlearned common persons and neophytes [*ad fidem indocti vulgi ac neophytorum corroborandam*], we have decreed this only: on that part of the altar where there is a space for it there shall be a representation as it were of a sepulchre, hung about with a curtain."[30] The cross is placed in the sepulcher guarded by two brethren "until the night of the Lord's Resurrection" (*usque dominicam noctem Resurrectionis*). The Mass of the Presanctified is celebrated, and the sequence ends with the instruction, "After the veneration of the Cross, let the ministers or children who are unoccupied [*quibus vacuum fuerit*] shave and bathe themselves if the number

---

[29] *DMC*, I, 586–87. For comment on the revised version, see Frere, *Winchester Troper*, pp. xxvii–xxix.

[30] *Regularis concordia*, ed., Symons, p. 44.

of the community is so great that the day of Saturday, the next day, would not suffice."[31]

The *Visitatio* part of the sequence occurs at the end of matins on Easter Morning:

> While the third lesson is being read, four of the brethren shall vest, one of whom, wearing an alb as though for some different purpose, shall enter and go stealthily to the place of the "sepulchre" and sit there quietly, holding a palm in his hand. Then, while the third respond is being sung, the other three brethren, vested in copes and holding thuribles in their hands, shall enter in their turn and go to the place of the "sepulchre," step by step, as though searching for something. Now these things are done in imitation of the angel seated on the tomb and of the women coming with perfumes to anoint the body of Jesus. When, therefore, he that is seated shall see these three draw nigh, wandering about as it were and seeking something, he shall begin to sing softly and sweetly,
>
> > *Quem quaeritis.*
>
> As soon as this has been sung right through, the three shall answer together,
>
> > *Ihesum Nazarenum.*
>
> Then he that is seated shall say
>
> > *Non est hic. Surrexit sicut praedixerat.*
> > *Ite, nuntiate quia surrexit a mortuis.*
>
> At this command the three shall turn to the choir saying
>
> > *Alleluia. Resurrexit Dominus.*

[31] *Ibid.*, pp. 45–46. I have followed Symons' translation, with the exception of the clause *quibus vacuum fuerit ministri vel pueri se radant ac balneent*, translated by him as "those ministers or children who can shall shave and bathe themselves." The *quibus* refers to both *pueri* and *ministri* rather than to *pueri* only; in addition, the idiom *vacuum* plus the dative usually connotes freedom from other obligations, rather than ability. The difference of interpretation may be significant. The provision for shaving and bathing is intended only for situations where "the number of the community is so great that the day of Saturday, the next day, would not suffice." In other words, it is a Holy Saturday rite. That the number of monks in the communities for which the *Regularis* was written would be so great that Holy Saturday "would not suffice" is questionable. Note the provision (p. 45) that "two or three" sepulcher guards should be posted on Good Friday "if the community is large enough." Another curious feature of the provision for shaving and bathing is that there is no other reference to bathing in the *Regularis*. In view of the secular influence observable elsewhere in the Easter sections, the provision is best considered not as a monastic rule but as a carry-over from earlier secular provisions that the neophytes and penitents, who are forbidden to shave and bathe during Lent, shall perform these acts on Holy Saturday in preparation for the vigil. This would explain (1) why the provision only occurs once in the *Regularis*, (2) why it is associated with Holy Saturday, and (3) why there is mention of the possibility of a group too large to be accommodated on Holy Saturday.

When this has been sung he that is seated, as though calling them back, shall say the antiphon

Venite et videte locum,

and then, rising and lifting up the veil, he shall show them the place void of the Cross and with only the linen [*linteamina*] in which the Cross had been wrapped. Seeing this the three shall lay down their thuribles in that same "sepulchre" and, taking the linen, shall hold it up before the clergy; and, as though showing that the Lord was risen and was no longer wrapped in it, they shall sing this antiphon:

Surrexit Dominus de sepulchro.

They shall then lay the linen on the altar.

When the antiphon is finished the prior, rejoicing in the triumph of our King in that He had conquered death and was risen [*congaudens pro triumpho regis nostri quod devicta morte surrexit*], shall give out the hymn *Te Deum laudamus,* and thereupon all the bells shall peal [*una pulsantur omnia signa*]. After this a priest shall say the verse

Surrexit Dominus de sepulchro

right through and shall begin Matins [i.e., lauds] saying

Deus in adiutorium meum intende. . . .[32]

Given the fact that 960 is the latest possible date for the *Regularis* source, the text is surprisingly full. The rubrics show a firm command of the significance of all parts of the ceremony, a sophisticated use of stage properties and dramatic gesture is evident, and the dialogue has a comparatively full complement of supplementary texts, two of which, the *Ite nuntiate* and the *Venite et videte,* are fully incorporated in the action. The details of the sepulcher, the night watch, the palm held by the angel, and the ringing of the bells all suggest that the ceremony may have been still more elaborate in performance than the rubrics themselves indicate. In sum, it is impossible to think of the *Regularis Quem quaeritis* as the product of more or less haphazard embellishment and improvement on a St. Gall original composed around 910.

Several features of the rubrics and text need further comment. Although the concept of clerical imitation of Biblical figures is almost unknown in tenth-century tropes other than the *Quem quaeritis,* it is a commonplace of Mass commentaries after Amalarius. The *Regularis* explains the actions of the Marys with the remark, "Now these things are done in imitation of the angel sitting on the monument and of the women coming with ointments to anoint the body of Jesus [*ad imitationem angeli . . . atque mulierum cum aromatibus venientium, ut ungerent corpus Ihesu*]." In the *Liber officialis* Amalarius explains the use of thuribles only for the Gospel procession of

[32] *Ibid.,* pp. 49–51.

the vigil Mass in an almost identical way: "The Resurrection of Christ is recalled and the speech of the angels to the women and the emotions of the women. . . . In my opinion the Roman book says that nothing but incense vessels are to be carried before the gospel on this night on account of imitation of the women [*propter mulierum imitationem*]. . . . Their sacrifice at that time was that they brought ointment to anoint the body of the Lord [*ferebant unguentum ad ungendum corpus Domini*]."[33]

It is noteworthy that this parallel leads us back—as did the Winchester troper—to the Easter vigil.

Another feature worth noting is the comment in the *Regularis* on the whole *Depositio-Visitatio* sequence. The *Regularis* version of the services from Maundy Thursday to Easter is based heavily on the first *Ordo Romanus* and the *Liber sacramentorum*. The services therefore retain many features characteristic of secular rather than monastic churches of the seventh to tenth centuries. There have, however, been modifications. Although the copyist occasionally slips into using secular titles, he normally uses monastic ones. The celebrant is called *abbas*, the congregation,

---

[33] *Ibid.*, p. 50; *Liber officialis*, ed. Hanssens, *Amalarii episcopi opera*, II, 159–61. Amalarius, in turn, draws on Bede, *Homilia evangelii de pascha* (*PL*, CXXIX, 1433): "Diluculo igitur aromata ad monumentum Domini feremus cum memores passionis ac mortis quam pro nobis suscepit. . . . Nec dubitari licet, ubi corporis et sanguinis Domini mysteria geruntur, supernorum civium adesse conventus . . . unde studiendum solertes est, fratres mei, ut . . . coeleste compleamus officium, in exemplum feminarum devotarum, quae apparentibus ad monumentum angelis, temuisse ad vultum declinasse narrantur in terram." Compare *PL*, XCII, 151–52, and *In Lucae evangelium expositio* (*PL*, XCII, 622–24); esp. 622[d]–23[a]:

Quod autem valde deluculo mulieres venient ad monumentum juxta historiam qui et magnus quaerendi et inveniendi Dominum fervor charitatis ostenditur; juxta intellectum vero mysterium nobis datur exemplum illuminata facie decussisque vitiorum tenebris ad sacrasanctum Domini corpus accedere. Nam et sepulcrum illud venerabile figuram dominiei (sic) habet altaris in quo carnis ejus acs anguinis solent mysteria celebrari. Unde ecclesia tenet cadem mysteria, non in serico, non in panno tincto, sed instar sidonis, qua eum Joseph involvit, in linteo puro deberi consecrari . . . candidumque . . . linum altari imponamus. Aromata autem quae mulieres deferunt, odorem virtutum et orationum quibus altari appropinquare debemus, suavitatem significant.

Note in these comments the interpretation of the Visit to the Tomb as an allegory of the Mass and, especially, the parallels that are emphasized. The angels are present at the sacrifice; the altar is the tomb; the Sacrament is the *corpus Domini;* the clergy and congregation are the Marys; their prayers and virtues are the *aromata;* and the corporal and altar cloth are the sindon in which Christ was shrouded by Joseph of Arimathea. All of the elements of the *Quem quaeritis* ceremony are apparent except the thuribles, which are first identified with the *aromata* of the Marys by Amalarius. The Amalarian interpretation is repeated by Pseudo-Alcuin, *De divinis officiis* (*PL*, CI, 1221[c]–22[a]). The close association between the Amalarian tradition and the ceremony is suggested by its inclusion in a manuscript of the *Liber officialis*—possibly of the ninth century—edited by A. Wilmert, *Revue benedictine*, pp. 161–62.

fratres, and so on.[34] The number of vigil service readings has been reduced from twelve to four, and they are in Latin rather than Latin and Greek. The Gregorian collects and chants are preserved, including the *Sicut cervus,* originally used for the procession of catechumens to the font. Here the *Regularis* diverges emphatically from secular forms. Although it provides for a blessing of the font, it has no provision for baptism. Mass immediately follows the blessing. The service is obviously much shorter than the secular equivalent, and Mass ends with a version of Holy Saturday vespers followed by compline. In other words, Mass is celebrated between 5:00 and 7:00 P.M.[35]

These alterations are understandable and, in fact, usual in monastic churches. The vigil was originally a secular service, and it was inevitably modified in situations where congregations were small and baptism was seldom performed.[36] The point is that the monastic version of the services directly contradicts the statement in the *Regularis* that the *Depositio-Visitatio* sequence is a device for "strengthening of the faith of the unlearned common persons and neophytes." All evidence points to the fact that the *Regularis* sequence is intended for monastic worship and that few, if any, "unlearned common persons" are expected to participate. Instructions for the Mass of the Presanctified and the Saturday Mass never mention the laity, and apart from the *Depositio* and *Visitatio* there is no trace of them in the other services for the Easter period. Even more puzzling is the reference to the neophytes. Used in connection with Easter services in the ninth and tenth centuries, *neophyti* is a technical term referring to newly baptized catechumens. It is never used in liturgical manuscripts of the period to mean simply novices. Yet the *Regularis* has, as we have seen, no provision for baptism.

---

[34] See *Regularis concordia,* ed. Symons, pp. 45, 49, 58, and notes. The errors are identical and are closely related. The first occurs in a comment on the *Depositio,* the second in a comment on the vigil Mass, and the third in a comment on the vigil Mass of Pentecost, which was originally a baptismal Mass for those who were not baptized at Easter. I suggest that the whole sequence is derived from the same source and that in the source *sacerdos* was consistently used where the *Regularis* scribe normally uses *abbas.*

[35] The Mass *ordo,* including vespers and followed by compline, is illustrated by the *Regularis concordia,* ed. Symons, pp. 48–49.

[36] Cf. Mabillon's note in his edition of the Gallican Lectionary (*PL,* LXXII, 198[d]): "Ex notis numericis apparet in Lectionario nostro nullas pro Dominica Paschae lectiones ad Vigilias seu Matutinum assignatas fuisse; nec fortasse tempus istis Vigiliis celebrandis reliquum esse poterat, cum omnia quae superius de Sabbato sancto retulimus, in multam noctem protraherentur. *Alia ratio est de monasteriis, in quibus baptismus non conferebatur*" (italics mine).

Only one conclusion accounts for the discrepancies. As the occasional use of secular for monastic titles (e.g., *sacerdos* for *abbas*)[37] also indicates, the source manuscript of the *Regularis* was secular. In the source, the *Depositio-Visitatio* sequence was explicitly described as a method of instructing the lay congregation and the newly baptized converts, and this description was copied by the *Regularis* scribe in spite of its inappropriateness. Moreover, in the source the *Visitatio* was associated with services following baptism (hence the reference to *neophyti* rather than *catechumeni*) and preceding Easter Mass. Only one service fits this requirement, the vigil Mass. In churches where the vigil service was not displaced by anticipation, no service is prescribed for the neophytes between the end of the vigil Mass and the Mass of Easter Day. Originally the long vigil precluded additional services; later the single nocturn of Roman Easter matins became important only in proportion to the decline in candidates for baptism and the consequent anticipation of the vigil Mass to Saturday evening, a process that occurred in the monasteries well before it influenced secular services.

The *Regularis Visitatio* has three further features. First, its dialogue is in what will henceforth be called the "abbreviated form." Instead of the familiar *Quem quaeritis in sepulchro, o Christicolae*, the rubrics give only *Quem quaeritis*, and the Marys reply only *Ihesum Nazarenum*. Editors have assumed that the dialogue is given as a series of *incipits*, but the frequent recurrence of the abbreviated form in later manuscripts suggests that versions using it should be considered a distinct type.[38] Since they have other features in common, they raise the possibility, first suggested by Klapper, that the dialogue was originally an extremely brief exchange of Biblical phrases supplemented by antiphons.[39] Second, two anomalies may be observed in the antiphons. *Surrexit Dominus* is sung twice, once before and once after the *Te Deum*. The doubling of this antiphon is superfluous and is evidently a device to emphasize the attachment of the piece to matins. After the first *Surrexit*, there is a further peculiarity. The rubrics describe the prior as *congaudens pro triumpho regis nostri quod devicta morte*

---

[37] See n. 34.

[38] For manuscripts with the abbreviated form, see *DMC*, I, 214, 215, 221, 230, 240, 247, 262, 300, 302–3, 306, 591, and *passim*.

[39] Klapper, "Der Ursprung der lateinischen Osterfeiern," pp. 53–55. Klapper makes the intriguing observation that in the Bible of Theodulph of Orleans, Luke 24:4 reads: "quem quaeritis. ihesum nazarenum. quum mortuis. non est hic sed surrexit." This is, of course, much closer to the text of the abbreviated form than the standard Vulgate reading. Theodulph was an older contemporary of Amalarius and, like him, wrote an essay on baptism in response to Charlemagne's *Interrogatio*. Klapper assumes that Theodulph's text is influenced by Eastern texts. This theory, whether valid or not, is surely less important than the fact that it was used in Carolingian France.

surrexit. The wording closely parallels the verse that begins the earliest Limoges version of the *Quem quaeritis: Psallite regi magno, devicto mortis imperio!* This verse, with variations, is fairly common in manuscripts of the *Quem quaeritis* and is also found independently, for example, as a prelude to the trope of the *Resurrexi* Introit in the Winchester troper.[40] It seems likely that the source of the *Regularis* included it as part of the spoken text and that it was demoted, either by accident or design, to the status of a rubric by the *Regularis* scribe. If so, it evidently came at the end of the piece rather than at the beginning, as in the Limoges version.

Finally, two events associated with the *Regularis Visitatio* appear significant. The placing on the altar of the *linteum* that covered the cross is a liturgical act without significance in the matins-lauds sequence. This act—a common feature of later versions as well—suggests preparation for Mass rather than the service of the hours. When we recall that in many later manuscripts a Host is placed on the altar along with the *linteum*, the likelihood of the interpretation is increased. The second event is the festive ringing of the church bells. The *Visitatio* rubrics require that at the end of the ceremony *una pulsantur omnia signa*. This repeats verbatim the *Regularis* rubric for the beginning of the vigil Mass: *pulsentur omnia signa*.[41] The doubling of the announcement of the Resurrection is awkward but understandable if the *Visitatio* originally introduced the Mass but was later separated from it by anticipation.

IV

Examination of tenth-century manuscripts demonstrates that there was no fixed place in the tenth century for the *Quem quaeritis*. The Winchester troper shows that one of its positions was in association with the Easter vigil; and the *Regularis* shows that at least one function of the piece was the instruction of the neophytes. Consideration of manuscript anomalies suggests the following hypotheses:

1. The *Quem quaeritis* began its career as a ceremony rather than as a trope.
2. In content it was a Resurrection ceremony in many ways similar to the ninth-century Visitation of the Font and closer to the *Regularis* version than any other tenth-century manuscript.

[40] *Winchester Troper*, ed. Frere, p. 17.
[41] *Regularis concordia*, ed. Symons, p. 48.

3. It functioned both as a device of instruction and as a means of preparing for the vigil Mass.

4. It was probably related to one of the candle ceremonies of the Easter vigil, though not necessarily to the blessing of the paschal candle, which took place on the afternoon of Holy Saturday rather than at night.

5. As a result of anticipation, especially in the monastic churches that are the source of all tenth-century manuscripts, it was detached from the vigil Mass and moved to the only other liturgical occasions associated closely with the Resurrection—the end of matins and Easter Mass.

6. When used with matins, it retained its identity as a representational ceremony, but when attached to Easter Mass it was normally used as a processional without rubrics and (evidently) without elaborate action.

Certain clues as to the shape and content of the original ceremony are already evident. Before these are considered, it will be well to test the preceding hypotheses. If the *Quem quaeritis* was originally associated with the vigil service, some evidence of this fact should be preserved in manuscripts later than the tenth century. Since the following analysis depends in part on the structure of the vigil Mass, it will be helpful to begin with an *ordo* representing tenth-century practice. In spite of anticipation and the elimination of the baptismal rite, the *Regularis* preserves the texts and at least part of the ceremony of the traditional Roman vigil service. It begins with the *Exsultet* and continues with the prophetic readings. The last chant in the sequence is the *Sicut cervus:*

Sicut cervus [is] followed by the collect: *Concede quaesumus omnipotens Deus.* After the prayer the sevenfold Litanies shall be begun at the entrance to the altar. Afterwards the abbot shall go down with the *schola* to bless the font, singing the five-fold Litanies. There follow the collect, *Omnipotens sempiterne Deus,* and the Preface. When these are finished they return to the altar singing the three-fold Litanies; and before the *Gloria in excelsis Deo* is sung the master of the *schola* shall sing on a high note *Accendite.*

And thereupon shall all the lights of the church be lit and, when the abbot has intoned the *Gloria in excelsis Deo,* all the bells shall peal. There follows the collect: *Deus qui hanc sacratissimam noctem;* then the epistle, *Si consurrexistis* [Col. 3:1–4] is read and *Alleluia, Confitemini Domino* and the tract *Laudate Dominum* are sung. No lights are borne before the gospel on the night itself, but incense only. When the gospel is finished the abbot shall say *Dominus vobiscum: Oremus.* On the day itself neither the Offertory, *Agnus Dei* nor Communion are sung . . . ;[42] but while Communion is being given *Alleluia* and *Laudate Dominum omnes gentes* are sung followed by the antiphon *Vespere autem sabbati* and the *Magnificat.*[43]

The service outlined is essentially a Mass fused with vespers, which substitutes for the missing Communion hymn and dismissal. Three collects are mentioned prominently, *Concede quaesumus*, *Omnipotens sempiterne*, and *Deus qui hanc.* Elimination of baptism has resulted in the loss of the ninth-century procession of neophytes, but several features of the ninth-century "Return from the Font" are retained. The Kyrie, although part of the Mass, has been assimilated into the last of the threefold litanies. As the *fratres* return from the font, the choirmaster sings *Accendite* in a loud voice. The church is suddenly illuminated, and the abbot begins the Gloria in Excelsis. There is a festive ringing of bells, and Mass continues with the collect.

From the standpoint of the association between the *Quem quaeritis* and the vigil Mass, the most intriguing text is from St. Martin of Tours. The date of the text is uncertain, and it exists only in the version printed by Martene in the eighteenth century. St. Martin, however, is one of the oldest and most famous shrines in France and was a center for pilgrims as early as the sixth century. The St. Martin *ordo* is secular, and the *Quem quaeritis* ceremony takes place, interestingly, at the tomb of St. Martin himself. The ceremony precedes Mass, but there is no indication in the rubrics as to which Mass is intended:

> Processionem sequebatur Missa, quae antequam incipiatur, inquit Turonese S. Martini ordinarium, veniat ordo Missae revestitus in chorum, et sit cantor cum succentoribus ante januam chori, duobus pueris albis in dalmaticis existentibus. Duo vero vicarii levitae revestiti in dalmaticis albis stantes ante Sepulchrum beatissimi Martini, versis vultibus ad cantorem, incipiant:
> > *Quem quaeritis?*
> Et duo pueri stantes ante cantorem respondent:
> > *Jesum Nazarenum.*

[42] So the earliest manuscript. The later manuscript (Tiberius A3, XI C.) adds "et pacem non debent dare nisi qui communicent" here. I have translated the beginning of the next clause (*sed*) by "but" rather than "and," the word used by Symons.

[43] *Regularis concordia*, ed. Symons, pp. 47–48. The ninth-century form did not include vespers, and matins was eliminated except in monastic churches. See n. 36. For more details concerning the ninth-century form, see below, n. 57.

Levitae:
> *Non est hic.*

Pueri:
> *Alleluja, resurrexit Dominus.*

Tunc unus puer solus dicat ter:
> *Accendite,*

exaltando vocem. Et alter puer respondet totidem vicibus:
> *Psallite, fratres.*

Sequitur solus puer una vice:
> *Accendite.*

Alter puer respondet:
> *Psallite, fratres.*

Puer:
> *Accendite.*

Alter puer respondet:
> *Psallite, fratres.*

Deinde puer:
> *Accendite.*

Alter puer:
> *Psallite, fratres.*

Et his peractis, simul pueri, versis vultibus ad cantorem, dicant:
> *Hora est; cantate Deo, eja!*

se inclinando. Quo dicto, incipit cantor officium Missae.[44]

(See Appendix)

Whatever the placement of this piece in the St. Martin *ordo* seen by Martene, it was evidently at one time part of the vigil service. In the first place, revesting is unnecessary before Easter Mass. It is necessary before the vigil Mass because the occasion is festive, but it follows an unbroken sequence of services that take place during the period of liturgical mourning extending from Good Friday through Holy Saturday. What is more important is that the repeated *Accendite* can only be related to the vigil Mass. It is both a summons to the celebrant and the command to the congregation to illuminate their tapers. We know from sources prior to the tenth century that the illumination of tapers was intensely dramatic.

[44] For the history and influence of St. Martin, see Wright, *The Dissemination of the Liturgical Drama in France*, pp. 42–44. St. Martin began as a monastic church but was changed to a chapter of secular canons at the end of the eighth century. Alcuin was abbot (the monastic title persisted) from 796–804 and made its school one of the great centers of Carolingian learning. It is noteworthy that the St. Martin *Quem quaeritis* is performed at the tomb of the saint, particularly when it is recalled that St. Martial of Limoges, the source of the earliest *Quem quaeritis* manuscript, was also the site of a famous tomb and a mecca for pilgrims (see Wright, pp. 25–26). The text of the St. Martin version was first printed by Martene, *De antiquae ecclesiae ritibus*, III, 17, and reprinted from that source by Young, *DMC*, I, 224–25.

Even in the *Regularis* vigil Mass special emphasis is placed on the *Accendite*. In the St. Martin text the command is repeated no less than six times. Evidently, this text preserves a form of the *Quem quaeritis* used as a transition between the procession of neophytes returning from the font and the beginning of the vigil Mass. It serves three functions: explicit provision is made for revesting, instruction is offered in the form of a dramatic representation of the historical events to be narrated in the Mass Gospel, and chants are provided for the time needed to illuminate the tapers of the faithful.

The chanted portions of the St. Martin ceremony are of particular interest. In the first place, there is no preamble. The ceremony begins not with an antiphon but with the query of the angels. In the second place, the *Quem quaeritis* dialogue is given in the abbreviated form used in the *Regularis concordia*. In the third place, the chants associated with the *Accendite*—the *Psallite* and the *Hora est*—relate the St. Martin text to a group of manuscripts that includes both of the tenth-century versions from Limoges. These chants have a clear function in the St. Martin ceremony. They are expressions of joy accompanying the lighting of the Easter candles, the *Hora est* being used also to emphasize the coincidence of liturgical and historical time. The first Limoges version (*ca.* 930) retains the chant but changes its placement. It begins with *Psallite*, filling out the command with a verse that is not quite so explicit a command for choral response: *Psallite regi magno, devicto mortis imperio!* The later Limoges text (*ca.* 990) conflates the two separate commands of the St. Martin version and also places them at the beginning: *Hora est, psallite; iubet dominus canere; eia, eia dicite!* The existence of several later manuscripts that include essentially the same chants strengthens the likelihood that they were part of the original ceremony. In these later manuscripts placement at the end of the dialogue is as common as at the beginning.[45] The fact that they have a clear liturgical function in the St. Martin version permits the inference that terminal placement is proper. A still more attractive possibility is suggested by the fact that in the Limoges troper of 988–96 the injunction *Hora est, psallite; iubet dompnus canere; eia, eia dicite* precedes the text of the *Laudes in die pasche*.[46] This text is a well-preserved example of the

---

[45] For examples of placement at the end, see *DMC*, I, 208, 209, 217, 223, 224, 245; for placement at the beginning, see *DMC*, I, 210, 211, 212, 213, 225. *Deo gratias* and *dicite eia* are extremely common and always appear at the end of the ceremony. Young (*DMC*, I, 211) suggests that *Hora est* may come from Rom. 13:11: "Hora est iam nos de somno surgere." It seems more likely that the phrase is part of a liturgical formula (see n. 46). The phrase *Psallite regi magno* has its closest parallel in the Mozarabic-Gallican version of Psalm 46: "Psallite Deo nostro; Psallite regi nostro psallite; quoniam rex omnis terrae Deus, Psallite" (*PL*, LXXXVI, 770ᵇ⁻ᶜ).

[46] *Winchester Troper*, ed. Frere, pp. 174–75.

extraliturgical compositions known as the *Laudes Gallicanae*, which were a feature of Gallican Mass in Carolingian times.[47] The injunction may therefore be considered a liturgical formula closely associated with Gallican worship and used to introduce an extraliturgical composition. It associates the versions of the *Quem quaeritis* in which it appears with Gallican tradition and, of course, with a period well before the tenth century. Since it was used to introduce a composition, its position at the end of the St. Martin text is improvisation, or it is intended to introduce the first text proper to the vigil Mass.

Although most texts of the *Visitatio* are for performance following matins, a few precede matins. These must have been performed around 3:00 A.M. Their position is, itself, of considerable interest. According to the usual explanation, the *Visitatio* was attached to the end of matins to coincide with the Resurrection. If so, the existence of texts preceding matins is difficult, if not impossible, to explain. On the other hand, it is easy to explain if the *Visitatio* were originally part of the vigil Mass. When separated from the Mass because of anticipation, it would have been attached to later parts of the liturgy in a variety of ways. If, as the St. Martin text indicates, the ceremony had an introductory function, making it a prelude to matins would have required a minimum of revision. Hence *Visitatio* texts preceding matins deserve particularly close examination. A fourteenth-century text from Udine, for example, begins with the following instructions:

> On the day of the Resurrection we should arise early for matins. Let all the bells be rung together, as for the service for the dead; but toward the end they should not continue in this way, but should ring as on other festivals. The bell-ringing over, let the priest and the people be readied in the church for the procession in albs, dressed in white robes and each holding a lighted taper. And let them proceed in an ordered procession with cross, candle-bearers, and thurible, saying nothing. And when the procession has arrived at the church, let there be two boys hidden in some high place in the church, and let them sing this verse in a high voice:
> *Quem quaeritis. . . .*[48]

The ceremony is definitely intended for the congregation as well as the clergy. Evidently, with the anticipation of the vigil Mass, Easter matins took on the qualities of a popular celebration. The ceremony begins with the ringing of bells, at first in the form used for the service of the dead and

---

[47] Jungmann, *Mass*, I, 388–89; Cabrol, "*Laudes Gallicanae*," *DACL*, VII, 1900–10. Includes texts from the eighth century and later.

[48] *DMC*, I, 298.

then in the form used for festive occasions. The transition is undoubtedly intended to symbolize the Resurrection. Yet beginning matins with the festive ringing of bells contradicts the more common practice, found in the *Regularis*, of deferring this action until the singing of the *Te Deum*. The Udine text is also of interest for its procession. Both clergy and congregation participate, and it is explicitly called *processionem albam*. It is preceded by cross, candles, and thuribles, and those involved are dressed in white (*superpellicis albis*) and carry tapers. The *Quem quaeritis* is sung as the procession enters the church; in other words, the angel's question is addressed to all participants rather than to the three Marys only. Dramatically speaking, all of the faithful are seekers after Christ, although they speak vicariously through the chorus. The procession is apparently a vestigial survival of the procession of the neophytes from the baptismal font to the church during the Easter vigil. The ringing of bells was, as we have seen, characteristic of the beginning of the vigil Mass. The references to the procession in albs and the white robes have no relation to the beginning of matins but have a very intimate relation to the albs assumed by the neophytes after baptism. The cross, thuribles, and candles were also used in the procession of neophytes, although in the original ceremony the candles were not illuminated until the *Accendite*. Finally, the dramatic arrangement whereby the members of the procession are addressed by the angels makes it clear why the *Regularis* explains the ceremony as good for "strengthening the faith of unlearned common persons and neophytes." The ceremony ends with another feature associating it with Mass. Although matins does not have a collect, the Udine rubrics instruct the bishop to conclude with the prayer *Presta, quaesumus, omnipotens Deus, ut intercedente*.[49]

An equally intriguing text comes from the Cathedral of Parma.[50] The ceremony begins *hora quasi nona*—about 3:00 A.M. It begins with the festive ringing of bells. While the bells are being rung, two other actions are going forward. First "all the lamps of the church are illuminated as on the Nativity" (*omnia luminaria ecclesiae ut in Nativitate accendantur*). Second, the altar is ornamented "as splendidly as possible" (*ornetur altare solemnius quam ornari possit*). Since there is no reason to ornament the altar for matins, the reference can only be a carry-over from a time when the ceremony was associated with Mass. The coincidence of the decoration of the altar, the festive ringing of bells, and the illumination of the church points directly

---

[49] Apparently, the first collect of Easter Mass, as in the *ordo* of Ratoldus of Corbie, *PL*, LXXVIII, 239°. Compare, however, the Gelasian Sacramentary, *PL*, LXXIV, 1113°. For detailed discussion of the collects, see below, pp. 211–12.

[50] *DMC*, I, 300.

to the vigil Mass. The fact that the Marys of the Parma version seek the *corpus Christi* in the sepulcher, rather than the Cross, relates it to the fairly large group of ceremonies known as the *Elevatio Hostiae*. At Parma the Host is removed from the sepulcher before the "visit," and the *linteamina* in which it is wrapped become evidence of the fact of the Resurrection, although they are not "displayed" like the *linteum* of the *Regularis concordia*. The dialogue of this version is in the abbreviated form of the *Regularis* and St. Martin texts. The ceremony ends with a feature which, though fairly common, has not been encountered in the manuscripts considered so far: "This finished, the first of the four clerics approaches the bishop without a taper and says softly *Surrexit Dominus*, and kisses him. And the bishop says *Deo gratias*. And next the bishop says in a loud voice *Te Deum laudamus*, and he censes the altar."[51]

If this is a matins ceremony, the *Te Deum* is obviously out of place. On the other hand, the exchange of the Kiss of Peace among the clergy and the censing of the altar (now splendidly decorated) suggest the beginning of Mass. The *Deo gratias*, today almost exclusively restricted to the Epistle and the final dismissal, was much more common in early medieval worship. It was, of course, the response to the ancient *Lumen Christi* chant of the Easter vigils and was apparently also used at the beginning of the vigil Mass. In conjunction with *Surrexit Christus* and the Kiss of Peace, it was also a formal Easter greeting.[52]

In two manuscripts intended for use at the beginning of matins some indication is given of the ceremonies associated with the Host. A sixteenth-century text from the Cathedral of Constance begins with the directions: "At matins, before the ringing of the bells, let there be a procession for removing the Blessed Sacrament [previously] placed in the sepulcher, with tapers, thurible, and holy water. First let the angel sing, *Quem quaeritis*. . . ."[53] A formal procession with candles, thurible, and holy water (*aqua benedicta*) is called for. Either the Host has been removed before the procession, or the ceremony is a confused version of an *Elevatio Hostiae* that originally involved returning the Host to the altar, a feature of the Laon manuscript, to be examined next. The reference to holy water is uncommon. The Constance text is immediately followed by the rubric *Ordo benedicendi agnum paschalem*, a ceremony associated in the ninth century with the Easter vigil.[54]

[51] *Ibid.*

[52] For the *Deo gratias*, see above, p. 158.

[53] *DMC*, I, 301–2.

[54] *Ibid.*, p. 302. Cf. the Winchester and Madrid versions, *DMC*, I, 254, 599, and above, n. 28.

A much more detailed version of the same ceremony, presumably closer to the original, is found in an early thirteenth-century manuscript from the Cathedral of Laon:

> In Pascha ad Matutinas due campane insimul pulsantur; sex cerei iuxta magnum cereum ante altare ponuntur. Dum campane pulsantur, processio ante altare in hunc modum ordinata vadit ad Sepulchrum. Precedunt clericuli cum cereis, duo cum thuribulis, duo diaconi, alij duo cantaturi *Dicant nunc*, cantor et succentor. Omnes isti albis capis induti; alij sequuntur in ordine, unusquisque cereum accensum deferens. Predicti vero diaconi ad ostium Sepulchri venientes incipiunt:
> *Ardens est.*
> Clericulus in Sepulchro:
> *Quem quaeritis?*
> Diaconi:
> *Ihesum Nazarenum.*
> Clericulus:
> *Non est hic.*
> Quo finito, sacerdos alba casula vestitus portans calicem cum Corpore Christi egrediens de Sepulchro repperit ante ostium quatuor clericulos pallium super baculos tollentes, et illo protectus incedit ante processionem, precedentibus clericulis cum cereis, astantibus alijs duobus iuxta ipsum cum thuribulis. Tunc diaconi predicti dicunt:
> *Surrexit Dominus vere, alleluia.*
> Post hec cantor et succentor incipiunt illam partem antiphone:
> *Cum rex glorie Christus.*
> *Advenisti desiderabilis.*
> Et sic cantando procedunt omnes in medio ecclesie ante crucifixum. Post antiphona:
> *Christus resurgens.*
> Duo canonici cum capis versum *Dicant nunc*. Post versum processio cantando *Quod enim vivit, vivit Deo*, intrat chorum. Sacerdos calicem super altare deponit. Interim campane insimul pulsantur. Episcopus stans in cathedra mitra et capa preparatus incipit *Domine, labia mea aperies*.[55]   (See Appendix)

Here, as in other versions already examined, there is a coincidence of several liturgical events associated with the vigil Mass: (1) ringing of bells; (2) illumination of the church (note the reference to the paschal candle, the *magnum cereum*); (3) a procession in which white robes (*albis capis*) are

---

[55] *Ibid.*, pp. 302–3. The text (XIII C.) is in the abbreviated form and is given without Young's additions. Several scribal revisions appear on the manuscript in a thirteenth-century hand. These are cited by Young in a note on p. 303.

prominently mentioned; (4) reference to thuribles, candles, and (according to a manuscript emendation of the rubrics) holy water.[56] The use of a chalice as the repository of the Host and the practice of carrying it beneath a canopy sustained by four staffs (*baculos*) strikingly parallels the Mozarabic procession for returning the Host to the altar on Good Friday. The question of possible influence is unimportant; what is significant is that the Mozarabic procession ends with the placing of the Host on the altar in preparation for celebration of Mass. The Laon text also ends with the placing of the Host on the altar. That this act was originally intended as preparation for Mass is indicated by the fact that the rubrics require the presence of the bishop in full regalia (*episcopus . . . mitra et capa preparatus*), a requirement that has no more relation to the matins service than the return of the Host itself.[57]

[56] This is one of the scribal revisions noted above.

[57] It will be helpful to cite here three versions of the transition from the baptism ceremonies to the vigil Mass, representing ninth-century practice. These may be considered a supplement to the *Regularis ordo* printed above, pp. 199–200.

First, the account in the *Liber sacramentorum* (PL, LXXVIII, 91[a]):

Quibus expletis [i.e., baptismal rites] jussi incipiunt in ecclesiam litaniam ternam. Et cum dixerint *Agnus Dei* magister scholae dicit, *Accendite*. Et illuminatur ecclesia, et procedit pontifex de sacrario cum duobus cereostatis sicut superius, et stant, sicut antea, a dexteris et a sinistris altaris. Litania expleta, dicit pontifex: *Gloria in excelsis Deo:* Quo finito, dicit: *Pax vobiscum.* Resp. *Et cum spiritu tuo.* Et dat Orationem: *Deus qui hanc sacratissimam noctem.* . . .

Second, the Mozarabic form (PL, LXXXV, 470[a-b]):

Et interim quo Litania perficitur: Sacerdos cum Ministris cruce et cereis et cereo paschali et serpente . . . descendent ad sacrarium. Et deponat Sacerdos cum ministris ornamenta quadragesimalia: et accipiant ornamenta alba et veniant ad altare isto ordine. . . . In primis precedant duo Ceroferarii cum cereis accensis. Scilicet cereo paschali et tribus lucernis quae sunt in serpente. Et cum pervenerint ad altare majus: Sacerdos faciat confessionem ut moris est. Et facta confessione Sacerdos solemniter dicat hymnum *Gloria in excelsis Deo.* Et statim pulsentur omnes campane tam majores quam minores. Et discooperiantur altaria frontalibus nigris: et retabula aurea: et omnia appareant solemniter. Et finito hymno angelorum Diachonus dicat. . . . *Concede Domine.*

Third, the form described by Pseudo-Alcuin in the *De divinis officiis* (PL, CI, 1221[b-c]): Finito . . . baptismo in Sabbato sancto, fiunt litaniae ex jussa pontificis ante altare. . . . Stat primicerius unus in dextro choro, et dicit cum ipso, *Kyrie eleison*, et respondet secundicerius cum sinistro choro, *Kyrie eleison*, usque quater. . . . His finitis, pulsantur signa ad missam publicam. Nam ministri ita debent esse praeparati ante ostium sacrarii, ut cum cantor dixerit: *Accendite*, absque mora procedant usque ad altare. Sequuntur litaniae trinae, *Kyrie eleison*, et reliqua. . . . Tunc egreditur pontifex de sacrario cum ingenti decore, et praedicta cerostrata ante illum cum thymiamateriis, et cum dixerit schola, *Agnus Dei*, dicat cantor excelsa voce, *Accendite*. Tunc primum illuminantur omnes cerei neophytorum, quos manibus tenent. . . .

These accounts all agree that the procession should be a solemn one. It begins in the sacristy and is led by two candles or (Pseudo-Alcuin) two candles preceded by thuribles.

Further light is cast on this ceremony by Bellotte in a comment reprinted by Karl Young:

Among the most ancient customs of the Church there is a procession which is annually celebrated with a solemn rite before dawn on Easter, by which the joy of the saving mystery is announced to the faithful through a token of happiness. Hence it is that in the church of Laon, at the start of the new day at the second hour after midnight, the bells are rung as a sign of the festive joy; and this occurs before the signal for matins is given. At this time the sacrist or some other priest . . . reverently, and with appropriate reverence and genuflexions, withdraws the Holy Sacrament which was reserved on the day before with the prescribed rite, . . . and carries it from the sepulcher to the altar, and on all sides it is illuminated with many candles, so that the place itself is brilliant and the night is as the day.[58]

The rite takes place at 2:00 A.M. and is emphatically designed for popular instruction. The Host is placed on the altar in conjunction with an illumination ceremony described in a phrase from the *Exsultet* text of the Easter vigil service (*nox ipsa quasi dies illuminetur*). That the Host used in this and kindred ceremonies was consecrated on Maundy Thursday

---

All emphasize the *Accendite*, through differences are observable concerning its timing. All three refer to the illumination and two (Mozarabic, Pseudo-Alcuin) refer to the ringing of bells. The church is illuminated and also the hitherto extinguished candles of the neophytes are lit. The *Liber sacramentorum* mentions the saying of *Pax vobiscum* after the Gloria, a point of some significance in view of the reference in *Quem quaeritis* manuscripts to the *Pax*, the kiss, and the response *Deo gratias*. The Mozarabic rubrics emphasize the need for revesting in white robes, the "discovery" of the altar, the golden *retabula*, and the festive decorations (*omnia appareant solemniter*). Pseudo-Alcuin illustrates the assimilation of the Mass Kyrie into the litany, the need for revesting before the procession, and the splendid effect of the procession (*cum ingenti decore*).

The use of candles, thuribles, and cross in the vigil procession may be taken as normal. The reference in *Elevatio* and *Quem quaeritis* manuscripts to banners, palms, and a canopy over the Host supported by four staffs, while irregular, is fairly frequent; e.g., *DMC*, I, 138–39, 159, 165, 261, 265, 279, 303, 305, 630. These elements, particularly when used together, clearly relate the ceremony to the Mozarabic procession restoring (not deposing) the Host to the altar for use in the Mass of the Presanctified. This text is given above, Essay III, pp. 134–35. Because the Mass of the Presanctified was a relatively late development—Amalarius is still somewhat confused about it in the ninth century—it is possible that *Elevatio* and *Quem quaeritis* manuscripts containing references to banners, palms, and canopies preserve traces of a procession restoring the Host reserved on Maundy Thursday at the vigil Mass, and that the Mozarabic Good Friday procession has been transposed to this position from the Holy Saturday vigil. This is merely a suggestion, however. The main point is that references to banners, palms, and canopies relate *Elevatio* and *Quem quaeritis* manuscripts to a procession explicitly intended to restore the Host to the altar in preparation for Mass.

[58] *DMC*, I, 620–21.

may be logically inferred from the fact that the Church does not permit Consecration on Good Friday. The Soissons ritual explicitly instructs the celebrant to consecrate three Hosts on Maundy Thursday, adding, *tertia reservetur usque ad diem Resurrectionis*.[59] The Bamberg agenda, printed in 1587, indicates that the practice of consecrating three Hosts on Maundy Thursday was associated with "major churches" rather than with the smaller parish churches: "In the major churches a third Host should be consecrated, which is placed in the sepulcher of the Lord on the next day and can there be venerated by Christian people up to the time of the Lord's resurrection."[60]

Two texts that lack the *Quem quaeritis*, one from Prüfening and the other from Dublin, are also suggestive. The Prüfening text specifies a Host consecrated on Maundy Thursday and requires that the elevation be performed at *hora undecima aut paulo antea*. Ordinarily this would mean 5:00 A.M. However, because the ceremony preceded matins, which began well before 5:00 A.M., and the text is late, the reference may mean simply 11:00 P.M.—close to the original time of the vigil Mass. The Host is carried to the altar in a candlelight procession with psalms and antiphons. A *capsa* containing the Sacrament is exposed to the congregation, and after further antiphons, the abbot "in his pontifical regalia" begins a collect, *Deus qui ad eternam vitam*. This is followed by the hymn *Ad coenam agni*. The *capsa* is taken to the choir and then to a reliquary behind the altar. While this is being done, the bells ring "as on the greatest feasts" (*sicut in maximis festis*). At this point, rather incongruously, the abbot and his assistants disrobe.

The Dublin text is quite similar, though apparently independent.[61] It begins in a church illuminated only by the lights before the sepulcher and the paschal candle (*cereo paschale*). While the participants hold extinguished candles in their hands, the chorus intones the antiphon *Cum rex glorie*, which is followed by the familiar *Eleuamini* sequence found in Palm Sunday ceremonies. The sequence is chanted before the "portals" of the sepulcher. The candles are then illuminated from the sepulcher light. While the cross is elevated, the *Ad coenam agni* is sung, followed by *Christus resurgens*. A procession with lights, thuribles, and the elevated cross now moves toward an altar on which the Host has been displayed. Before its arrival, the Host is placed in a tabernacle. The antiphon *Surrexit Dominus* and the collect *Deus, qui pro nobis Filium* are said, and all reverence the cross. As the

[59] *Ibid.*, p. 624. For Parma, see *ibid.*, p. 125, n. 1.

[60] *Ibid.*, pp. 564–65. Compare Bamberg (*ibid.*, p. 173): "Et haec quoque Domenicae Resurrectionis commemoratio celebrioribus servit ecclesiis."

[61] For Prüfening, see *DMC*, I, 157–60; Dublin, *DMC*, I, 169–72.

procession returns to the choir, the crosses and images of the church are revealed and the bells are rung.

Both the Prüfening and Dublin ceremonies are somewhat obscure, and neither includes the *Quem quaeritis*. However, the candle, the procession, the altar with the Host, the *Ad coenam agni*, the use of a collect, the "discovery" of images, and the ringing of bells are all familiar in versions of the *Quem quaeritis* and are all associated with the vigil Mass.

The ceremonies that precede matins have several common features. They usually involve a Host, a procession to the altar, the ringing of bells, and a more or less emphatic illumination. Although not all of them include the *Quem quaeritis* dialogue, the *Elevatio* texts lacking the dialogue are related by their rubrics to those that have it. Other significant features— also associated with the vigil Mass rather than with matins—are the prominence given to revesting in white robes, emphasis on participation by a bishop or abbot in festive vestments, the occasional use of collects, including collects associated with the vigil service, the singing of the hymn *Ad coenam agni*, and references to holy water (from the newly blessed font) and the paschal candle. No adequate explanation of these features has been offered. The best one is that they are survivals from the time when the ceremony was associated with the vigil Mass. The need for a ceremony that involved transporting the Host to the altar is explained by the fact that as originally celebrated the vigil Mass was a Solemn Mass offered only in major churches and involving, as has been shown, the use of a sancta or fermentum consecrated either on Saturday before Palm Sunday or on Maundy Thursday. [62]

V

Although texts associated with the end of matins and the Introit of Easter Mass are generally less suggestive than those coming before matins, they too frequently have features unrelated to their liturgical positions. For convenience these features may be considered under the following heads: (1) references to baptism and related "events" associated with the vigil; (2) use of texts associated with the vigil service; (3) reference to all or part of the bells-illumination-procession sequence; (4) reference to liturgical acts associated with the beginning of Mass.

Two texts preserve prominent references to baptism. The first is from St. Gall. [63] In it the *Quem quaeritis* dialogue follows two antiphons associated

---

[62] See above, Essay IV, pp. 158–59.

[63] *DMC*, I, 227–28. The antiphons from the "Visitation of the Font" are *In die resurrectionis meae* and *Vidi aquam egregientem* (see *PL*, LXXVIII, 771).

with the Gregorian Easter vespers and referring to the *Visitatio Fontis*. The piece is evidently confused, and the confusion is instructive. It is manifestly a processional introducing Mass, but the antiphons relate it to the return of the neophytes from the font prior to the vigil Mass rather than to Easter Mass. The second, from Berlin, describes an apparently routine use of the *Quem quaeritis* at matins.[64] It begins with a candle procession, calling the candles *cerei Paschales*. The procession does not, however, lead to the altar. The participants, we are informed, stand "here and there around the baptismal font" (*Hii stabunt circa baptismum hinc et inde*), while two canons with thuribles visit "the imaginary Sepulcher" (*Sepulchrum ymaginarium*). The font, in other words, is either the sepulcher itself, as it is for the Easter vespers, or associated with it by position. The Marys approach the sepulcher, cense it, and "standing between the font and the choir" (*inter locum baptismalem et conventum*), sing the antiphon *Ad monumentum venimus*. After further action (the display of two *lintea*) the archbishop intones *Surrexit Dominus* and is answered with *Te Deum laudamus*. The procession then returns to the choir, the bells are rung, and the *lintea* are deposited on the altar.

The use of Mass texts as part of the *Elevatio* and *Quem quaeritis* ceremonies, while not general, is common enough to deserve notice. A surprising number of manuscripts include collects. Because matins does not have a provision for collects, their inclusion suggests that they are relics of a time when the ceremonies using them led directly to Mass. A variety of collects are used, not all of them identifiable. The most frequent one (found in seven manuscripts) is *Deus qui hodierna die per unigenitum tuum*, the Gregorian collect for Easter Mass.[65] It is somewhat incongruous for a ceremony performed in association with matins, and is perhaps best understood as a substitute for a vigil collect originally used but later transferred to Saturday evening or afternoon along with the rest of the vigil Mass. Two manuscripts preserve the Gregorian vigil collect *Deus qui hanc sacratissimam noctem*, and two others contain the earlier vigil prayer, found in the Gallican and Gelasian Sacramentaries, *Omnipotens sempiterne Deus qui hanc sacratissimam noctem*.[66] Of the other collects that can be

---

[64] *Ibid.*, p. 630.

[65] For the collect, see *PL*, LXXVIII, 92. Found in the following manuscripts (all in *DMC*, I): Moosburg (p. 141), Zurich (p. 154), *Liber officialis*, ed. Wilmert (p. 555), Klosterneuburg (p. 558), St. Florian (p. 559), Nuremberg (p. 564), Venice (p. 623), and perhaps also Aquileia (p. 560).

[66] For the Gregorian vigil collect, see *PL*, LXXVIII, 91ᵃ. In Sainte-Croix (*DMC*, I, 571) and Paris MSS (*DMC*, I, 575). For the Gelasian collect, *PL*, LXXIV, 1112ᵇ. In Aquileia (*DMC*, I, 145) and Venice (*DMC*, I, 623). Because both texts have *hac sacratissima nocte* rather than *hanc sacratissimam noctem*, the identification is not certain, but probably the variation results from scribal omission of the *n* and *m* abbreviations.

identified with any certainty, three are optional prayers from the Gregorian Sacramentary and two from the Gelasian Postcommunion benediction.[67] The remainder are presumably prayers devised for the ceremony after the tenth century. Another text originally associated with Mass and appearing in *Elevatio* and *Quem quaeritis* manuscripts is the hymn *Ad coenam agni.*[68]

The Bamberg *Elevatio* (1587) and the Venice *Processio in nocte pasche* (1523) may be taken as representative of a group of twelve manuscripts containing all or substantial parts of a sequence of prefatory texts.[69] The full sequence begins with the *Confiteor* and *Misereatur*, continues with two Psalms, *Domine, quid multiplicati* (3) and *Domine, probasti* (128), follows these with the Kyrie, the Pater Noster, and a response, and concludes with one or more collects. The Bamberg version specifies that the ceremony is for *celebrioribus ecclesiis* and takes place before matins at *horam undecimam*. The reference to "nobler" or "more frequented" churches would, according to the present hypothesis, be a vestige of the rule limiting Solemn Mass to cathedral churches, and the time, which may be 11:00 P.M. rather than 5:00 A.M., relates the ceremony to the vigil Mass. In both texts the ceremony begins with a candlelight procession to the sepulcher led by the clergy in full regalia. The Psalms are chanted at the sepulcher and are followed in the Bamberg text by the Kyrie, Pater Noster, and responsory *In resurrectione tua*. The Venice text omits the Kyrie and Pater Noster but includes a responsory (*Surrexit pastor bonus*). Both texts continue with a collect: the Bamberg uses the Gelasian Postcommunion benediction *Gregem tuum, Pastor bone*, and the Venice, the vigil collect *Omnipotens sempiterne Deus, qui ha[n]c sacratissima[m] nocte[m]*.[70] In both texts a procession now forms to carry the Host to the altar, using as its frame the *Tollite portas* antiphons of Palm Sunday. In the Bamberg manuscript this is concluded with *Ad coenam agni*, whereas in the Venice manuscript the *Quem*

---

[67] For the Gregorian optional prayers, see *PL*, LXXVIII, 98[b]. In Prüfening (*DMC*, I, 160) and *PL*, LXXVIII, 201[e]. In Barking (*DMC*, I, 166) and Dublin (*DMC*, I, 169). For the Gelasian benediction, see *PL*, LXXIV, 1198[d]. In Bamberg text (*DMC*, I, 173) and *Liber officialis*, ed. Wilmert (*DMC*, I, 555). Texts including unidentified collects (all in *DMC*, I): Moosburg (p. 141), Aquileia (p. 145; includes four unidentified), Barking (p. 166), Indersdorf (p. 559; includes two unidentified), Nuremberg (p. 564), Venice (p. 623).

[68] E.g., *DMC*, I, 160, 171, 175.

[69] Bamberg, *DMC*, I, 173–75; Venice, 622–24. The other manuscripts in this group (all in *DMC*, I) are Moosburg (p. 141), Aquileia (p. 145), Zurich (p. 154), Prüfening (p. 160), *Liber officialis*, ed. Wilmert (p. 555), St. Florian (p. 559), Klosterneuburg (p. 558), St. Florian (p. 559), Indersdorf (p. 559), Nuremberg (p. 564), and St. Gall (p. 621). Venice and St. Gall MSS include the *Quem quaeritis*.

[70] Assuming that the ablative is a scribal error for the accusative. See n. 66.

quaeritis dialogue follows. Both ceremonies end with Resurrection texts, *Christ ist erstanden* for Bamberg and *Surrexit Christus* for Venice. What is particularly striking about the prefatory sequence in manuscripts of the Bamberg-Venice group is that it preserves recognizable outlines of the preliminary parts of Mass. The *Confiteor* and *Misereatur* are the prayers of the clergy at the foot of the altar; it is impossible to interpret them as anything other than preparation for Mass.[71] The psalms parallel the normal Mass Introit, which is always followed by the Kyrie. The response is a substitute for the Gloria in Excelsis, presumably eliminated when the ceremony was separated from the Mass proper, and the collect is simply the next Mass text after the Gloria. Manuscripts of the Bamberg-Venice group thus suggest the existence of a clerical ceremony preceding the *Quem quaeritis* and having the double function of a preparation for Mass and the transfer of the Host from the sepulcher to the altar.

As might be expected, the sequence of bells, illumination, and procession is extremely common. The sequence is much the same whether it occurs at the beginning of matins or at the end. In other words, it is independent of the liturgical time of its performance, a fact that points to a common source for the texts using it. Among texts calling for a sudden illumination are those from St. Blaise, Sarum, Zurich, St. Gall, Bamberg, Dublin, Augsburg, and Soissons.[72] The ringing of bells is prominent in texts from St. Blaise, Moosburg, Sarum, Dublin, Soissons, Laon, and St. Gall.[73] The ceremonial placement of the Sacrament on the altar is a feature of texts from St. Blaise, Sarum, Hungary, Prüfening, Dublin, Metz, Aquileia, Bamberg, and Augsburg.[74] As is evident from these manuscripts, as well as from manuscripts examined in detail, the events are not isolated but related; the inclusion of one tends to produce the others. In several manuscripts the sequence leads directly to actions that appear to be preparations for Mass. Thus in a Hungarian *ordo* (XV C.) the Host is transported in a chalice (as in the *Quem quaeritis* from the Cathedral of Constance) and placed on a paten at the altar, suggestive of preparation for Communion.[75] In the Soissons, Prüfening, and Metz *ordines* the

---

[71] *Confiteor* and/or *Misereatur* appear in Moosburg (*DMC*, I, 141), Prüfening (*DMC*, I, 160), and Troyes (*DMC*, I, 603). The Psalm *Domine probasti* is used in the Easter Introit. A third Psalm that occurs frequently is *Miserere mei Deus*. For the Kyrie, see *DMC*, I, 154, 174, 222, 564, 621.

[72] *DMC*, I, 113, 146, 154, 164, 165, 169, 560, 573, 624. Here and below, see the texts and discussion of ninth-century forms for the beginning of the vigil Mass in n. 57.

[73] Cf. *DMC*, I, 113, 141, 146, 164, 169, 295, 460, 573, 620, 621, 624–25.

[74] Cf. *DMC*, I, 113, 145, 146, 148, 159, 169, 173, 261, 560.

[75] *DMC*, I, 148.

receptacle for the host is called a capsa, the term used in the *Liber sacramentorum* for the repository transporting the sancta to the altar at the beginning of Solemn Mass.[76] Finally, in the Augsburg *ordo* (XII C.) there are explicit instructions that the Host is to be kept on the altar until used in Communion: "donec alicui detur ad consumendum."[77]

Less common but equally striking are various minor liturgical observances normally associated with the vigil Mass. The Dublin *Elevatio* manuscript (XIV C.), for example, follows the bells-illumination-procession sequence with a collect (*Deus qui pro nobis*) and instructions for the "disclosing" of the cross and images: "His itaque gestis, discooperiantur cruces per ecclesiam et omnes ymagines."[78] Again, the *Visitatio* of St. Stephen of Besançon (XIII C.) ends with instructions that the entire choir change from black and red copes to white, an act unrelated to the normal transition from matins to lauds.[79]

An additional ceremonial element is provided in many texts of the *Quem quaeritis* by the singing of the *Deo gratias* and the giving of the Kiss of Peace. Both are puzzling if we assume that they originated in a ceremony intended to precede or follow matins. On the other hand, they are entirely appropriate to Mass. The *Pax* is today most closely associated with Communion, and the *Deo gratias* with the dismissal. If the *Quem quaeritis* ceremony were originally a part of Mass, it may occasionally have been used either as a substitute for the missing Communion hymn of the Roman vigil or—in scattered cases—at the end of the service. On the other hand, both the *Pax* and the *Deo gratias* have associations with the beginning of the vigil Mass. The kissing of the altar and the exchange of the *Pax* among the clergy were regular parts of the preliminary ceremonies described by Amalarius of Metz.[80] *Deo gratias* was the congregational response to the entry of the *Lumen Christi* during the vigil, and an early Spanish *ordo* cited by Duchesne shows that it was also used, at least in some churches, at the illumination ceremony preceding Mass itself. The facts, then, are consistent with the hypothesis that the *Quem quaeritis* was originally related to the vigil and are not consistent with the theory that it originated as an Introit trope of Easter Mass or in connection with matins.

---

[76] *Ibid.*, pp. 159, 261.

[77] *Ibid.*, pp. 560–61.

[78] *Ibid.*, p. 169.

[79] *Ibid.*, p. 615. The use of black and red copes was a feature of *Depositio* ceremonies.

[80] *Liber officialis*, ed. Hanssens, *Amalarii episcopi opera*, II, 278. Recall also the reference to the *Pax vobiscum* following the Gloria in the *Liber sacramentorum*, n. 57.

VI

If the *Quem quaeritis* ceremony originated in the ninth century or earlier, it must have developed variants well before anticipation detached it from its parent service. Any attempt to reconstruct the original must therefore be extremely tentative, but it need not be mere guesswork.

The conditions that "frame" the vigil Mass itself considerably limit the possibilities. Early *ordines* show that the Roman form of the vigil Mass differed from other forms such as the Gallican and Mozarabic and that the other forms also differed among themselves. The most important difference is that the Roman form was abbreviated, lacking preliminary chants and prayers, Offertory, and Communion, whereas in other liturgies these elements were included. All unanticipated forms have the following elements.[81] First, the congregation is divided into two separate components until the beginning of Mass. The pontiff and his assistants, the catechumens, and their sponsors proceed from the church to the baptistery at the end of the prophetic readings, while the remainder of the congregation and (presumably) a large number of clerics remain in the church proper. After baptism and confirmation a second procession leads the neophytes back to the church. It is preceded by two deacons carrying illuminated tapers (one of them the paschal candle) and followed by a cross, the pontiff and his assistants, and the catechumens (now neophytes) clothed in their white baptismal robes. Before their return the church must be prepared for a festive Mass. The images must be revealed, the crosses unshrouded, and the altar, bare since Maundy Thursday, redecorated for the paschal sacrifice. Because the early vigil Mass was a Solemn Mass which used a sancta or fermentum, a preconsecrated Host must have been brought from its place of repose to the altar. In the absence of instructions explicitly intended for the vigil Mass, it seems likely that the procession with the Host was similar to the sancta procession prescribed for Solemn Mass in the first *Ordo Romanus*.[82] The Host, it will be recalled, is carried from the sacristy in a capsa either by the pontiff or by a deacon. During the vigil the pontiff leads the procession of neophytes, and we may therefore suppose that a deacon carries the sancta. The Host is ultimately placed in a receptacle or paten on the altar for use during the commingling. Finally, as the neophytes rejoin the congregation, a deacon cries *Accendite*, and there is a general illumination of tapers; in at least one *ordo* this is followed by the response *Deo gratias*. At

---

[81] The following description is based on the *Regularis* and the *ordines* cited in n. 57.
[82] See Essay IV, pp. 159–60.

the same time there is a festive ringing of bells, and the exchange of the *Pax* among the clergy occurs. Mass then begins with the Gloria and collect, the Kyrie having been assimilated into the litany.

This outline has two separate but interrelated parts: the first is associated with preparations for Mass that occur prior to the return of the neophytes; the second, with the procession of neophytes from the font to the nave. If we rely on the logic of the angel's *Non est hic; surrexit*, we must assume that the Host is taken from the sepulcher to the altar before the neophytes enter the church. The removal is primarily a clerical rather than a popular function. The Host, reserved from Maundy Thursday, is transported by two or three deacons (the "sepulcher guards" of the *Regularis*) preceded by the sepulcher lights.

Soon after the Host is removed, the procession of white-robed neophytes enters. The neophytes carry unlit tapers and are preceded by the bishop, two illuminated candles (one the paschal candle), and one or more clerics with thuribles. On the basis of the St. Martin, Laon, and Udine versions it seems likely that the procession originally visited the place of repose of the Sacrament (the sacristy or perhaps a side altar) before entering the nave.[83] The function of the *Quem quaeritis* dialogue is, as the *Regularis* indicates, to instruct the "unlearned common persons and neophytes." This function is fulfilled in a simple and direct way by having the angel's query (*Quem quaeritis?*) addressed to the procession as it reaches the "sepulcher," and by having the answer given by the thurible-bearers, who act as surrogates for the neophytes. Since *Ite nuntiate*, *Venite et videte*, and *Cito euntes* appear in the Winchester version, which is explicitly associated with the vigil, we may assume that they were often part of the dialogue in its original position. *Ite nuntiate* regularly follows the announcement of the Resurrection in all *Quem quaeritis* manuscripts and is addressed to the Marys. The Marys obey the command by turning to the neophytes and singing *Alleluia. Resurrexit Dominus.* The subsequent texts are never found in Introit versions of the *Quem quaeritis* but are common in *Visitatio* versions. They imply definite actions. *Venite et videte*, found in Gregorian Easter vespers, the Winchester manuscript, and the *Regularis*, is an invitation to the neophytes to view the empty sepulcher (or the baptismal font in the vesper ceremony) for themselves. *Cito euntes*, found in the Winchester text and in Easter vespers, instructs them to resume their procession in order to "tell the disciples," i.e., the congregation.[84] The antiphon

---

[83] Above, pp. 200–7.

[84] The "ineptitude" of the *Cito euntes* of which Young complains (*DMC*, I, 254) disappears when the text is related to the original ceremony rather than interpreted out of context.

Surrexit Dominus fulfills this command and was probably used as a processional. The reason for the omission of *Cito euntes* from the *Regularis* is that the ceremony is performed at the altar in front of the congregation rather than at the sacristy. The command would be superfluous. The inclusion of the *linteum* in the *Regularis* suggests that the ceremony included a display of "graveclothes"—the cloth originally used to cover the Sacrament—which were then transported to the altar where they served either as altar cloth or as corporal and pall (*linteum,* sudarium) for the Mass that followed. The two phases of the ceremony merge as the neophytes reach the nave and the deacon cries *Accendite.*

This reconstruction, while admittedly theoretical, explains several otherwise puzzling features of *Elevatio* and *Quem quaeritis* manuscripts, most obviously their use of Mass texts and ceremonies. It also explains the variant forms and positions of the ceremonies. When the vigil Mass came to be celebrated on Saturday afternoon or evening, the introductory rites were not transferred bodily to another position. There was a tendency to separate the primarily clerical elements from the popular ones. This was, of course, not universal, but it was frequent enough to produce two markedly different groups of manuscripts. The clerical elements, which preceded the popular ones, are preserved in manuscripts of the *Elevatio Hostiae. Elevatio* ceremonies almost always precede the *Visitatio* in *ordines* having both, and they retain a position close to the original time of the vigil Mass—between 11:00 P.M. and 3:00 A.M. Occasionally *Elevatio* texts retain the *Quem quaeritis* dialogue and the tradition of popular participation; but usually the dialogue has been eliminated, and the people are either ignored or explicitly excluded. On the other hand, texts and actions associated with Mass—bells, illumination, procession to the altar, the Kyrie, the collect, etc.—are retained more frequently and in a more coherent sequence than in *Visitatio* ceremonies.

Unlike the clerical elements, the popular elements lose their meaning without the presence of the congregation; hence they were usually transferred to times that permitted lay participation and were popularly associated with the Resurrection. One such time was between the end of matins and the beginning of lauds. The end of Easter matins apparently was not treated as a moment symbolizing the Resurrection until well after the *Visitatio* had become traditional in that position. In fact, the first symbolic explanation is from the *Gemma animae* of Honorius of Autun (d. *ca.* 1150).[85] However, the daily service of lauds had always drawn on

---

[85] *PL,* CLXXII, 677. The interpretation is repeated by Sicardus of Cremona (d. 1215) and Durandus of Mende (d. 1296). It is not, however, found in Amalarius or Pseudo-Alcuin, who are the best evidence for ninth- and tenth-century interpretations.

the parallel between the rising of the sun and the Resurrection, and in the absence of alternative explanations Easter lauds may be considered the source of the association between the *Visitatio* and the end of matins.

At the end of matins the vigil ceremony tended to retain those elements intended for instruction and to drop the clerical ones. The *Quem quaeritis* dialogue is almost always preserved. References to popular participation, while by no means universal, are frequent. On the other hand, the Host appears far less frequently, the cross being used in its place. Mass texts are also infrequent, but Mass ceremonies announcing the Resurrection are kept. Illuminations and candle processions occur, although they are somewhat superfluous because the *Visitatio* takes place at daybreak, and the ringing of bells is generally called for. The graveclothes are frequently displayed, but the procession carrying them to the altar is less common than in the *Elevatio*. Popular participation is further encouraged by the inclusion in many German manuscripts of the vernacular *Christ ist erstanden* before the *Te Deum*.

The third position of the *Quem quaeritis* is just before the Easter Mass. In this position it retains its original character as an introduction to Mass. The Easter Mass is, however, quite different from the vigil Mass. There is no procession of neophytes, no illumination, no special ceremony for preparing the altar. Furthermore, the sancta was all but forgotten by the eleventh century. Accordingly, the rubrics of the original are dropped and the dialogue is simplified to serve as an Introit trope. The *Ite nuntiate* is retained, often as a part of the *Non est hic* rather than as a separate sentence. The commands *Venite et videte* and *Cito euntes* are dropped. This is not because they are late developments; they appear in the ninth-century Easter vespers and in the Winchester troper. It is simply because they imply action which is inappropriate to the beginning of the Easter Mass.

Returning now to the original of the *Quem quaeritis*, the following extremely tentative suggestions may be made regarding its text. The initial procession carrying the sancta to the altar may have been silent, but all or part of the sequence of texts introducing the Bamberg-Venice group of manuscripts may have been used. If so, the *Confiteor* and Psalms were recited as part of the adoration of the reserved Host and, perhaps, during the procession to the altar. Shortly thereafter, the neophytes returned from the font to the accompaniment of either the threefold litany or antiphons associated with the "Visitation of the Font," as in the eleventh-century St. Gall version. The dialogue was in the abbreviated form but included the sequence *Ite nuntiate, Alleluia. Resurrexit, Venite et videte*, and *Cito euntes*. After the last command the procession of neophytes moved to the nave, probably singing *Surrexit Dominus*. At this point the command *Accendite* was given. It seems likely that the St. Martin text preserves at least one early form for this command. If so, it was repeated several times, and choral responses were given. Coincident with the cry, the illumination occurred. At the same time the clergy (perhaps the congregation as well) exchanged the Kiss of Peace and the Easter greeting *Surrexit Christus . . . Deo gratias*. The command *Hora est; psallite; iubet Dominus canere eia, dicite eia!* may have been used to introduce the Gloria in Excelsis, followed in turn by the regular Gregorian texts.

VII

Recovering a lost tradition is at best a hazardous enterprise, but it is one that cannot always be avoided. An unsatisfactory historical theory remains an obstacle to scholarship as long as no alternatives are available. The "simplest version" hypothesis concerning the origin of the *Quem quaeritis* is unsatisfactory. It is based on the analogy between evolution and the development of literary forms rather than on historical evidence, and it has resulted in an arrangement of manuscripts so arbitrary as to conceal rather than reveal their significant features. The alternative is to begin not with evolution but chronology. The *Quem quaeritis* manuscripts assignable to the tenth century both invalidate the "simplest version" hypothesis and provide a basis other than that of increasing complexity for classifying later versions. Further light is shed on extant manuscripts by the history of early medieval liturgy. An analysis of *Quem quaeritis* manuscripts in these terms consistently leads to the conclusion that the dialogue originated not as an Easter trope but as a ceremony associated with the vigil Mass. Its subsequent displacement and modification are explained by three major factors: the anticipation of the vigil Mass to a time no longer even approximately coincident with the Resurrection, the characteristics of monastic as against secular worship, and the special requirements of those ceremonies with which the *Quem quaeritis* became associated in the tenth century. Enough features of the original may be dimly observed in the texts and rubrics of extant manuscripts to justify a tentative reconstruction, but this reconstruction is offered only as a suggestion. Concerning the date and place of origin of the ceremony there is no evidence at all. Here scholarship must yield to pure speculation.

ESSAY VI

From *Quem quaeritis* to
Resurrection Play

I

ETWEEN THE TENTH and the twelfth centuries there is a marked increase in the number, variety, and complexity of extant liturgical dramas. This increase cannot be taken as evidence of gradual, incremental growth. As far as manuscript chronology goes, the history of the *Quem quaeritis* is one of long periods of stagnation alternating with abrupt and unexplained changes. To make the situation still more complicated, during the eleventh century, when the *Quem quaeritis* shows little or no change from tenth-century forms, Christmas plays appear both in simple and highly elaborate versions having the qualities of self-conscious drama. One complex Latin Resurrection play survives from the twelfth century; yet along with several elaborate Christmas plays this century produced complex Latin dramas on Lazarus, Daniel, and St. Nicholas, and two highly finished vernacular plays, the *Seinte Resureccion* and the famous *Mystère d'Adam*, which incorporates episodes on Cain and Abel and the prophets of Christ in what looks like a fragmentary Old Testament cycle.

This summary raises at least three fundamental questions. What justification is there for speaking of the development of liturgical drama as a slow, continuous growth from simple to elaborate forms? What evidence exists that the complex Resurrection play can be studied without consideration of the fact that complex Christmas plays precede it by as much as a hundred years? And is it proper to assume that Latin plays regularly precede their vernacular equivalents, in view of the fact that the earliest plays on Adam and Cain and Abel are in French?

Knowledge of the history of liturgical drama is heavily dependent on the manuscripts that have survived. Since the survival of manuscripts is a matter of chance, it is limited and tentative. On the other hand, the fact that many important manuscripts have undoubtedly been lost cannot justify indifference to the chronology of those we have. While chronology cannot solve all of the problems involved in the development of the Easter play, it can serve as a frame to limit speculation by telling the critic, "This approach is contrary to available evidence"; or "This approach fails to take into account important precedents." Once the chronological frame is established, the critic can proceed with some assurance to matters of literary form, dramatic technique, themes, influences, and the like—in short, to matters involving the relation of liturgical drama to drama in general.

II

The situation indicated by tenth-century manuscripts of the *Quem quaeritis* is extremely fluid. The nine surviving manuscripts are evenly divided between those intended for Easter Mass, those intended for matins, and those with ambiguous liturgical associations. The Mass texts have brief rubrics or none at all, and their dialogue consists of the angel's query, the reply, the *Non est hic; ite nuntiate*, and either the *Resurrexit (Surrexit)* antiphon plus the *Resurrexi* Introit, or the *Resurrexi* by itself. Supplementary material is limited to commands (*Psallite, dicite, iubet Dominus*) and exclamations (*Hora est, eia, alleluia*). The *Regularis concordia* text, associated with matins, is much more elaborate. It has detailed instructions as to the method of presentation and acting of the piece, and it includes the *Resurrexit* antiphon, the angel's command *Venite et videte*, and a second resurrection antiphon, *Surrexit Dominus*. The Winchester text is associated with the *Benedictio cerei*. Its rubrics are brief, but it has the fullest dialogue of any tenth-century version, and, in fact, is more developed than all but two eleventh-century versions. In addition to *Resurrexit Dominus* and *Venite et videte*, it includes the command *Cito euntes dicite*, followed by *Surrexit Dominus*. No Christmas or other plays survive from the tenth century, and it is probable that none existed.

There are a great many contrasts between the tenth and eleventh centuries. In contrast to the nine versions of the *Quem quaeritis* definitely assignable to the tenth century, some forty-five versions survive from the eleventh century.[1] Almost all of these are associated with either Easter Mass or matins. In other words, the fluidity of tenth-century placement has been replaced by a quite definite convention, a situation contrary to

[1] This and later counts are based on the texts and references in Young, *DMC*, I, *passim*. It is impossible to make an absolutely accurate count because several manuscripts are either of uncertain date or dated X–XII C. For simplicity, I have assigned texts dated XI C. and XI–XII C. to the eleventh century, and texts dated XII C. and XII–XIII C. to the twelfth century. For a more exact enumeration of the manuscripts, see Appendix II.

what one would expect if the origin of the *Quem quaeritis* were the Mass Introit or matins. The texts of the eleventh-century versions—with one exception—show no advance whatsoever over tenth-century versions. The Introit versions have few rubrics or none, and no Introit version carries the dialogue beyond the *Ite nuntiate* and the reply (*Resurrexit, Surrexit, Resurrexi*). Some slight experimentation is evident in the supplementary antiphons. A text from Bobbio includes *Pascha nostrum . . . immolatus est* and *Hodie exultent iusti*.[2] Texts from Limoges and Ripoll (XI–XII C.) include *En ecce completum est*, and three manuscripts, two from St. Gall and one from Bonona, include several antiphons evidently used as processionals. One text, from Limoges, begins with *Ubi est Christus meus*.[3]

The *Visitatio* manuscripts are equally undeveloped. Most are simply adaptations of the Introit version and lack even the elements found in the *Regularis concordia*. Only seven *Visitatio* texts are as complete as the *Regularis*. One of these is simply the eleventh-century manuscript of the *Regularis*, and four others are dated XI–XII C.[4] No other *Visitatio* manuscripts unambiguously assignable to the eleventh century include the *Venite et videte*, and the only text which includes this and the *Cito euntes* together is the eleventh-century copy of the Winchester troper.[5] Four texts show the same sort of experimentation with antiphons that is evident in the Introit versions. In three, *Et dicebant invicem: Quis revolvet* precedes the dialogue proper.[6] The fourth is the *Visitatio* from Aquileia.[7] This text, for which there is no tenth- or eleventh-century precedent, begins with *Quis revolvet*, emends *o Christicolae* to *o tremule mulieres*, and substitutes *cito euntes* for the traditional *Ite nuntiate*. In place of *Resurrexit Dominus*, the Marys sing *Ad monumentum venimus;* and in place of *Venite et videte* and *Cito euntes*, there are two antiphons related to the "race" of Peter and John (*Currebant duo* and *Cernitis, o socii*)—the first appearance of these texts in liturgical drama.

This concludes the brief register of eleventh-century experiments with the *Quem quaeritis*. On the record, eleventh-century versions are less "developed" than tenth-century ones. Since only nine tenth-century manuscripts survive, in contrast to approximately forty-five eleventh-

---

[2] *DMC*, I, 207. These are marked *Item Trophi* and hence may be separate compositions.

[3] *DMC*, I, 207, 209, 212, 226, 570, 571. The Ripoll text (p. 570) also begins with *Ubi est Christus*.

[4] *DMC*, I, 581 (*Regularis*); and 263, 583, 590, 598.

[5] *DMC*, I, 586.

[6] *DMC*, I, 259, 263, 590.

[7] *DMC*, I, 628.

century ones, it is impossible to ascribe this situation entirely to the vicissitudes of manuscript survival. The proper conclusion is that between the tenth and eleventh centuries, at the time when the placement of the *Quem quaeritis* was becoming codified, the dialogue of the piece was simplified along the lines established by the St. Gall manuscript of *ca*. 950. The Aquileia version suggests some slight progress toward increasing freedom of treatment, but it remains isolated. The tradition behind it cannot have been widespread.

The lack of development in the eleventh-century *Quem quaeritis* is placed in the sharpest possible relief if contrasted to the Christmas drama produced in the same period. Some twenty Christmas plays can be definitely assigned to the eleventh century. They are almost evenly divided between plays on the visit of the shepherds (*Officium Pastorum*) and plays on the adoration of the Magi (*Officium Stellae*). The shepherd plays are uniformly simple. They are all attached to the Introit of Christmas Mass, and their dialogue is modeled on the *Quem quaeritis*. The Magi plays are most frequently attached to matins and are much more diversified. Three texts, one of them dated X–XI C., are fragments of what must have fairly complete Nativity plays,[8] and two texts, from Compiègne and Freising, are elaborate, self-conscious dramas that differ from all eleventh-century Easter texts in quality as well as length.[9] Finally, the Freising manuscript, by joining the visit of the Magi to the visit of the shepherds, with a reference to the Slaughter of the Innocents, provides an early instance of the impulse to combine episodes into larger dramatic units. This same impulse is evident in manuscripts from Limoges and Einsiedeln (both XI–XII C.) in which Christmas episodes are grouped together instead of being separated by intervening liturgical texts.[10] Although the number of eleventh-century Christmas manuscripts is less than half that of Easter manuscripts, five highly developed Christmas plays survive, as against not a single complex Easter play. The obvious conclusion is that no complex Easter plays have survived because none were written.

The situation in the twelfth century confirms this view. There are some thirty-five *Quem quaeritis* manuscripts from the period. Only one of these, a text from Ripoll, is in any way comparable in scope and technique to the five eleventh-century Christmas plays previously mentioned.[11] All but nine of the texts simply continue the tradition established in the tenth

[8] *DMC*, II, 443–46.

[9] *DMC*, II, 53–56 (Compiègne), 93–97 (Freising).

[10] *DMC*, II, 453–54, 456 (Limoges); I, 598 (Einsiedeln fragments).

[11] *DMC*, I, 678–81. I have not included the Einsiedeln text (I, 390–92) because it is dated XII–XIII C.

century, exhibiting no greater tendency to experiment with supplementary antiphons than is observed in eleventh-century texts. In the nine complex texts the race between Peter and John appears six times; the scene between Mary Magdalene and Christ in the garden (*Hortulanus*) appears four times, twice in conjunction with the *Peregrini* rather than the Resurrection play; and the *Victimae Paschali* appears three times.[12] In one of the texts, from Augsburg, the antiphon *Currebant duo* is the only addition to the traditional *Visitatio* text, and it is therefore less developed than the eleventh-century version from Aquileia.[13] Three others (Vienna, Cracow, Graz) add the race and supplementary antiphons.[14] A text from Sicily adds only the *Planctus Mariae*. In the other four texts innovations occur in groups. The St. Lambrecht *Visitatio* includes the race between Peter and John, the *Victimae Paschali*, and two vernacular songs.[15] This version marks the first use of vernacular singing in the Latin Easter play, although there is rather extensive French dialogue in the Limoges *Sponsus* (XI–XII C.) and French is used throughout the *Trois Maries, La Seinte Resureccion*, and the *Mystère d'Adam*. The Prague *Visitatio* includes the *Hortulanus* episode, followed by the race between Peter and John.[16] The Ripoll manuscript, the most complex of the group, includes the *Planctus Mariae*, a spice-merchant scene with dialogue, the *Hortulanus* scene, and the scene on the road to Emmaus, the latter two separated from the earlier material by the rubric *Versus de Pelegrinis*.[17] Finally, in a Sicilian manuscript following Norman usage, the *Hortulanus* and *Victimae Paschali* are incorporated into an elaborate play labeled *Versus ad faciendum Peregrinum*.[18]

All of these versions seem timid when placed against the background of developments in twelfth-century drama apart from the Latin Easter play. Rather full Latin plays survive on the themes of the appearance of Christ on the road to Emmaus (*Peregrini*), the visit of the Magi (*Stellae*), the Antichrist, Daniel, Lazarus, and St. Nicholas. The highly finished *Mystère d'Adam*, which is written in French and includes episodes on Cain and Abel and the prophets of Christ, comes from the twelfth century. If Grace Frank's dating of the vernacular *Seinte Resureccion* in the late twelfth century is accepted, a vernacular Easter play covering the period from the Deposition from the Cross to the appearance at Emmaus was

12 *DMC*, I, 269, 310, 363–65, 476–80, 629, 632, 634, 664–65, 678–81.
13 *DMC*, I, 310.
14 *DMC*, I, 32, 34, 629.
15 *DMC*, I, 363–65. For the Sicilian text, see I, 269.
16 *DMC*, I, 664–65.
17 *DMC*, I, 678–81.
18 *DMC*, I, 476–80.

being performed on a fairly elaborate stage before the common people well before any hint of a comparable Latin play can be found.[19] In sum, while only one moderately complex version of the Latin Easter play can be ascribed definitely to the twelfth century, elaborate dramas with cyclic overtones survive on several other topics in both Latin and the vernacular, the latter being more developed than the former.

The situation in the thirteenth century is still more complex than that in the twelfth. Fortunately, it has little bearing on the chronology of liturgical drama. By the thirteenth century Latin precedents exist for the complex forms of all but one of the important Christmas and Easter dramas, vernacular dramas have appeared as well as Latin ones, and the tendency to consider individual dramas to be components of larger cycles is becoming marked. The single innovation is the Passion play, which appears for the first time in the Benediktbeuern manuscript of the *Carmina Burana*.[20] It is clear that the use of the vernacular illustrated by the *Sponsus* (XI–XII C.), the St. Lamprecht *Visitatio* (XII C.), and the *Mystère d'Adam* (XII C.) persisted and increased. Jean Bodel, Adam le Bossu, and Rutebeuf wrote noncyclic vernacular plays in the thirteenth century, and although *La Seinte Resureccion* is dated in the twelfth century, the two surviving manuscripts come from thirteenth-century France and England. Thirteenth-century fragments from Kloster Muri and Kloster Himmelgarten suggest the appearance of the German cycle during this period, although complete plays and developed cycles do not appear in German manuscripts before the fourteenth century (i.e., the plays from Innsbruck, 1391, and Vienna, XIV C.).[21]

What is most distinctive about the development of the theater in the thirteenth century is the tendency to consolidate and elaborate the complex forms and cyclic tendencies that arose in the eleventh century in connection with the Christmas plays. Fairly substantial Christmas cycles

[19] Frank, *Medieval French Drama*, p. 88. The reference by Gerhoh of Reichersberg (1093–1169) to "theatrical spectacles performed in the church" suggests the existence of some sort of cycle with a fairly well-developed Resurrection play in the twelfth century. This and similar references are, however, ambiguous. The plays may have been vernacular or Latin adaptations of vernacular dramas, and in the absence of manuscripts it is impossible to determine how substantial they were. If elaborate Latin Resurrection plays were common in the twelfth century, it is extremely hard to understand why only one of the thirty-five extant texts is at all developed, whereas several complex Christmas plays survive from a much smaller total number of manuscripts. Gerhoh's comment is reprinted in Young, *DMC*, II, 524–25. See also Craig, *ERD*, pp. 102–5.

[20] *DMC*, I, 518–33.

[21] For French drama of the period, see Frank, *Medieval French Drama*, pp. 66–113; for German drama, see Craig, *ERD*, pp. 102–5.

exist from the cathedrals of Laon and Rouen, while the Fleury playbook and the *Carmina Burana* preserve the most polished examples of liturgical drama that survive, grouped together in a manner indicating that— whatever the time of performance of the plays—they were considered parts of a larger cycle. In addition, references to the theater and ecclesiastical records from the twelfth and thirteenth centuries prove conclusively both the existence and popularity of religious plays throughout Europe. Perhaps the most famous of these is the reference in the *Cronaca Friuliana* to a complete cycle of religious plays performed at Cividale in northern Italy at Pentecost in 1298 and 1303. No matter what its progress elsewhere, the Corpus Christi cycle had reached something like its full dimensions in Italy by the end of the thirteenth century.[22]

To recapitulate, the Easter play was the first of the liturgical dramas to appear in Europe. Examination of the manuscripts suggests that it originated as a liturgical ceremony, rather than as a brief trope of the St. Gall type, and that in the tenth century there was some uncertainty about its proper placement, its mode of performance, and its text. In the eleventh century these questions were solved, and the *Quem quaeritis* became a formal and rigidly limited liturgical embellishment. The only significant eleventh-century additions are two antiphons relating the race of Peter and John. The Christmas play was produced by analogy to the Easter play. Because it was a free composition, unencumbered by tradition, its forms are far more various than those of the Easter play. Logically, one would assume that simple forms preceded complex ones, but there is no evidence of this. Until such time as manuscripts are dated more accurately or fresh texts are discovered, the possibility must be kept in mind that the Christmas play originated as a fairly elaborate composition, and that parts of this composition were extracted by clerics who wished to use them in connection with Christmas services in the same way that the *Quem quaeritis* was used at Easter.[23]

In the twelfth century, along with some thirty-five versions of the *Quem quaeritis* in its traditional form, there is one fairly elaborate version. There are no "transitional" manuscripts to show that this version was produced by gradual elaboration of simpler forms. In view of the proliferation of complex non-Easter plays in the twelfth century, there is a strong possi-

[22] Craig, *ERD*, pp. 100–1.

[23] There is one Christmas text that may be as early as the tenth century. This text, reprinted in *DMC*, II, 443, is evidently a fragment of a complex Magi play. In other words, the text that may be the earliest of all Christmas plays is not simple but relatively elaborate. The dating, however, is approximate, and the play may be from the eleventh rather than the tenth century.

bility that this play was produced self-consciously in imitation of another drama, perhaps the *Magi*. Another possibility that cannot be rejected flatly is that the Latin drama was an imitation of a vernacular drama, intended either as competition for the vernacular play or simply as a Latin redaction for the edification of a learned—hence Latin-oriented— monastic community. These possibilities are suggested by the nature of the historical evidence that survives, and if they are to be rejected, con- vincing reasons must be offered against them.

Because the major forms of liturgical drama, including cyclic combina- tions, are found in thirteenth-century manuscripts and references to dramatic productions, we may assume that by the year 1300 the "devel- opment" of Latin religious drama was complete. Later elaborations must be understood in the context of the vernacular cycles.

Manuscript chronology can take us no further. For additional under- standing of the Latin Resurrection play, we must turn to the internal features of the plays themselves. Because they represent the earliest appearance of important innovations, three manuscripts are especially interesting: the *Visitatio* from Aquileia, containing the earliest form of the race between Peter and John; the *Visitatio* from St. Lambrecht, the only twelfth-century Latin Resurrection play with vernacular singing; and the Resurrection play from Ripoll, the only twelfth-century example of a complex Latin Easter play, the only one with an *unguentarius*, and the only one having cyclic qualities. Each of these plays is a definite step in the direction of increasing complexity. Criticism cannot assure us that they are the earliest instances of the innovations that they illustrate, but it can tell us something about the methods—and perhaps the motives—that produced them.

III

The Aquileia *Visitatio* stands out against a background of a century or more of highly stylized drama which was fixed in text and in liturgical placement. If the *Quem quaeritis* originated, as has been suggested, in a ceremony intended to enhance the transition between the baptism and Mass of the Easter vigil, its meaning must have been almost purely liturgical. The sequence of its dialogue, the actions performed, and the costumes and stage props employed were dictated not by the needs of representational drama but by the sequence of events and ceremonies peculiar to the early vigil service. Nevertheless, like the Palm Sunday procession and the Maundy service, the *Quem quaeritis* ceremony has strong representational elements. If it dramatized the transition from baptism to Mass, it also instructed the "unlearned common persons and neophytes" in the rudiments of divine history.

Teaching divine history is not as simple as it might at first seem. The *Quem quaeritis* teaches the facts of the Resurrection as recounted by three of the four Gospels—Matthew, Mark, and Luke. Because these accounts are not perfectly consistent among themselves, a certain amount of conflation—such as might be found in a harmony of the Gospels—characterizes even the earliest *Quem quaeritis* texts, and minor variations occur in the number of angels, their placement, and so forth. But sacred history does not exist in a vacuum. By the ninth century the important events in the New Testament had been glossed, analyzed, interpreted, and reinterpreted in countless sermons, homilies, commentaries, and theological treatises. Being perhaps the central event of Scripture and of the Church year, the story of the Resurrection had accumulated a particularly rich store of associations. These may be considered the *dianoia* of the *Quem quaeritis* play. Although they may have had little significance for the "unlearned common persons," it is clear from the surviving texts that they influenced both the shape of the dialogue and the mode of presentation. They may have furnished a motive for the continued performance of the piece as strong as that of popular appeal, especially in monasteries.

Amid the numerous and varied interpretations of the Visit to the Tomb, three are particularly widespread and authoritative. For Augustine, the most important feature of the Visit to the Tomb is that it furnishes "ocular proof" of the miracle on which the entire fabric of Christianity depends. In an Easter sermon addressed to the entire congregation, he wrote: "Let us believe in the Christ who was crucified and in the Christ who arose on the third day. This is the faith that distinguishes us from the pagans . . . and Jews. I know that you believe: you will be saved."[24] The theme recurs in sermons to the neophytes, in sermons to the faithful, and in sermons attacking the Gentiles, the Donatists, and the Manichees.[25] It leads to emphasis on the "evidences" of the Resurrection—the abandoned graveclothes and, particularly, the appearance of Christ himself to Mary Magdalene.[26]

Symbolic elements also enter Augustine's interpretations. The moment of the Resurrection is a turning point in history, symbolized by the light

---

[24] Sermon 234, *PL*, XXXIX, 1115.

[25] E.g., Sermons 116, 219–23 (all vigil sermons), 237, 238, 240–44, etc. (all in *PL*, XXXIX, 1070–1150).

[26] Especially Sermons 234, 238, 243.

that turns night into day.[27] The interpretation emphasizes the importance of the dramatic peripeteia and points the symbolism of the candle ceremonies so often incorporated into the *Visitatio*. Again, in a vigil service sermon, Augustine stresses the parallel between the Marys watching at the tomb and the faithful keeping watch throughout Easter Eve.[28] This view anticipates the function of the Marys in the *Visitatio* as representatives of the congregation, through whom the people participate directly in the dramatized history. Finally, in his commentary on John, Augustine asserts that Mary Magdalene symbolizes the Church of the Gentiles (i.e., the Western Church), which did not worship Christ before the announcement of the Resurrection. Christ's *Noli me tangere* means "do not believe in me as I am now; believe in me as I will be when I ascend to the Father."[29]

A second major contributor to interpretations of the Visit to the Tomb is St. Gregory. Gregory's twenty-first homily on the Gospels, read during matins of Easter Day, is an extended interpretation of Mark's account (16:1–7). Perhaps because he lived in an age after the great heresies of the early Church had been quelled, Gregory stresses the devotional symbolism of the visit rather than ocular proof. The parallel between the Marys and the Christian congregation is prominent: "We also, who believe in Him That was dead, do come to His sepulchre bearing sweet spices, when we seek the Lord with the savour of good living. . . . Those women, when they brought their spices, saw a vision of Angels and, in sooth, those souls whose godly desires do move them to seek the Lord . . . do see the countrymen of our Fatherland which is above."[30] The position of the angel on the right side of the tomb symbolizes eternity: "For what signifieth the left, but this life which now is? or the right, but life everlasting?"[31] His white garment symbolizes both eternity and the joy of the Resurrection. Like Augustine, Gregory offers more particularized symbolic interpretations of various parts of the story. In the twenty-fifth homily, read at matins on Thursday of Easter Week, Mary Magdalene is interpreted as a symbol of the penitent who tearfully seeks Christ and is finally rewarded.[32] In the twenty-second homily, read at matins of Low Saturday, Peter and John are interpreted as representatives of the Church

---

[27] Sermon 221, 231, 233, *PL*, XXXIX, 1090, 1104, 1112.

[28] Sermon 221, *PL*, XXXIX, 1090.

[29] *In Joannis evangelium*, *PL*, XXXV, 1956–57. According to this interpretation the two angels at the head and foot of the tomb represent "the beginning and the end," while Mary represents mankind's acknowledgment of the sovereignty of Christ with her *Rabboni quod dicit magister*.

[30] *The Roman Breviary*, II, 388.

[31] *Ibid.*

[32] *Ibid.*, pp. 396–97.

of the Gentiles and the synagogue: "They run both of them together, for from the time of her birth until now . . . the Church of the Gentiles hath run in a parallel road . . . with the Synagogue. . . . The Synagogue came first to the Sepulchre, but she hath not yet entered in; for . . . she will not believe in Him who died for her."[33]

With Gregory we first encounter the type of detailed allegorical exegesis that is characteristic of the later Middle Ages. By the tenth century allegorical interpretations can be found for every detail of the Visit to the Tomb, but they do not seem immediately relevant. The third interpretation of sufficient importance to be an element in the *dianoia* of the *Quem quaeritis* play is what may be called the liturgical interpretation. It is characteristic of Bede, Amalarius, and Pseudo-Alcuin and therefore may be taken as fairly typical of the period between the eighth and tenth centuries. In his commentary on Luke, Bede draws an emphatic parallel between the visit of the Marys and the priest's approach to the altar during the Eucharistic sacrifice.[34] This, says Bede, is the meaning of the episode *juxta intellectum* in contrast to its meaning *juxta historiam*. Amalarius and Pseudo-Alcuin elaborate this interpretation in their commentaries on the Mass. At the climax of the Mass, according to Amalarius, the clerics at the altar represent the Marys, the corporal and pall represent the graveclothes, and at the moment of transition from sacrifice to Communion, the angel announces, *Non est hic; surrexit.*[35] This interpretation closely links the *Quem quaeritis* to the Mass, and it appears in the period contemporary with the appearance of the *Quem quaeritis*. It may have been involved in the composition of the original ceremony and almost certainly contributed to its initial appeal to the clergy.

Whether or not the *Quem quaeritis* originated as a vigil ceremony, by the tenth century it is liturgically independent. If the exigencies of liturgical ceremony determined its original content and mode of presentation, these are no longer operative. In other words, it has passed over the line dividing ceremony from representation. Its new function is to present a number of facts derived from an historical source in as comprehensible a manner as possible. Freed of the limits of ceremony, it can include more history than the original, and it can substitute representational elements— costumes, realistic stage props, etc.—for liturgical ones. The more clearly the implications of the new situation are realized, the more prominent

[33] *Ibid.*, pp. 400–1.

[34] *In Lucae evangelium expositio, PL*, XCII, 622–24. For the relevant text, see Essay V, n. 33.

[35] *Liber officialis*, ed. Hanssens, *Amalarii episcopi opera*, II, 160–61.

these elements become. A ceremony is neither true nor false in the normal sense of those terms, but a representation is by definition an imitation, a replica of the thing represented. Its effectiveness depends on its closeness to its subject, which, in the case of the *Quem quaeritis,* is sacred history. Two factors limit the development of representational elements in the *Quem quaeritis.* The first is the conservative force of tradition. The second is *dianoia*—the symbolic meanings attached to the scene. In general, symbolic meanings are best expressed in forms that are simple and stylized. In complex forms symbolic meanings are easily lost because of the interest in the forms themselves. The spectator is encouraged to ask "What happens next?" and to forget or ignore the question "What does it mean?"

Tradition and a lingering sense of the *Quem quaeritis* as symbolic statement help to explain why it remained static for two—and perhaps three— centuries, during which other Latin dramas reached a high degree of sophistication. The earliest signs of experimentation in the *Quem quaeritis* are so slight that thus far they have passed without comment. They are evident in a unique eleventh-century *Visitatio* doubtfully ascribed to Aquileia:

Finito tertio responsorio, visitatur Sepulchrum cum versibus, duo fratres in vice Mulierum sanctarum dicentes:
> *Quis reuoluet nobis ab hostio lapidem quem tegere sacrum cernimus sepulchrum?*

Angeli dicant:
> *Quem quaeritis, o tremule mulieres, in hoc tumulo plorantes?*

Respondent fratres:
> *Iesum Nazarenum crucifixum querimus.*

Angeli:
> *Non est hic quem queritis, sed cito euntes dicite discipulis eius et Petro quia surrexit Iesus.*

Fratres vice Mulierum uenientes convertant se ad populum et ad chorum dicentes:
> *Ad monumentum venimus gementes, angelum Domini sedentem uidimus et dicentem quia surrexit Iesus.*

Chorus cantet antiphonam:
> *Currebant duo simul.*

Deinde ostendunt linteamina duo fratres aliis dicentes:
> *Cernitis, o socii, ecce linteamina et sudarium, et corpus non est in sepulchro inuentum.*

Deinde
> *Surrexit.*

Chorus:
>   *Te Deum laudamus.*

Populus:
>   *Kyrieleison,*
> alta uoce.[36]   (See Appendix)

The most important feature of this text is its elimination of ceremonial elements. Procession, candles, thuribles, illumination, ringing of bells, and bishop (or abbot) in full regalia, all found in early *Visitatio* texts, have disappeared. This is understandable. They are meaningful in relation to the Easter vigil, not matins. Their absence results in a kind of realism by default. As vestigial ceremonial associations are pruned away, representational elements necessarily are thrown into sharper relief.

The Aquileia text, however, is not just dramatized history; in fact, it involves historical falsification. According to John 20:1–10, Peter and John visit the tomb, see the graveclothes, and "believe"; but they do not "display" the graveclothes to the Marys or the disciples. The Aquileia display of graveclothes is justified not by the desire to teach history but by the Augustinian interpretation of the Visit to the Tomb as ocular proof of the Resurrection. Since the graveclothes are displayed to the entire congregation and responses *alta uoce* are supplied for the people as well as for the chorus, the idea that the scriptural characters are representatives of the Christian community is also a part of the play's meaning. In responding, the people become actors in the drama—the *socii* of Peter and John. In addition to justifying a departure from history, the emphasis on symbolism thus causes a certain indifference to realism, in that realism (or pure representation) postulates a sharp line between audience and actors.

In spite of its symbolism, the Aquileia *Visitatio* is a much more obvious dramatization of history than anything preceding it. A new line of scriptural dialogue is given to the Marys at the beginning. Unlike *Cernitis, o socii,* the antiphon *Quis reuoluet* is Biblical, drawn from Mark 16:3. It extends the history backward a step from the angels' query, and it serves as exposition by identifying whatever structure the Marys are approaching as a tomb closed by a stone. The substitution of *o tremule mulieres, in hoc tumulo plorantes* for the traditional *o Christicolae* is a case of historical improvisation. Neither form of address is justified by Scripture, but *o tremule mulieres* carries out the implication of Mark's statement (16:5), "and they were affrighted." The traditional form is appropriate to a ceremony in which representation is secondary (it is serviceable enough in any context), but the Aquileia form realizes more fully the implications

---

[36] *DMC,* I, 628.

of the representational mode. Instead of identifying the Marys as *Chris-ticolae* before they have spoken, the angels call them *mulieres* and comment on the fact that they appear fearful and sad. In other words, the nexus between action and dialogue, a fundamental condition of the representa-tional mode, is tightened.

The same principle is evident in the treatment of the second statement of the angels and the response of the Marys. The traditional text as found in the *Regularis concordia* has *Ite nuntiate, Resurrexit Dominus, Venite et videte*, and *Surrexit Dominus* sung alternately by the angels and the Marys. Judged by representational standards, this sequence is (as Young has pointed out) awkward and illogical.[37] It is best understood as a ceremonial survival rather than as an addition to an already representational form. The Aquileia text freely revises the entire sequence. The angels' speech is a conflation of Mark 16:7 and Matthew 28:7. It expresses the command to announce the Resurrection in a way that foreshadows the concluding episode, the race between Peter and John. The response of the women is far more logical than in any earlier version. It is a traditional antiphon based on Matthew's statement (28:8), "they did run to bring his disciples the word." Like *o tremule mulieres* it must be considered improvisation. The point is that it is not a flat statement—"He is risen, Alleluia!"—but a description of what has occurred: "We came sorrowing to the tomb, and we saw an angel of the Lord sitting there announcing that Jesus has risen." The realism of the announcement is enhanced by the fact that before it is made the Marys, obeying the injunction *cito euntes dicite discipulis*, move (correlative to *euntes*) toward the chorus and *populus*.

The concluding episode illustrates the tendency to amplify the history presented in the drama by adding to the end as well as to the beginning. "What happened after?" is as important a question as "What led up to it?" The race between Peter and John is introduced by an antiphon which,

---

[37] As Young says (*DMC*, I, 246–47):

A more decisive enlargement of the essential action of the little play arises with the adoption of the antiphon *Venite et videte locum ubi positus erat Dominus*. This utterance of the angels supplies a motivation for the act of raising the altar-cloth, or of peering within the sepulchre, on the part of the Marys. In disposing of this speech within the fabric of the performance, however, the writers seem not to have been very adroit. . . . In the great majority of the plays the words *Venite et videte* are spoken after the Marys have left, or turned away from, the sepulchre in order to make their announcement to the chorus and congregation. This inept arrangement arises apparently from a reverent unwillingness to disturb the original simple structure of the trope *Quem quaeritis*—and from a lack of dramatic resourcefulness.

For an alternative explanation according to which the antiphon and its awkward arrangement arise from the original ceremonial context of the *Quem quaeritis*, see above, Essay V, p. 216.

like the introductory *Quis reuoluet*, serves as exposition. There is no indication that a formal race occurred, and there is no suggestion that verisimilitude in the treatment of Peter and John extended beyond having *duo fratres* rather than one. The possibility cannot, of course, be ruled out, but it appears that the motif of ocular proof outweighs representation in the display of graveclothes and the concluding anthems.

IV

Only two twelfth-century Latin texts are sufficiently elaborate to be considered transitional forms between the Aquileia *Visitatio* and the Ripoll Resurrection play. These are from St. Lambrecht and Prague. Since the Ripoll play is also from the twelfth century, there is no way of proving that the simpler texts represent a stage of development chronologically prior to the complex Resurrection play. They may well be *centos* of pieces used in other Easter plays; they may also be consciously simplified versions of a complex play, adapted for performance in the traditional manner. The Prague text is in essence the Aquileia version with the *Hortulanus* scene added. Its chief interest lies in the fact that it illustrates the tendency to amplify the story by adding at the end new episodes from Scripture. The St. Lambrecht text is more informative. It has substantial rubrics and is the only twelfth-century Latin Resurrection play to include vernacular singing. It is also one of the three twelfth-century texts to include the sequence *Victimae Paschali*:

Interim autem, dum est circa finem tercie lectionis, distribuat custos singulas candelas singulis fratribus, et diaconus reuestiat se stola candida, vadatque residere super lapidem iuxta Sepulchrum. Cum uero secundo tercium responsorium fuerit inceptum, candelis omnibus accensis quas habent in manibus, cantor processionem ordinet ita. Primo scolares cum pedagogo, deinde abbas, post illum seniores, dehinc iuniores et indocti; sed illi qui in personis sanctarum Feminarum uisitare debent Sepulchrum remaneant in choro et uelent capita sua humeralibus uel capitiis capparum quas habent in se. Reliquus uadat, ut predictum est, ad locum Sepulchri conuentus, ibique silentio facit. Illi predicti tres remissa voce cantant:
> Quis reuoluet nobis ab hostio lapidem quem tegere sacrum cernimus sepulcrum?
Quibus respondeat leuita uice Angeli dicens:
> Quem queritis, o tremule mulieres, in hoc tumulo plorantes?
Ad hec illi:
> Iesum Nazarenum crucifixum querimus.

Quibus ille subiungat:

Non est hic quem queritis, sed cito euntes nunciate discipulis eius et Petro quia surrexit Iesus.

Post hec illis accedentibus surgat et subleuet cortinam et Sepulchrum patefaciat, dicatque ad illos:

Venite et uidete locum ubi positus erat Dominus, alleluia, alleluia.

Qui uenientes inclinatis capitibus considerare debent intra Sepulchrum, et tollentes inde filacterium quo inuoluta Crux fuerat et sudarium quod fuerat super Crucis caput, ac inde recedentes stent ante proximum altare et uersi contra conuentum canant alta uoce:

Ad monumentum venimus gementes, angelum Domini sedentem uidimus et dicentem quia surrexit Deus.

Quo dicto, totus conventus concinat dicens:

Dic nobis, Maria, quid uidisti in uia?

Et unus ex illis tribus qui uisitabant Sepulchrum dicat clara uoce:

Sepulchrum Christi uiuentis, et gloriam uidi resurgentis.

Alter uero dicat:

Angelicos testes, sudarium et uestes.

Et tercius subiungat:

Surrexit Christus, spes mea; precedet suos in Galilea.

Post hec totus conuentus concinat ita:

Credendum est magis soli Marie ueraci, quam [Iudeorum turbae fallaci].

Versus:

Scimus Christum [surrexisse ex mortuis vere; tu autem, victor rex, miserere].

Tunc incipiat ipsa plebs istum clamorem:

Giengen dreie urovven ce uronem grabe.

Interim uero, dum plebs clamorem istum concrepat, cantor ordinet duos, unum senem et alterum iuuenem, qui, postquam finitus fuerit clamor populi, ueniant ad Sepulchrum, iuuenis primo et subsistat, senex uero subsequens prospiciat in Monumentum, et alter cum eo. Et illis factum incipientibus imponat cantor antiphonam:

Currebant duo simul.

Qua finita, ueniant illi tres supradicti ante aram proximam subleuantes linteamina, ut ab omnibus uideantur, ita concinentes:

Cernitis, o socii, ecce linteamina et sudarium, et corpus non est in sepulchro inuentum.

Atque mox extollant Crucem in altum sonora uoce conclamantes ita:

Surrexit Dominus de sepulchro.

Quam simul cum eis concinat totus conuentus. Post hanc incipiat abbas uel prior *Te Deum laudamus;* et hunc ymnum canendo reuertantur in chorum, plebe conclamante *Christ ist erstanden.*[38]   (See Appendix)

---

[38] *DMC*, I, 363–65,

In two respects this text is more conservative than the Aquileia version of the eleventh century. The rubrics preserve a substantial amount of material that is ceremonial rather than functional. Candles are distributed, there is an illumination ceremony and procession, the graveclothes are transported to the altar for display instead of being shown at the tomb, and it is still important that a deacon and no other cleric shall represent the angel. The dialogue also retains ceremonial elements that conflict with the logic of representation. In the Aquileia text the command *Cito euntes* is immediately obeyed by the Marys, who turn to the congregation and recite the *Ad monumentum*. The St. Lambrecht text also substitutes *Cito euntes* for *Ite nuntiate*, but it does not drop the *Venite et videte* of the early ceremonial version. The result is a logical contradiction. The angel orders the Marys to "go quickly to the disciples" and in the next breath countermands the order with "come and see the sepulcher." Only after they have inspected the graveclothes do they move to the altar to sing the *Ad monumentum*.

In addition to preserving a strong ceremonial flavor, the St. Lambrecht *Visitatio* places considerable emphasis on the motif of proof. The *Victimae Paschali*, although best understood in connection with representative elements, emphasizes the truth of the announcement of the miracle by repeating it. Conventual and vernacular responses provide confirmation while incorporating the congregation in the drama as "disciples." As in the Aquileia version, the race between Peter and John is used to justify a public display of graveclothes, and is followed by two anthems, one for the clergy and one for the *populus*.

The representational aspect of the St. Lambrecht text, however, remains prominent. In the *Regularis concordia* the cleric representing the angel is described as *alba indutus* ("wearing an alb"), a ceremonial garment closely associated with the Easter vigil. In the St. Lambrecht text the angel wears a *stola candida* ("white stole"). In other words, it is not expressly required that the garment be a liturgical robe. The generalized reference suggests that the robe is understood in relation to the drama rather than to the liturgy—that, whatever its history, it is regarded as a costume. Again, the *Regularis* requires that the clerics playing the Marys be "vested in copes" (*cappis induti*). At St. Lambrecht they can wear either humerals or copes, and the important point is not what they use but that their heads be covered (*uelent capita*) in the manner of the women.

Verisimilitude of costume complements verisimilitude of dialogue and setting. The Marys are instructed to speak in a soft voice (*remissa voce*), and the ensuing exchange uses the Aquileia rather than the traditional speeches. The rubrics indicate that the sepulcher is conceived realistically. It has a "stone" on which the angel sits and a curtain that can be raised for a dramatic revelation of the graveclothes. In spite of the awkward contradiction caused by the retention of *Venite et videte*, the inspection of the tomb is also intended as representational action: the Marys bow their heads, look inside, and remove the *linteum* (here called a *filactarium*— a fillet) and sudarium.

We now come to the *Victimae Paschali*. Interestingly, the St. Lambrecht text is the only *Visitatio* of the twelfth century that includes it. In both of the other twelfth-century manuscripts in which it occurs, it is part of the *Peregrini* rather than the Resurrection play and is sung by Mary Magdalene alone.[39] Its primary function is to provide dialogue for the scene, only mentioned in Scripture, in which the Marys tell the disciples of the Resurrection. It is thus a substantial instance of historical improvisation. Such improvisation is a necessary consequence of the dramatic representation of an historical source. Scripture is explicit about major events, but minor ones are mentioned briefly or ignored. This is quite acceptable in a history intended for reading, but when the history is acted out "just as it must have happened," minor events cannot be omitted without creating gaps in the action. The Aquileia text uses the *Ad monumentum* antiphon to fill the gap left by the scriptural account. The St. Lambrecht manuscript retains this antiphon but increases the realism of the episode by providing a full dialogue between the Marys and the disciples. In this case the dialogue was already at hand in the form of a popular sequence used in the Mass that could easily be broken into the form of a question, a reply, and a joyous response to the reply.[40] The fact that the *Victimae Paschali* is a Mass text may be irrelevant, but its use with the *Quem quaeritis* may indicate a survival of the Bede-Amalarius interpretation of the Visit to the Tomb as symbolic of the Mass sacrifice.

As has been noted, the response to the announcement of the Marys includes a *versus* for conventual singing and a vernacular song. These work against the logic of representation by making the congregation a participant in the drama. After the vernacular piece, the drama returns to the representational mode. The St. Lambrecht rubrics specify that the two clerics representing Peter and John be "an old man" and "a young man," respectively, that the young one arrive first but wait outside the tomb, and that the old one arrive later and enter it. The action faithfully

---

[39] *DMC*, I, 479, 681.

[40] For the *Victimae Paschali* as a sequence, see Raby, *Christian Latin Poetry*, pp. 217–18. The hymn is usually assigned to Wipo and dated in the eleventh century. See also *DMC*, I, 273–75.

duplicates the historical source (John 20:3–8) and is explained by the *Currebant duo* antiphon, which is purely expository.

Curiously, the women at the altar sing *Cernitis, o socii* and display the graveclothes. In this detail the St. Lambrecht text is closer to the *Regularis concordia* than to Aquileia, where the graveclothes are displayed by Peter and John. The *Regularis* sequence has been amplified by a new antiphon (historical improvisation), but it still ends at the altar rather than the sepulcher. Evidently, it is a survival of the procession carrying the *linteum* and sudarium from the "sepulcher" to the altar for liturgical use. On the other hand, it is significantly less realistic than the sequence used at Aquileia. The variation illustrates a fact of considerable importance in the development of complex forms of liturgical drama. Although the dramatist is bound to his source when treating major episodes that are fully described, he has considerable freedom when treating minor ones that were created solely by the need for a smooth, uninterrupted sequence of events. Because his source gives him no assistance in such cases, he must be guided by the inner logic of representational drama. How much he should include, what order he should follow, what stage props should be used, and what dialogue should be provided are problems that can only be solved in terms of what seems dramatically effective. The St. Lambrecht text simply adds lines without changing the traditional form of the *Visitatio*. The race is arbitrarily inserted between the announcement of the Resurrection and the display of the graveclothes by the Marys. The Aquileia text, though considerably earlier, is much bolder. By having Peter and John display the graveclothes, it changes the ceremonial action into a smooth plot, in which the race and the display are a self-contained episode.

The Aquileia and St. Lambrecht texts illustrate both the limitations and the options present as the *Quem quaeritis* changed from a liturgical ceremony to a representative drama. The core of the play remains the same. It is essentially an objectification in historical terms of the transition from *tristia* to *gaudium*—from sorrow to joy—which is objectified in the Mass ritual and the cycle of the Church year. If the pattern is, as cultural anthropologists have claimed, an archetype, its connotation in medieval culture is wholly Christian. The first effect of the *Quem quaeritis* is to give this Christian form a local habitation and a name, to show that it exists in history as well as in the timeless present by expressing it in terms of linear time, fixed space, and logical cause and effect.

The implications of the shift from ritual to representation were not realized in the eleventh and twelfth centuries, nor, for that matter, are they fully realized in the drama of Shakespeare. What we have at the beginning is a series of groupings that reveal the first influences of the new mode on the medieval dramatists. Because the *Quem quaeritis* is linked to an historical source, the most obvious option of the playwright is historical amplification; because the middle of the drama is complete in the earliest manuscripts, expansion takes the form of adding new parts at the beginning or the end. When this is done, certain gaps appear in scriptural accounts that must be filled by means of historical improvisations in order to keep the action continuous. Because such improvisations are not limited by source, they can be treated freely, in terms of the didactic or dramatic effect required.

Complementing the sense of the *Quem quaeritis* as imitation of events in the past, various devices of verisimilitude are used to enhance the illusion. Garments are understood as costumes; the sepulcher is shaped like a tomb and equipped with a stone; instructions require that the actors physically resemble the historical figures they represent. Equally important, the dialogue is interpreted in terms of cause and effect. A person who is supposed to be sad speaks sorrowfully; a happy one utters a joyful lyric. When a command is given, it is obeyed; and when a question is asked, an answer is given. In this suiting of the action to the words, a concern for characterization—especially for consistency of character—is evident. Finally, because representational drama is pointless unless it is understood by the audience, exposition appears in the form of antiphons explaining who the characters are, what the stage props represent, and what the action signifies. To define and intensify the response, lyrics are added that incorporate the audience in the action.

V

The earliest complex Latin Resurrection play is a twelfth-century text from Ripoll, first edited by Karl Young.[41] It is disordered, has no rubrics, and may be two plays rather than one. What it shows beyond doubt is that a complex Resurrection play was in existence in the twelfth century and that it was associated closely with (if it did not include) the *Peregrini* play depicting the appearance of Christ on the road to Emmaus. Because all other complex Resurrection plays are later, there seems to be no point

---

[41] "Some Texts of Liturgical Plays," *PMLA*, XXIV (1909), 303–8. Reprinted in *DMC*, I, 678–81.

in attempting, with Wilhelm Meyer and K. Dürre, an elaborate reconstruction of the history of its various parts.[42] In the Ripoll play these are:

1. An introductory speech by the Marys;
2. A lament by the Marys in which they state their intention to purchase ointment;
3. A speech by the ointment-vendor (*mercator, unguentarius*);
4. A reply by one of the Marys;
5. A long *planctus*;
6. The *Quem quaeritis* dialogue;
7. The *Hortulanus* scene;
8. The *Victimae Paschali*; and
9. A truncated version of the scene on the road to Emmaus, followed by the rubric *Versus de Chrismate in Cena Domini*.

Young's text is as follows:

Verses Pascales de III Mariis

Eamus mirram emere
cum liquido aromate,
ut ualeamus ungere
corpus datum sepulture.

Dicunt [Mariae:][43]

Omnipotens Pater altissime,   5
angelorum rector mitissime,
quid facient iste miserime!

Heu, quantus est noster dolor!

Amisimus enim solatium,
Ihesum Christum, Marie filium;   10
iste nobis erat subsidium.
    Heu,

Set eamus unguentum emere,
quo possimus corpus inungere;
non amplius posset putrescere.   15
    Heu,

---

[42] Meyer, *Fragmenta Burana* (Berlin, 1901), pp. 106–20; Dürre, *Die Mercatorszene im lateinisch-liturgischen, altdeutschen und altfranzösischen religiösen Drama* (Göttingen, 1915), pp. 15–24. Meyer invented the term *Zehnsilberspiel* ("ten-syllable play") for the hypothetical original form of this drama; Dürre argues on the basis of the Ripoll text that the earlier form of the play was in lines of eight syllables.

[43] I have transposed and emended this rubric. For the manuscript form, see *DMC*, I, 678.

         Dic tu nobis, mercator iuuenis,
         hoc unguentum si tu uendideris;
         dic precium, nam iam habueris.
           Heu,   20

Respondet Mercator:
         Mulieres michi intendite.
         Hoc unguentum si uultis emere,
         datur genus mirre potencie,
         quo si corpus possetis ungere,
         non amplius posset putrescere   25
         neque uermes possent comedere.

         Hoc unguentum si multum cupitis
         unum auri talentum dabitis;
         nec aliter umquam portabitis.

Respondet Maria:
         O mercator, unguentum libera.   30
         Ecce tibi dabimus munera.
         Ibimus Christi ungere uulnera.
           Heu,

         Cuncta, sorores, gaudia
         deflorent in tristicia   35
         cum innocens opprobria
         fert et crucis suspendia
         Iudeorum inuidia,
         et principum perfidia!
         Quid angemus et qualia!   40

         Licet, sorores, plangere,
         plangendo Christum quererere,
         querendo corpus ungere,
         ungendo mente pascere
         de fletu, uiso uulnere,   45
         dilecto magno federe
         cor monstratur in opere.

         Cordis, sorores, creduli
         simus et bene seduli,
         ut nostri cernant oculi
         corpus Christi, uim seculi.   50
         Quis uoluet petram cumuli
         magnam sive uim populi?
         virtus celestis epuli.

Tanta, sorores, uisio 55
splendoris et lustrascio
nulla sit stupefatio,
vobis sit exultatio.
Mors et mortis occasio
moritur uita uicio. 60
Nostra, surge, surreccio.

Hoc, sorores, circuitu,
lecto, dicite, sonitu
illis qui mesto spiritu
et proditio transitu 65
dux uicto surgit obitu
querantur lecto strepitu
. . . scis . . . . dux ortitu.

Quid faciemus, sorores,
graues ferimus dolores? 70
Non est, nec erit seculis,
dolor doloris similis.

Iesum gentes perimere,
semper decet nos lugere,
set ut poscimus gaudere, 75
eamus tumbam uidere.

Tumbam querimus non lento,
corpus ungamus unguento,
quod extinctum uulneribus
uiuis preualet omnibus. 80

Regis perempti premium
plus ualet quam uiuencium,
cuius amor solacium
iuuamen et presidium
et perenne subsidium 85
sit nunc et in perpetuum.

Vbi est Christus, meus Dominus et filius excelsi?
Eamus uidere sepulcrum.[44]

[44] Printed by Young, *DMC,* I, 680, in association with the *Ubi est Christus.* Apparently in the manuscript the *Ubi est* antiphon is also given following the *Eamus uidere,* raising the possibility that its inclusion before the *Eamus* is a scribal error and that in the original the last of the seven-line stanzas was given as a unit preceding the *Quem quaeritis* dialogue. On the other hand, the conscious interruption of lyric units appears as a regular feature of the Ripoll text. See below, p. 247.

Respondet Angelus:

 Quem queritis in sepulcro, Christicole?

Respondet Mariae:

 Ihesum Nazarenum crucifixum, o celicole.   90

Respondet Angelus:

 Non est hic, surrexit sicut predixerat; ite, nunciate quia surrexit dicentes.

Respondent Mariae:

 Alleluia, ad sepulcrum residens angelus nunciat resurrexisse Christum.
 Te Deum laudamus.

Versus de Pelegrinis

Rex in acubitum iam se contulerat,
et mea redolens nardus spirauerat;   95
in hortum veneram in quem descenderat,
at ille transiens iam declinauerat.

Per noctem igitur hunc querens exeo;
huc illuc transiens nusquam reperio.

Angeli:

 Mulier, quid ploras? Quem queris?   100

Maria:

 Occurrunt uigiles ardenti studio,
 Quos cum transierim, sponsum inuenio.

Ortolanus:

 Mulier, quid ploras? Quem queris?

Maria:

 Tulerunt Dominum meum, et nescio ubi posuerunt eum. Si tu sustulisti
 eum, dicito michi, et eum tollam.   105

Ortolanus:

 Maria, Maria, Maria!

Respondet Maria:

 Raboni, Raboni, Raboni!

Maria rediens dicat:

 Dic, impie Zabule, quid ualet nunc fraus tua?

Discipuli:

 Dic nobis, Maria, quid uidisti in uia?

Maria:

 Sepulcrum Christi uiuentis, et gloriam uidi resurgentis;   110
 Angelicos testes, sudarium et uestes.

Angeli:

 Non est hic, surrexit sicut predixerat uobis.

Discipuli:

> Credendum est magis soli Mariae ueraci quam Iudeorum turbe fallaci.
> Scimus Christum surrexisse a mortuis uere: tu nobis, Christe, Rex,
> miserere.
> Qui sunt hij sermones quos çonfertis ad inuicem ambulantes, et estis
> tristes?   115
> Alleluia.

Respondent duo:

> Respondens unus cui nomen Cleophas dixit ei: Tu solus peregrinus es in
> Iherusalem et non cognouisti que facta sunt in illa his diebus? Alleluia.

Respondet:

> Quibus ille dixit: Que?

Respondet duo:

> Et dixerunt: De Ihesu Nazareno, qui fuit uir propheta, potens in opere et
> sermone coram Deo et omni populo, alleluia. Euouae.   120

(See Appendix)

If we begin with the middle of this drama, we find the *Quem quaeritis* (ll. 89–92) in the form established in the tenth century, retaining even the *Te Deum*. In other words, all amplification consists of additions to the beginning and end of the drama. Additions are of two kinds. Non-Biblical material, consisting of lyric stanzas, is used for the lament of the Marys and for a substantial scene in which they purchase ointment from the *mercator*. This material is quite different in tone from the stiff, formalized mixture of antiphons and quasi-Biblical dialogue used in the *Quem quaeritis*. Its rhyme schemes and eight- and ten-syllable accentual verse were familiar in twelfth-century vernacular poetry, as well as in Latin hymns and sequences, and must therefore be considered to be more "realistic" than the *Quem quaeritis* proper. The end of the *Quem quaeritis* is amplified in part by lyric material (*Rex in acubitum*), but chiefly by the addition of two brief dramatic episodes in the traditional formalistic manner—the *Hortulanus* and the *Peregrini*. The two quite different methods of amplification illustrate a point made in connection with the St. Lambrecht *Visitatio*. Whereas episodes dealt with fully in Scripture limit the dramatist, episodes created by historical improvisation can be treated with considerable freedom and shaped in ways that conform to the logic of representational drama rather than to historical sources.

The lyric material is of interest in itself. It comprises 94 of the 120 lines of the play. One group of stanzas (ll. 1–4, 69–80) consists of octosyllabic quatrains rhymed alternately a-a-a-a and a-a-b-b (ll. 69–72, 77–80). These stanzas are primarily a lament of the Marys as they proceed to the tomb to anoint the body, and they are unique to the Ripoll play. A second group of stanzas found in both Latin and French in thirteenth-century plays recounts the purchase of the ointment from the *mercator* (ll. 5–33). These stanzas consist of three ten-syllable lines rhyming a-a-a with the refrain *Heu, quantus est noster dolor,* which is omitted in the stanzas assigned to the *mercator.* A third block of seven-line stanzas (ll. 34–68, 81–86, 88) has octosyllabic lines rhyming a-a-a-a-a-a-a. These stanzas are unique to the Ripoll play. They are unified by their prosodic form and also by the fact that all but the last begin with the word *sorores* used as a nominative of direct address. The last of the seven-line stanzas does not use this form and is interrupted after the sixth line with the nonmetrical *Quem quaeritis* line *Ubi est Christus.* . . . The fourth lyric block is the hymn *Rex in acubitum,* consisting of twelve-syllable quatrains rhymed a-a-a-a. This hymn appears at the beginning of the *Peregrini* episode (ll. 94–99, 97–98). It is apparently sung by Mary Magdalene as she proceeds from the tomb to the garden (*in hortum veneram,* l. 96), and it is interrupted by the angels' query, *Mulier, quid ploras?* (l. 100). It also is unique to the Ripoll play. The last lyric block is the *Victimae Paschali,* sung by Mary after seeing Jesus and used as a transition to the scene on the road to Emmaus. It is interrupted by a repetition of the angelic cry *Non est hic* (l. 112).

The bulk of the Ripoll play thus consists of formal lyrics used to amplify episodes only mentioned in Scripture or not mentioned at all. The most striking instance is the *unguentarius* scene. Mark mentions (16:1) the purchase of spices, but the details of the transaction are obviously a matter of indifference to him. On the other hand, the form of representational drama makes some depiction necessary as soon as the play is extended backward in time to a point before the purchase has been made. In the ceremonial version of the *Quem quaeritis* the clerics representing the Marys are already carrying the thuribles that represent the ointment boxes. This remained the case as long as a procession "with candles and thuribles" was part of the matins performance. When the procession was eliminated, as at Aquileia, the Marys either had to be given thuribles or had to acquire them on the way to the tomb. Although slightly awkward, the improvisation need have created no difficulty. In a ceremony actions are performed because they are necessary, not because they are logical. On the other hand, as soon as the *Quem quaeritis* comes to be regarded as historical representation, its actions are referred not to ceremony but to its source. From the representational point of view, the fact that the Marys begin their trip to the sepulcher without thuribles can only mean that they have not yet purchased the ointment. Moreover, since the actors are real people performing on the physical stage of the church, they must acquire the thuribles by a physical action performed during their journey.

This action can only be understood as the purchase of ointments mentioned by Mark. Once the action is understood in such terms, the ceremonial thuribles are transformed into imitation ointment boxes, just as the sepulcher has already become an identifiable tomb; and the cleric offering them is transformed into a spice merchant.

The logic of this process is quite clear. What cannot be known is whether it occurred in a series of steps or all at once. Meyer and Young believe that it began with a trip to a side altar to collect thuribles, was amplified by lyrics in which the Marys refer to purchasing ointments, and that these lyrics in turn suggested lines for a spice merchant. Unfortunately, the texts cited to illustrate the early stages of the process are from the thirteenth century, whereas the spice-merchant scene is already well developed and incorporated in a complex Resurrection play in the twelfth-century Ripoll manuscript.

However it originated, the mode of presentation of the spice-merchant scene is up to the dramatist. Latin texts containing the scene show a wide variety of treatments. In some cases the merchant appears but does not speak. In others, he demands exorbitant payment. In still others, he is a pious believer who offers his wares free of charge. He is sometimes alone, but sometimes has competition from another merchant or is rebuked by a shrewish wife. In contrast to these later treatments, the Ripoll text is surprisingly down to earth. The merchant praises his wares (there is no suggestion here either of satire or of the medicine man of folk drama whom Stumpfl considers his prototype), and quotes his price. Mary pays without comment and resumes her lament. The sequence is almost banal in its realism. It shows that where historical improvisation is necessary the medieval dramatist resorts to anachronism. He does not ask himself how merchants acted in the first century B.C. Instead he uses contemporary behavior as his guide, in the same way that illuminated manuscripts show Biblical characters dressed in medieval costumes and residing in medieval villages or castles. Anachronism is a form of verisimilitude in medieval drama and remains so in the drama of Shakespeare.

The beginning of the Ripoll play, then, is a rather substantial historical improvisation extending the action backward in time to a point before the Marys purchase their spices. The congregational procession of earlier *Visitatio* texts such as the *Regularis concordia* and St. Lambrecht has become a representation of the journey of the Marys to the tomb, and the inner logic of the representation mode has necessitated the creation of a scene in which the Marys purchase ointment. To provide dialogue the dramatist has used a method different in kind from the method of the episodes based on Scripture. In the place of antiphons and bits of scriptural paraphrase he has adopted three lyrics, each using a rhyme scheme and prosody found in vernacular as well as Latin compositions, and each distinguished from the other two. Because of its dialogue form the decasyllabic poem (*Omnipotens Pater . . .*) has intrinsic representational qualities. The octosyllabic poems, on the other hand, are more purely lyric. Since both refer to a journey, they appear to be processional hymns. Although they may have been composed explicitly for the *Quem quaeritis* play, the fact that they are different in form and that each can stand alone as a complete poem suggests that—like the *Victimae Paschali*—they were originally independent of liturgical drama.

In any case, the Ripoll dramatist was aware of the difference between lyric and representation. The most interesting feature of the introductory lyrics is the way in which they are used. Instead of giving one lyric in its entirety, then the second, and then the third, the dramatist has freely intermixed the four- and seven-line octasyllabic stanzas, has eliminated the refrain line from the decasyllabic stanzas assigned the merchant,[45] and (apparently) has interrupted the last seven-line stanza with the non-metrical *Quem quaeritis* line, *Ubi est Christus*. The effect of each of these devices is to reduce the self-identity of the lyrics. They no longer stand out as set pieces but begin to resemble continuous dialogue. The treatment, though still highly formal, shows a conscious desire for verisimilitude. The dialogue is understood as a continuous development rather than as a series of recitations, and where the source material would give the latter effect if used in its original form, changes have been introduced. That these changes are made consciously is indicated by the fact that the *Rex in acubitum* and *Victimae Paschali* lyrics at the end of the play are similarly handled.

If the beginning of the Ripoll play is developed by historical improvisation, the end is developed by historical amplification. The *Hortulanus* and *Peregrini* episodes are derived from Scripture and presented with the same combination of antiphons and scriptural paraphrase used in the traditional *Quem quaeritis*. The episodes are found in two other twelfth-century plays, one a *Visitatio* and the other a *Peregrini* drama.[46] Since the rubric *Versus de Pelegrinis* precedes the two episodes in the Ripoll text, it is likely that the dramatist simply added a pre-existing *Peregrini* drama containing the *Hortulanus* episode to the end of the *Quem quaeritis*. This raises the question of whether the *Resurrection* and *Peregrini* plays are to be considered a unit. The use of *Rex in acubitum* as a transition from the tomb to the garden

---

[45] For versions retaining the refrain line, see *DMC*, I, 413–14, 439–40.

[46] *DMC*, I, 479, 664.

suggests continuous action, but it could also be an expository introduction
to a separate piece. For present purposes the question may be ignored.
The Ripoll play anticipates several thirteenth-century versions in which
the *Hortulanus* scene is unambiguously linked to the Resurrection, and the
Ripoll scene of the meeting on the road to Emmaus is quite clearly
continuous with the *Hortulanus*. Observations made on the assumption
that it is a continuous play are probably valid for the Ripoll text and are
certainly valid for the unambiguously continuous versions that it anticipates.

The *Hortulanus* episode enlarges the play historically. It is drawn from
John 20:11–18. The motive for including it is doubtless that it is "part of
the story." A second motive, which cannot be evaluated from extant versions, may be that it provides even more vivid ocular proof of the Resurrection than the race between Peter and John. Its inclusion, however, is
not an unmixed blessing. It increases the length of the play at the expense
both of the unity of the dramatic structure and of the logic of representation.

The clouding of the play's logic by the *Hortulanus* episode is evident in
the inconsistency of Mary Magdalene. On hearing the angelic announcement of the Resurrection, she joins the other Marys in singing the joyful
antiphon *Alleluia, ad sepulcrum residens*. Immediately thereafter she begins
a lament. The Ripoll text emphasizes the sudden change in mood by
having the question *Mulier, quid ploras* asked twice, as in John 20:13, 15.
Evidently the episode is presented not because it is logical but because
"that is the way it happened." The point has implications for Renaissance
as well as medieval drama. If character consistency is one of the requirements of representative drama, then drama based on a source considered
to be historically true must often settle for something less than pure
representation. In the *Hortulanus* episode fidelity to source results in what
is pretty clearly a blemish. Mary has to be at the same time joyful and sad,
believing and sceptical. In later drama, however, the same motive can
result in a certain richness—a suggestion of some of the mystery of
experience—that disappears in drama that conforms rigorously to didactic
theories of behavior or "scientific" systems of psychology.

In addition to considering sources and techniques of representation,
dramatic criticism involves aesthetic questions. No matter how a drama
originated, a critic can always ask whether it is a good play. There is no
evidence that aesthetic considerations entered into the ceremonial or early
representational forms of the Resurrection play, but in spite of this fact
the early forms inherit the well-defined comic structure of the Mass and

the Church year. The additions at the beginning of the Ripoll play enhance this structure by intensifying the threnos—the mood of despairing sorrow—that precedes the reversal objectified in the *Quem quaeritis* dialogue. In the St. Lambrecht *Visitatio*, the *Victimae Paschali* and the race between Peter and John have a similar effect at the end, since they enhance the joyous theophany. The *Hortulanus* episode is different from both of these earlier additions. John's Gospel omits the angelic announcement at the tomb, and, consequently, the *Hortulanus* in its original location has the same function as the visit of the Marys in Matthew, Mark, and Luke. It is the moment of reversal from sorrow to joy on which the narrative hinges. The effect of adding it to the *Quem quaeritis* episode is not intensification but anticlimax. The outburst of joy associated with the Visit to the Tomb must be truncated, and the mood must shift abruptly back to lament. The lament leads, in turn, to a second "announcement," with its own reversal and joyous conclusion. Both episodes are blunted. The visit episode cannot be properly "celebrated," and the *Hortulanus* episode loses force because it has been anticipated. The placement of the *Victimae Paschali* after the *Hortulanus* episode, as a speech of Mary Magdalene rather than of all the Marys, may be a rather lame attempt to compensate for this flaw. More probably, it is simply because the dramatist found this arrangement in his source.

The last unit in the Ripoll play is an incomplete scene of the meeting on the road to Emmaus. There are three other twelfth-century versions of this episode, all of them more elaborate and all of them separated from the Resurrection play.[47] Quite possibly the rubric *Versus de Pelegrinis* is misplaced and belongs properly between the last line of the *Hortulanus* (l. 114) and the first of the Emmaus episode (l. 115). If the play is read just as it stands in the Ripoll manuscript, the Emmaus episode involves exactly the same problems as does the *Hortulanus*. It is added because it is part of the story. On the other hand, it blurs the logic and structure of the play. The garden where Christ appears to Mary must suddenly become the road to Emmaus; the disciples who have just proclaimed the truth of the Resurrection (*Credendum est magis soli Mariae . . . Scimus Christum surrexisse a mortuis uere*) must once again appear to doubt it; and the plot is diluted by still another reversal-recognition scene.

One final word on the plot of the Ripoll play. Just as pure representation seeks character consistency and logical sequence based on cause and effect, it also strives for rationally defined unity, a point nicely illustrated by the neoclassic insistence on unity of action as well as unity of time and

47 *DMC*, I, 459–60, 467–69, 476–80.

space. The desire to depict events because they happened rather than because they are dramatically appropriate conflicts with the ideal of pure representation. Like indifference to character consistency, it can produce an extremely episodic structure, as witness the Ripoll manuscript, the Corpus Christi cycles, and Shakespeare's *Henry VI* trilogy. At the same time, it preserves elements of the ritual and mythic modes of drama against the incursions of rationalistic theories. Although little can be said for the Ripoll play when contrasted to the St. Lambrecht *Visitatio*, a great deal can be said for Shakespeare's *Antony and Cleopatra* in contrast to Dryden's *All for Love.*

VI

The development of the Resurrection play between the tenth and the twelfth century provides a unique case history of how the forms of ritual and myth are re-embodied in the modes of representational drama. It is of interest not only in relation to medieval drama but also in relation to later drama which preserves marked ritual elements. The principles governing this development are: (1) continuity of ritual form with amplification from the center outwards, (2) historical amplification, (3) historical improvisation, (4) verisimilitude, (5) fidelity to source a primary concern, and (6) aesthetic effect a minor concern or simply ignored.

Continuity of form is evidenced in the tendency of the *Quem quaeritis* dialogue to retain its original wording and central position in all stages of the development of the Resurrection play. In fact, when the Resurrection play becomes a part of the vernacular cycles, the episodes that precede and follow it have the character of enormous amplifications of its beginning and end. The Resurrection remains what it is in both Augustinian theology and the cycle of the Church year—the pivot on which the whole gigantic pattern of human history turns—and the center of the Resurrection play remains the depiction of the Visit to the Tomb. Whether the cycle takes the form of the German Passion play, which omits the Nativity episodes, or the English Corpus Christi play, its structure remains comic and its climax is the peripeteia of the Easter miracle.

Historical amplification is seen in the elaboration of the Resurrection play by the addition of episodes from Scripture. Because time is linear in representational drama, it extends backward and forward from the moment of the Resurrection. What events prepare for the Resurrection and what follow from it? From a Christian point of view, the answer is simple and inevitable. Ultimately, everything that has happened since the beginning of time is in some sense a preparation. The fall of Lucifer is the first preparatory event, and the fall of Adam the second. Between Adam and Christ the sacred history of the Chosen People is so crucial that other histories may be ignored. The Old Testament is thus the primary or secondary source for plays preceding the Nativity, and from it are taken episodes having special didactic or typological significance—Cain and Abel, the Flood, Abraham and Isaac, the prophets of Christ, and the like. By the same token all events after the Resurrection are relevant to an understanding of its effects. Here sacred history is less useful. The Acts of the Apostles furnish some material (e.g., "The Conversion of St. Paul"), but for the most part the consequences of the Resurrection are symbolized by plays that foretell the final moments of human history—*Antichrist* and the *Last Judgement*. Medieval drama begins, as we have seen, in the timeless present of ritual. Curiously, the effect of the largest of the medieval cycles is that of a return to the timeless present. Human history emerges from eternity in the first episode and is lost within it once again in the last.

If historical amplification leads inevitably to a past and a future eternity, historical improvisation leads to the world of the here and now. Improvised scenes must be composed without scriptural precedent, and they are usually theologically unimportant. The dramatist must compose them by reference to what is probable and familiar. Because scriptural precedent is lacking, he can be brief and general, or he can invent characters, expand dialogue, and include satire or propaganda. Hence, while the Visit to the Tomb and the Adoration of the Shepherds remain stable throughout the history of medieval drama, tangential characters such as the *unguentarius*, Herod, Noah's wife, and Mac and Tyb multiply in number and variety. Indeed, in the *Second Shepherds' Play* the tangential action is far more elaborate than the Nativity episode, a fact that reveals not secularization but pious devotion to purity of source and tradition.

Verisimilitude is a corollary of the shift from ritual to representation. Its manifestations include imitative costumes and stage props, correlation of action with dialogue, use of popular lyric forms instead of liturgical antiphons and scriptural paraphrase, character consistency, anachronism, and elimination of ceremonial and symbolic elements. Strict verisimilitude is never achieved on the stage unless, perhaps, in the dramas of the school of Ibsen. Needless to say, it is found only in tentative and irregular forms in medieval drama, and when conflicts develop, it takes a second place to fidelity to source.

Like verisimilitude, concern for aesthetic effect is rudimentary in medieval drama and regularly yields to fidelity to source. In both cases the immediate results are unfortunate. From a rationalistic point of view, medieval drama is a tissue of impossibilities strung together on an absurd parody of a plot and staged with a bizarre mixture of improvisation and crude realism. This, of course, is not the attitude with which its contemporaries regarded it, nor is it the tradition bequeathed by medieval drama to the Renaissance. As study of the Resurrection play shows, liturgical drama is the outcome of a search for representational modes which preserve a vital relation to ritual. The contrast between the conservative drama of Renaissance England and the drama of sixteenth-century Italy, which was written in conscious rebellion against medieval tradition, suggests that this relation was worth preserving.

ESSAY VII

The Vernacular Tradition:
Form, Episode, Dialogue

I

ONLY ONE COMPLEX Latin Resurrection play can be dated with certainty in the twelfth century. Yet this century boasts two vernacular dramas sufficiently complex to bear comparison with the cycle plays of the fourteenth century. Both of these plays are Anglo-Norman. The deservedly famous *Mystère d'Adam* survives in a unique manuscript from the thirteenth century but is dated, on the basis of language and versification, between 1146 and 1174.[1] It contains 942 lines written in octosyllabic and decasyllabic couplets and is punctuated with Latin stage directions, readings, and responsories. Although titled "the play of Adam" (*Ordo representacionis Ade*), it consists of three dramatic pieces, the Fall of Man (ll. 1–590), the Murder of Abel (ll. 591–744), and the Prophets of Christ (ll. 745–942).

La Seinte Resureccion was written around 1175. It survives in two manuscripts. The earliest ("C") is from Canterbury and dates from around 1275. The second ("P") is from the Bibliothèque Nationale in Paris and has been dated as late thirteenth or early fourteenth century.[2] In spite of its earlier date, "C" is an amplified and redacted version of the original, whereas "P" is relatively uncontaminated. Neither manuscript is complete. "P" contains 371 lines of octosyllabic verse carrying the Easter drama from the request of Joseph of Arimathea for the body of Christ to the setting of the watch around the Holy Sepulcher. "C" contains 522

---

[1] *Le Mystère d'Adam*, ed. Paul Studer (Manchester, 1949), p. lvi. Although first published in 1917, Studer's edition remains the best one available. All later references are to this edition, abbreviated as *Adam*. An English translation was made by E. N. Stone, "Adam, a Religious Play of the Twelfth Century," *Washington University Publications in Language and Literature*, IV (1928), 159–93. For later comment see Frank, "Genesis and Staging of the *Jeu d'Adam*," *PMLA*, LIX (1944), 7–17; Frank, *Medieval French Drama*, pp. 76–84; Craig, *ERD*, pp. 64–65, 67–69, 97–99.

[2] *La Seinte Resureccion*, ed. T. A. Jenkins, J. M. Manly, M. K. Pope, Jean G. Wright, Anglo-Norman Text Society (Oxford, 1943), IV, lxx. Later references are to this edition, abbreviated *Resureccion*. For discussion, see Frank, *Medieval French Drama*, pp. 86–92.

lines. It adds to the dialogue in "P" and continues the plot beyond the setting of the watch to the capture of Joseph by Pilate's soldiers. Estimates of the length of the original play vary from a minimum of 2,000 lines to a maximum of 4,000.[3]

Length is an exceedingly crude standard for literary judgments, but on the basis of length alone the *Mystère* and the *Resureccion* are the most elaborate Biblical dramas that survive prior to the fourteenth century. They are unique in another, more important, respect. They both show marked independence from the liturgical tradition. The prophet play of the *Mystère* is an adaptation of a Latin *Ordo prophetarum* of the type commonly used in liturgical drama to introduce the plays of the Nativity cycle. No Latin analogue can be found, however, for the Adam and Cain sections that comprise over two-thirds of the *Mystère*. Not a single liturgical play on either of these subjects survives, and there is no reason to believe that they were regular parts of the Latin cycle. Moreover, the dialogue, *mise en scène*, and action of the *Mystère* are qualitatively different from their liturgical counterparts. The only links between the Adam and Cain sections of the *Mystère* and the liturgical tradition are their use of Latin responsories and the fact that they were staged in or in front of a church.[4]

La Seinte Resureccion is also markedly independent of the liturgical tradition. It has no Latin passages, no suggestion of attachment to a church festival or service, and no reference indicating that it was performed in or near a church. It requires an elaborate *mise en scène* involving fourteen "places," a minimum of forty-two performers, and sophisticated stage props such as a cross with a detachable figure that can be made to "bleed" when struck with a spear.[5] Of the 371 lines of "P," 80 are stage directions, yet in these 80 lines there is not a single suggestion of liturgical costumes, clerical actors, a choir, or such liturgical properties as thuribles, sindon, or candles. The movements of the actors are evidently representational

---

[3] Alfred Jeanroy, *Le théâtre religieux en France* (Paris, 1923), p. 68, n. 1, estimates three to four thousand lines. Manly, in *Resureccion*, p. cxiv, estimates "at the most not more than two thousand lines."

[4] The most authoritative account of the staging is that by Frank, "Genesis and Staging," pp. 7–17. Studer (*Adam*, pp. xxiv–xxv) simply quotes Sepet's impressionistic description. All scholars agree, however, that the *Adam* is "transitional" and "semi-liturgical." Cf. Studer, *Adam*, p. xxi; Frank, *Medieval French Drama*, pp. 74–76. Craig's comment (*ERD*, p. 64) is typical: "Certainly the *Jeu d'Adam* was caught in the very act of leaving the church and had been developed, like other dramatic offices, within the church itself." It should be stressed that the use of the church as setting and the responses are the only justification for this fanciful theory. In fact, the responses, properly understood, are evidence that the play was *not* derived from the liturgical tradition as is shown below, pp. 259–60.

[5] See below, p. 268.

rather than ceremonial, and the audience never becomes involved in the play's action. In short, while all surviving Latin Easter plays have obvious ceremonial vestiges, *La Seinte Resureccion* has none.

The contents of the play are as independent of the liturgical tradition as is its technique. It includes several episodes never treated in Latin drama and omits details that were usually emphasized. In those few places where its action overlaps the action of liturgical drama, its mode of treatment is unique. The setting of the watch around the sepulcher, for example, is prominent in the *Resureccion* and in four Latin plays from the thirteenth and fourteenth centuries. In the Latin plays actions and dialogue are standardized. The Klosterneuburg and Benediktbeuern plays show the Hebrew priests paying the soldiers, who then chant a set piece consisting of a four-line stanza beginning *Defensores erimus tumuli* and a five-stanza processional with the macaronic refrain *Schowa propter insidias*.[6] The Tours Easter play and the Sulmona Passion omit the detail of the payment and provide a chant beginning *Ergo eamus*.[7] If the *Resureccion* were influenced by the liturgical tradition, one would expect reminiscences of one of these pieces: the only other twelfth-century Easter play in the vernacular, the forty-line *Les Trois Maries*, is simply a translation of an expanded *Quem quaeritis*.[8] Yet the setting of the watch in the *Resureccion* is unique. Instead of being bribed or commanded by Pilate, the soldiers volunteer. Their speeches are neither chants nor processionals, and have nothing in common with the Latin texts beyond a certain boastfulness.

The best evidence of the independence of the *Resureccion* is its plot. The play begins with a versified prologue giving directions for the stations required in the ensuing action. The last lines of the prologue introduce the first episode, a long dialogue between Pilate and Joseph. Before giving permission to bury the body of Jesus, Pilate sends his soldiers to the Cross to make certain that Jesus is dead. On their way they meet Longinus, portrayed as a blind beggar, who agrees to pierce the side of Christ for twelve farthings (*dener*). When he does, blood and water flow from Christ's side. Longinus touches the mixture to his eyes, and his vision is miraculously restored. He then falls in prayer before the Cross. While he prays, the soldiers return to Pilate, who silences them until he has granted

---

[6] Texts in Young, *DMC*, I, 422, 434.

[7] *Ibid.*, pp. 439, 707.

[8] Text edited with comment by Paul Meyer, "*Les Trois Maries*, mystère liturgique de Reims," *Romania*, XXXIII (1904), 239–45. The play includes the lament of the three Marys on the way to the tomb, the dialogue with the angel, and the *Victimae Paschali*. It does not include the *Hortulanus* episode. The French verses vary from paraphrase to straightforward translation.

Joseph's request. After Joseph's departure he hears their story and orders Longinus imprisoned to keep him from announcing the miracle.

Joseph now asks Nicodemus to assist him in the last rites, but Nicodemus refuses until he has spoken to Pilate. After being reassured, he accompanies Joseph to the Cross, from which he removes the body. The two men anoint the body, place it in the tomb, and cover the entrance with a stone. Caiaphas, who has learned of the interment, now warns Pilate that the disciples may steal the body and claim that Christ has arisen as He predicted. Pilate agrees that a guard should be posted at the tomb. Four soldiers volunteer, and Caiaphas decides to accompany them. To make sure of their fidelity, he requires that they swear an oath on "the law of Moses," which is conveniently brought forward by the priest Levi. They then station themselves around the tomb. The "P" text ends here, but the "C" version includes a scene where the soldiers capture Joseph and bring him before Caiaphas. From references in the prologue it is evident that the complete play included the Harrowing of Hell, the Visit to the Tomb, and the Appearances at Emmaus and Galilee.

Among the unusual features of this sequence are the following:

1. Joseph asks permission to bury Christ before His side is pierced, thus reversing the usual order of Latin and later vernacular drama.
2. Joseph is presented as a *decurio*—a man of importance—rather than as Pilate's knight.
3. Pilate is reluctant to grant the request. Usually he does not hesitate.
4. The silencing of the soldiers before Joseph's departure is unique to the *Resureccion*.
5. Longinus is a blind beggar rather than a knight or soldier. He is unaware of Christ's divinity, and he agrees to pierce Christ's side for a money payment.
6. The imprisonment of Longinus is unique to the *Resureccion*.
7. Longinus does not utter the phrase attributed to the centurion in the Bible, "Vere filius Dei erat iste." In other respects, however, the roles of Longinus and the centurion are conflated.
8. Although the *Resureccion* refers to ointments and anointing, the "P" version contains no reference to the gravecloth in which Joseph wrapped the body of Christ. Usually the gravecloth is emphasized, and sometimes Joseph buys it from a cloth merchant.
9. The disciples and Marys are not present at the Deposition, and there are no strophic "laments" provided for the scene.
10. The character of Nicodemus is highly developed; usually he is undeveloped.

11. The soldiers are part of Pilate's guard and are volunteers. Usually they are hired by the Hebrew priests. Where they are not hired, they are commanded to guard the tomb by Pilate. There are four soldiers in contrast to the five of the German liturgical plays and the three of most later vernacular plays.

12. The episode in which the guards swear fidelity on the "law of Moses" is unique.[9]

A few of these features occur in later plays. When this happens, the later plays are themselves deviations from the medieval norm. It is probably significant that most parallels occur in works written in the British Isles. The reversal of the order of the Joseph-Longinus episodes, for example, is found only in the *Resureccion*, the Coventry *Burial*, and the English version of the *Passion des Jongleurs* known as *The Northern Passion*.[10] The English plays agree with the *Resureccion* in depicting the soldiers as Pilate's men rather than as mercenaries hired by the priests, and the *Cornish Passion* shows them volunteering for duty.[11]

Jean Wright, one of the editors of the Anglo-Norman Society edition of the *Resureccion*, concludes that "the effort to discover sources for our *Resureccion* and to relate it to plays treating the same theme only establishes more clearly the independence and originality of the author and revisors."[12] Grace Frank reaches a similar conclusion about the *Mystère*: "The work is one of the most delightful and original compositions of the Middle Ages. . . . Its author has seldom been given sufficient credit for the originality of his whole composition."[13] These observations, while entirely just, miss an important point. We have not one but two lengthy vernacular dramas from the twelfth century. They are apparently both from England and in Anglo-Norman, they use similar staging techniques and the same verse form, they are both independent of the liturgical tradition, and they are both far more complex than any of the surviving Latin Biblical plays. The logical conclusion is that a strong vernacular tradition existed in Norman England in the twelfth century. This tradition undoubtedly was a branching off from the liturgical tradition, but the branching must have occurred before liturgical drama developed its typical complex forms. After the branching, the vernacular drama followed a course of development quite different from that of the Latin drama. The *Mystère* and *Resur-*

---

[9] See *Resureccion*, pp. xcvi–cvii, for more extended discussion.

[10] *Ibid.*, p. xcviii.

[11] *Ibid.*, p. cv.

[12] *Ibid.*, p. cvii.

[13] *Medieval French Drama*, pp. 76, 80.

reccion appear original only because they are being compared to Latin plays on the assumption that every vernacular mystery play must be derived from a liturgical source. In fact, they cannot be original. A clever author in the twelfth century could easily have written a long narrative poem on the Fall or the Resurrection, but he could not have invented out of whole cloth the elaborate conventions of staging and acting required for the production of the *Mystère* and the *Resureccion*.

The early history of the Anglo-Norman vernacular tradition is beyond recovery. Its typical features, however, can be inferred from the *Mystère* and the *Resureccion*. Both plays reveal a good deal about the medieval playwright's method of organizing his materials. The *Resureccion* also provides a case history of the relation between scene and episode in early vernacular drama and some interesting hints about the technique of composing dialogue.

II

In Chapter XVII of the *Poetics* Aristotle asserts that the playwright should reduce his material to its "universal form" before proceeding to the more particular phases of composition. The "universal form" of a drama is the outline of the main steps of its action. This outline may or may not be identical with the arrangement of the episodes in the finished work. In drama based on aesthetic criteria the universal form is intrinsic to the action imitated. In drama written to illustrate didactic or psychological principles—homily and allegory, for example—the universal form is extrinsic to the action, which is shaped to fit it. Drama based on fidelity to source, historical or otherwise, occupies a middle position between these extremes. The source is the universal form. If this source is aesthetically coherent, the drama will be coherent; if it is formless, the drama will be, as well.

Both the *Mystère* and the *Resureccion* belong in the third category. The universal form of the first is provided by a liturgical text, that of the second by the New Testament.

Current opinion about the *Mystère* starts from the belief that it is three separate "plays": an Adam play, a Cain play, and a prophet play. The prophet play has always been recognized as a redaction of a Latin original. Sepet proposed that the Adam and Cain plays resulted from backward expansion of the prophet play and went on to contend that the whole Old

Testament cycle originated in this way.[14] Almost all later scholars agree that the *Mystère* is "an early and incomplete attempt at cycle-building,"[15] but Sepet's attempt to show that the origin of the cycle was the prophets has been rejected. Following the lead of Hardin Craig and A. M. Jenney, scholars now believe that the Old Testament cycle is a result of the liturgy itself.[16] According to this view, the Adam and Cain sections of the *Mystère* are the first two episodes in an open-ended series that would eventually grow to include all of the Old Testament figures heavily stressed in the liturgy of the Lenten season. The two plays, then, are separate compositions, not backward amplifications. Their subjects were suggested by the liturgy and their substance was derived from Genesis. The Latin responsories are evidence of the transitional character of the *Mystère* and substantiate the theory of its liturgical origin. They are a somewhat haphazard collection of texts used in the Roman breviary for Sunday and Monday of Septuagesima, and they are inserted more or less arbitrarily into the action. Finally, although the author of the *Mystère* moved abruptly from Cain to the prophets, there is no reason why he could not have interpolated other Old Testament plays after the Cain play if he had so desired.

A consideration of the responses in the *Mystère* suggests a quite different view of its origin and form. Responses are used nine times in the Adam-Cain section. Seven responses are labeled and are chanted by the chorus so that they divide the action into distinct units. Two others, hitherto ignored, are unlabeled, and one of these is part of the dialogue. Because Sepet and his successors used the modern breviary, they found no significant pattern in the responses beyond the fact that they are associated with various Septuagesimal services. It is clear, however, that the author of the *Mystère* referred not to a high medieval or modern form of the breviary but to the Gregorian *Liber responsalis*. During the Lenten season the *Liber responsalis* provides seven lengthy responsories on Old Testament themes. The first of these is the responsory of Sexagesima, which occupies fifty-two lines in the *Patrologia* edition. It begins with the creation, depicts the Fall of Man, and ends with the murder of Abel. It includes each of the nine

[14] Marius Sepet, *Les prophètes du Christ* (Paris, 1878), *passim;* followed by Studer, *Adam*, pp. xii–xviii.

[15] Craig, *ERD*, p. 68; Frank, *Medieval French Drama*, p. 80.

[16] Craig, "The Origin of the Old Testament Plays," *MP*, X (1913), 473–87; Jenney, "A Further Word as to the Origin of the Old Testament Plays," pp. 59–64; Frank, *Medieval French Drama*, pp. 80–81.

responses found in the *Mystère* and follows exactly the same order as the *Mystère*.[17]

The Gregorian responsory is more than the source of a few Latin verses in a vernacular play. It is the outline of the play itself. The Cain section is not included in the *Mystère* because (as Craig and Jenney believed) the author anticipated the form of the high medieval vernacular cycles, but simply because the outline—the responsory—required its inclusion. This fact in turn shows that the Adam and Cain sections are conceived as a single unit—at best, as two episodes—rather than as two individual acts or plays. The Adam-Cain play is formless by aesthetic standards. The source of its "universal form" is neither dramatic nor narrative but lyric, and the play suffers accordingly.

Obviously, the author of the *Mystère* was indifferent to aesthetic matters. When composing the *Mystère* he ignored the dramatic tradition embodied in Latin Easter and Christmas plays and relegated the narrative history supplied by the Old Testament to a secondary position, using it to fill in the sequence defined by the responsory. The closest analogue to the Adam-Cain section of the *Mystère* is an elaborately troped or farsed responsory with the interpolations in dramatic rather than lyric form. This parallel is at best remote. Three points, however, are certain: (1) The technique of plot construction as well as the content of the Adam-Cain play is independent of liturgical drama. (2) The inclusion of two Old Testament episodes does not warrant the notion that the *Mystère* is "an early and incomplete attempt at cycle-building." (3) The "universal

---

[17] Migne (ed.), *PL*, LXXVIII, 748–49. The other Old Testament responsories (all in *PL*, LXXVIII) are Noah (p. 749), Abraham (pp. 749–50), Jacob (pp. 753–54), Joseph (pp. 755–56), Moses (p. 757), and Joshua (pp. 757–58), followed by the *Responsoria de passione Domini* of Passion Sunday. The nine responses found in the Gregorian text and the *Mystère* are as follows: (1) *In principio fecit Dominus*, the first Gregorian response; it appears as a *Lectio* preceding the action of the *Adam* (*Adam*, p. 2). The second Gregorian response simply repeats it. (2) *Formavit igitur Dominus*, the third Gregorian response, used in *Adam*, p. 2, and marked R̂. (3) *Tulit ergo dominus hominem*, the fourth Gregorian response, used in *Adam*, p. 6, and marked R̂. The fifth response, *Dixit Dominus Deus, non est bonum hominem esse solum*, is not quoted in *Adam*, but is echoed in the dialogue. The sixth, describing the creation of Eve, is omitted for the simple reason that Eve is already created. (4) *Dixit Dominus ad Adam*, the seventh Gregorian response, used in *Adam*, p. 6, and marked R̂. (5) *Dum ambularet*, the eighth Gregorian response, used in *Adam*, p. 20, and marked R̂. (6) *Adam, ubi es?*, part of the eighth response, appears in *Adam*, p. 20, as part of the dialogue: ". . . dicet FIGURA: Adam, u es?" (7) *In sudore vultus tui*, the ninth Gregorian response, used in *Adam*, p. 25, and marked R̂. (8) *Ecce Adam quasi unus*, the tenth Gregorian response, used in *Adam*, p. 25, and marked R̂. (9) *Ubi est Abel, frater tuus?* The eleventh and last Gregorian response, used in *Adam*, p. 36, and marked R̂. In addition to furnishing the outline for the play, the Gregorian responsory furnished hints for the dialogue, particularly through the versicles following each response.

form" of the drama is provided by a set liturgical piece; instead of organizing his play around a single action, the dramatist turned to an already extant outline and filled it in with dialogue based partly on suggestions in the responsory itself and partly on relevant passages in Genesis.

The surviving fragment of *La Seinte Resureccion* is less than half as long as the *Mystère*. Nevertheless, it gives the impression of being far more episodic. This is surprising because the liturgical Resurrection plays, whatever their weaknesses, retain the strong comic pattern bequeathed them by ritual. Continuity of ritual form and amplification from the center outwards are two fundamental principles in the development of the liturgical tradition. By contrast, the author of the *Resureccion*, like the author of the *Mystère*, appears to have begun with a nondramatic source. This source is easily identified as the New Testament through four quotations that appear as marginal notes in the "P" manuscript and serve to demarcate the four main divisions of the action. They are:

1. "Tunc acessit ad Pilatum et peciit corpus Jesu" (Matt. 28:58). This quotation is the basis of the first sixty lines of dialogue in the play (ll. 29–88). Essentially the same statement is found in Mark 15:43 and Luke 23:52, so that the action may be considered an essential part of Gospel history.

2. "Lancea latus eius aperuit et continuo exiuit sanguis et aqua" (John 19:34). The quotation provides a basis for the summoning of the soldiers by Pilate, the journey to the Cross, the hiring of Longinus, the piercing of Christ's side, the report to Pilate, and the imprisonment of Longinus (ll. 89–182). To give the piercing of Christ's side dramatic weight, the author has added apocryphal and legendary material and has fused the centurion of Luke 23:52 with Longinus. The arrangement of the Joseph-Pilate and Longinus episodes is explained by the fact that the piercing of Christ's side is mentioned only by John. Its place in Matthew's chronology is therefore ambiguous. Evidently, the tradition that it occurred before Joseph's interview with Pilate had not solidified at the time that the *Resureccion* was composed.

3. "Posuit eum in monumento nouo quod excideratur a petri" (Matt. 27:60). This quotation justifies the conversation between Joseph and Nicodemus, the Deposition, and the burial (ll. 183–276). Again, this is an essential part of Gospel history mentioned by Mark (15:46), Luke (23:53), and John (19:39–42). John is the only Evangelist to state that Nicodemus assisted Joseph.

4. "Jube custodire sepulchrum ne furentur eum discipuli eius et dicant plebi quia surrexit, et erit nouissimus error peior priore" (Matt. 27:64). The desire of the Hebrew priests for a sepulcher guard, mentioned only by Matthew, accounts for the interview between Caiaphas and Pilate and the setting of the watch (ll. 277–371).

The scriptural quotations divide the play into four movements of approximately equal length. Each movement has as its climax an important event of the period between the death of Christ and the Visit to the Tomb. The chronology follows Matthew, and three quotations are taken from his account. John's account furnishes one movement (the second) and provides the figure of Nicodemus in the fourth. Taken together, the quotations provide an outline of the action identical in function to the outline of the *Mystère* provided by the Gregorian responsory. There are two differences. First, the source of the *Resureccion* is narrative history rather than lyric. Second, while the divisions of the responsory parallel the divisions in the action of the *Mystère*, the movements of the *Resureccion* are complicated by subdivision into episodes.

III

The arrangement of episodes in the *Mystère* is relatively simple. The action of the Adam-Cain play requires only two stations, Paradise and "the world," plus two locations, heaven and hell, from which nonhuman characters appear and to which human characters are led. The action moves from the first to the second station after the Fall, and the human characters do not travel back and forth between stations. For this reason the dialogue is not continually interrupted by movements from station to station. Practically speaking, the stage is identical with the station. The divisions of the action—its episodes—are marked by the seven Latin responses that are sung by the choir. The episode structure of the *Mystère* is thus identical with its universal form.

The *Resureccion* involves an entirely new set of conditions. Unlike the *Mystère*, it requires multiple stations and continual movement between them, so that the stage is, in effect, the space containing the stations. What Aristotle refers to as "insertion of episodes" is not a simple matter of dividing four large movements into convenient subsections. In fact, the division of episodes in the *Resureccion* is independent of the play's universal form. It is based not on plot but on the physical arrangements required for the *mise en scène*, and its episodes are not units of action but passages of dialogue between stage directions. There are no less than twenty-three such episodes in the 371 lines of the "P" manuscript. The effect, while extremely crude, is reminiscent of the division of Greek dramas into episodes separated by choral passages. If the stage directions separating the dialogue were recited, as is possible, the speaker would have a decidedly choral function. Unlike the Greek choral interludes, however, the stage directions of the *Resureccion* are brief and limited to exposition. If they did not arise spontaneously, they may be modeled on the expository antiphons of liturgical drama, such as the *Currebant duo* chanted during the race of Peter and John.

To understand the arrangement of episodes in the *Resureccion*, it is necessary to visualize the "stage" on which the play was presented. The prologue of the "P" version contains much useful information:

> En ceste manere recitom
> La seinte resureccion.
> Primerement apareillons
> Tus le lius e les mansions,
> La crucifix primerement   5
> E puis aprés le monument;
> Vne jaiole i deit aver
> Pur les prisons enprisoner;
> Enfer seit mis de cele part
> Es mansions del altre part   10
> E puis le ciel; e as estals
> Primes Pilate od ces vassals—
> Sis u set chivaliers avra;
> Cayphas en l'altre serra—
> Od lui seit la Juerie—   15
> Puis Joseph d'Arunachie;
> El quart liu scit danz Nichodemus —
> Chescons i ad od sei les soens—
> El quint les deciples Crist;
> Les treis Maries saient el sist.   20
> Si seit purveu que l'om face
> Galilee en mi la place;
> Iemaus uncore i seit fait,
> U Jesus fut al hostel trait.[18]   (See Appendix)

The presentation requires a fairly large neutral area, which is, properly speaking, the stage. There is no indication that the shape of this area is influenced by, or related to, a church. In it are located a series of stations,

[18] Pp. 1–3.

called variously *lius*, *mansions*, and *estals*. The *mansions* appear to be places without characters, whereas the word *estal* is used for places at which various performers stand. The *mansions* are listed first. The Cross is the most important object, and the other *mansions* are arranged on either side of it, a system that also seems to be followed for the *estals*. In addition to the Cross there must be a monument, a jail, hell, and heaven. The first *estal* is occupied by Pilate and "six or seven knights." Caiaphas and the Jews occupy the second *estal*. The third and fourth are for Joseph and Nicodemus, each with six retainers. The fifth and sixth are for the disciples and the Marys. Two additional places are mentioned, Emmaus and Galilee. Later, we learn that Longinus has a place (*liu*) and that a figure known only as *aliquis in via* participates in the action. Simple addition shows that the play calls for fourteen stations and a minimum of forty-two performers. The performers are usually grouped at the *estals*, which typically have one major character and several subordinate ones who carry out his wishes. How the *mansions* and *estals* were constructed is unknown. On the basis of the *Mystère* and complex Latin plays it seems possible that they were platforms, but even this is conjecture. They could equally well have been circles drawn on the ground of an open field and marked with flags.[19]

Two quite different plans have been offered for the stations. Assuming that the stations were arranged according to the interior plan of a church, E. K. Chambers suggested that they were placed in two parallel rows extending from the Cross toward the audience.[20] As Professor Jean Wright observes, however, "The spectators would follow with difficulty the movement of the players from station to station in such an arrangement."[21] Professor Wright's alternative plan is shown on the following page as Plan I.

There are several defects in her arrangement. The stage directions of "P" indicate that the Cross was centered and that the *mansions* and *estals*

---

[19] "C" uses the word *estage* once (l. 15), which may indicate a formal structure. Otherwise there is no foundation for the almost universal assumption that *mansions* were platforms. Neither text of the *Resureccion* has any reference to actors ascending or descending in spite of the constant stational movement in the play. This would indicate that the *mansions* of the *Resureccion* are at ground level. All suggestions about the construction of the stations in the *Resureccion* are based on analogies to either the *Adam* or to much later plays. Chambers, in fact, bases his theories on the plan of the sixteenth-century Donaueschingen Passion (*MS*, II, 84).

[20] *MS*, II, 83.

[21] *Resureccion*, p. cxviii.

Plan I:

| Heaven | Cross | Monument | Jail | Hell |

| Pilate, Caiaphas | | Joseph, Nicodemus | | Disciples, Marys |

Galilee and Emmaus

[Audience]²²

were deployed symmetrically on either side of it. The phrase *puis après* (l. 6) may mean that the monument is constructed "next after" the Cross, but it also means "further back" in the sense of nearer the audience. Placing Pilate and Caiaphas together is questionable, and if their stations were located in front of the Cross, the meeting of the soldiers with Longinus on their way to the Cross would be awkward. Finally, the emphasis on right-and-left symmetry in the prologue suggests medieval positional symbolism associating "right" with paradise and the Gentiles, and "left" with hell and the Jews, and this symbolism is lost in Professor Wright's plan. The arrangement proposed in Plan II draws on the suggestions of both Chambers and Wright but is, it is hoped, more consistent with the play than either of theirs.

In Plan II the *mansions* are indicated by rectangles, the *estals* by ovals, and ambiguous "places" by circles. The right-and-left grouping accords with positional symbolism (right means to the right of the Cross as it faces the audience) and with the order and precedence of the prologue. The stage is dominated by the Cross and divided symmetrically between sepulcher and heaven on the one hand, and jail and hell on the other.

²² *Ibid.*, p. cxix. A slightly modified plan is offered on the same page for the "C" version. The plan is based on a miniature by Fouquet and an illustration of the Valenciennes Passion, both much later than the *Resureccion*. That the audience faces the "stage" rather than circulating among the stations is indicated by the preface (l. 21), by the requirement that the spaces between the stations be left open to permit the journeys from one station to the next, and by the fact that in two instances "actions" occur in the space between stations.

Plan II:

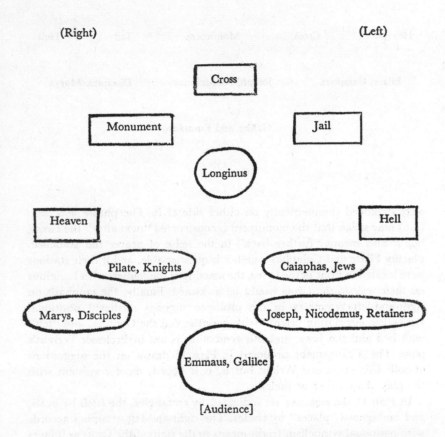

(Right)   (Left)

Cross

Monument   Jail

Longinus

Heaven   Hell

Pilate, Knights   Caiaphas, Jews

Marys, Disciples   Joseph, Nicodemus, Retainers

Emmaus, Galilee

[Audience]

The whole stage can be kept before the audience, and the compromise between horizontal and vertical placement of the stations reduces obstruction to a minimum. The action of the play naturally falls into movements across the stage—i.e., in front of the audience—or movements toward or away from the Cross. The positional symbolism is, it will be noted, closely related to that discovered by Amalarius of Metz in the placement and movements of clergy and liturgical objects during Mass.

We now turn to the use of this stage in the action of *La Seinte Resureccion.* The play consists of twenty-three units of dialogue ("D") separated by twenty-three stage directions ("S") varying from two to six lines each.

The stage directions always refer to the unit that follows, never to the one preceding. They are introductions rather than summaries. Each stage direction combines reference to an action to be performed (usually movement from one station to another) with a formula phrase equivalent to ". . . and he said the following." The result is the following pattern of stage directions ("S") and dialogue ("D"):

[Prologue: 24 lines]	S 2; D 14	S 2; D 12
S 4; D 60	S 2; D 8	S 2; D 8
S 4; D 8	S 2; D 28	S 2; D 16
S 2; D 4	S 4; D 8	S 2; D 8
S 6; D 8	S 2; D 12	S 2; D 16
S 4; D 6	S 2; D 4	S 2; D 10
S 2; D 4	S 2; D 2	S 2; D 18
S 4; D 16	S 2; D 2	S 2; D 18 (fragmentary)

The play formally begins with a four-line stage direction (ll. 25–28) requiring Joseph to cross the stage in order to address Pilate:

> Cum la gente est tute asse
> . . . .
> Dan Joseph, cil de Arunachie,
> Venge a Pilate, si lui die:

The movement is thus from left to right stage if the proposed composite plan is valid. The next sixty lines are an extended dialogue between Pilate and Joseph, at the end of which Pilate orders his soldiers to visit the Cross to make certain that Christ is dead. Before the soldiers depart, a new stage direction is inserted: "Dunt s'en alerent dous des serganz" (l. 89). On their way to the Cross the soldiers pass the place of Longinus: "Si un dit a Longin le ciu / Que unt trové seant en un liu" (ll. 91–92). The "place" of Longinus should therefore probably be located between the station of Pilate and that of the Cross, as in the proposed composite plan. After an eight-line exchange, Longinus joins the soldiers, who resume their journey to the Cross. Since this requires movement between stations, another stage direction is necessary: "Quant il vendrent devant la croiz, / Une lance le mistrent es poinz" (ll. 101–2).

Thus far, all stage directions have referred to movement between stations. A second justification for stage directions, less well defined than the first, is to introduce significant events involving physical action. After Longinus has accepted the lance, he must plunge it into Christ's side, causing blood and water to flow over his hands. This is obviously a high point, and it is preceded by the statement:

> Il prist la lance. ci.l feri
> Al quer, dunc sanc et ewe en issi;
> Si li est as mainz avalé
> . . . E quant a ses oils le mist,
> Dunc vit an eire, e puis si dit (ll. 107–12).

Although the episode derives most of its effect from the spectacle of the bleeding figure of Christ, the convention that each episode must have dialogue is observed. Longinus delivers an eight-line prayer while kneeling before the Cross. After this prayer, stational movement is resumed. The soldiers must report the miracle to Pilate: "Les chivalers s'en vunt en arere" (l. 123). The phrase *aler en arere* may simply mean "return," but the possibility that it refers to movement back from the Cross (i.e., toward the audience) cannot be discounted. It echoes the phrase *puis après* in the prologue and provides some slight additional justification for E. K. Chambers' theory of vertical deployment of the stations. At any rate, since Pilate is the principal speaker in the ensuing dialogue, the soldiers have to move from the Cross to Pilate's station, leaving Longinus bowed in prayer. After a brief exchange, Pilate turns to Joseph to dismiss him: "Vers Dan Joseph dunc se turna" (l. 131). This stage direction is omitted in "C" and was probably considered of marginal importance by the "C" scribe. On the other hand, the "P" version consistently interprets an episode as dialogue between two major characters or a major character and members of a group. The turning of Pilate involves a shift from one dialogue (Pilate-the soldiers) to another (Pilate-Joseph), and hence to a new episode. "P" and "C" agree that a stage direction is necessary for Joseph's trip to the station of Nicodemus: "Quant Joseph ont pris le congé . . . Vers Nichodem fut alé" (ll. 137–38).

As Joseph passes across the stage, Pilate commands the guards to imprison Longinus. The soldiers must again move to the Cross: "Dunt alerent tost a Longin" (l. 157). At this point in the play true simultaneous action occurs. Longinus is praying at the Cross, Joseph is proceeding to the station of Nicodemus, and the soldiers are approaching the Cross. None of these situations involve dialogue, however, and the playwright consistently avoids having characters at different stations speak simultaneously.

The episode of the imprisonment of Longinus is presented before the meeting of Joseph and Nicodemus. Longinus is apprehended and taken to jail, where he is threatened by the soldiers: "Quant il vindrent al gaiole / Si lui distrent ceste parole" (ll. 173–74). The stage directions now return to the arrival of Joseph at the station of Nicodemus: "Entre ces feiz Joseph li pruz / A Nichodem esteit venuz" (ll. 183–84). A rather long conversation follows in which Nicodemus timidly refuses to assist Joseph unless they first speak to Pilate. Accordingly, the next episode requires movement back to Pilate's station: "A Pilate en vunt ambesdouz" (l. 213). Some interest is added to this journey by the fact that the pair are accompanied by vassals carrying the tools to be used in the Deposition and an ointment chest (according to John 19:39, this chest weighed "about an hundred pound"). After Pilate has confirmed his permission to remove Christ's body, the group resumes its trip to the Cross: "Quant il vindrent devant la cruis, / Joseph criat od halte voiz" (ll. 225–26).

The Deposition sequence is obviously a high point, and each of its actions is significant. It is broken into five episodes involving (1) the extraction of the nails, (2) the lowering of the body from the Cross, (3) the anointing of the body, (4) prayer for a worthy burial, and (5) placing the body in a coffin. Only the prayer episode has more than four lines of dialogue. The stage directions are:

(1)	Nichodem ses ustilz prist E Dan Joseph issi lui dist:	239–40
(2)	Quant Nichodem l'out fait issi, Dist a Joseph qui le cors saisi.	245–46
(3)	Dunt mistrent bel le cors aval E Joseph dit a son vaissal:	249–50
(4)	Tant cum l'oinnement lui baut, Nichodem dit tut en haut.	253–54
(5)	Quant le cors enoint aveient, Sur la bere il le metient.	267–68

(See Appendix)

After the Deposition Joseph and Nicodemus move to the monument, where they inter the body and seal the entrance with a stone. Curiously, there is no dialogue accompanying the action at the monument. This action is mentioned in the first line of the stage direction in "P" and immediately followed by a reference to the movement of Caiaphas to the station of Pilate: "Quant il fut enterrez et la pere mise, / Caiaphas, qui est levez, dit en ceste guise" (ll. 277–78). The suspicion that an episode may have been lost in "P" is strengthened by the fact that "C" provides two episodes and two stage directions for the same sequence ("C," ll. 311–94). Whatever the case, after Caiaphas urges that a watch be set on the sepulcher, two short episodes occur in which the soldiers volunteer: "Un des serganz dunc s'esdresça / E a Pilate issi parla"; and "Treis des altres dunc leverent" (ll. 295–96 and 305, respectively). The volunteering must have been considered a significant action because it has a stage direction even though it does not involve stational movement. After boasting of their prowess, the soldiers move with Caiaphas to the sepulcher. As on their journey to the Cross, they encounter an unexpected personage: "Dunt si cum il alerent la / Un par vei lur demanda" (ll. 323–24). The episode is interesting because the new character, labeled only *aliquis in via*, does not seem to have a station. This is the only instance in the *Resureccion* of use of the neutral space between the stations for anything other than movement. In spite of this fact, the episode is treated according to the stational conventions. After a brief exchange, a new stage direction is inserted: "Quant Caiphas les i ont mené, / Si lur ad dit e comandé (ll. 335–36). The command is that the soldiers shall swear an oath on "the law of Moses." This necessitates bringing forward a manuscript of the "law," and hence another movement between stations: "Est vus un prestre, qui out a non Levi, / Si out escrite la lei Moysi" (ll. 354–55). The "P" version of the *Resureccion* breaks off in the middle of the dialogue provided for this episode. "C" continues with the episode of Caiaphas' departure (ll. 429–30), a visit to Joseph by a character labeled *quidam homo* (1. 453), the journey of Joseph to the sepulcher (1. 489), the capture of Joseph (ll. 495–96), and the departure of all concerned to the station of Pilate (ll. 513–14). Five of these six episodes involve movement between stations, and the sixth (ll. 495–96) is clearly a significant action.

The principle of creating episodes on the basis of movement between stations is so regularly observed in *La Seinte Resureccion* that it must have been a well-established convention at the time the play was written. Like the dramatic conventions of later ages, it was doubtless accepted by playwright and audience as the inevitable and right way to present action realistically. It seems extremely artificial to the modern reader, but then the conventions of modern cinema will probably seem equally artificial to scholars eight hundred years hence.

Whether or not conventional in the twelfth century, the episode technique of the *Resureccion* is an attempt to cope with the problem of imitating action. Here, the word "action" refers not to plot but to the activity of the characters—the motions and tasks they perform before the audience. The dramatic mode of imitation requires the author to provide for this sort of action throughout his play. The acts performed by the characters become, cumulatively, the action of the play in the Aristotelian sense. But how does one imitate acts? Because we live at a time when drama of all sorts is commonplace—we grow up with it—it is hard to realize that this is a serious question, and harder still to discuss it meaningfully. Yet it *is* a serious question and a very basic one. The conventions of dramatic imitation, of what constitutes acceptable stage representation of human acts, have changed radically since the Renaissance, as witness the differences between the Shakespearean and the proscenium stage, or the realism of Ibsen's *Ghosts* and that of Arthur Miller's *Death of a Salesman*. The conventions of twelfth-century vernacular drama are particularly important because they are the first medieval conventions that are relatively free of liturgical influence.

The natural way to imitate an object in language is to describe it. This is possible because the object is static. It exists in one place and one time, the present. But an action is not static. It is a process involving movement in space and time. The simplest way to imitate action is to tell a story, but this is narrative, not drama. To imitate action dramatically, the play-wright must place it in a context of physical space and time, and this context is necessarily the result of his assumptions about space and time, in the same way that intelligible speech is the result of a complex but usually unconscious set of assumptions about grammar.

Ritual action occurs in the context of the timeless present and un-localized space. At the moment of the Mass sacrifice, past, present and future are one, and the congregation is united with Christians everywhere in the mystical body of Christ.[23] Liturgical drama represents the first sustained crossing of the boundary between ritual and representation in the Middle Ages. The effect of the shift to linear time and localized space is apparent in the clarified sequence of events, consistency of character identity, verisimilitude, and elimination of ceremonial elements unrelated to the historical event represented. In no liturgical plays, however, is the ceremonial element entirely eliminated.

In contrast to liturgical drama, *La Seinte Resureccion* appears to have been conceived from the beginning as representation. Its stage is an almost too literal reproduction of the neutral space of geometry, which is simply the bounded area within which all real points may be located. Not all points are of interest to the dramatist. Those that are receive labels and are marked off as the *mansions* and *estals* around which the play is built. The rule for the points is: one "place" or character group, one station. That is, the stational technique is a dramatic analogue to the brute fact that a place or human being occupies physical space in the natural world. The rule of identity—that two points cannot occupy the same place—is

[23] See Essay II, *passim*, for more extended comment.

symbolized by having a different place for each group. Thus the stage of the *Resureccion* is not the Protean stage of the Elizabethans, which can be a palace one moment, a tavern the next, and the rebel camp a few moments later. Rather, it is the bounded container of all that exists. That it is geometrical rather than geographical space is easily seen from the fact that there is no attempt in the play to reproduce the geography of Jerusalem in the deployment of stations. That it is universal space is shown by the fact that it includes heaven and hell as well as the Cross, the monument, and the jail in which Longinus is imprisoned.

The deployment of stations in space provides one of the co-ordinates necessary for imitation of action. The second co-ordinate is time. Because action is a continuous process, a convention is necessary that represents continuity while permitting emphasis on significant moments. In *La Seinte Resureccion* time is represented as literally as space. The analogue for a process occurring in time is a line the components of which are points arranged sequentially: A–B–C–D, etc. Since time is unidirectional, the sequence is fixed. No order is possible that involves inversion, flashback, or folding, as, for example, A–C–B–D or D–C–A–B. Continuity is represented by avoidance of gaps between episodes. In Elizabethan or modern drama, if A–B–C–D represents a logically necessary sequence in which A and D are significant and B and C trivial, the author usually employs discontinuous action. A and D are represented, but B and C are left to the imagination. Shakespeare, for example, omits a considerable period of time between Hamlet's interview with the ghost of his father (Act I) and his next appearance in the interviews with Polonius and Rosencrantz and Guildenstern (Act II). In the *Resureccion*, on the other hand, discontinuity is ruled out. If the action imitated is represented by A–B–C–D, and A and D are significant, A and D are presented as episodes, and B and C are symbolized as a journey between the stations at which A and D occur.

Again, in real time, actions involving different groups occur simultaneously. Literal reproduction of this situation would require the performance of two or more episodes at the same moment. Such action is, however, confusing to the audience, although occasionally it is found in Shakespearean and modern drama, when, for example, two groups hold simultaneous conversations on different parts of the stage. The typical Shakespearean solution, however, is alternation. In *Henry IV, Part I*, for example, the groups associated with Prince Hal and Hotspur engage in actions that are simultaneous in time but separated in space. If the sequence of Hal's actions is labeled A, and the sequence of Hotspur's actions, A_1, the Shakespearean technique is to alternate between groups in the form A–A$_1$, B–B$_1$, C–C$_1$, etc. The trouble with this arrangement is that it violates continuity. The dramatist of the *Resureccion* cannot avoid some violation of continuity in shifting from one group to another, but he reduces it to a minimum by concentrating on sequence A and following it to its completion before dealing with sequence A$_1$. When Pilate hears of the miraculous cure of Longinus, for example, he initiates two distinct sequences by (1) sending his soldiers to imprison Longinus, and (2) allowing Joseph of Arimathea to depart for the station of Nicodemus. The dramatist chooses to follow the shorter of the two sequences first. The soldiers are dismissed (episode A), they apprehend Longinus at the Cross (B), and they imprison him (C). Only after his imprisonment has concluded the sequence does the dramatist return to Joseph. Joseph speaks with Nicodemus (episode A$_1$), they revisit Pilate (B$_1$), move to the Cross and remove the nails (C$_1$), and perform the burial (D$_1$–E$_1$–F$_1$–G$_1$).

In the light of the preceding considerations the episode structure of *La Seinte Resureccion* can be understood as the result of an effort to represent actions as they occur in natural space and time. The stage itself is a model of space. Characters and places are deployed in this space, each occupying a point distinct from other points. Actions involve motion from one point to another, and significant moments are symbolized as episodes requiring dialogue. The journeys between stations are denotatively neutral, i.e., they are not furnished with dialogue or mimetic byplay. Their only function is to sustain continuity. They preserve the moments on the time line that the dramatist does not choose to emphasize. If a typical sequence of episodes in modern drama is A–C–F–K, with the missing letters representing gaps in the time line, the typical sequence of the *Resureccion* is A–b–C–d–e–F–g–h–i–j–K, with the capital letters representing episodes at stations, and the lower-case letters representing journeys between stations. The *Mystère d'Adam* follows this convention, but because its events are confined to two stations, Paradise and the world, it has the extremely simple structure A–B, the division being the expulsion from Paradise.

One further observation: the deployment of characters means that there must be at least as many episodes as there are stations. In practice, the number of episodes is multiplied enormously by the fact that characters can visit the same station more than once[24] and that, even when they remain at a given station, the arrival of a new character requires a new episode—a situation illustrated by the arrival of Levi at the sepulcher with the law of Moses. By the same token, an action both logically necessary and involving a station cannot be suppressed. No matter how trivial

---

[24] This does not hold true for the *Mystère* because the movement from Paradise to "the world" is emphatically a one-way trip.

it may be, it must be presented in an episode and provided with dialogue. Joseph does not need to purchase a gravecloth for the simple reason that there is no station for a cloth merchant. On the other hand, the episode of the meeting of the soldiers and Longinus is necessary because Longinus has a station—this in spite of the fact that a rudimentary sense of dramatic economy would suggest combining it with the episode at the Cross in which Longinus accepts the lance (ll. 103–6). The result of these conventions is that the number of episodes is out of all proportion to the natural dramatic form of the events represented. The simple four-part movement which is the play's "universal form" is obscured by twenty-three episodes, many of which are at best trivial and at worst pointless or tangential.

IV

Thus far we have been concerned with accounting for the general form and the peculiar episodic structure of *La Seinte Resureccion*. An equally important factor is dialogue technique. The playwright who inherits a well-established convention for what constitutes realistic dialogue need only ask, "What shall the characters say?" For the historian of drama, however, the convention itself is important. Different ages and cultures accept radically different forms of dialogue as realistic. For the Greeks and Romans quantitative iambic verse seemed the natural form of dialogue. The cycle plays of the fifteenth century often use strophic stanzas for dialogue. During the Renaissance blank verse, *versi sciolti*, and the Alexandrine were in favor for serious drama. In England blank verse was replaced first by the heroic couplet, and later by prose. Evidently, the form of dialogue is as closely related to the assumptions a culture makes about reality as is the form of dramatic action.

For French and Anglo-Norman authors of the twelfth century the octosyllabic couplet was a normal and proper vehicle for narrative poetry. It is therefore not surprising to observe that this form influenced drama. What is surprising is that when used in drama the octosyllabic couplet loses its importance, becoming secondary to other, more complex, forms.

A casual examination of the verse of *La Seinte Resureccion* suggests that the basic module is the octosyllabic couplet, with considerable variation permissible in syllable count. More careful analysis, however, shows that the basic module is not the couplet but the quatrain. This arrangement is reflected in several ways. In the first place, the author is fond of mono-rhyme. When monorhymes occur, they are usually in groups or multiples of four. Examples in the "P" manuscript of the *Resureccion* include lines

57–64 (double monorhymed quatrain in -ie), 65–68 (quatrain in -ait), 113–16 (-ire), 117–20 (-i), 133–36 (-i), 137–40 (-e), 197–200 (-u), 201–4 (-re), 205–8 (-se), 209–12 (-ai), 235–38 (-enz), 255–64 (triple monorhyme in -ent), 297–300 (-ure), 301–4 (-oille), 307–10 (-um), and 319–22 (-i). There is only one six-line monorhyme in the play (ll. 227–32), and ten-line monorhyme does not occur.

Another indication that the quatrain rather than the couplet is the basic module of the dialogue in the *Resureccion* is the length of the episodes. Of the twenty-three episodes, sixteen have dialogue in multiples of four, ranging in length from four lines to a maximum of sixty. Individual speeches are also frequently quatrains, for example, "P" lines 29–32, 73–76, 77–80, 85–88, 103–6, 141–44, 175–78, 179–82, 217–20, 211–14, 269–72, 273–76, 307–10, 311–14, 315–18, 356–59, and 362–65. When variations from this norm occur, they are usually based on the quatrain module. The quatrain can be divided between two or more speakers in arrangements such as 1, 1, 1, 1 (ll. 81–84); 1, 1, 2 (ll. 93–96); 2, 2 (ll. 133–36); and 3, 1 (169–72). Alternatively, long speeches can be written in multiples of four, as, for example, lines 49–56, 57–64, 185–96, and 255–66. The most common exceptions to the quatrain rule are isolated couplets (ll. 247–48, 251–52) and six-line speeches (ll. 37–42, 43–48, and 113–18). There are no ten- or fourteen-line speeches. A seventeen-line speech occurs once in "P" (ll. 337–53, according to the line numeration), but it is recognized by the editor as defective.[25] In one case an episode of sixteen lines has the abnormal division 15, 1 (ll. 279–94).

These statistics make it plain that the author of the *Resureccion*, while not absolutely faithful to the quatrain, considered it, rather than the couplet, the normal verse module. As such, it is slightly less flexible than the couplet but far more so than the complex strophic stanzas used by the poet of the English *Second Shepherds' Play*.[26] In spite of minor disadvantages it permits the poet to invent dialogue with relative freedom and does not require frequent padding to complete the form. The most severe restriction on the poet of the "P" version is that he is not permitted to subdivide the line itself. In this respect the "P" version differs slightly from the "C" version, in which the line is divided on four occasions ("C," ll. 141, 461, 507, 508), and differs markedly from the *Mystère d'Adam*, where line division and *stichomythia* are common.[27]

---

[25] *Resureccion*, p. 35.

[26] Many English cycle plays use the quatrain; e.g., the Shrewsbury fragments, the Chester *Deluge*, the Brome *Abraham and Isaac*, etc.

[27] *Adam*, ll. 1–2, 81–84, 86, 113–27, etc.

A second convention influencing the verse form of the *Resureccion* is symmetry. As Grace Frank observes, the characters "frequently address each other in balanced phrases built on similar verbal and rhythmic patterns."[28] The reason for the symmetry goes beyond the mere desire for rhetorical display, which is never very important in the *Resureccion*. The symmetry reflects the dramatist's recognition of the dialectic quality of dramatic speech. In normal speech and in the dialogue of post-Renaissance drama the dialectic element is obscured. A statement may be extremely long and the reply brief or expressed in action rather than words. Three or four people may participate in a conversation, so that the statement-response pattern is fragmented, or a given statement and response may be insignificant links in a chain of dialectic extending over several speeches.

The poet of the *Resureccion* ignored these complicating factors. His dialogue expresses literally the dialectic quality of dramatic speech. First, it is usually restricted to two characters or one character and a group (e.g., Pilate and the soldiers). Second, it often balances statement against response; that is, if character A makes a statement, character B often replies in the same number of lines, frequently using the same rhymes and parallel rhetorical form. The effect is similar to that of the *débat* as found in Virgil's *Eclogues* and in medieval poetry.

The corollary of this technique is that speeches tend to fall into paired units. The typical episode consists of two speeches, a statement and a reply, or, when the episode involves a named character and a group, a statement by the character and parallel replies by the members of the group. The episodes are sometimes extended to four units (i.e., statement-reply, statement-reply), but except for the Joseph-Pilate dialogue at the beginning, they are never longer. The only consistent exception to the rule of paired units is the episode involving a single speaker, which produces monologue, not dialogue. There are six monologues in the *Resureccion*, three of which are extended speeches (ll. 101–6, 113–20, 251–52, 255–56, 297–304, 337–53).

The effect of these requirements can be seen in the Joseph-Pilate episode that begins the play. The episode is atypical in that it consists of sixty lines and attempts to present something like a dialectic chain. It does not develop, however, in the normal A–B–C–D pattern of everyday speech. Instead, it develops by paired speeches. The first pair consists of an A stanza of four lines rhymed a-a-b-b and a reply by Pilate (B) which is also in four lines and uses the same rhymes and sentence structure as A.

---

[28] *Medieval French Drama*, p. 87.

Pilate's speech does not lead naturally to a reply by Joseph. The next stanza (C) is in six lines and uses new rhymes. Although it is logically the consequence of B, it is related by form to D, which is also in six lines and uses the same rhymes. After D the form changes again. E and F are in eight-line stanzas preserving rhetorical parallelism but differing in rhyme. The first thirty-six lines of dialogue thus take the form A–B, C–D, E–F, rather than the continuous form of normal conversation.

After Pilate's eight-line speech (F) the symmetry becomes more complex. The remaining speeches in the episode are: Joseph, 8 lines; Pilate, 4; Joseph, 4; Pilate, 1; Joseph, 1; Pilate, 1; Joseph, 1; Pilate, 4. Two speeches in the series, the first and last, are not paired. The symmetry may simply be defective here, but a more likely explanation is that it is observed in the unit, though not in the speech division. In this case the proper interpretation would be sixteen lines divided 8,8, and eight lines divided 4,4.

The most common episode in the later sections of the play is that of eight lines with 4,4 symmetry. Four episodes are of this type (ll. 93–100, 175–82, 217–24, and 269–76). Variations include couplet episodes with 1,1 symmetry (247–48), quatrain episodes with 1,1,1,1 or 2,2 symmetry (ll. 241–44, 133–36), and larger units. Only five episodes are over sixteen lines. The longest of these, the dialogue between Joseph and Nicodemus ("P," ll. 185–212), is asymmetrical in "P" but symmetrical in "C," where it consists of two twelve-line speeches, two one-line speeches, and two two-line speeches ("C," ll. 211–40).

Evidently, for the author of *La Seinte Resureccion*, composing dialogue involved considerations quite different from those that would concern a modern dramatist. The quatrain module and symmetry are requirements that are independent of the particular situation being treated. They both limit and define the possibilities for dialogue in the same way that the eight-tone scale limits possibilities for musical composition. If they give the *Resureccion* the stylized and archaic quality noted by Professor Frank, they also provide convenient guidelines. Their most serious defect is that, like the conventions for creating episodes, they blur the dramatic focus. Thus the author of the *Resureccion* uses sixty lines for the conversation between Joseph and Pilate and twenty-eight lines for the conversation in which Joseph and Nicodemus decide to return to Pilate to confirm his permission to bury Jesus; but he uses only four lines for the episode in which Longinus spears Christ and four more lines for the episode in which Nicodemus removes Christ from the Cross. Part of the effect of these four-line scenes was undoubtedly created by spectacle, but even so, the lopsided emphasis is egregious. The best and perhaps the only explanation is that the author conceived of dialogue as a form and believed that when he had completed the form he had done enough, regardless of whether or not the lines he had written adequately reflected the significance of the events to which they were related.

V

By modern standards *La Seinte Resureccion* has little characterization. The main figures have large motives determined by their part in the action. Pilate is cautious and political, the soldiers are ferocious and boastful, Caiaphas is malicious, and Joseph and Nicodemus are pious. Longinus is the only character whose motives change. He is avaricious at the beginning and devout at the end. The dramatist does not emphasize motive by rhetoric, nor does he attempt the sort of differentiation in terms of age, sex, and social status that goes under the heading of decorum. The language of the *Resureccion* is surprisingly uniform. It is never either florid or racily colloquial. Pilate, the soldiers, Joseph, and Caiaphas use the same grammar, the same syntax, and the same vocabulary. There are none of the interpolated lyrics common in the Latin Easter drama, no quaint anachronisms, no vivid metaphors. The soldiers are boastful but never engage in buffoonery, and Caiaphas is malicious but never bombastic or comic. The effect is that of scrupulously correct, rather pallid, dialogue intended for an upper middle-class audience.

Within these limits there occasionally appear hints of dramatic ingenuity. The first exchange between Joseph and Pilate is a case in point:

Joseph: Deus, qui des mains le rei Pharon
        Salva Moysen e Aaron,
        I sault Pilate, le mein seignur,
        E dignetez lui doinst e honur.
Pilate: Hercules, qui occist le dragon
        E destruist le viel Gerion,
        Doinst a celui ben e honur
        Qui saluz me dit par amur.   29–36
                      (See Appendix)

Here the symmetry is functional. It reflects the different outlooks of two of the principal characters, Joseph the pious Jew and Pilate the affable pagan. The formal parallel of stanza and rhyme is echoed in the rhetoric. Joseph invokes God in two lines and then asks His blessing for Pilate. Pilate reciprocates by invoking Hercules in two lines and then asking his blessing for Joseph.

Contrast is provided by the different deities invoked. The choice of *Deus* and Hercules not only reveals the difference between the two speakers but also shows some slight concern for historical accuracy. The miracles cited by Joseph also appear to be functional. The salvation of the Israelites from Egypt is the most important Old Testament type of salvation by baptism and is a recurrent theme in Lent. The Gregorian responsory for Quadragesima emphasizes the theme: "In mari viae tuae, et semitae tuae in aquis multis. Deduxisti sicut oves populum tuum in manu Moysi et Aaron."[29] At the very least, Joseph's reference to Moses and Aaron foreshadows the Resurrection. Since it is a part of a prayer for Pilate's salvation (*I sault Pilate*), it may also be intended as an ironic prayer for his conversion.

Pilate's reply is contrasted to this prayer as the True God of Moses is contrasted to the false god Hercules. Again, further symbolism may be intended. The labors of Hercules were regularly allegorized in the Middle Ages to accord with the idea that Hercules is a type or adumbration of Christ. The slaying of the dragon probably refers to the second labor, the slaying of Hydra, a type of deceit; while the victory over Geryon refers to the tenth labor, in which Geryon is a symbol of fraud.[30] If these observations are relevant, Pilate's blessing may foreshadow Christ's rescue of Joseph from the deceit and fraud of the Jews.

Could the dramatist of *La Seinte Resureccion* have sustained the quality of his first eight lines, his work would have been remarkable indeed. Unfortunately, he could not. The rest of the dialogue between Joseph and Pilate is slowed by the need to observe symmetry and has only occasional touches of interest. The fact that Joseph shows no awareness of Christ's divinity is an unusual bit of verisimilitude for a medieval play. The curses heaped on the perfidious Jews by Pilate and Joseph (ll. 53–60) are hardly characterization, but Pilate's justification for allowing Christ's execution helps to individualize him:

> Jol consenti par veisdie,
> Que ne perdisse ma baillie:
> Encusé m'eussent in Romanie,
> Tost en purraie perdre la vie.   61–64

(See Appendix)

---

[29] *PL*, LXXVIII, 757ᵇ. Cf. Essay III, *passim*.

[30] For the medieval legend of Hercules, see Erwin Panofsky, *Hercules am Scheidewege* ("Studien der Bibliothek Warburg," Vol. XVIII; Berlin, 1930). Geryon appears in Dante's *Inferno*, Canto XVII, where he is a dragon-like monster and guardian of the fraudulent. It is therefore possible that the "dragon" of Pilate's first line and the "Gerion" of his second are one and the same.

Pilate is not the all-powerful proconsul of liturgical drama but a politician whose security depends on keeping order in Palestine. The image is further developed by Pilate's reply to Joseph's request for the body: "Quidez vus qu'il vivre poisse?" (l. 76). A hint of pagan scepticism is introduced that recurs when Pilate hears of the miracle of Longinus.

The treatment of Longinus is disappointing. In the right hands, the blind beggar forced to pierce the side of Christ might have been a moving figure. In the *Resureccion* he accepts the offer of twelve farthings (*dener*) in a four-line speech ending with the rather irrelevant sentence, "Povres sui, despense ne faut; / Asez demand, mes poi me vaut" (ll. 99–100). Still less satisfying is the perfunctory eight-line prayer which he utters after the miraculous recovery of his sight. The lyric element of this prayer is limited to its first line: "Ohi, Jesu! ohi, bel sire!" When contrasted to the *Victimae Paschali* and *Planctus Mariae* of the Latin drama, the speech seems particularly inadequate.

After the soldiers report the miracle to Pilate, interest revives momentarily. His abrupt "Taise us, bricons, ne ditez plus" (l. 130) and his dismissal of Joseph recall his political acumen. His explanation of the miracle as a *fantosme* (l. 152) reinforces the earlier suggestion of his pagan scepticism. Finally, his decision to imprison Longinus to prevent him from spreading the story of the alleged miracle once again shows him sacrificing justice for political expediency.

The most barren dialogue in the play is the conversation between Joseph and Nicodemus. Its twenty-eight lines add nothing except the utterly useless information that Nicodemus is timid. Because of this timidity a second trip to Pilate is necessary and a second request is made that simply repeats the first one. The sequence of episodes at the Cross is promising in the abstract but, as already observed, trivial in execution. One might expect a lyric lament before or after the Deposition. Instead, the poet has provided a twelve-line prayer by Nicodemus asking God's help in making the burial a worthy one: "Dune nus faire dignement / A cest seint cors enterment" (ll. 265–66). The only faintly intriguing feature of the prayer is that its rhetorical structure parallels the *Deus qui . . praesta quaesumus* formula of liturgical prayer. If the parallel is intentional, however, its purpose is not evident.

The remainder of the play involves Caiaphas and the soldiers. The fact that the soldiers volunteer is curious but neither realistic nor especially dramatic. Their promises to guard the sepulcher are stretched out through three repetitive episodes (ll. 297–334). Perhaps the medieval audience found them comic, but if so, the comedy must have been in the performance rather than in the dialogue. Their speeches contain nothing to indicate that they are not to be taken seriously. The last mildly ingenious event in the play is the appearance of Levi with the law of Moses. The swearing-in speech by Caiaphas is empty enough, but the introduction of Moses' law appears to carry forward Joseph's initial reference to Moses and Aaron. If the parallel is significant, the soldiers are swearing by a law already superseded and a tradition about to be transformed. But because the "P" manuscript ends here, it is impossible to be sure how the reference should be interpreted.

VI

Returning now to the general subject of the vernacular tradition in the twelfth century, we can say with assurance that at some point before the middle of that century the liturgical drama branched off in two directions. The first direction led to the complex Latin plays of the thirteenth century such as those from Fleury, Rouen, Klosterneuburg, and Benediktbeuern. Plays in this tradition preserved ceremonial features, and the Easter plays uniformly retained the dramatic structure inherited from ritual. Liturgical drama was spread throughout the continent and England, largely via monasteries. The second direction led to the *Mystère d'Adam* and the *Resureccion*. The meager evidence that exists indicates that it reached a complex level of development a century before Latin drama and that it remained localized in Norman England.

In subject matter and technique the plays of the vernacular tradition are independent of the liturgy. They lack the ceremonial elements found in Latin drama, they are based on nondramatic sources rather than on traditional ritual patterns, and they are consciously constructed in the representational mode.

The *Mystère d'Adam* and the *Seinte Resureccion* show that three quite different techniques were used by the vernacular playwright to achieve representation. The first is a technique for arriving at the universal form of the drama. The fact that it is used at all indicates that the vernacular plays were composed rather than adapted from pre-existing dramas. Both plays turn to convenient and authoritative sources for their universal form—the *Mystère*, to the Gregorian responsory of Sexagesima, and the *Resureccion*, to the Gospels of Matthew and John. Because the responsory is lyric, the *Mystère* lacks a coherent over-all structure; it treats two distinct actions, Adam and Cain, as a single unit. The fact that the Gospels are historical narrative makes the over-all structure of the *Resureccion* somewhat more coherent. In its complete form it would necessarily have had a ritual element because ritual structure is inherent in the Gospel narratives as well as in the Mass and the plays of the liturgical tradition.

The second technique is that involved in the creation of episodes. The outline furnished by the Gregorian responsory was already quite detailed, consisting of nine parts. For this reason and because the action of the Adam-Cain play does not require constant movement between stations, the episode division of the *Mystère* generally follows its universal form. In *La Seinte Resureccion* the episode division is different from the universal form. It depends on a set of conventions regarding the space and time in which the action occurs. In effect, the stage is a model of space and time, and the conventions are an attempt to reproduce on it the geometric space and linear time attributed to nature by philosophy. The result is that the simple four-part movement provided by the Gospels is lost in a twenty-three-part division, the units of which are stational episodes furnished with dialogue and denotatively insignificant journeys between stations. Although hints of this technique are found in liturgical texts, the *Resureccion* has developed these hints so elaborately as to be qualitatively distinct from plays of the Latin tradition. The arrangement is admittedly awkward. Its awkwardness is a reflection of the bondage of the playwright to the representational mode. The greater freedom of the later vernacular theater is a compromise with the rules of pure representation that was made possible by the accumulated experience of dramatists, actors, and audience.

The third technique determines the form of dialogue. Here again convention is important. For the author of *La Seinte Resureccion* dramatic speech was a dialectic based on a unit consisting of a single statement and a single response, and composed in four-line modules. The one episode involving extended dialogue moves jerkily forward in paired speeches. Most other episodes consist of one or two paired speeches, or monologues. The formality of the convention is softened, in episodes involving a named character and a group, by the practice of allowing members of the group to respond individually. For the playwright, filling out the form was a primary object, and fitting the dialogue to the action was secondary. Characterization in the modern sense was haphazard, and some of the realistic touches that intrigue the modern reader may have been sheer accidents, produced by the need for an additional couplet or a rhyme. Of character, in the sense of comment on moral issues involving choice, there is only the quatrain in which Longinus asserts that he will die rather than renounce his faith.

Spectacle is harder to assess than the other elements. The stage directions of the *Mystère* require elaborate settings and costumes. Frequent instructions to the players also indicate an advanced acting technique. The *Resureccion* begins with instructions for deploying the stations but does not say how the stations are to be constructed. Costumes are not mentioned, but the soldiers carry swords and spears, Joseph supplies hammer and tongs, Nicodemus has an ointment box, and Levi carries a scroll of the Mosaic law. The Cross has a detachable figure, presumably life-sized, that can be made to bleed when struck. The monument is large enough to contain the figure of Christ and is equipped with a stone that can be moved to close its entrance. These details indicate a large, complex production with considerable emphasis on verisimilitude but do not prove that the stations were elevated like those in the *Mystère* or that the characters all wore appropriate costumes. Acting the play would require a good deal of pantomime—the Longinus episodes and the Deposition show this—but there is much less emphasis on it than in the stage directions of the *Mystère*. Quite possibly, at the time that the *Resureccion* was written acting technique was sufficiently stylized to allow the author to assume it.

The existence of a strong, highly conventionalized vernacular tradition in the twelfth century raises a serious question about the dependence of later vernacular drama on the liturgical tradition. The first definite record of an English cycle is 1377. Yet we have clear proof that the basic problems of representational drama were solved in England by 1175. What happened to this drama during the intervening two centuries? Was the tradition entirely lost, or has preoccupation with the liturgical tradition simply caused evidence of its survival to be ignored? If it survived, what influence did it have on the cycles? In 1928 Professor Gustav Cohen remarked that the scenic arrangement of *La Seinte Resureccion* anticipates all essentials of the *grands mystères* of the fourteenth and fifteenth centuries.[31] The chief difference between the staging of the *Resureccion* and that of the English guild cycles two hundred years later is that in the fourteenth century the stage has been enlarged to include the entire town, and the stations have been mounted on pageant cars. If the Norman French drama of the twelfth century did not prepare the way for the later religious drama of France and England, one would like, at the very least, to know what happened to it. The fact that the Canterbury manuscript of the *Resureccion* dates from around 1275 suggests, however, that Anglo-Norman influence may have persisted even as the language of the popular drama of Britain was changing from French to English.

[31] *Le théâtre en France au Moyen Age* (Paris, 1928), I, 23–24.

EPILOGUE

A Note on the Continuity of
Ritual Form in European Drama

I

ROM THE POINT OF VIEW of the literary critic, perhaps the most important fact about the early history of medieval drama is that the ritual structure characteristic of the Mass and the Church year carries over unchanged into representational plays. This structure is comic, not tragic. The mythic event celebrated is rebirth, not death, although it is a rebirth that requires death as its prelude. The experience of the participants is transition from guilt to innocence, from separation to communion.

In addition to a persistent formal pattern, we find a technique developing for representational performance. Some elements of this technique can be observed in liturgical plays, especially those not a part of the Resurrection group, but the major steps, which allow for the artificial construction of plots, their formulation into episodes, and their expression in nonceremonial dialogue (i.e., dialogue that is neither Biblical, lyric, nor derived from liturgy), appear to have been taken first by vernacular playwrights.

The story of the development of religious drama from the thirteenth to the fifteenth century is reasonably clear in outline, although complex and often obscure in detail. Isolated segments of the story of man's salvation were combined into immense vernacular cycles of two major types, the Continental Passion play, which includes Old Testament episodes and episodes of Christ's ministry and Resurrection, and the English Corpus Christi cycle, which adds to these a group of episodes of the Nativity.

Craig and Jenney are doubtless correct in their conclusion that the form of the Old Testament phase of the cycle was determined by the responsories of Lent. The nonexistence of Latin dramas for most of the standard Old Testament episodes indicates further that they were the work of vernacular rather than liturgical dramatists. The principle may be extended to episodes of Christ's ministry and to the Nativity and Resurrection episodes that have no close Latin cognates.

However, the vernacular cycles are not independent of liturgical tradition in the manner of the *Mystère d'Adam* and *La Seinte Resureccion*. To the degree that they return to the liturgy of Lent for their structure, they return to the ritual "plot" of the Church year. They must therefore be considered a fusion of the techniques of representation derived from vernacular tradition with the ritual form characteristic of Latin religious drama. The combination accounts for both their episodic quality and their larger unity.

The meaning of the phrase "ritual form" as used here is essentially that which has been standard since Gilbert Murray's "Excursus" on ritual forms preserved in Greek drama, first printed in Jane Harrison's *Themis* (1912). Murray lists six elements: an agon (a struggle or contest); a pathos involving suffering (including a *sparagmos*—a "tearing apart") and death; a messenger who announces the death; a threnos (lament); an anagnorisis and peripety (recognition and reversal); and a theophany (a period of joy occasioned by rebirth). The Aristotelian orientation of this pattern is obvious from its terms. One qualification is necessary. Because it was formulated to deal with Greek drama, it is both too specific and too limiting for medieval drama. Medieval writers habitually speak of the Mass and the Lenten sequence in terms of a transition from *tristia* to *gaudium*. The *tristia* phase is objectified in a variety of ways that include Murray's agon, pathos, and threnos, as well as elements not found in Greek drama—penance, alienation, Old Testament typology, and the like. The *tristia* may be presented *in extenso*, as in the liturgy of Lent, or it may be extremely brief. The same is true of the theophany, which may include any or all of such elements as purification, rebirth, union in Christian love, marriage, and lyric rejoicing. In its most general form the Christian pattern consists of three parts. These may be labeled pathos, peripety, and theophany, with the understanding that the more extended the pathos and theophany phases, the more numerous the devices used to objectify them. In the *Quem quaeritis* the pattern is presented in its entirety but in the briefest possible manner. The Marys show sorrow for Christ's death (pathos), they are informed of the Resurrection (peripety), and they rejoice (theophany). Partly to satisfy the desire to tell the story and partly to make the peripety more significant by the enlargement of pathos and theophany, the drama is extended backward and forward from its center. In Latin drama the extension is limited by inadequacies of technique and conditions of performance. A hint of more ambitious development is provided by manuscripts in which groups of plays appear together rather than being attached to widely separated church services, but there is little or no evidence of the performance of several plays together prior to the thirteenth century.

The *Mystère d'Adam* and *La Seinte Resureccion* use techniques that permit a radical extension of the scope of religious drama. Combining these techniques with the concept of history as a providential drama centering on the Resurrection, dramatists extended the time line of the Resurrection play back to the beginning of time and forward to the Last Judgment. Did this extension occur in one step or as a result of gradual aggregation? There are allusions to performances of cycles at Riga and Cividale in the thirteenth and early fourteenth centuries, but there are no references to continuous performances of unrelated plays. The play that is usually considered an example of a transitional work, halfway between liturgical drama and the cycles, is the *Mystère d'Adam*. Upon inspection, however, the Adam and Cain episodes prove to be associated arbitrarily, because of the responsory that was their source, rather than because they are the first episodes of an incomplete drama of redemption. A transition cycle is, after all, a contradiction in terms. Either the author thinks of his work as having unity or he thinks of it as a series of separate plays. The concept of unity (though not its achievement) is absolute. As the concept of a unified cycle spread through Europe, authors reworked older plays in cyclic form or composed new ones, incorporating traditional material where suitable. Early allusions indicate that initially there were wide variations among the cycles of different regions in choice of episodes and manner of treatment. Later, when a few cycles became "authoritative," the variations diminished, and the pattern of a few dominant "types" emerged, with specific cycles showing local variation and cross-influence. Thus the evidence favors the idea that the movement from isolated play to cycle was brought about by a new way of regarding the subject matter rather than by a gradual, unconscious process of aggregation.

As we have noticed, the cycles represent a movement back to liturgy. Their liturgical quality can only have been intensified by the common practice of presenting them on Corpus Christi day. Numerous documents dating from the sixth to the fifteenth century show that the body of Christ had two equally important meanings for the medieval Church. First, of course, the *corpus Christi* is the Host. This meaning is the dominant one in the liturgy composed for the feast by Thomas Aquinas. But the *corpus Christi* is also the mystical body of Christ, which is the whole body of the faithful from the beginning to the end of time. Both meanings are present in St. Cyprian's comparison of Christians united in Christ to the grains of flour united in the oblation loaf. The first—the *corpus Christi* as Host— is the basis of the Corpus Christi procession, during which the Sacrament is carried through the community and displayed at various stations. The second—the *corpus Christi* as the mystical body—finds its expression in cycle plays that present the whole history of the faithful from creation to judgment.

Considered from the medieval point of view, the stories composing the typical cycle are episodes in a single drama. The practice of calling them plays is, in fact, a modern one. Medieval and sixteenth-century writers normally refer to the cycles in the singular. We hear of "the play of Corpus Christi," not "the plays of Corpus Christi," and the *Ludus Coventriae*, not the *Ludi Coventriae*. When approached in this way, the typical cycle, no matter what its size, is an enlargement of the Resurrection play. The beginning or pathos phase extends from creation (or the fall of Lucifer) to the ministry of Christ. The reversal is the Resurrection— often a recognizable adaptation of the *Quem quaeritis*. The end, or the-ophany, extends from the appearances of Christ to the disciples to the Last Judgment. The effort to express ritual form in representational terms is thus completed in an historical drama that emerges from eternity in the first episode and disappears into it once again in the last. It may be added that regardless of digressions and irrelevancies the cycle play is also aesthetically complete. The action is one, whole, and entire, and the "universal form" has a beginning, middle, and end, as it did in the briefest plays of the tenth century.

II

To extend these notes beyond the cycles is to confront the problem of the transition between medieval and Renaissance drama. There can be no thought here of offering a solution to this problem, but a few suggestions seem relevant. At present the traditional view of the Renaissance as a rebirth of secular interests antithetical to the medieval period persists: it is evident even in the work of some historians who consciously admit its inadequacies. At the same time, other historians insist that the Renaissance is an artificial concept and that medieval attitudes remained dominant throughout Europe at least until the seventeenth century. It is natural that these conflicting views should affect approaches to the drama.

On the level of practical criticism, for which Shakespeare criticism may be considered the touchstone, the spectrum of positions extends from those that stress Christian elements inherited from the Middle Ages (E. M. W. Tillyard, Willard Farnham) through qualified secularism (Theodore Spencer, E. W. Talbert) to pure historicism on the one hand and myth-ritual criticism on the other. There is an equally marked lack of agreement among studies concentrating on medieval influences. Tillyard, C. S. Lewis, and a host of American critics stress the influence of a Christian world view presumed to persist from the Middle Ages through the sixteenth century. Willard Farnham and L. B. Campbell stress the importance of a specific nondramatic influence, the "fall of princes" motif. Spivack, Ribner, and others stress the influence of the morality play. And although it has ceased to be a major factor, the idea that the comic and digressive elements of the Corpus Christi cycle influenced or prepared the way for the secular theater can also still be found in handbooks and short histories of the drama.

I suggest that recognition of the persistence of ritual form inherited from the Mass and the liturgy may provide a way of coming to terms with the variety of views now current. This form is, after all, the dominant form for medieval drama. As such, it both fulfilled the expectations of audiences conditioned by their experience of Christian worship and educated them in what to expect from representational drama.

In attempting to bridge the gap between medieval and Renaissance drama, at least four complicating factors must be considered.

First, the emergence of noncyclic religious plays must be examined closely. The cyclic concept permits the writing of one, and only one, play. When taken out of context, the episodes of the cycles lose their meaning, in the same way that the play of the murder of Gonzago from *Hamlet* would lose its meaning if presented alone. To restate the point in different terms, logically, the line of time is continuous from beginning to end. Every event has a past extending back and a future extending forward to eternity, and any interruption of the sequence is arbitrary. Yet the writing of a noncyclical play requires just such an interruption. One segment of the time line must be treated as complete in itself. The first scene must somehow be made independent of what comes before, and the last must have the quality of finality: e.g., "they were married and lived happily ever after."

One late medieval form, the saint's play, was traditionally presented in isolation from other plays, and it is probable that many of the problems involved in composing noncyclical dramas were first solved here. The Digby *Conversion of St. Paul* is a case in point. At the same time certain cyclical episodes, of which the Brome *Sacrifice of Isaac* is an outstanding example, show a degree of unity that would justify individual production. It appears significant that both the *Conversion of St. Paul* and the *Sacrifice of Isaac* draw on the pathos-peripety-theophany structure of ritual. Paul passes from intolerance and brutal persecution through a miraculous conversion to zealous piety, and, again, from adversity through angelic consolation to hope of salvation. In like manner Abraham passes from agonized sorrow through angelic deliverance to joyful praise of the Lord. The Brome play is far more successful than the *Conversion of St. Paul* because its parts are organically unified around a single peripety. Because the sacrifice of Isaac was always considered a type of the sacrifice of Christ, the use of ritual form to dramatize it may have been quite intentional.

Second, it must be recognized that the morality play is qualitatively different from the cycle play and that Renaissance drama was heavily indebted to its techniques. The morality play is not history but fiction. It is not based on fidelity to an historical source but on fidelity to doctrine, and its episodes are invented and arranged to illustrate this doctrine. Since the doctrine is moral and depends on the sacraments (grace, in Protestant cognates), the morality play is of necessity psychological drama. The characters do not act in such and such a way because history says they did but because a sacramental psychology requires them to do so. Since the characters in a morality play are personified motives, the form is also psychological in a literal sense: it takes place within the mind of the central character, who appears in the action as a personification of the soul, or what would now be called the ego.

The morality play introduces two new elements: a method of constructing plays on the basis of doctrine (akin to Aristotelian *dianoia*) and a psychological concept of character portrayal. For both theoretical and practical reasons, however, the "universal form" of the morality play is the same as that of the liturgical play. The liturgy of baptism and Communion makes it abundantly clear that the individual Christian (Mankind or Everyman) recapitulates in his own life the ritual pattern of alienation, suffering, death, and resurrection. Thus the "full scope" morality begins with a period of innocence terminating in a fall, reaches its climax at a reversal whereby the central character is saved or reborn, and ends with reconciliation and hope. *Everyman* is unique only in that it concentrates on the "Summons of Death" phase of the action and symbolizes the pathos phase by a series of episodes in which various characters desert Everyman prior to the change in his fortunes. With this reservation, the pathos-peripety-theophany sequence in *Everyman* is both clear and effective.

Third, the influence of classical drama during the sixteenth century had a profound effect on traditional forms. The dramatists imitated—Seneca, Plautus, Terence—had inherited a ritual tradition somewhat different from that of Christian Europe and, in addition, had all but buried this tradition beneath an overlay of philosophy, psychology, rhetoric, intrigue, and the conventions of five-act structure. In Italy and France the alien classical influence was strong enough to replace medieval forms. In Spain its effect was relatively slight. In England it permitted an enlargement of the scope of traditional drama but—except for isolated experiments in neoclassic comedy and tragedy—was absorbed into the traditional frame.

Fourth, there is the matter of the shift of orientation brought about by the complementary forces of nationalism and the Reformation. As Father Gardiner has shown, the medieval cycles did not die out spontaneously but were suppressed by Protestant reformers. As they disappeared, dramatists turned from solely religious subjects to secular ones. Classical history and the history of the national state replaced sacred history as prime sources for dramatic plots. Ethical, political, and protopsychological doctrine vied with, and for some authors replaced, the older sacramental psychology. Rhetoric, wit, intrigue, complex stage effects, and brilliant display added an element of gorgeousness entirely lacking in medieval plays.

For all these changes, the persistence of ritual form is obvious both from the plays themselves and from the mass of scholarship and criticism that has accumulated in the last thirty years on such matters as Shakespeare's religious imagery, his use of morality-play techniques, and archetypal and ritual patterns in his plays. In the cycle of plays from *Richard II* to *Richard III* it is evident that we have a secular equivalent to the sacred cycle of the Middle Ages. The protagonist of the cycle is *respublica* rather than Holy Church, and its rationale is the religio-political synthesis of the Tudor apologists rather than Catholic theology. Insofar as the plays participate in a larger unity, they are episodes in a drama extending from England's "fall from grace" by the murder of Richard II to her "rebirth" under the Tudors. After all qualifications based on order of composition, departures from the larger pattern, and ambiguities of Tudor political theory have been accepted, the plays remain something more than a haphazard collection, and their unity is that of the cycles.

The parallel between the Corpus Christi cycle and Shakespeare's histories is evidence of the persistence of medieval tradition in the Renaissance but is of minor significance in itself. The appearance of ritual pattern in individual plays is more important and more useful to criticism. Without entering into extended comment, I suggest that *Henry V* is a clear example of the use of ritual form for a secular subject. The play begins with challenge and conflict, turns on what Henry insists is the "miracle" of Agincourt, and ends with a political and social marriage—the union of France and England and the wooing of Katharine. The implications of

the form are brilliantly realized in the imagery of death and peril, providential salvation, and finally, in Burgundy's speech, natural rebirth. The
same pattern is so marked in *The Winter's Tale* that at least one critic has
interpreted it as conscious Biblical allegory. While the allegory may, I
think, be discounted, the ritual pattern is most emphatically there.
Because it has close analogues in sacred history, it encourages allegorical
reading in the same way that the Mass pattern encouraged the Amalarian
interpretation. The error of the allegorical reading is that it equates
structure with subject matter (an error less serious in the case of the Mass,
where ritual and sacred history are intimately related) and ends by
diverting attention from the play as written to ingenious and strained
parallels between its episodes and events in the New Testament. On the
other hand, an approach based on the concept of the representation of
secular materials in ritual form preserves the valuable insights of the
allegorical reading while avoiding its liabilities. The themes of fertility
and rebirth, for example, can be treated as analogues, rather than
disguised equivalents, of the Christian archetype.

It is in the case of tragedy that recognition of the continuity of ritual
form is perhaps most needed. The form of Shakespearean tragedy is usually
understood—consciously or unconsciously—in terms of the Freytag
pyramid, according to which its typical shape is that of rising action,
climax-catastrophe, and falling action. The reading based on the "fall of
princes" tradition, while historically more sophisticated, repeats and
reinforces this view. Yet scholars have been forced to abandon the Freytag
pyramid when dealing with individual plays. In what sense do Othello,
Hamlet, and Lear rise before they fall? More important, it is generally
recognized today that Shakespearean tragedy tends to end with a sense
of uplift. At times this uplift is equated with Aristotelian catharsis,
although it seems unrelated to the meanings normally read into "purga-
tion of pity and fear." At other times it is explained in terms of Renaissance political philosophy: the state is healed (or order restored) at the
expense of individual suffering. Herbert Weisinger has gone beyond these
explanations to equate the uplift with the paradox of the Fortunate Fall.

We can, I think, extend Weisinger's insights by admitting that the
archetypal form of Christian drama is not tragic, in the sense defined by
Freytag's pyramid, but comic. The uplift is neither accidental nor
cathartic, in the usual sense of that term, but the first hint of rebirth—of a
movement toward theophany. Properly speaking, many Shakespearean
plays that we call tragic—the list includes *Romeo and Juliet*, *Hamlet*, and
Othello—are comic in structure and tragic in tonality; that is, the episodes,
the rhetoric, and the imagery stress darkness, sorrow, alienation, suffering,

and death. The theophany is limited to the last scene or even to the last few lines and is suggested (not stressed) by imagery of creative sacrifice (*Romeo*), restoration of social health (*Hamlet*), or lovers reunited in death (*Othello*)—this in contrast to the emphatic theophanies symbolized by lyric rejoicing, marriage, reconciliation of opposed factions, and the like, in the romances and pure comedies. If it seems strange to speak of comic structure and tragic tonality in *Romeo*, *Hamlet*, and *Othello*, a parallel can be found in the shifting tonalities of the Mass itself, which is joyful on Christmas and deeply somber on Passion Sunday, although the same comic structure is used on both occasions.

The preceding notes (and they are no more than that) are intended to suggest that the forms and techniques used in the earliest drama of the Middle Ages are important not only to later medieval drama but to Renaissance drama as well. The task of relating them to the data of history and criticism remains for the future. Even as notes, however, they offer the promise of a measure of unity among conflicting positions—a unity in which opposing views can be understood in terms of "both/and" rather than "either/or."

APPENDIX I

Translations

Page 165:

At the end of the Sabbath, when it began to dawn towards the first day of the week, came Mary Magdalene and the other Mary to the sepulcher, alleluia.

And behold there was a great earthquake. For an angel of the Lord descended from heaven, alleluia.

For an angel of the Lord descended from heaven, and coming, rolled back the stone, and sat upon it, alleluia, alleluia.

And his countenance was as lightening, and his raiment as snow, alleluia, alleluia.

And for fear of him the guards were struck with terror, and became as dead men, alleluia.

And the angel answering said to the women: Fear you not; for I know that you seek Jesus who was crucified; he is risen, alleluia.

Jesus whom you seek is not here, but he is risen; remember how he spoke to you, when he was in Galilee, alleluia.

Come and see the place where the Lord was laid, alleluia.

Going quickly, tell His disciples that he is risen, alleluia.

Page 166:

PRIEST: *Rejoice, O people, and be happy: an angel sat on the stone of the Lord: he himself brought the good news to you. Christ has arisen from the dead: the Savior of the world: and he has sweetly fulfilled all: rejoice and be happy.*

CHOIR: *And his face was shining: and his clothing like snow: and he said.*

PRIEST: *Christ has arisen from the dead.*

CHOIR: *And the women hastily left the monument with fear and great joy: running to announce to His disciples that he has arisen.*

PRIEST: *Christ.*

CHOIR: *Glory and honor to the Father, Son, and Holy Ghost, world without end. Amen.*

PRIEST: *Rejoice, O people, and be happy.*

COMMUNION: *Fed with the body and blood of Christ: we praise you, Lord. Alleluia, alleluia, alleluia.*

Page 171:

RESPONSE: *An angel of the Lord descended from heaven, and approaching rolled away the stone; and sat on it, and said to the women: Fear not; I know that you seek the man who was crucified. He has arisen. Come and see the place where the Lord was placed, alleluia.*

VERSE: *An angel of the Lord spoke to the women saying: Whom do you seek, do you seek Jesus? He has.*

RESPONSE: *An angel of the Lord spoke to the women saying: Whom do you seek; do you seek Jesus? He has arisen, come and see, alleluia, alleluia.*

VERSE: *Lo he precedes you in Galilee, there you will see him, as he told you. He has.*

RESPONSE: *While the Sabbath was passing, Mary Magdalene, and Maria Jacobus and Salome purchased ointment, and approaching they anointed Jesus, alleluia, alleluia.*

VERSE: *And early on the Sabbath they came to the sepulcher, when the sun had just risen. And approaching.*

RESPONSE: *Angels were sitting on the stone by the sepulcher, and they sang of the Resurrection of the Lord; and before the sepulcher of Jesus stood Mary saying: Master, if you have taken him, tell me where you have placed him, alleluia.*

VERSE: *But she, thinking he was a gardener, said to him, Master, if.*

Page 172:

ANTIPHON: *And early on the Sabbath they came to the sepulcher, when the sun had just risen, alleluia.*

ANTIPHON: *And they said to one another; Who will roll the stone for us from the entrance of the sepulcher? Alleluia, alleluia.*

ANTIPHON: *And looking again they saw the stone was rolled away, it was indeed huge, alleluia.*

ANTIPHON: *Do not fear, you seek Jesus of Nazareth who was crucified; he is not here; he has arisen, alleluia.*

ANTIPHON: *I will precede you in Galilee; there you will see me as I told you, alleluia.*

ANTIPHON: *Go quickly, tell the disciples that the Lord has arisen, alleluia, alleluia. After the Passion of the Lord the covenant has been completed, since the body is not in the sepulcher. The rock supports eternal life, the sepulcher has given up the pearl of heaven, alleluia.*

ANTIPHON: *Mary Magdalene and the other Mary came to see the sepulcher, alleluia.*

Page 173:

The choir having assembled at the proper time with the bishops and deacons in a major [i.e., stational] church they begin the Kyrie eleison at the place of the cross, and proceed up to the altar; and the deacons ascending the pulpit [*pogium*] . . . the archdeacon nods to the leader of the choir, and let him bowing begin the Alleluia with the Psalm *Dixit Dominus Domino meo.* . . . This finished . . . let the archdeacon begin:

ANTIPHON: *I know that you seek Jesus who was crucified; he has arisen, alleluia.*

ANTIPHON: *Jesus whom you seek, is not here; but he has arisen. Remember what he said to you when he was still in Galilee, alleluia.*

After this let the priest say the collect, and let them proceed to the font with the antiphon. *On the day of my resurrection . . . I will pour pure water over you, alleluia.* Next let the second deacon read the Gospel.

ANTIPHON: *Come and see the place where the Lord was placed, alleluia.*

Then let the priest say the collect, and then let them go to the vestry of St. John [Lateran?], singing. . . . *This is done by the Lord, and it is a miracle to our eyes, alleluia, alleluia.* Then . . . the Psalm *In exitu Israel.* . . . After this the deacon says.

ANTIPHON: *Go quickly; tell the disciples that the Lord has arisen, alleluia, alleluia.*
Then let him say [*oret*] the Kyrie eleison continually. And then they go to Saint
Andrea of the Cross, singing: *I saw water flowing from the temple from the right side,
alleluia: and all to whom this water has come, are saved, alleluia, alleluia.* . . . . This finished,
the leader of the choir begins *alleluia. Come let us rejoice.* . . ."

ANTIPHON: *Go quickly, say to the disciples* . . .
Then the priests of the church proceed to the refectory. . . .

Page 179:

Whom seek you in the cradle, O shepherds, tell me?
Christ the Lord and Savior, the infant wrapped in swaddling clothes, as the angel has said.
The babe is here with Mary, His mother. . . . .

Whom have you seen ascending to the stars, O followers of Christ?
Jesus who came from the tomb, O Heaven-Dwellers.
He has ascended, as he foretold. . . . .

Page 200:

Mass follows after the procession. According to the Ordinal of St. Martin of
Tours, before Mass begins, the choirmaster [?], having changed vestments, should
come to the choir, and the chief singer with assistants should stand before the
entrance of the choir, along with two boys in white dalmatics. And two deacons
revested in white dalmatics, standing before the tomb of the Blessed Martin,
turning their faces to the chief singer, should begin:
    Whom do you seek?
And two boys standing before the singer reply:
    Jesus of Nazareth.
Deacons:
    He is not here.
Boys:
    Alleluia, the Lord has risen.
Then one should sing three times:
    Accendite ["Ascend!" or "Kindle!"],
each time more loudly.
And the other should respond the same number of times:
    Sing, O brothers.
The first boy next should say once:
    Accendite.
Second boy:
    Sing, O brothers.
First boy:
    Accendite.

The second boy should reply:
> Sing, O brothers.

Then the first boy:
> Accendite.

The second boy:
> Sing, O brothers.

And these things done, the two boys, their faces turned to the chief singer, should say:
> The time is here; sing to the Lord, eia!

bowing. This completed, the singer should begin the Mass.

Page 206:

On Easter at matins two bells are rung together; six candles are placed next to the great [paschal] candle before the altar. While the bells are being rung, a procession goes from the altar to the sepulcher in this order. Two acolytes with candles, two with thuribles, two deacons, another two to chant *Dicant nunc*, a chief singer, and one assistant. All these are dressed in white copes; the others follow in order, each one carrying a lighted candle. The aforesaid deacons, coming to the door of the sepulcher, begin:
> My heart burns.

An acolyte in the sepulcher:
> Whom do you seek?

Deacons:
> Jesus of Nazareth.

Acolyte:
> He is not here.

This finished, a priest, dressed in a white alb and emerging from the sepulcher carrying a cup with the Corpus Christi, finds the four acolytes before the door carrying a canopy on staffs, and covered by this, moves to the head of the procession. The acolytes with candles precede him; the other two stand next to him with thuribles. Then the aforesaid deacons say:
> The Lord has risen, alleluia.

After this the singer and his assistant begin this part of the antiphon:
> When Christ the King of Glory.
> You have come, O adorable one.

And singing thus all proceed to the middle of the church before the crucifix. Afterwards the antiphon:
> Christ arising.

Two canons with copes [sing] the versicle *Dicant nunc*. After the versicle the procession enters the chorus, singing *Because he lives, he lives in God*. The priest places the cup on the altar. Meanwhile the bells are rung together. The bishop, standing at his chair in miter and cope, begins *Lord, open my lips*.

Page 231:

When the third response is finished, the sepulcher is visited with the chants. Two brothers in the role of the women say:

Who will remove the stone from the door that we see covering the holy tomb?

The angels should say:

Whom seek you, O fearful women, weeping at this tomb?

The brothers should reply:

We seek Jesus of Nazareth who was crucified.

Angels:

He whom you seek is not here; but go swiftly, tell the disciples and Peter that Jesus has arisen.

The brothers playing the women should come foreward and turn to the people and to the choir, saying:

We came to the tomb lamenting, we saw an angel of the Lord seated there and saying that the Lord has arisen.

Let the choir sing the antiphon:

Two ran together.

Then two other brothers should hold forth the graveclothes, saying:

Behold, O companions, behold the graveclothes and sudary, and the body is not in the tomb.

Then

He has arisen.

Choir:

Te Deum laudamus.

People:

Kyrie Eleison,

in a loud voice.

Page 234:

Meanwhile, toward the end of the third lesson, [let] the sacrist [give] a candle to each brother, and the deacon should vest himself in a white stole, and go to sit on the stone of the tomb. When the third response has been begun for the second time, all the candles having been lit, the chief singer should form a procession in the following order: first the scholars with the teacher, then the abbot, next the older [clerics], then the junior ones and the untaught. But those who are to visit the sepulcher in the person of the holy women should remain in the choir and veil their heads with humerals or with the hoods of their copes. The rest of the convent should go, as stated, to the place of the sepulcher and [stand] there in silence. The aforesaid three should say three times in a subdued voice:

Who will remove the stone from the door that we see covering the holy tomb?

To whom the deacon playing the angel should reply, saying:

Whom seek you, O fearful women, weeping at this tomb?

And they to him:

We seek Jesus of Nazareth.

To whom he replies:

He whom you seek is not here; but go swiftly; tell the disciples and Peter that Jesus has arisen.

After this, as they draw near, he should rise and withdraw the curtain and show the sepulcher, and say to them:

Come and see the place where the Lord was placed, alleluia, alleluia.

The [women], approaching with bowed heads, should look within the sepulcher, and, taking from there the veil in which the cross was wrapped and the sudary which was over the top of the cross, and returning, they should stand near the altar and before it and sing in a loud voice:

We came to the tomb lamenting, we saw an angel of the Lord seated there and saying that the Lord has arisen.

This said, the whole convent should sing together, saying:

Tell us, Maria, what did you see on the way?

And one of the three who visited the sepulcher should say in a loud voice:

I saw the sepulcher of the living Christ, and the glory of His rising.

The second should say:

An angel was witness, and the sudary and the graveclothes.

And the third should add:

Christ has risen, my hope; he precedes His [disciples] in Galilee.

After this the whole convent should say:

A single truthful Mary is more to be believed than [the lying tribe of the Jews].

Then the people should begin this song:

Three women went to the holy grave.

Meanwhile, while the people sing this song, the chief singer of the choir should select two, an old man and a youth, who, after the people's song is over, should go to the sepulcher. The youth [should be] first and should wait; the old man should follow and look into the tomb, and the other with him. And as they are doing this, the chief singer should begin the antiphon:

Two ran together.

This over, let the three aforementioned [women] come before the near altar displaying the graveclothes, so that all can see them, singing:

Behold, O companions, behold the graveclothes and sudary, and the body is not in the tomb.

And next they should raise the cross on high, singing in a loud voice:

The Lord has arisen from the sepulcher.

The whole convent should sing along with them. After this the abbot or prior should begin *Te Deum laudamus;* and, singing the hymn, they should return to the choir, the people singing *Christ has arisen.*

Page 240:

AUTHOR'S NOTE:

The text of the Ripoll play is extremely poor. Many readings are conjectural, and in places the manuscript is unintelligible. This is particularly true of the processional song of the Marys. In the following translation certain liberties have been taken with the Latin text. These are based on silent emendations necessary for grammatical or dramatic sense. As Young remarks, "The temptations to emend are numerous. . . . Parts of the text are unintelligible" (DMC, I, 678). Those passages which are especially uncertain are bracketed.

EASTER VERSES OF THE THREE MARYS

[Marys]:

Let us go to buy myrrh
with perfumed ointment
that we may anoint
the body given to burial.

[? Angel]:

Omnipotent, most high Father,
gentlest ruler of angels,
what shall these most miserable women do!

[Marys]:

Alas, how great is our sorrow!

We have lost our solace,
Jesus Christ, son of Mary;
he was our aid and refuge.
  Alas,

But let us go to buy ointment
that we may anoint the body;
no further will it be able to decay.
  Alas,

Tell us, young merchant,
if you will sell this ointment;
tell its price and you will have it.
  Alas,

Merchant:

Women, listen to me.
This ointment, if you wish to buy it,
has a marvelous potency,
whereby, if you anoint a body with it,
the body will be unable to decay further,
nor can worms eat it.

If you truly want this ointment
you will give one talent of gold;
you will not have it otherwise.

Mary: O merchant, give the ointment.
                Here, we will give you money.
                We will go to anoint Christ's wounds.
                    Alas,

                O sisters, all joys
                wither in sorrow
                when innocence suffers
                disgrace and crucifixion,
                the envy of the Jews,
                and the treachery of princes!
                How deeply we grieve!

                It is proper, sisters, to weep;
                and weeping, to seek Christ;
                and seeking, to anoint the body;
                and anointing, to gratify [the mind
                after weeping, the wound having been seen;
                the great law having been adored,
                the heart is shown in works.]

                We are, O sisters,
                believing in our hearts and eager
                that our eyes see Christ
                the power of the ages.
                Who can move the great stone
                of the tomb [? "of the summit"]
                or the malice of the people?
                The power of the heavenly banquet.

                So great a vision, sisters,
                of splendor and ceremony,
                should not amaze you;
                to you be exaltation.
                Death and the life of death
                die [vice having been slain].
                Arise, our Resurrection.

[? Angel]:   [During this procession, sisters,
                speak in chosen words
                to those who are sad in spirit
                and wander wretchedly;
                their Lord arises, death conquered;
                they grieve with careful plaint
                . . . you know . . . your Lord arises.]

What shall we do, sisters,
enduring such heavy sorrows?
There is not, nor will there ever be,
sorrow like our sorrow.

Since the nations slew Jesus,
we should ever mourn;
but that we may rejoice,
let us go to see the tomb.

We are not slow to seek the tomb;
let us anoint the body with ointment,
which, though dead from its wounds,
outvalues all things living.

The value of the lost King
is greater than all the living,
whose love was a refuge,
an aid and a protection,
and an eternal support,
both now and forever more.

Where is Christ, my Lord and the son of the Most High?
Let us go to see the tomb.
The angel should reply:
  Whom do you seek in the sepulcher, O followers of Christ?
The Marys should reply:
  Jesus of Nazareth, crucified, O Heaven-Dweller.
The angel should reply:
  He is not here, he has arisen as he foretold; go, announce that he has arisen, saying:
The Marys should reply:
  Alleluia, the angel at the sepulcher says Christ has arisen.
  We praise thee, O Lord.

VERSES OF THE PILGRIMS

The King had taken himself to rest,
and my fragrant nard had perfumed the air;
in the garden I came where he had been,
but he had already left.

Through the night therefore I seek him;
going here and there I cannot find him.

Angels:
> *Woman, why do you lament?*

Mary:
> *There must be vigils with burning zeal;*
> *When these are done, I will find my spouse.*

Gardener:
> *Woman, why do you lament? Whom do you seek?*

Mary:
> *They have taken my Lord, and I do not know where they have placed*
> *him. If you have removed him, tell me, and I will take him.*

Gardener:
> *Mary, Mary, Mary!*

Let Mary reply:
> *Raboni, Raboni, Raboni!*

Let Mary, returning, say:
> *Say, impious Zabulon, what use is your trickery now?*

Disciples:
> *Tell us Mary, what did you see on your way?*

Mary:
> *I saw the sepulcher of the living Christ, and the glory of His rising;*
> *Angels were witness, the shroud and graveclothes.*

Angels:
> *He is not here, he has risen as he told you.*

Disciples:
> *A single true Mary is more to be believed than the race of the deceitful Jews.*
> *We know Christ has truly risen from the dead: have mercy on us, Christ, our King.*

[Pilgrim]:
> *What words are these that you exchange as you walk, and you are sad?*
> *Alleluia.*

Let two reply:
> *One whose name was Cleophas replied and said to him: Are you a pilgrim in Jerusalem*
> *and you do not know the things that have been done there in these days? Alleluia.*

Let him reply:
> *To whom he said: What things?*

Let two reply:
> *And they said: The things that concern Jesus of Nazareth, who was a prophet,*
> *powerful in deed and word before God and all the people, alleluia. Euouae.**

* [The vowels of the closing formula, *in saecula saeculorum amen.*]

Page 263:

> In this manner we recite
> The holy Resurrection:
> First we prepare
> All the places and the mansions,

And the crucifix first
And afterwards the tomb:
A jail is necessary
For imprisoning the prisoners.
Hell should be put on that side
And the mansions on the other
And then heaven; and at the stations
First Pilate and his vassals—
He will have six or seven knights,
Caiaphas should be on the other side—
And with him Jewry—
Then Joseph of Arimathea;
The fourth place should be for Nicodemus—
Each one having six followers—
And fifth the disciples of Christ;
The three Marys should be sixth.
Arrange it so that the spectator faces
Galilee in the middle of the stage;
Emmaus should also be placed there,
Where Jesus was brought to the inn.

Page 269:

(1) Nicodemus took his tools
  And Dan Joseph said to him thus:
(2) When Nicodemus had done it thus,
  Joseph, who took the body, said.
(3) Then they put the sweet body down
  And Joseph said to his vassal:
(4) When he had anointed him with the ointment
  Nicodemus said in a loud voice.
(5) When they had anointed the body,
  They placed it on the bier.

Page 278:

JOSEPH: God, who from the hands of King Pharoah
    Saved Moses and Aaron,
    Save Pilate, my lord,
    And grant him dignity and honor.
PILATE: Hercules, who slew the dragon
    And killed old Gerion,
    Grant to him good and honor
    Who wishes me health through love.

Page 279:

> I consented to it through guile,
> In order not to lose my office:
> They accused me in Rome,
> I could have easily lost my life because of i t.

APPENDIX II

Chronological Index of
Early Liturgical Plays

Plays of the Tenth through the Thirteenth Century
Cited in Karl Young, *The Drama of the Medieval Church*

Quem quaeritis Plays

Page numbers refer to DMC, Volume I.

TENTH CENTURY

"First Stage"

201	St. Gall (*ca.* 950)
569	Bamberg
569	Vienna
210	St. Martial (923–34)
211	St. Martial (988–96)

Visitatio

249	*Regularis concordia* (965–75)
578	St. Vito
254	Winchester troper (*ca.* 980; position ambiguous) [Bamberg troper; not mentioned by Young but dated ninth century by Lange.]

TENTH TO ELEVENTH CENTURY

"First Stage"

569	Paris (996–1024)
207	Abruzzi
212	Apt

Visitatio

578	Paris
259	Reichenau

ELEVENTH CENTURY

"First Stage"

207	Bobbio
568	St. Gall
569	Paris
569	St. Martial (5 MSS)
570	Rome
570	Nonantuliere
208	Vercelli
209	Monza
209	Limoges
210	Mantua
214	Cassino (? eleventh century)
215	Cassino
215	Novalesa
223	Ivrea
225	Heidenheim
226	St. Gall

"First Stage" (cont'd)

227	St. Gall
570	Zurich
571	Place uncertain
577	Silos (2 MSS)

Visitatio

243	Minden
245	Arras
582	*Regularis concordia*
577	London
578	Fredeslarensis
578	Paris
579	Nevers
586	Winchester
628	Udine

ELEVENTH TO TWELFTH CENTURY

206	Ravenna	241	Place uncertain
208	Vercelli	263	Place uncertain
569	Huesca	578	Metz
570	Ripoll	583	Zurich
212	Limoges	590	Munich
578	Piacenza	598	Einsiedeln

TWELFTH CENTURY

"First Stage"

205	Vercelli
207	Bobbio
215	Benevento
226	Monza

Visitatio

242	Utrecht (2 MSS)
246	St. Gall
248	Remiremont
248	Budapest
560	Remiremont
577	Besançon
579	Angers
580	Mauri
580	Paris
590	Munich
590	Udine
595	Oxford
596–97	Munich
599	Madrid

Visitatio (cont'd)

262	Holy Sepulchre (1160)
266	Zwiefalten
269	Sicily

Includes Race of Peter and John

310	Augsberg
629	Vienna
632	Cracow
634	Graz

Complex Versions

263	St. Lambrecht
664	Prague
678	Ripoll (includes spice merchant)

[Also in this period: the vernacular *Trois Maries*]

TWELFTH TO THIRTEENTH CENTURY

212–13	Ripoll	389	Einsiedeln (complex)
584	Bamberg	592	Rheims
304	Soissons		

THIRTEENTH CENTURY

"First Stage"

228	Monza

Visitatio

579	Frauenfeld
580	Bellovacensin
580	Paris
585	Bamberg
587	London
591	Italy
595	Gotha
602	Münster
603–5	Troyes
265	Toul
271	St. Martial

Visitatio and
Victimae Paschales

279	Châlons-sur-Marne
280	Treves
293	Place uncertain
294	Padua
302	Laon
608	Paris
609	Paris
610	London
614	Besançon
615	Sens
620	Laon
628–29	Oxford
629	Würzburg

Visitatio and *Victimae*
Paschales (cont'd)

632	Graz
632	Nuremburg
633	Klosterneuburg
639	Graz
647	Vorau
651	Munich
656	Graz
658	Sicardus of Cremona
658	Durandus

Includes Race of Peter and John

309	Germany
312	Germany
314	Zurich
319	Harlem
659	Rouen

Mary and Jesus

370	Rouen
385	Rheinau
393	Fleury
403	Prague
398	Nuremburg

Complex Versions

421	Klosterneuburg
432	Benediktbeuern
438	Tours
665	Fleury playbook

Page numbers refer to DMC, Volume I.

Peregrinus Plays

Tenth to Eleventh Century	Twelfth Century		Thirteenth Century	
No plays extant	459–60	Sicily	461–62	Rouen
	467–69	Beauvais	463–65	*Carmina Burana*
	678–81	Ripoll	481–82	Padua
			694	Lille

Ascension Plays

No plays of period extant.

Pentecost Plays

No plays of period extant.

Page numbers refer to DMC, Volume II.

Nativity Plays (*Pastores*)

Tenth Century	Eleventh Century	Twelfth Century	Thirteenth Century
No plays extant	4 Limoges	6–7 Bobbio	427 Ripoll
	6 Ivrea	427 Ref. to plays at Niverness, Oscense, Ravenna, Piacenza, Vercelli (2 MSS), Pistoia, Limoges, Huesca, Sammaglorianum	427 Vicenza
	7 Mantua		9–10 Padua
	8 Novalesa		16 Rouen (complex)
	427 Ref. to plays at Limoges (2 MSS), Nevers, Moissac, Vercelli, Volterra, Martial (3 MSS)	12–13 Rouen	172–90 *Carmina Burana*

Page numbers refer to DMC, Volume II.

Magi Plays (*Officium Stellae*)

Tenth Century	Eleventh Century	Eleventh to Twelfth Century	Twelfth Century	Thirteenth Century
No plays extant	50 Nevers	447–48 Einsiedeln	34–35 Limoges	435–36 Rouen
	53–54 Compiègne (complex)		440 Nevers	437 Rouen
			445 Munich	
Tenth to Eleventh Century	439 Nevers			
	443–44 Malmédy			
	445 Lambach			
443 Paris	*Includes Pastores*		*Includes Pastores*	*Includes Pastores*
			59–62 Sicily	64–65 Strassburg
			68–72 Montpellier	84–89 Fleury
			75–80 Bilsen	99 Padua (includes Herod)
	93–97 Freising (Includes Herod)		448 Place uncertain	172–90 *Carmina Burana*

Slaughter of Innocents Plays
(includes Rachel's lament)

Tenth Century	Eleventh Century	Eleventh to Twelfth Century	Twelfth Century	Thirteenth Century
No plays extant	93–97 Ref. in Freising *Magi*	109 Limoges 117–20 Freising; *Ordo Rachelis*	No plays extant	103–6 Laon 110–13 Fleury 172–90 *Carmina Burana*

Prophet Plays

Tenth Century	Eleventh Century	Eleventh to Twelfth Century	Twelfth Century	Thirteenth Century
No plays extant	No plays extant	138–42 Limoges 458–60 Einsiedeln 462 Ref. to Regensberg play	Prophet section of French *Mystère d'Adam*	145–50 Laon 462 Riga 172–90 *Carmina Burana*

Other Extant Latin Plays

199–208	Lazarus: Fleury (twelfth century)
212–18	Hilarius (twelfth century)
219–22	St. Paul: Fleury (thirteenth century)
172–90	Annunciation: *Carmina Burana* (thirteenth century)
259–64	Isaac and Rebecca: Vorau (twelfth century)
267–74	Joseph and His Brothers: Laon (thirteenth century)
276–86	Daniel: Hilarius (twelfth century)
311–14	St. Nicholas: Hildesheim (eleventh to twelfth century)
316–21	Fleury (thirteenth century)
325–27	Hildesheim (eleventh to twelfth century)
330–32	Fleury (thirteenth century)
335	Einsiedeln (twelfth century)
337–41	Hilarius (twelfth century)
344–48	Fleury (thirteenth century)
351–57	Fleury (thirteenth century)
361–69	Wise Virgins: Limoges (eleventh to twelfth century)
371–87	Antichrist: Tegernsee (twelfth to thirteenth century)

Note: There are no Latin Adam or Cain and Abel plays, although both are included in the *Mystère d'Adam* (twelfth century).

Index

(NOTE: "t" in parentheses following an entry indicates that the citation is of the text of a liturgical ceremony or play.)

A

Abruzzi (t), 69

Accendite: as exclamation during Mass, 157, 159, 160, 199, 200, 201, 202, 204, 215, 217, 219

Acolyte, 42, 49, 70, 159

Actio, 30

Adam, 88, 99, 109, 164, 220, 251, 253, 258, 259, 260, 262, 281, 282, 286

Adam le Bossu, 225

Adams, Henry, 2

Ad coenam agni: as hymn, 95, 161, 210, 212

Ad monumentum: as antiphon, 211, 222, 231, 235, 236, 237

Adoration of the Cross, 86, 130–34, 170, 174

Advent, 87

Aelred, Abbot of Rievaulx, 78

Aeschylus, 182

Aesthetic: of Benedetto Croce, 27

Agnus Dei. *See* Mass texts, selected; Paschal lamb

Agobardus of Lyons, Bishop, 78, 80

Agon. *See* Easter liturgy

Alb, 83, 86, 156, 157, 169: removal of, 86, 175–76; procession in, 169–70; relation to drama, 193, 200, 203, 210, 215, 234, 236, 286, 287

Alcuin, 80

Allegory: in Mass, 36–40, 45–47; method of Amalarius, 43–44; in Easter liturgy, 87–89, 88n, 97, 150–53, 153–63, 164, 166; recapitulation symbolism, 88n, 92, 97, 105; of Visit to the tomb, 228–30

Alleluia, the, 45, 56, 164, 165, 199, 200, 216, 218, 221, 233, 243, 244: "Farewell" to, 86, 89–91, 176; "Return" of, 90, 162; as source of *Quem quaeritis*, 183

Alleluia dulce carmen: hymn, 90–91

Allen, P. S., 21

All for Love, 250

Amalarius of Metz, Bishop, 37–79 *passim*, 80, 81, 82, 89, 90, 96, 98, 111, 115, 116–17, 117–18, 122, 123, 124, 128, 129, 130, 131, 144, 145, 146, 147, 149, 150, 153, 155, 159, 161, 162, 163, 164, 173, 187, 194, 214, 230, 237, 266, and notes *passim*: influence of, 38, 78; sources of *Liber officialis*, 41n; love of music, 48; doctrine of triple sacrifice, 63–64, 66, 67, 69; doctrine of triform body, 75. *See also Liber officialis*

Ambrose, St., 97, 161

Ambrosian missal, 97

"Angelic sacrifice," 63–64, 67

Angels: relation to drama, 24, 193, 194, 231, 233, 236; in Mass, 35, 36, 45, 52–53, 63, 72, 76, 230; in Easter liturgy, 90, 101, 147, 157, 161, 164, 168, 171, 174, 175, 216, 229

Angelus Domini descendit: as antiphon, 165, 171

Anselm of Canterbury, 81–82

Antichrist: as theme of Latin play, 224, 251

Anticipation, doctrine of, 82, 141, 170, 197, 198, 199, 215, 219

Antony and Cleopatra, 250

Apertio Aurium, 105, 106–7

Apology for Actors, 32

Apt (t), 184, 188

Aquileia (t), 213, 222, 223, 224, 227–34, 236, 237, 238, 245

Archbishop. *See* Bishop

Archer, William, 33

Aristotle, 17, 30, 139, 178, 258, 270, 285, 289, 291

Arnold, Matthew, 14, 27

Arras (t), 185

Articulation, principle of, 86, 97–98, 115

Ascension, 47, 52, 53–54, 59, 76, 120, 176, 178, 179

Ascham, Roger, 10, 11

Ash Wednesday, 87, 92–93, 94, 97–100, 119

Atonement, the, 82, 139

Augsburg (t), 136–37, 187, 213, 214, 224

Augustine, St. *See* St. Augustine

Aulén, Gustaf, 81

B

Bale, John, 25
Bamberg (t), 188, 209, 212, 213, 218
Baptism, 141, 145, 148, 150, 151, 153, 169, 196, 204: in Carolingian period, 80–81; in Easter liturgy, 81–82; rebirth symbolism, 81, 95, 108; decline of adult form, 95–96; as *photismos*, 102–3; rites of, 153–56; commemorated in Easter vespers, 174; relation to drama, 210, 211, 215, 227, 228
Baptismal font. *See* Font
Baptistery of Constantine, 154
Baudot, Jules, 122
Bede, Venerable, 72, 147, 230, 237
Bellotte, A., 208
Bells: silenced, 126; rung at vigil Mass, 161, 199, 200, 207*n*; relation to drama, 194, 198, 203–18 *passim*, 232
Benediktbeuern (t), 225, 255, 281
Benevento (t), 185
Berlin (t), 211
Bible: source for religious drama, 194–95, 232–33, 239, 245–46, 250–51, 261–62
—Old Testament passages cited: Bar., 150; Dan., 150; Deut., 150; Exod., 150; Ezek., 104; Gen., 150; Hos., 129; Isa., 107, 116, 142, 150; Joel, 100; Jonah, 150; Ps., 67, 87, 141, 142, 165, 174, 175, 212; Ruth, 53
—New Testament passages cited: John, 63, 70, 106, 110, 113, 127, 128, 169, 232, 238, 248, 261; Luke, 45, 53, 60, 64, 66, 70, 75, 76, 96, 169, 261; Mark, 60, 71, 72, 163, 169, 171, 229, 232, 233, 245, 261; Matt., 49, 60, 63, 64, 66, 70, 92, 100, 101, 102, 107, 112, 163, 169, 172, 233, 261, 262
—Epistles: Col., 102, 107; I Cor., 91, 92, 96, 173; II Cor., 96, 100; Gal., 105; Heb., 110; Phil., 49, 116; Rom., 95, 152; I Thess., 101; I Tim., 72; II Tim., 53
Bishop: in Mass, 42, 48, 49, 50, 51–52, 53–55, 54*n*, 73*n*, 74–75; in Easter liturgy, 98, 112, 113–14, 118, 120, 129, 146, 156, 158, 174, 216, 232; relation to drama, 204, 205, 206, 207, 210, 216, 232
Blessing of the rose, 106
Bobbio (t), 184, 222
Bodel, Jean, 225
Boeckh, August, 3

Bonona (t), 222
Brescia (t), 185
Breslau (t), 181, 187
Brooks, Neil C., 166
Brunetière, Ferdinand, 4
Burckhardt, Jacob, 13, 16, 29
Burial of Christ: Coventry play, 257

C

Caiaphas, 256, 262, 265, 269–70, 278, 280, 281
Cain and Abel, 220, 224, 251, 253, 254, 258, 259, 260, 262, 281, 282, 286
Campbell, L. B., 288
Canon: of Mass, 40, 42, 44, 59, 63, 64–71, 163. *See also* Mass
Canticum triumphale, 142
Capsa, 112, 123, 159–60, 209, 214, 215. *See also* Chalice; *Conditorium*
Caput jejunii. *See* Ash Wednesday
Carmina Burana, 225, 226
Cassino (t), 185
Catechumens, 59, 93–95, 102, 103, 104, 105–6, 105–8, 109, 119–20, 140, 141, 143, 150, 151, 152, 153, 155, 157, 164, 174, 196, 197, 215. *See also* Neophytes
Celebrant: during Mass, 39, 42, 70, 162; represents Christ, 64, 67, 78; blessing of font, 153–54
Centurion, the, 69–70, 256, 261
Cernitis, o socii: as antiphon, 222, 231, 232, 235, 238
Chalice, 59, 70, 73 and *n*, 75, 79, 126, 135, 206. *See also* Capsa
Chambers, E. K., 1–18, 19, 20, 24, 26–34, 180, 182, 183, 191, 264, 268. *See also Mediaeval Stage, The*
Chances of Death, The, 5
Charlemagne, 37, 80
Chrism, 119–21, 153, 154, 155, 156
Christ, 24, 40, 52, 75, 139, 140, 142, 144, 228, 229, 239, 267–68: in Mass allegory, 35–77 *passim*; mystical body, 42, 44, 62, 75, 271, 286–87; in Easter liturgy, 101, 106, 109–10, 116, 117–18, 120, 126–27, 129–30, 140, 143–44, 146, 147–48, 154, 157, 158, 163–64, 167–70, 174–75
Christ ist erstanden: as hymn, 213, 218, 235
Christmas, 26, 122, 159, 292: plays, 19, 45, 52, 178, 179, 204, 220, 221, 223i 225, 226, 250, 260, 284. *See also* Mag, play; Shepherds' plays

Christus resurgens: as antiphon, 141, 206, 209

Christus Victor, 81

Chronology of early MSS, 307–16

Cito euntes: as antiphon, 165, 172, 174, 216, 217, 218, 221, 222, 231, 233, 235, 236

Cividale cycle, 226, 286

Clermont-Ferrand (t), 185

Cloetta, W., 7

Codex Ratisponensis, 122, 123, 159

Codex Ratoldus, 132, 164

Coena Domini. See Maundy Thursday

Coffman, George R., 21

Cohen, Gustav, 283

Coincidence, principle of, 86, 115, 121, 141, 172

Coleridge, S. T., 5, 27

Collect, the: in Mass, 42, 53, 100, 104, 107, 115–16, 130, 138, 150, 151, 152, 162, 168, 200; in relation to drama, 209, 210, 211–12, 217

Collingwood, R. G., 26

Commingling, 42, 45, 72–73, 75, 139, 141, 164, 166

Communion, 40, 42, 46, 47, 53, 61–62, 65, 71–77, 78, 83, 158, 160, 161, 164, 166, 167, 214. *See also* Mass

Compiègne (t), 223

Comte, Auguste, 3

Concelebration, 42, 54, 119

Concordia regularis. See Regularis concordia

Conditorium, 123, 160. *See also* Capsa

Confirmation, 156, 215

Consecration, 42, 43, 64–71, 119–20, 123, 163, 164. *See also* Mass

Constance (t), 191, 205, 213

Constantine, Emperor, 103

Conversion of St. Paul: play, 288, 289

Cornish Passion, 257

Corpus Christi. *See* Host

Corpus Christi cycle, 12, 18, 26, 226, 250, 284, 286, 288, 290

Council of Mayence, 81

Council of Trent, 39

Coventry *Burial of Christ*, 257

Cracow (t), 224

Craig, Hardin, 1, 21, 25, 26, 29, 259, 260, 284

Creed: "Transmission," 41, 94, 106–8; "Return," 143

Creizenach, Wilhelm, 7

Critical theory: scientific, 2–5, 7–11, 26–31; "play," 31–32; basis for alle-gorical exegesis, 77–79; Freytag pyramid, 291–92. *See also* Allegory; Drama; Evolution

Criticism and Fiction, 20

Croce, Benedetto, 27

Cronaca Friuliana, 226

Crucifixion: in Mass, 40, 46, 62, 64–66, 68; in Easter liturgy, as Adoration of the Cross, 83, 86, 96, 130–34

"Crucifixion of Christ, The," 14

Cum rex gloriae: as antiphon, 137, 206, 209

Cur Deus homo?, 81

Currebant duo: as antiphon, 222, 231, 235, 238, 263

Cycles, 251, 283, 284, 286, 287, 288, 290: tendencies toward, in early MSS, 220, 223, 225–26, 259, 260, 274

Cyprian, St., 62, 286

D

Daniel: play, 220, 224

Dante, 170

Darwin, Charles, 4, 12, 20, 21, 22, 23, 27, 28

Deacon: in Mass, 42, 49, 50, 56, 58, 62, 64, 65–66, 68, 69, 70, 72, 73, 76, 78; in Easter liturgy, 107, 110, 113, 115, 118, 119, 120, 128, 130, 135, 137, 138, 143, 147, 149, 150, 160, 163, 164, 174, 215, 216; relation to drama, 200, 206, 215, 230, 234–35, 236

Débat, 30

De divinis officiis: of Pseudo-Alcuin, 163

De Julleville, L. Petit, 7

De la littérature considérée dans ses rapports avec les institutions sociales, 3

De officiis ecclesiasticis, 113

Deo gratias: as exclamation, 40, 47, 76, 158, 166, 190, 205, 214, 215, 219

De ordine baptismi, 82

Depositio crucis, 24, 159, 195, 196, 197: of *Regularis ordo*, 137–38

Deposition, 69, 70: in *Seinte Resureccion*, 224, 261, 269, 280, 283

De scrutinio et baptismo, 81

De Staël, Madame, 3

De Vries, Hugo, 22, 183

Dialogue: see Drama; Representation *vs.* ritual; Ritual

Dialogues of Gregory the Great, 36

Diderot, Denis, 33

"Disenchantment of the Elizabethans, The," 11

Donne, John, 142

Drama: definitions of, 17, 23, 30–33, 39–40; verisimilitude in, 47, 239, 246, 251, 271; dialogue technique in, 246–47, 274–81; "universal form" in, 258–62
—in Mass, 35–79 *passim*: in Easter liturgy, 80–177 *passim*; development of, 250–51
—ritual *vs.* representation in, 39–44, 47, 77–79, 83–84, 85–86, 178, 230–31, 233, 236–37, 248–50, 250–52, 270–73, 285: ritual influence, 286–92. *See also* Representation *vs.* ritual; Ritual
Drama of the Medieval Church, The, 1, 2, 18–25, and notes *passim*
Dryden, John, 250
Dublin (t), 209, 210, 214
Duchesne, L., 7, 214
Du Méril, E., 7
Durandus of Mende, Bishop, 44, 65
Dürer, Albrecht, 35, 36, 39, 44, 68, 79
Dürre, K., 240

E

Easter liturgy, Easter phase, 139–76: history and form, 139–41, 166–67, 176; agon motif, 139, 142–43, 151, 163–64, 167, 168; exodus motif, 146, 148–49, 151, 161, 168–69, 175; light imagery, 145, 148, 151, 157–58, 162, 167
—phases: vigil service, 141, 144–67; lauds, 142–43; seventh scrutiny, 143; new fire, 145–46; paschal candle, 146–47, 149, 154; *Exsultet*, 147–49; prophetic readings, 149–53; blessing of font, 153–54; baptism, 154–57; confirmation, 156; vigil Mass, 157–67; fermentum and sancta, 158–60; "paschal lambs," 160–61; Communion antiphons, 165, 166; Easter octave, 167–76; appearances of Christ, 169–70; Easter matins, 170–72; Easter Mass, 172–73; Easter vespers, 173–74; Low Sunday, 175–76
Easter liturgy, Lenten phase, 86–138: history and form, 82–87, 109, 259, 284–85; agon motif, 91, 91*n*, 92, 94, 96, 98, 101, 103, 108–9, 110, 114, 116, 129–30, 133, 138; exodus motif, 92, 94, 95, 97, 105; light imagery, 95–97, 102–3, 107; Tenebrae, 117–18
—phases: Septuagesima, 87–96; "Farewell" to Alleluia, 90–91; Sexagesima, 96; Quinquagesima, 96–97; Ash Wednesday, 97–100; dismissal of penitents, 98–99; Quadragesima, 100–1; second Sunday of Lent, 101–2; third Sunday, 102–3; first and second scrutiny, 102–5; Laetare Sunday, 105–6; third scrutiny, 105–8; Passion Sunday, 109–11; Palm Sunday, 111–15; procession, 112–14; Wednesday of Holy Week, 115–16; Maundy Thursday, 116–28; Tenebrae, 117–18; reconciliation of penitents, 118–19; *Missa chrismalis*, 119–21; reservation of Host, 122–26; Maundy service, 127–28; Good Friday, 128–34; solemn prayers, 130; Adoration of Cross, 130–34; Mass of Presanctified, 134; procession with Host, 134–35; "Burial of Host," 136–37; Deposition of Cross, 137–38
Easter Mass, 82, 83, 95, 122, 142, 145, 167–68, 169, 172–73: relation to drama, 189–90, 199, 211, 214, 218, 221
Easter matins, 137, 141, 170–72: relation to drama, 187–88, 189, 197, 199, 203, 204, 206, 210, 214, 217, 221, 222, 231, 232, 245
Easter Monday, 189
Easter plays, 225, 226, 234, 250–51, 260, 278. *See also* Passion play; *Peregrini* play; Resurrection play
Easter vespers: in vigil Mass, 164; special form for Easter octave, 173–74, 175, 186, 211, 216, 218
Easter vigil, 81, 82, 85, 95, 103, 109, 117, 119, 122, 123, 136, 139, 144–67: relation to drama, 190–91, 205, 208, 215, 232, 236
Easter vigil Mass, 45, 144, 157–67, 170, 172; relation to drama, 197, 199–200, 201, 203, 207*n*, 209, 210, 211, 212, 214, 215, 216, 217, 218, 219, 227
Eclogae de ordine Romano, 37, 45–46, 52, 54, 56, 67, 72
Eclogues: of Virgil, 276
École des chartes, 7
Einsiedeln (t), 223
Elevatio: *Crucis* and/or *Hostiae*, 24, 84, 136–37, 170, 171, 187, 205, 209, 211, 212, 214, 217, 218
Elevation, 64–65, 70, 79
Elton, Oliver, 11
Emmaus, 45, 75, 169, 224, 239, 249, 256, 264
Encyclopädie und Methodologie der philologischen Wissenschaft, 3

English Poets, The, 14
English Religious Drama, 1, 21, 25
Episcopus. See Bishop
Etheria, 112, 116, 129
Eusebius of Caesarea, 145
Everyman, 25, 289
Evolution: in literary studies, 4, 10, 18, 20–21, 22–23, 24, 27–28, 219
Évolution des genres dans l'histoire de la littérature, L', 4
"Excursus," 285
Exorcism, 103, 104, 143: of oils, 120
Exsultet: as chant, 145, 147–49, 208

F

Fall and Expulsion of Adam. *See* Adam
Farnham, Willard, 287
Feast of Fools, 12
"Feast of the Seven Sorrows," 111
Fermentum, 42n, 122, 123, 136, 158, 159, 210, 215. *See also* Sancta
Fiske, John, 21
Fleury (t), 186, 226, 281
Florus of Lyons, Deacon, 38, 78
Foerster, Norman, 34
Folk drama, 12, 15, 16, 179, 246
Font: blessing of, 153; as sepulcher, 174–75, 211
Fontanelle, 27
Fortunatus, 120, 133
Fraction of the Host, 45, 72, 73, 75, 79, 125, 166, 168
Frank, Grace, 224, 257, 276, 277
Franke, Kuno, 21
Frazer, Sir James, 12, 14, 28, 32, 139, 177
Freising (t), 223
Frere, Walter, 181–82, 190, 191
Freud, Sigmund, 28
Freytag pyramid, 291
Frye, Northrop, 28
Fulda (t), 185

G

Gallican rite, 41, 49, 53, 70, 79, 80, 85, 107, 146, 203, 211, 215
Gardiner, Father Harold, 290
Gaster, T. H., 28
Gaudium, 40, 46, 71, 72, 83, 89, 139, 238, 285. *See also Tristia*
Gelasian Sacramentary, 147, 150, 211, 212
Gemma animae, 39, 40, 217
Geschichte des neueren Dramas, 7
Gibbon, Edward, 11

Gloria. *See* Mass texts, selected
Gloria, laus, et honor: as hymn, 112, 113
Golden Bough, The, 12, 14
Gonzalo de Berceo, 77
Goode, Sister Teresa Clare, 43, 77
Good Friday, 83, 86, 109, 115, 116, 117, 123, 124, 125, 128–38, 140, 144, 145, 159, 170, 174, 181, 201, 207, 209
Gospel: ambo, 56, 58; in Mass, 57–59; "presentation" of, 107; procession, at vigil Mass, 163; during Easter octave, 169; as sacred history, 228, 232–33, 250–51; as source of *Seinte Resureccion,* 261–62. For gospel texts used in liturgy, *see* Bible
Gottschalk of Fulda, 38
Graz (t), 224
Gregorian Antiphonary, 85, 132
Gregorian Responsory, 85, 173, 259–60
Gregorian Sacramentary, 36, 41, 49, 85, 119, 122, 134, 144, 150, 155, 157, 189, 195, 212, 214
Gregory, Pope. *See* St. Gregory the Great (Pope)
Grindal, Archbishop, 16
Groos, Karl, 31
Grosseteste, Bishop, 16

H

Hallam, Henry, 13
Hamlet, 31, 32, 272, 288, 291, 292
Handbook to Literature, 21
Harper's Magazine, 20
Harrison, Jane, 285
Harrowing of Hell, 72, 139, 141, 142, 256
Hegel, Georg Wilhelm Friedrich, 3, 6, 8, 9, 13
Heidenheim (t), 185
Henry IV, 272
Henry V, 47, 290
Henry VI, 250
Hercules, 278–79
Herder, Johann Gottfried von, 27
Hermannus Alemannus, 40
Heywood, Thomas, 32
Hincmar of Reims, 80
Histoire du théâtre en France au Moyen Age, 7
History of English Dramatic Literature, 17
History of English Literature, 3
History of English Poetry, 4, 10
Holy Saturday, 71, 83, 94, 95, 107, 117, 119, 122, 141, 144, 145, 159, 165, 168, 175, 190, 199
Holy Thursday. *See* Maundy Thursday

Holy Week. *See* Easter liturgy, Lenten phase
Holy women. *See* Marys, the
Homer, 182
Honorius of Autun, 39, 41, 44, 46, 217
Hora est: as chant, 201, 202, 219, 221
Hoskins, John P., 21
Host, the, 35, 42, 61, 64–65, 70, 72, 74, 75, 76, 79, 112, 208, 209, 218, 286: "Burial" of, 124–26, 136–37, 138; reservation of, 121, 122, 123, 124, 136, 158; "Return" of, to altar, 134–35, 136, 160, 207, 209, 210, 212, 213; *Regnum* particle of, 166; relation to drama, 205, 206, 207, 209, 210, 212, 214, 216, 218. *See also* Fraction of the Host; Fermentum; Sancta
Hortulanus play, 169, 224, 234, 240, 243, 244, 247–49
Howells, William Dean, 20
Hugh of St. Victor, 39
Hungary (t), 213
Hunningher, Benjamin, 16
Huxley, T. H., 3, 4
Hyman, Stanley, 28

I

Ibsen, Heinrich, 251
Illumination: during vigil, 158; relation to drama, 201, 204, 209, 210, 213, 214, 215, 217, 218, 219, 232, 236
Impersonation, theory of, 17, 23, 31–32
Improperia: as chant, 131–32, 137
Innocent I, Pope, 144
Innsbruck (t), 225
Introduction to the Study of Literature, 3, 8, 10, 14
Introit, 46, 48–55: relation to drama, 180, 183, 185, 187, 189, 190, 210, 214, 216, 218, 221–22, 223
Isidore of Seville, 113
Ite nuntiate: as antiphon, 33, 193, 194, 216, 218, 221, 222, 233, 235, 236, 243
Ivrea (t), 185

J

Jenney, A. M., 259, 260, 284
Jerome, St., 144
Jerusalem, 47, 58, 61, 77, 83, 88, 90, 95, 105–6, 109, 157, 161, 167, 181
Jesse of Amiens, 81, 155
John Beleth, 39
John the Baptist, 45, 57
Jones, H. S. V., 21

Jonson, Ben, 4
Joseph of Arimathea, 44, 70, 253–81 *passim*
Jubilus. *See* Melisma
Julleville, L. Petit de, 7
Jumièges (t), 187
Jung, Carl, 28, 177
Jungmann, Father Joseph, 122, 150, and notes *passim*

K

King Lear, 31, 291
Kiss of Peace, 40, 42, 45, 46, 49, 50, 53, 74, 78, 121, 156, 160, 205, 214. 216, 219
Klapper, Joseph, 180–81, 197
Kloster Himmelgarten (t), 225
Kloster Muri (t), 225
Klosterneuburg (t), 225, 281
Kluckhohn, Clyde, 28
Kretzmann, Paul, 181
Kyrie eleison: relation to drama, 161, 199, 200, 212, 217, 232. *See also* Mass texts, selected

L

Laetare Sunday, 94, 105–6, 107, 140, 157
Lamb, Charles, 31
La méthode scientifique de l'histoire littéraire, 3
Lang, Andrew, 28
Langlois, Charles, 3, 7, 8, 9, 14, 19
Laon (t), 205, 206, 208, 213, 216, 226
Last Judgement, The, 251
Latin: *vs.* vernacular. *See* Vernacular, the
Laudes Gallicanae, 53, 203
Laudes in die pasche, 202
Lauds: Holy Saturday, 141, 142–43; Easter, 172; resurrection symbolism, 217–18
Le Bossu, Adam, 225
Leduc, Camille, 122
Legenda aurea, 35
Leidrad of Lyons, 81
Lent. *See* Easter liturgy, Lenten phase
Leo X, Pope, 106
Levi: in *La Seinte Resureccion*, 256, 270, 273, 281, 283
Liber antiphonarius, 85, 132
Liber officialis, 37, 45, 47–77 *passim*, 79, 82, 85, 122, 124–25, 144, 156, 170, 187, 195: influence of, 38; sources of, 41 and n. *See also* Amalarius of Metz, Bishop
Liber responsalis, 85, 173, 259–60
Liber sacramentorum. *See* Gregorian Sacramentary

Limoges (t), 182, 183, 184, 186, 188, 189–90, 198, 202, 222, 223, 224, 225

Linteamina. See Linteum

Linteum, 157, 194, 198, 205, 211, 217, 237, 238. *See also* Sindon; Sudarium

Litany of the Saints, 153, 156, 157, 158, 199, 200, 207*n*, 218

"Literary Forms and the New Theory of the Origin of Species," 21–24

Longinus, 255–56, 261, 264, 265, 267–68, 273, 274, 277, 278, 280, 283

Lord's Prayer, 65, 69, 71, 72, 212: symbolism in, 71–72; "received" and "returned," 94, 106, 108, 143

Louis the Pious, 37, 38

Lowell, James Russell, 27

Low Sunday, 86, 143, 167, 169, 175–76, 229

Ludi, 12, 15, 16, 179, 246

Lumen Christi, 147, 205. *See also* Paschal candle

M

Macbeth, 25

Madrid (t), 191

Magi play, 223, 224, 227. *See also* Christmas

Magnus of Sens, 81

"Manifestation of the Blood," 121

Manly, J. M., 7, 13, 21, 22, 23, 24, 26–27, 33, 183

Mantua (t), 184

Manual of the History of French Literature, 4

Marlowe, Christopher, 4

Marshall, M. H., 180

Martene, E., 201

Mary Magdalene, 111, 179, 224, 228, 229, 237, 248, 249

Marys, the: in the Mass, 35, 64, 66, 69, 71, 72, 74, 78; in the Easter liturgy, 141, 142, 143, 163, 165–66, 171, 175; relation to drama, 178, 193–95, 197, 204, 205, 211, 216, 222, 229, 230, 231, 232, 233, 234–37, 240–42, 245–46, 263, 264, 285

Mass, 35–79, 80–177 *passim*: history and forms of, 42–43, 77, 82–83, 85; historical interpretation of, 23–24, 29, 38; allegorical interpretation of, 36–41, 43–44, 45–47, 50*n*, 77–79, 291

—parts: Introit, 48–55; readings, 56–59; Offertory to Canon, 59–64; Consecration, 64–71; Communion, 71–77

For particular Masses, *see* Easter liturgy; Mass texts

Mass of Easter vigil. *See* Easter vigil Mass

"Mass of Pope Gregory": woodcut of Dürer, 35, 39, 79

Mass of the Presanctified, 124, 134, 136, 192, 196

Mass texts: in dramatic MSS, 211–12, 213

Mass texts, selected: Agnus Dei, 75, 153, 157, 164, 200; Alleluia, *see* Alleluia, the; *Benedictus qui venit*, 59, 60, 64; collects, *see* Collect, the; creed, *see* Creed; *Deo gratias, see* Deo gratias; embolism, 71, 72; Gloria, 45, 46, 50, 52, 55, 58, 89, 91, 119, 164, 219; Gospel, 45, 46, 56–58, 78; *Ite, missa est*, 40, 71, 76, 166; Kyrie, 45, 52, 161, 199, 200, 212, 217, 232; Lord's Prayer, *see* Lord's Prayer; *Nobis quoque*, 45, 69; *Pax Domini*, 50, 72, 74, 159, 168; *Per omnia saecula*, 63, 70, 71; *Qui pridie*, 64, 65, 67, 79; Sanctus, 59, 64, 65, 67, 74, 164; *Secreta*, 40, 45, 61, 62, 63; *Sursum corda*, 63, 70, 148; *Te igitur*, 65, 66, 67, 71

Matins. *See* Easter matins

Maundy Thursday, 93, 98, 111, 116–28, 130, 135, 136, 140, 145, 158, 159, 161, 164, 195, 208, 209, 210, 215, 216, 227

Maxentius of Aquileia, 81

Mediaeval Stage, The, 1, 2, 5, 6–18, 180. *See also* Chambers, E. K.

Melisma, 56, 183

Ménard, Hugo, 159

Meredith, George, 5

Metz (t), 213

Meyer, Wilhelm, 240, 246

Milton, John, 101

Minden (t), 185

Missa chrismalis, 119–21, 127, 128

Missale mixtum: Palm Sunday rite, 113–14; "Burial" of Host, 125–26; procession to altar, 134–35; Communion, 166; beginning, 207*n*. *See also* Mozarabic rite

Molien, Father, L. A., 103, 150

Monza (t), 184, 185

Moosburg (t), 213

Morality play, 289

Mozarabic rite, 75, 79, 80, 85, 113–14, 125–26, 128, 134–35, 137, 166, 207*n*, 215. *See also Missale mixtum*

Müller, Max, 28

Murray, Gilbert, 139, 285

Mystère d'Adam, Le, 220, 224, 225, 253, 254, 257–61, 262, 273, 275, 281–83, 285, 286

N

Nativity play. *See* Christmas, plays
Neophytes, 57, 137, 156, 157, 158, 161, 162, 164, 168–69, 173, 174, 175–76, 192, 193, 196, 197, 198, 202, 204, 211, 215, 216, 217, 218, 228. *See also* Catechumens
"New Criticism, The," 27
New fire, 145–46, 153–54
Nicholas, St., 215, 220, 224
Nicodemus, 44, 70, 256, 261, 262, 264, 268–69, 273, 277, 280, 283
Nietzsche, Friedrich, 16
Nocturn. *See* Easter matins
Northern Passion, The, 257
Notker Balbulus, 180, 185, 187

O

Oberammergau play, 32
Octava in albis, 83, 167–76
Octave of Easter, 83, 167–76
Oedipus Rex, 32
Offertory, 59–63, 77, 78, 142, 160, 163
Oils: blessing of, 119–21; use in baptism and confirmation, 154, 155, 156
Ointments: symbolized, 71, 157, 163, 194–95; purchase of, in Ripoll play, 240–41, 245, 246
"On the Application of Evolutionary Principles to Art and Literature," 4
Ordines Romani, 85, 93, 116, 119, 122, 124, 130, 144, 146, 155, 158, 163, 187: *OR* I, 115, 123, 125, 130, 150, 153, 159, 195, 215; *OR* VII, 94, 104, 106–7; *OR* X, 119, 125, 126, 150
Origin of Species, The, 4, 28
Osculum pacis. See Kiss of Peace
Othello, 33, 291, 292

P

Palm Sunday, 24, 45, 46, 59, 86–87, 111–15, 116, 123, 136, 158, 176, 181, 186, 190, 192, 209, 210, 227
Pange lingua: as hymn, 132–34, 138
Paraphrase of the Poetics of Aristotle, 40
Paris (t), 188
Parma (t), 204–5
Pascal, R., 16
Paschal candle, 141, 146–49, 153, 154, 157–58, 169–70, 175, 209, 210, 211, 214, 215, 216
Paschal lamb, 143–44, 160–61, 168, 169, 205
Paschasius Radbertus, 80, 81
Passion, the: symbolized in religious ceremony, 40, 46, 59, 64–67, 68, 69, 71, 109–11, 114–15, 117, 131–34
Passion des Jongleurs, La, 257
Passion play, 16, 19, 25, 26, 32, 225, 250, 284, 292. *See also Peregrini* play; Resurrection play
Passion Sunday, 83, 109–11, 128, 292
Passover, 152
Pastores. See Shepherds' plays
Paten, 70, 71, 72, 79
Pater Noster. *See* Lord's Prayer
Payne, W. M., 21
Pearson, Karl, 5, 16
Penance, public, 86, 92–93, 96, 98–99, 118–19, 140
Pentecost, 45, 87, 122, 159, 176, 226
Peregrinatio Etheriae, 112, 131
Peregrini play, 169, 224, 237, 239, 243–44, 247, 248, 249
Perry, Thomas S., 20
Peter and John: race of, 24, 222, 224, 226, 227, 229–30, 231, 232, 233, 234, 235, 236, 237–38, 248
Piacenza (t), 185
Pilate, 254–81 *passim*
Pilgrims play. *See Peregrini* play
Planctus Mariae, 24, 224, 240–42, 280
Plautus, 289
Poenitentes. See Penance, public
Poetics. See Aristotle
Polybius, 26
Pope Gregory. *See* St. Gregory the Great (Pope)
Pope Innocent I, 144
Pope Leo X, 106
Powell, Frederick York, 7, 8
Praefatio altera, 47
Prague (t), 224, 234
Preface: of Mass, 40, 63, 148, 163–64, 168, 173
Primitive Culture, 28
Processions: in dramatic texts, 203, 204, 206, 207, 209–10, 211, 212, 216–17, 218, 232, 234, 236, 245
Prooemium, 47
Prophets play, 220, 224, 253, 254, 258, 259
Prosser, Eleanor, 1

Prudentius, 101, 102
Prüfening (t), 209, 210, 213
Pseudo-Alcuin, 130, 155, 230
Purvis, J. S., 1

Q

Quadragesima, 87, 100–1, 109, 140. *See also* Ash Wednesday
Quem quaeritis, 12, 13, 18, 26, 40, 72, 81, 85, 96, 124, 125, 130, 137, 140, 157, 162, 163, 164, 176, 255: early history of, 178–219; in tenth century, 188–98, 221–22; in eleventh century, 221–23; in twelfth century, 223–24; chronology of early MSS, 184–85, 188, 190–91; theories of origin, 182–84, 198–99; associated with vigil Mass, 190–91, 194–97, 199–210; tentative reconstruction of, 215–19; texts discussed and/or reprinted: Limoges, 178; Wakefield, 179; *Regularis*, 193–94; St. Martin, 200–1; Udine, 203; Parma, 204–5; Laon, 206; St. Gall, 210–11; Berlin, 211; Aquileia, 231–32; St. Lambrecht, 234–35; Ripoll, 242–43
Quinquagesima, 96–97, 101, 102
Quis revolvet: as antiphon, 222, 231, 232, 234

R

Rabanus Maurus, 80
Race of Peter and John. *See* Peter and John
Rahner, Father Hugo, 43, 177
Ratold, Abbot of Corbie, 131, 148
Ravenna (t), 184
Realism: in religious ceremony, 47, 84, 230–31; in Aquileia text, 232–33; in St. Lambrecht text, 236–37, 239; in Ripoll play, 239 50. *See also* Representation *vs.* ritual
Real Presence: doctrine of, 43, 164
Regularis concordia, 95, 113, 128, 137, 164, 171, 185, 186, 187, 188, 192–98, 199–200, 202, 204, 205, 216, 217, 221, 222, 233, 236, 238, 246
Reichel, Oswald, 122
Reichenau (t), 188
Remigius of Corbie, 81
Remiremont (t), 185
Renard, Georges, 3
"Renewal of the Altar," 121
Representation *vs.* ritual, 67–68, 230–31, 238–39, 248–49, 250, 251–52, 271–73, 274, 284, 287: in Palm Sunday rites, 111–14; in Maundy rites, 121–22; in Good Friday rites, 130–34; in Easter rites, 176; in Aquileia text, 232–33; in St. Lambrecht text, 236–37; in Ripoll play, 246–47; in *Mystère and Seinte Resureccion*, 270–72, 277, 281–82. *See also* Ritual
Resurrection: symbolized in Mass, 45, 46, 59, 64, 71, 72–73, 74, 75; in Easter liturgy, 81, 82, 83, 95, 96, 108, 109, 125, 137, 139, 140–41, 149, 151, 153, 157, 158, 163, 166, 169–70; in Easter matins and lauds, 171–72, announced with bells, 198, 203–4; related to lauds, 217–18; dramatic relations, 228–29, 232, 249, 250–51
Resurrection play, 179, 220, 224, 227, 234, 237, 239, 246, 249, 250–52, 253. *See also* Ripoll Resurrection play
Resurrexi et adhuc tecum: as antiphon, 137, 167, 172, 173, 198, 221, 222; emendation of *Resurrexit*, 189–90
Resurrexit: as antiphon, 189–90, 218, 221, 222, 233
Rex in acubitum: as hymn, 243, 244, 245, 247
Ribner, Irving, 288
Richard II, 290
Riga cycle, 286
Ripoll Resurrection play, 185, 222, 223, 224, 227, 234, 239–50
Ritual: in Mass, 43–44, 47, 67–68, 78; in liturgy, 83–84, 139, 150–51, 153, 176–77; *vs.* representation, 238–39, 271, 274, 283–92. *See also* Drama; Representation *vs.* ritual
Robertson, J. M., 14
Robertson Smith, W., 28
Romeo and Juliet, 291, 292
Rossiter, A. P., 2
Rouen (t), 226, 281
Rutebeuf, 225

S

Sacrament. *See* Host, the
Sacrifice of Isaac, 288, 289
"Sacrifice of Penance," 69
"Sacrifice of the angels," 63–64, 67
"Sacrifice of the elect," 66
St. Ambrose, 97, 161
St. Augustine, 48, 89, 92, 117, 144, 228, 229, 232
St. Blaise (t), 213

St. Cornelius (t), 90

St. Cyprian, 62, 286

Sainte-Beuve, Charles Augustin, 3

St. Gall (t), 180, 182, 183, 184, 185, 186, 187, 188, 190, 194, 210–11, 218, 222, 223, 226

St. Gregory the Great (Pope), 35, 36, 37, 43, 44, 50, 68, 80, 82, 97, 127, 168, 171, 176, 182, 229, 230

St. Jerome, 144

St. Lambrecht (t), 224, 225, 227, 234–39, 244, 246, 249, 250

St. Martial of Limoges (t). *See* Limoges

St. Martin of Tours (t), 185, 200–1, 202, 205, 216, 219

St. Nicholas, 215, 220, 224

St. Stephen of Besançon (t), 214

St. Theodulphus of Orleans, 81, 82, 112, 155, 157

St. Thomas Aquinas, 39, 286

St. Ulrich: *Life* of, 136, 187

St. Vito (t), 188

Sancta, 42, 73, 75, 122, 123, 136, 158, 159–60, 210, 215, 218

Sappho, 182

Sarum (t), 213

Saturday after Laetare Sunday, 108–9

Schelling, Felix, 21

Scherer, George, 2

Schiller, Johann Christian Friedrich von, 27

Scotus Erigena, 38

Scrutiny, 94, 97–103, 104–5, 106–8, 141, 143, 162, 168

Second Shepherds' Play, 29, 251, 275

Second Sunday in Lent, 101–2

Seignobos, Charles, 3, 7, 8, 9, 14, 19

Seinte Resureccion, La, 220, 224, 225, 253–83, 285, 286: "C" and "P" MSS, 253–54, 263, 264, 268, 269, 270, 275, 281, 283; originality of, 254–58; prologue, 263; staging, 265, 266; episodes, 266–74; dialogue, 274–78

Seneca, 289

Senlis (t), 185

Sepet, Marius, 7, 258, 259

Septuagesima, 86, 87–96, 101, 102, 109, 110–11, 140, 161, 162, 167, 259

Sepulcher: associated with altar, 70, 71, 72, 75; place of reserved Host, 124–25, 135, 137, 208; relation to drama, 137–38, 171, 175, 193, 194, 200, 205, 206, 208, 212, 234–35, 237, 238; symbolism of, 229–30; in *Seinte Resureccion,* 262, 265, 269–70, 283

Sexagesima, 96, 259, 281

Seydel, Rudolf, 14

Shakespeare, 4, 25, 29, 33, 47, 239, 246, 250, 272, 287, 290

Shakespeare's Predecessors, 4, 10

Shepherds' plays, 13, 29, 223, 251, 275. *See also* Christmas

Shrouding of images, 110

Sicardus of Cremona, 39

Sicily (t), 224

Sicut cervus: as chant, 153, 199

"Simplest version" hypothesis, 186, 219

Sindon, 59, 61, 66, 67, 68, 71, 79, 125, 130, 254. *See also Linteum;* Sudarium

Slaughter of Innocents play, 223

Soissons (t), 209, 213

Soldiers at sepulcher, 255, 257, 262, 270, 280: *Regularis* "watch," 137–38

Solemn Mass, 41–42, 54, 73–74, 122, 158, 210, 212, 214

Specimens of Pre-Shakespearean Drama, 7

Spectacula, 12, 15, 16, 179, 246

Speculum charitatis, 78–79

Spencer, Herbert, 4, 31

Spencer, Theodore, 287

Speyer (t), 185

Spice merchant. *See Unguentarius*

Spiers, John, 2

Spivack, Bernard, 288

Staël, Madame de, 3

Stanislavski, 33

Stations: St. Lawrence, 102; Santa Croce, 106, 131; St. Mary Major, 115, 189; St. John, 137, 154, 156; St. Peter, 189

Stations of the Cross, 111

Stedman, E. C., 21

Stellae plays, 223, 224, 227

Stendhal, 3

Stonyhurst pageants, 25

Strauss, David, 14

Stripping of altar, 126

"Studies in the Evolution of Dramatic Species from the Beginnings of English Drama to the year 1660," 21

"Study of English Literature, The," 5–6

Stumpfl, Robert, 16, 246

Subdeacon, 38, 42, 49, 57, 64, 66, 68, 69, 70, 71, 72, 73, 78, 118, 119, 160

Sudarium, 59, 62, 63, 66, 67, 68, 70, 79, 217, 237, 238. *See also Linteum;* Sindon

Sulmona Passion, 255

Sumner, William Graham, 20

Surrexit Dominus: as antiphon, 171, 190, 192, 194, 197, 205, 206, 209, 211, 219, 221, 222, 231, 233, 235

Symonds, J. A., 2, 4, 7, 10, 13, 16

Synod of Quiercy, 38, 66, 75

T

Taine, Hippolyte, 3, 4, 13, 16

Talbert, E. W., 287

Taylor, George C., 21

Te Deum: as chant, 197, 204, 205, 211, 218, 232, 235, 243, 244

Tenebrae, 117–18, 127, 128, 138

Terence, 289

Tertullian, 13, 16

Texts of liturgical ceremonies and commentaries: *Gemma animae*, 39; *Regularis* Palm Sunday *ordo*, 113; Mozarabic Palm Sunday *ordo*, 113–14; Amalarius on Tenebrae, 117–18; Vatican ceremonies, 121n; Mozarabic "Burial" of Host, 125–26; Good Friday chants, 132–34; Mozarabic "Restoration" of Host, 134–35; Augsburg elevation, 136; *Regularis Depositio crucis*, 137–38; *Exsultet*, 148–49 and n; vespers antiphons, 165; Mozarabic Communion chants, 166; Easter matins antiphons, 171–72; Easter lauds antiphons, 172; *ordo* of Easter vespers, 173–74; *ordines* of Easter vigil, 207n; prologue to *Seinte Resureccion*, 263

Texts of liturgical plays. *See Quem quaeritis*

Themis, 285

Theodore, Archdeacon, of Rome, 145

Theodulphus of Orleans, St., 81, 82, 112, 155, 157

Theophany: in Mass, 76–77; in Easter liturgy, 83, 139, 140, 167–70, 177, 285, 289, 291–92

Third Sunday of Lent, 102

Thomas Aquinas, St., 39, 286

Thrall, William F., 21

Thucydides, 26

Thurible: in religious ceremony, 47, 59, 125, 135; relation to drama, 203, 205, 206, 207, 209, 232, 245, 254

Tillyard, E. M. W., 287, 288

Time: in Mass, 44, 47, 67; in Easter liturgy, 82–84; relation to drama, 251, 271–73, 288

"Timelessness of Poetry, The," 5

Tollite portas: as antiphon, 114, 137

Tom Jones, 32

Tours (t), 185, 255. *See also* St. Martin of Tours

Townley cycle, 29

Tract: of Easter vigil, 150–51; of Easter, 152, 173

Transfiguration, 102

Translations of Latin texts, 295–306

"Tretise of Miraclis Pleyinge, A," 16

Trisagion, 132

Tristia, 46, 71, 72, 83, 139, 238, 285. *See also Gaudium*

Trois Maries, Les, 224, 255

Tutilo of St. Gall, 180, 183, 187

Tylor, E. B., 4, 28

U

Ubi est Christus: as antiphon, 222, 242, 245, 247

Udine (t), 203, 204, 216

Ulrich, St.: *Life* of, 136, 187

Unguentarius, 224, 227, 240, 241, 244, 245, 246, 251

Utrecht (t), 185

V

Venice (t), 212, 213, 218

Venite et videte: as antiphon, 24, 165, 174, 194, 216, 218, 221, 222, 233, 235, 236, 237

Vercelli (t), 184

Verisimilitude. *See* Realism; Representation *vs.* ritual; Drama

Vernacular, the: in drama, 213, 218, 220, 224, 225, 226–27, 235, 237, 238

Vernacular drama: twelfth-century, 253–83

Vespere autem sabbati: as antiphon, 165, 166, 200

Vespers. *See* Easter vespers

Vico, Giambattista, 27

Victimae Paschali: as sequence, 24, 173, 224, 234, 235, 236, 237, 240, 243, 245, 247, 249, 280

Vienna (t), 188, 224, 225

Vienne (t), 185

Vigil Mass. *See* Easter vigil Mass

Virgil, 276

Visitation of Font. *See* Easter vespers

Visitatio Sepulchri, 23, 24, 84, 170, 174, 181, 184, 185, 186, 187, 188, 189, 196, 197, 198, 203, 214, 216, 217, 218, 222, 224, 227, 228–30, 237, 244, 246, 247, 249,

250–51, 256, 262: *Regularis* text, 193–94; symbolism of, 228–30; Aquileia text, 231–32; St. Lambrecht text, 234–35. *See also Quem quaeritis*

Visit to the tomb. *See Visitatio Sepulchri*

Von Herder, Johann Gottfried, 27

Von Schiller, Johann Christian Friedrich, 27

W

Wakefield *Resurrection,* 179

Walafrid Strabo, 39, 80

Ward, A. W., 6, 7, 14, 17

Warton, Thomas, 4, 10, 11

Weber, Paul, 181

Wednesday of Holy Week, 115–16

Weiser, Father Francis X., 98, 109

Weisinger, Herbert, 291

White, Charles A., 22

Wilson, F. P., 8, 16

Winchester Troper, 182, 188, 190–91, 192, 195, 198, 216, 218, 221, 222

Winter's Tale, The, 47, 291

Wright, Edith, 181, 183

Wright, Jean, 257, 264

Y

Young, Karl, 1, 2, 5, 8, 13, 18–25, 26, 28, 29, 30, 31, 32–33, 115, 130, 182, 183, 184, 186, 188, 190, 191, 208, 233, 239, 240, 246. *See also Drama of the Medieval Church, The*

Z

Zola, Émile, 4

Zurich (t), 213